THE SINGING-MASTERS

AIDAN NICHOLS, O.P.

The Singing-Masters

*Church Fathers from
Greek East and Latin West*

IGNATIUS PRESS   SAN FRANCISCO

Cover art:
The Final Judgement
Anonymous artists
Fresco painting at Voronet Monastery
Moldova, Romania
Photograph © iStock/svcoco

Cover design by Roxanne Mei Lum

To the members of the English Dominican Province,
in gratitude for half a century of companionship.

O sages standing in God's holy fire
As in the gold mosaic of a wall,
Come from the holy fire, perne in the gyre,
And be the singing-masters of my soul.

—W.B. Yeats, "Sailing to Byzantium"

CONTENTS

PREFACE

I have been studying the Fathers—not (for the most part) in a professional way but with the love of the amateur—since I sat, in my early twenties, in the North Oxford study of Metropolitan (then Archimandrite) Kallistos Ware. His students read out the weekly essay to a tutor who was surrounded by the texts of the Fathers and sundry relevant monographs on shelves surmounted by a lithograph of the monasteries of the Meteora (and a large framed photograph of the Russian imperial family). Here I offer some fruit of that study thus begun.

It takes the form of sixteen vignettes: one eight-some for the Greek East, the other for the Latin West. As such, it cannot of course be a comprehensive guide.[1] Instead, I have selected for treatment those patristic figures who have the best claim to the attention of modern theology students, or who were in other ways the most influential in Church tradition. I also find these Fathers to be, in words of William Butler Yeats, "singing-masters of my soul". Anyone who prays through the year the Office of Readings in the Roman Liturgy of the Hours will understand why.

In recent decades no one has done more to alert ordinary Catholics to the significance of the Church Fathers than Pope Benedict XVI.[2] The texts of his General Audiences on the Fathers, translated into a number of languages and widely distributed, whet the reader's appetite for nourishment on patristic food. In the present book, space has permitted the teaching of some of his heroes to be set forth more

[1] The notable omissions would be, for the earliest period, the "Apostolic Fathers" and the Apologists, forerunners of Irenaeus and Tertullian, and in the middle of the age, John Chrysostom, important as a preacher of the moral life, and those monastic writers, especially the Rule-givers, who figure in the history of spirituality.

[2] For his assignation to the Fathers of a crucial role in the reception of biblical revelation, see the Conclusion to the present work.

fully. Accordingly, I see this attempt at patristic *ressourcement* as in continuity with the pope's own.

St. Michael's College
Kingston, Jamaica
Pentecost 2021

Witness against the Gnostics: Saint Irenaeus

Ever since New Testament times, claims to esoteric knowledge have been a major obstacle to the dissemination of the Church's faith. In the twenty-first century, one might cite in this connexion the diverse irrationalisms of post-Modernism and New Age, the claims to "special revelation" (so Catholic theology would term it) made by historic paganisms on the global stage, and, not least, the pretensions of the physical sciences to have superseded the metaphysics of the common man. In the first two centuries of the Christian era, one word will suffice: "Gnosticism". The enduring character of the problem of false gnosis makes it appropriate to begin this account of the great Fathers by invoking the name of Saint Irenaeus.

About Irenaeus we do not know as much as we might wish, but what we know is by no means nothing.[1] In a letter preserved in *Church History* by Eusebius of Caesarea, theological adviser to Constantine, the first Christian emperor and "the great 'archivist' of Christian beginnings",[2] Irenaeus remarks that when he was young he listened to Saint Polycarp, disciple of Saint John the Evangelist.[3] Polycarp, bishop of Smyrna, was martyred in 155 (or 156) at what Irenaeus calls the "royal court" there. (Smyrna, now Izmir, on the Aegean coast of Turkey, was never the capital of the Roman Empire; Irenaeus may

---

[1] Eric Osborn, *Irenaeus of Lyons* (Cambridge: Cambridge University Press, 2001), pp. 2–4.

[2] Pope Benedict XVI, *Church Fathers: From Clement of Rome to Augustine* (San Francisco: Ignatius Press, 2008), p. 8.

[3] Eusebius, *Church History* V, 20. Eusebius' work, dating from the 290s, describes the history of the Church from the apostles to his own time; its reproduction of such documents is its most valuable feature. See Andrew Louth, "Eusebius and the Birth of Church History", in *Cambridge History of Early Christian Literature*, ed. Francis Young, Lewis Ayres, and Andrew Louth (Cambridge: Cambridge University Press, 2004), pp. 266–74.

be referring to the residence there of the future emperor Antoninus Pius, who had been proconsul of Asia, meaning the western portion of what geographers would call Asia Minor.) A manuscript of *The Martyrdom of Polycarp* now at Moscow claims that at the time when Polycarp was executed Irenaeus was engaged in teaching in Rome. Most Christian teachers in Rome in the second century were indeed native Greek speakers. So on this—rather slender—evidence, it is assumed that Irenaeus was a Romanised Greek from Asia Minor.

It may seem strange to find an Asiatic Greek operating as teacher of the Christian faith on the river Rhône, but this would be to overlook the excellence of the communications system of the Roman Empire, with its well-made, if uncomfortable, paved roads and its generally peaceful sea-lanes. Eusebius reports that Irenaeus served as an intermediary between the Church of Lyons and the Roman see, both before and after he became bishop of Lyons, the capital of Roman Gaul (Gaul being the Roman name for what is now France). In Lyons, too, the Church appears to have been essentially Grecophone, though some of its martyrs have Latin names, while Irenaeus speaks of himself as living among the Celts, as indeed he was.

In his *Commentary on Isaiah*, Saint Jerome records that Irenaeus died in a persecution triggered by the emperor Septimius Severus in 202 or 203—or, if this mention be, as some think, a scribal error, the first indication of his status as a martyr is late sixth century, from the chronicler Gregory of Tours in his *History of the Franks*.[4] So some scholars are not convinced that Irenaeus met a martyr's death, though the Western liturgical tradition insists that he did.

Irenaeus left behind two works: the *Proof of the Apostolic Preaching*, a fundamental statement of the truths of the faith, now extant only in Armenian, and *Against the Heresies*, which is an attack on Gnosticism as well as a positive statement of the contents of Christian theology.[5] This is a work that survives in fragments in the original Greek

[4] Denis Minns, O.P., *Irenaeus* (London: Geoffrey Chapman, 1994), p. 8n11.

[5] Irenaeus, *Proof of the Apostolic Preaching*, trans. Joseph P. Smith, S.J., Ancient Christian Writers (New York: Newman Press, 1952); citations from *Proof of the Apostolic Preaching* are from this translation. Irenaeus, *Against Heresies*, trans. Alexander Roberts and William Rambaut, in *Ante-Nicene Fathers*, ed. Alexander Roberts, James Donaldson, and A. Cleveland Coxe, vol. 1 (Buffalo, NY: Christian Literature Publishing, 1885). Irenaeus' original Greek title for the longer work reads *The Detection and Overthrow of the False Gnosis*. On the vexed question of the origins of Gnosticism (and its definition) in twentieth-century scholarship,

and otherwise in Latin and Armenian translations. Though a potted description of the five books of *Against the Heresies* can make it sound like a straightforward read, this is far from being the case. The work has been compared to a "virgin forest" or a "primeval jungle".[6] Not for nothing has a modern writer produced a "condensation" of Irenaeus' main work.[7] On the whole, it is better to begin with the *Proof of the Apostolic Preaching*, the shorter writing.

The *Proof of the Apostolic Preaching*

Called by Benedict XVI "the oldest 'catechism of Christian doctrine'", the *Proof of the Apostolic Preaching* is the best place to get an initial grasp of what Irenaeus thinks Christian theology is and how it functions.[8] The *Proof* opens by situating its desired reader: he is someone who walks in the way of "piety", which alone, says Irenaeus, can "lead man to eternal life".[9] Setting out to "please" God, the Creator, one must "keep the faith intact".[10] Just as there is a "bodily purity", consisting of the "continence" that "abstains from shameful things and all unjust actions", so likewise there is a "purity of soul", consisting in "keeping intact faith in God without either adding anything or taking anything away"—that is, without doctrinal augmentation or subtraction. Just as piety is "withered" when "contaminated by bodily impurity", so likewise piety ceases to be "intact" when "error enters the soul". Piety, writes Irenaeus, "will keep itself in its beauty and measure, when truth is constantly in the soul and purity in the body".[11]

   In the *Proof*, Irenaeus proposes to "expound the preaching of the truth so as to affirm your faith".[12] "We send you," he writes, "a sort of reminder of the capital points, in such a way that ... you will find

---

see Karen L. King, *What Is Gnosticism?* (Cambridge, MA: Harvard University Press, 2005); King, however, shares some of the Gnostics' animus against the Christian heresiologists (not excluding Irenaeus).

   [6] Osborn, *Irenaeus of Lyons*, p. 9.

   [7] James R. Payton Jr., *Irenaeus on the Christian Faith: A Condensation of "Against Heresies"* (Cambridge: James Clarke, 2012).

   [8] Benedict XVI, *Church Fathers*, p. 22.

   [9] Irenaeus, *Proof of the Apostolic Preaching* 1.

   [10] Ibid.

   [11] Ibid., 2.

   [12] Ibid., 1.

you have grasped in brief form all the members of the body of the truth, and by this summary, you will be in possession of the proofs of the divine things. The fruit thereof will be your salvation, at the same time as [the capacity to] confound all those who hold opinions that are false."[13] It is generally agreed that, by "the proofs of the divine things", Irenaeus means the content of the Holy Scriptures. But the Scriptures need to be interpreted according to what he terms the "rule of faith", the oral (word-of-mouth) version of what later Christians would call the creeds. Furthermore, so as to be applied salvifically, the Scriptures, read according to the rule of faith, require the carrying out of the commandments they contain. As Irenaeus writes, "We must hold inflexibly the rule of faith and accomplish the commandments of God, fearing him because he is Lord and loving him because he is Father."[14] While it is truth that "procures faith", it is faith, rightly lived, that "enables the accomplishment of the commandments".[15] The faith in question is that which, in Irenaeus' words, "the presbyters, the disciples of the apostles, have transmitted [or 'traditioned'] to us", and he links this introduction of the theme of tradition to baptismal initiation. For the sentence from which I just quoted about the presbyters (a term he seems to use interchangeably with "bishops") goes on: "First and foremost, [faith] recommends us to remember that we received Baptism for the forgiveness of sins in the name of God the Father and the name of Jesus Christ, the Son of God incarnate, dead and risen, and in the Spirit of God—to remember too that this Baptism is the seal of eternal life and the new birth in God, in such a way that it is no longer of mortal human beings but of the eternal God that we are the sons."[16] So for the Irenaeus of the *Proof of the Apostolic Preaching*, all doctrinal study—all theological research—must be regarded as an outcome of baptismal grace, implying its radically ecclesial character. It must be in perpetual dialogue with Tradition. Like Tradition, it must work with the Scriptures and the essential points of the faith as contained in what we should call the creeds.[17]

---

[13] Ibid.

[14] Ibid., 3.

[15] Ibid.

[16] Ibid.

[17] Jacques Fantino, *La théologie d'Irénée: Lecture des Ecritures en réponse à l'exégèse gnostique; Une approche trinitaire* (Paris: Cerf, 1994), p. 14.

Against the Heresies

In *Against the Heresies*, where the Gnostics are in view, Irenaeus prefers the expression "the rule of truth" instead of the phrase "the rule of faith" in *Proof of the Apostolic Preaching*. That is probably because for Gnostics, unlike for the Great Church,[18] faith is an inferior—a less valuable—kind of knowing. But whether he speaks of the rule of *faith* or the rule of *truth*, he consistently implies that at the very starting point of theology is a body of knowledge consisting of the essential articles of faith in their interrelation, a body of knowledge derived from Scripture read in Tradition and transmitted in the baptismal catechesis of the Church.[19]

Irenaeus stresses the coherence and harmony of this body of knowledge, reflecting (for him) the coherence and harmony of the physical cosmos.[20] It is a parallel emphasised by the twentieth-century Swiss theologian and patristic scholar Hans Urs von Balthasar in his monograph on Irenaeus in his theological aesthetics, *The Glory of the Lord*: "[The] cosmic beauty, which tells of the art of the creator, can never be contemplated in isolation from its true artistic intention, from the mystery of *anakephalaiôsis* [recapitulation in Christ]", the goal as well as the heart of the apostolic preaching.[21] The concept of "recapitulation" is one to which we shall return.

In Irenaeus' judgment, Gnosticism lacks an awareness of both kinds of harmony and coherence—in the case of the cosmos that is because of a distorted cosmology, and in the case of the rule of truth, it is owing to a habit of interpreting the Scriptures via their most obscure passages, rather than, as is the way of ecclesial catechesis, taking the clearer texts in Scripture as primary and interpreting more cryptic passages in their light. The latter procedure is, he says, how the successors of the apostles do things. In Book II of *Against the Heresies*, he recommends that, to understand the Bible aright, one start from the clear passages "in such a way that the whole Scripture,

[18] The term "Great Church" is the body of orthodox Christians as distinct from the members of sects in the wider quasi-Christian environment of the early centuries.

[19] Ibid., pp. 20–21.

[20] Ibid., pp. 70–71.

[21] Hans Urs von Balthasar, *The Glory of the Lord: A Theological Aesthetics*, vol. 2, *Studies in Theological Style: Clerical Styles* (Edinburgh: T&T Clark, 1984), p. 70.

which has been given us by God, appears to us concordant; the parables will agree with the clear passages and the clear passages will furnish the explanation of the parables; through the polyphony of the texts, one sole harmonious melody will resonate in us, singing to the God who made all things."[22] He notes, however, that some exegetical puzzles may never be sorted out this side of the grave. Some things in the Scriptures we must leave "in the hands of God and that not only in this present world, but also in that which is to come, so that God should forever teach, and man should ever learn the things taught him by God."[23] It was Irenaeus' conviction that, in what Latin theology terms the "Beatific Vision" (Irenaeus calls it "passing into the Father's glory"[24]), we shall never stop growing in both love and understanding, "for neither does God at any time cease to confer benefits upon, or to enrich man; nor does man ever cease from receiving the benefits, and being enriched by God."[25]

To sum this up, then, *Against the Heresies* confirms what has been said in *Proof of the Apostolic Preaching*: Scripture, doctrinal teaching, and apostolicity constitute the obligatory reference points of the theological enterprise.[26] As Irenaeus writes in the prologue to Book III of *Against the Heresies*, the book that begins his positive exposition of the faith in that work: "The Lord of all things has indeed given his apostles the power to announce the Gospel, and it is by them that we have known the truth, that is to say, the teaching of the Son of God.... It is not by means of others that we have known the economy of our salvation, but really by them through whom the Gospel reached us. This Gospel they first preached, then, by the will of God, they transmitted to us in the Scriptures so that it might be the ground and the pillar of our faith."[27] The word "economy", included in this citation, is crucial to Irenaeus' understanding of the faith (it is his most distinctive term), so we shall want to explore it at some length when considering the content, as distinct from the formal basis, of his theological work.

---

[22] Irenaeus, *Against the Heresies* II, 28, 3. Here and subsequent translated passages from this work are the present author's via the French versions of citations in Fantino, *La théologie d'Irénée*.

[23] Ibid.

[24] Irenaeus, *Against the Heresies* IV, 20, 4.

[25] Ibid., IV, 11, 2.

[26] Fantino, *La théologie d'Irénée*, p. 15.

[27] Irenaeus, *Against the Heresies* III, 1, 1, Prologue.

Meanwhile we can note that Irenaeus is the first of the Fathers to give the concept of Tradition its full weight as what he calls the "deposit of great price".[28] "This faith we have received from the Church we guard it with great care for under the action of the Spirit like a deposit of great price—kept in an excellent vessel it rejuvenates the very vessel that contains it", the vessel of the Church herself.[29] Faith understood as Tradition rejuvenates the Church, giving her youth back to her. Irenaeus' "tradition, uninterrupted Tradition, is not traditionalism, because this Tradition is always enlivened from within by the Holy Spirit, who makes it live anew, causes it to be interpreted and understood in the vitality of the Church."[30] Irenaeus emphasises the unity of Tradition. Since there is only one Holy Spirit that animates the Church, there can be only one Tradition. Already in Book I of *Against the Heresies*, he remarks:

Having thus received this preaching and this faith ... the Church, though dispersed in the entire world, keeps it with care, as indwelling only one house; she believes it in an identical manner, as having only one soul and the same heart; and she preaches, teaches and transmits it with a unanimous voice, as possessing only one mouth. For if languages differ across the world, the content of Tradition is one and identical.... And not the most powerful in speech among the heads of the churches will say anything other than that, since no one is above the Master, nor will he who is weak in words lessen this Tradition, for, the faith being one and identical, he who can speak about it abundantly does not have more of it, nor does he who can only speak of it a little have any less.[31]

Tradition is thus the unitary transmission of the faith accompanied by the Scriptures and their interpretation.[32] Scripture and Tradition teach the same thing, carry the same revelation, and find expression in a single doctrine.[33] They express together the reality

---

[28] Ibid., III, 24, 1.

[29] Ibid.

[30] Benedict XVI, *Church Fathers*, p. 26.

[31] Irenaeus, *Against the Heresies* I, 10, 2. In a later book, Irenaeus draws attention to the "preeminent authority" in this context of the Church of the city of Rome, owing to the role in her making of the apostles Peter and Paul. Ibid., III, 3, 2.

[32] Fantino, *La théologie d'Irénée*, p. 31.

[33] Ibid., p. 32.

of salvation. Readers of *Dei Verbum*, the Second Vatican Council's 1965 Dogmatic Constitution on Divine Revelation, will find this picture remarkably familiar.

Formal Similarities between Orthodoxy and the False Gnosis

One of Irenaeus' problems in *Against the Heresies* begins with the discovery that heterodox groups also claimed an apostolic succession, a tradition passed down from the apostles through what they termed the "masters" to contemporary members of the Gnostic assemblies. The most impressive of the Gnostic sects, that of Valentinus and his disciple Ptolemy,[34] seem quite deliberately to have borrowed the vocabulary of apostolic succession from the Great Church, though the notion of succession, taken by itself, was already found in the philosophical schools of the Hellenistic age just as, contemporaneously with Irenaeus, it will also be invoked by the Jewish rabbis. As Irenaeus remarks, "[The Gnostics] imitate our phraseology."[35] The weakness of the Gnostic successions lay in the admission that their claimed successions were secret, occult, rather than historically demonstrable. They were not public like the succession of the presbyter-bishops (or of philosophical teachers in the schools, or the rabbis in the synagogues, come to that).

Irenaeus is inclined to counter that if the Gnostics *do* have a succession, it is from Simon of Samaria, the Jewish sorcerer regarded by his followers as the "Great Power [of God]" and opposed to his face by the apostle Saint Peter in the Acts of the Apostles (8:9–25): "All those who in any way corrupt the truth, and injuriously affect the preaching of the Church, are disciples and successors of Simon Magus of Samaria...."

---

[34] "The Valentinians mingled with believers, and must have held themselves to be Christians, though of a rare and privileged kind. Hence it was that, while Irenaeus could write of the Gnostics as though the mere rehearsal of their opinion would render them odious, the Valentinian heresy, which because it was both more profound and more orthodox, was much the more alluring, could be refuted only by longer arguments and an exposure of its real or supposed antecedents." M.J. Edwards, "Gnostics and Valentinians", *Journal of Theological Studies*, n.s., 40, no. 1 (1989): 46.

[35] Irenaeus, *Against the Heresies* III, 5, 2.

They set forth, indeed, the name of Christ Jesus as a sort of lure, but in various ways they introduce the impieties of Simon."[36] It was a suggestion already made by Justin Martyr, one of the earliest post-apostolic writers. Modern scholars tend to agree with Justin and Irenaeus to this extent: they find the origins of Gnosticism to lie in heterodox versions of Jewish Christianity. That said, pagan Greek poets also produced "theocosmogonic" schemes, claiming to show the origin of the gods and the world,[37] while the importance the Gnostics gave to numbers— especially in their version of the Genesis creation account, which they read as an elaborate code for enumerating entities in the heavens—may reflect the view of the ancient Greek sage Pythagoras and his later disciples that numbers can explain the universe.[38]

The substantive difference here between the bishop in the apostolic succession and the Gnostic master is that the latter transmits with the Scriptures not the rule of faith but the theocosmogonic myth—a myth about the birth of the divine realm as it currently exists and the created world with it. It is a myth that seeks to explain both the low and the high points in human experience. In the words of the Irenaean scholar Denis Minns, an Australian Dominican,

> It sought to explain all these things in terms of a cosmic drama long since finished. All the distress we suffer is simply part of the cosmic rubbish left behind by the primordial near-catastrophe within the divine realm. The true Gnostic knows this, and knows that he or she does not belong to this shadowy world of matter and soul, multiplicity and diversity, but to the divine *Plêrôma* [Fulness] of light and spirit, where universal harmony and unity have long since been restored.[39]

This is the myth described, in various versions, in the opening books of *Against the Heresies* and very largely confirmed from the discovery of Gnostic documents at Nag Hammadi in Egypt in 1945. Irenaeus emphasises that the myth takes several—or even many— forms. "Let us now look at the inconsistent opinions of those heretics (for there are some two or three of them), how they do not agree in

[36] Ibid., I, 27, 4.
[37] Cf. II, 14, 1.
[38] Cf. II, 14, 6.
[39] Minns, *Irenaeus*, p. 18.

treating the same points but alike, in things and names, set forth opinions mutually discordant."[40] He continues: "Every one of them generates something new, day by day, according to his ability, for no one is deemed 'perfect' who does not develop among them some mighty fictions."[41] Eventually, then, he drops the idea of only "two or three" versions, reporting that "a multitude of Gnostics have sprung up, and have been manifested like mushrooms growing out of the ground".[42] In particular, "a many-headed beast has been generated from the school of Valentinus."[43] Among the Gnostic teachers, Valentinus was the most serious threat to Christianity, not least because he was the closest to Christianity in content and spirit.[44]

The canonical Scriptures could be amplified for the Gnostics by apocryphal or pseudonymous works, such as the *Gospel of Judas* mentioned by Irenaeus himself. But for Gnostic Christians it was the theocosmogonic myth that was the indispensable complementary revelation, absolutely required if scriptural texts are to be interpreted aright. Consequently, while the mode of transmission of the Scriptures may be parallel, as between Gnosticism and the Church, the content of the teaching given is very different.

In Irenaeus' own hermeneutic, which he takes to be that of the Great Church herself, the Bible is to be read as a whole, the Old Testament together with the New in their most basic "harmony and continuity".[45] Following the apostolic preaching, the Scriptures are to be read in their entirety as, more especially, centred in Jesus Christ. Irenaeus organises his writing by appealing to the accredited witnesses to the biblical revelation in the following quite reasonable—not to say inevitable—chronological order: the Old Testament prophets, Jesus Christ, the apostles. The Scriptures are to be read as Old Testament prophecy of the Incarnation, which took place as the central event of the entire economy, described in the four Gospels and subsequently proclaimed in the apostolic letters.

[40] Irenaeus, *Against the Heresies* I, 11, 1.

[41] Ibid., I, 18, 1.

[42] Ibid., I, 29, 1.

[43] Ibid., I, 30, 15.

[44] The great study of this is François M-.M. Sagnard, *La Gnose valentinienne et le témoignage de saint Irénée* (Paris: Vrin, 1947).

[45] Minns, *Irenaeus*, p. 36.

Corresponding to the baptismal catechesis, the whole is to be understood in terms of faith in the Father, Son, and Holy Spirit, three agents who by their activity furnish salvation. The Father, Son, and Holy Spirit were already operative in the Old Testament, as Irenaeus explains in *Against the Heresies*, where he writes, "In each epoch a truly spiritual man will recognize the same God [Irenaeus means the Father]; at each epoch too he will recognize the same Word of God, even if now [Irenaeus means since the Incarnation] he [the Word] has been manifested to us; in each epoch again he [the 'truly spiritual man'] will recognize the same Spirit of God, even if in the last times [Irenaeus means since Pentecost] he [the Holy Spirit] has been poured out on us in a new manner."[46] Irenaeus insists that, thanks to this coordinated action of Father, Son, and Spirit, we possess a real knowledge of salvation. The Church, therefore, has her own gnosis which is authentic knowledge, to which he contrasts the pseudo gnosis of the Gnostics, the knowledge falsely so called.

The object of true gnosis is God even though it is also the case that for Irenaeus God remains in a certain sense unknowable. As he writes, "One cannot know God according to his greatness, for it is impossible to measure the Father; but one can know him according to his love, for it is this which leads us to God by his Word."[47] Here the similarities between Orthodoxy and the false gnosis go beyond the formal question of how the Scriptures are to be "traditioned" in the succession. The Gnostics too, like the Great Church, held that the Father, whom they also termed "the Depth", is known by means of the "Son" or the "Only-begotten", whom they also termed "Intellect" or "Mind". But the original recipients of such mediated knowing are not entities recognised by the Church. On the basis of their interpretation of Genesis 1, Gnostics posited a series of "aeons" or "Everlasting Ones", in each case a set of gendered pairs bearing vaguely divine-sounding names—of which the single most noteworthy, for the theocosmogonic myth, is the name "Sophia". Irenaeus reports on belief in two Tetrads or groups of four, equalling one Ogdoad or group of eight, one Decad or group of ten, and one Duodecad or group of twelve, making thirty in all, from

---

[46] Irenaeus, *Against the Heresies* IV, 33, 15.
[47] Ibid., IV, 20, 1.

which there followed a search through the biblical text for further significant occurrences of the numbers 4, 8, 10, 12, and 30.[48] (That may sound a very odd proceeding—and it is—but the general procedure is hardly unknown; thus, some people consider the plays of Shakespeare coded signals to recusant Catholics, or—as I was once told by an ardent believer in this thesis—Jane Austen's novels coded accounts of English politics during the Napoleonic wars.) The Son, said Gnostics, at the Father's request, transmits to these world-transcending beings—coming forth from the Father in a descending hierarchy of emanations, and constituting around him the "Fulness" (*Plêrôma*) of the divine world—whatever it is that these beings, the "aeons", can grasp of God. And what the aeons can grasp of God is, precisely, the Son, who is himself emanated by the Father for this purpose. In the Gnostic world picture, the Son comes into existence, then, for the purpose of the divine plan: the purpose of making the Father known.

So the Father wills that the aeons should desire to know him—but this must be through the Son. Unfortunately, the Father's will, faithfully done by the Son, was definitely not done by all the aeons. In a meta-event comparable to the fall from pride of Lucifer in Western angelology, the aeon "Sophia" yielded to an arrogant desire for total knowledge of the Father not mediately, through the Son, but immediately, as the Father is in himself. In one of Irenaeus' simplest formulations, "A higher power went astray."[49] This act of passionate but ignorant hubris, not knowing or keeping her place, had appalling results. Sophia's desire, turning to fear and bewilderment, set in process a series of negative events. Distortions (ruptures) appeared in the divine realm, and these, for the Gnostic, explain, ultimately, the existence of our fallen world. (Irenaeus has little patience with this feature of the myth. He points out the incongruity of locating "passion"—passibility—in the divine realm, suggesting that "those who have invented such opinions have rather had an idea and mental

---

[48] Though he himself was not averse to number symbolism, arguing for the appropriateness of, for instance, four Gospels, Irenaeus will warn that "to prosecute enquiries respecting God by means of numbers, syllables, and letters ... is an uncertain mode of proceeding" (ibid., II, 25, 1). He draws attention to the unclear status of the aeons: either they are consubstantial with the Father or they are separate substances. Ibid., II, 17, 2–9.

[49] Ibid., II, 1, 3.

conception of some unhappy lover among men, than of a spiritual and divine substance."[50]) For the Gnostic narrative, in the changed circumstances that follow from this disturbance in the heavenly world, a created universe eventually emerges. Essentially, it is what is left of Sophia's disorientation, now embodied in time and space. But among its human members it includes some people who, like the everlasting aeons, can also profit from gnosis, with the prospect of knowing the Father through the Son.

Just so the Church too holds out that same prospect to her faithful. Yet the way the restoration of godly order is expected to happen for such human persons—the soteriological schema represented by Gnosticism—is markedly different from that of the Great Church.

Differences between Orthodoxy and the False Gnosis

To begin with, only one category of people can adequately profit from gnosis, from divine revelation as Gnostics understand it. Salvation consists in transmitting the gnosis of the Father through the Son to those outside the *Plêrôma* who are capable of receiving it. But only one limited segment of the human race *is* capable of receiving it—namely, human persons in the category of "pneumatics", or "spirituals", those who carry within them a "seed" or "spark" from the *Plêrôma*, as a consequence of the disturbance or indeed disintegration in the *Plêrôma* caused by Sophia's fall, the supracosmic Fall that took place before the creation of the world. Pneumatics can be reintegrated into the divine realm, and this makes them distinct from those people who are merely "psychics", "ensouled ones". The latter can have at best knowledge of the "Demiurge", principal offspring of Sophia, the artisan of a nondivine world. It is a word taken from the *Timaeus*, one of Plato's dialogues where the Demiurge is the power that orders the chaos of a material world by reference to the "Forms" or "Ideas". Unaware of the Father, or indeed of the *Plêrôma*, the Demiurge thinks himself to be the one and only God, "God the Creator", as in the Old Testament. In reality, he is just a cosmic craftsman. The best psychics can hope for is that, by the

[50] Ibid., II, 18, 5.

practice of continence and good works, they will enter after death an intermediate state, halfway between this world and the *Plêrôma*. In this Limbo they will have the Demiurge's company, time without end.[51] Pneumatics are even more distinct from "hylics" or "material ones", those incapable of salvation even in the reduced sense of life in the intermediate state. The category of the hylics includes, for Valentinus and Ptolemy, the Devil and his angels, grouped together with humans who lack spiritual or even moral aspiration. The fallen angels have no such aspirations, having surrendered themselves entirely to evil. All hylics are destined to be annihilated at the end of the temporal process. So that is the first really major difference from the Church that follows from reading the Bible in the light of the theocosmogonic myth. The Church does not know this categorization of the human race into three types of people, only one of which counts as candidates for "true" salvation.

Then secondly, the Christ on whom salvation turns is not, for the Gnostics, the Word-made-flesh, the Father's Son. Irenaeus was aware that Gnostic Christology was hardly uniform.[52] Yet typically for Gnostic opinion, the Christ became who he is not at the Annunciation, as the Church holds, but at the Baptism in the Jordan (Mt 3:13–17; Mk 1:9–11; Lk 3:21–22; cf. Jn 1:31–34). In that episode, there descended onto the pneumatic human Jesus of Nazareth another of the aeons:—a quasi-angelic figure called "Saviour", sent by the Father's Son to form the composite personality "Jesus Christ". So for Gnostics, or at any rate for Valentinian Gnostics, Jesus is a pneumatic man plus the aeon "Saviour". The divine aim, in the descent of the aeon at the Baptism, was to transmit gnosis to pneumatics everywhere. Readers of the Synoptic accounts of the Baptism would know, of course, that the Gospel text speaks here, rather, of the *Holy Spirit* descending on Jesus (Mt 3:16; Mk 1:10; Lk 3:22; cf. Jn 1:32). Gnostics therefore called the descending aeon, sent by the Son, both "Saviour" and "Holy Spirit". On a variant Gnostic scheme, the Holy Spirit, coming down at the Jordan, is actually the aeon Sophia, now purged by disassociation from her own disordered desire and given the task of guiding the lower world, which came into being by her fault. It may not be pure coincidence that Irenaeus

---

[51] Cf. ibid., IV, 1, 1.
[52] Ibid., III, 11, 3.

identifies the biblical figure of Wisdom (in Greek, the word is *sophia*) not with the Son (the consensus position among the Church Fathers) but with the Holy Spirit. Be that as it may, we can at least say that Gnostic Christology is very different from anything ever known in the Great Church. So that is the second major difference.

And thirdly, when contrasting the soteriological schemes of gnosis and the Great Church, Gnostic salvation—salvation in its fullness as enjoyed by pneumatics—does not require charity. Gnosticism is, for the elect, the ultimate Gospel of faith without works. Salvation occurs when the spiritual seed that is the pneumatic's true self awakens. This happens when he at once hears the theocosmogonic myth and reads or listens to the narrative of the Saviour's descent. Recognising the truth of the combined message of myth and Gospel, the Gnostic Christian is then indeed saved—that is, reunited with the *Plêrôma* where his seed, their essential self, originated.

The Irenaean Response

Over against this scenario, Irenaeus counterposes the teaching contained in the rule of faith. No prior classification of human persons impedes the Gospel proclamation that, through love aroused by the Holy Spirit, men and women (and children) are brought through knowledge of the Son to knowledge of the Father. The true gnosis is, therefore, far simpler than the false.

To begin with, there is only one God. There is no "Pleroma" of divine emanations emerging from the "Depth", nor, as taught by Marcion (discussed by Irenaeus but not, strictly speaking, a Gnostic), is there a duality of Gods: a lesser God who created the material world and is disclosed in the Old Testament, and a greater God, revealed in the New Testament, a God disdainful of the natural creation.[53] "The rule of truth which we hold is that there is one God Almighty, who made all things by His Word, and fashioned and formed, out of that which had no existence, all things which exist,... He who, by

---

[53] Over against the Creator-god "deficient in competence and good will", Marcion "called the merciful kind deity, above and unknown to this Creator, 'the Stranger', and Marcionite believers were to live as aliens in the dark world of law." Henry Chadwick, *The Church in Ancient Society: From Galilee to Gregory the Great* (Oxford: Oxford University Press, 2001), p. 90.

his Word and Spirit, makes and disposes and governs all things, and commands all things into existence."[54] Monotheism is a truth that, for Irenaeus, can be known in three ways. The ancients remembered it from Adam; the Jewish prophets taught it openly; pagans learn it from creation.[55]

Likewise, just as God is one, Jesus Christ is one: one Person, that is. He is the Father's Word, now incarnate—made flesh—or, what amounts to the same claim, made man. There is not a combination of the man Jesus and the aeon Saviour (or Holy Spirit) sent by the Son. For Irenaeus the incarnate Son is "what is visible of the Father", just as the Father is "what is invisible of the Son".[56] This makes Jesus Christ the only Revealer of the Father. In Minns' words, "Because the Son 'comprehends' the incomprehensible Father, because he has, or rather is, the 'measure' of the immeasurable Father he is able to reveal the Father, to make him known."[57] Seeing Jesus, the Son incarnate, we see the divinity of the one and only God. The Spirit descends upon him at his Baptism not to change his ontological status (he is already, at the Baptism, the "God-man"), but to "become accustomed in fellowship with Him [the incarnate Son] to dwell in the human race".[58] The Spirit descends to begin the pneumatic presence in men, a presence that spreads out from the humanity of Christ.

Finally, the true gnosis, unlike the false, is universal. It is directed to the human race in its unity. It does not exclude those who are— temperamentally, we might say—psychics and hylics, those not habitually conscious of spiritual or even maybe ethical aspirations. Though the true gnosis is genuinely cognitive—a "communion" of mutual knowledge between God and man—it works by means of love in a way all can share, by contrition and repentance if need be. As Irenaeus writes in the final book of *Against the Heresies*, and without knowing the background, this remark could seem just commonplace, "Indeed, there is only one Son who has accomplished the will of the Father, and only one humankind, in which are accomplished the mysteries of God."[59]

---

[54] Irenaeus, *Against the Heresies* I, 22, 1.

[55] Ibid., II, 9, 1.

[56] Ibid., IV, 6, 6.

[57] Minns, *Irenaeus*, p. 40, commenting on Irenaeus, *Against the Heresies* IV, 4, 2.

[58] Irenaeus, *Against the Heresies* III, 17, 1.

[59] Ibid., V, 36, 3.

The Key Irenaean Concept—Economy

The term "economy" is the most characteristic feature of Irenaean theology—and yet it is also a favoured term of its bitter opponents, the Gnostics. Likely enough, Irenaeus saw enhanced opportunities in the word and concept from its use in their writings.

The word *oikonomia*, known from the Greek fragments of *Against the Heresies*, is rendered in the Latin of the full text as *dispositio*, or less commonly, *dispensatio*; though occasionally *dispositio* is translating a related term in the Irenaean vocabulary, *pragmateia*, the difference being (apparently) that for Irenaeus *oikonomia* means primarily an action that corresponds to a plan (the divine plan), while *pragmateia* indicates the productive result of such planned action. *Oikonomia* is plainly the more basic of these two words: it governs Irenaeus' entire presentation of the content of the "true knowledge". Its overall denotation has been defined as follows: "an organizing action that consists in producing and ordering realities according to a divine design".[60] The obvious New Testament source is the opening chapter of the Letter to the Ephesians at verses 9 to 12:

> For he has made known to us in all wisdom and insight the mystery [*mystêrion*] of his will, according to his purpose which he set forth in Christ as a plan [*oikonomia*] for the fulness [*plêrôma*] of time, to unite [literally, "recapitulate", from the verb *anakephalaiôômai*] all things in him, things in heaven and things on earth. In him, according to the purpose of him who accomplishes all things according to the counsel of his will, we who first hoped in Christ have been destined and appointed to live for the praise of his glory.

This text is surely the single most important biblical text for Irenaeus' theology.

For the Gnostics the *economy* entails the organisation of the *Plêrôma*, the "fullness" surrounding the Father, and the need to reconstitute that *Plêrôma* on the fall of one of its constituent members. According to Gnosticism as Irenaeus describes it, the Christ has a threefold task. Firstly, and most importantly, he is to announce to pneumatics their true identity, thus enabling them to return to the *Plêrôma* so that they can know the unknowable Father through the Son. Secondly,

---

[60] Fantino, *La théologie d'Irénée*, p. 93.

he is to invite psychics to identify with his soul, the only dimension of his being accessible to them. That gives them the chance to share life with the Demiurge, the creative Artisan of the cosmos who, like the psychics, is merely subpneumatic, not a spark from the *Plêrôma*. Thirdly, the Christ is to warn hylics of their coming annihilation along with that of the Devil and his angels, the "archons" or "rulers" (cf. Col 2:15), who, though more potent than any human being, are also, on the Gnostic scheme, just as hylic as materially minded people.

For Irenaeus, the aim of the *economy* can be stated much more simply than any of this: it is to bring all human persons into the divine life, knowing the Father by love and doing so through the Son by the gift of the Spirit. To be aware of this economy (and no other) and to reflect upon it, this is the true gnosis.

The mysteries that unfold in the economy, as set forth in the Scriptures when read according to the rule of faith preserved in Tradition and guarded by the presbyter-bishops, enable the economy to point to the ultimate mystery. And this is the mystery of God himself in his own inner life into which human persons are invited. The economy unfolds through a series of covenants—under Adam, under Noah, under Moses[61]—or at any rate of phases, as the patriarchs (notably Abraham) and the prophets receive their calls.

But the central or crucial economic mystery is the Incarnation, which not only reveals but realises the entire plan of God, enjoying as it does a universal efficacy. This is expressed by Irenaeus as *anakephalaiôsis*, the recapitulation of all the economies of God in the new Head of humanity, the Second Adam, Jesus Christ, in whom all God's previous productive work for the salvation of mankind is brought to completion, to fullness.[62] Explaining the recapitulation concept, Jeremy Holmes writes:

---

[61] Irenaeus, *Against the Heresies* III, 2, 8.

[62] "God rehabilitates the earlier divine plan for the salvation of mankind which was interrupted by the fall of Adam, and gathers up his entire work from the beginning to renew, to restore, to reorganize it in his incarnate Son, who in this way becomes for us a second Adam" (Johannes Quasten, *Patrology* [Utrecht: Spectrum Publishers, 1950], 1:296). Let us not forget the role for Irenaeus, using this same typology, of the Second Eve. See Irenaeus M. C. Steenberg, "The Role of Mary as Co-Recapitulator in St. Irenaeus of Lyons", *Vigiliae Christianae* 58 (2004): 117–37.

"Recapitulation" is a term coined originally to describe something we do when we write: a *capitulum* ("little head") is the heading or description of the beginning of a chapter so *recapitulate* means to go over the main points again. After a long discourse it is helpful to state again briefly the essential points so that the whole work, as it were, stands before the audience. Similarly Christ carries out in his brief earthly life and small human nature the essential contents of the whole of cosmic and human history. But there is a difference: in a book or lecture, recapitulation condenses the whole by leaving out a great deal, that is, by having less perfection than the book or lecture, whereas Christ condenses the whole by constraining it all in a more perfect and simple manner.[63]

In the plan of God, the consequences are extraordinary, both for the revelation of God as man and for the destiny of the human—and not only the human—world. As Irenaeus explains,

He took up man into Himself, the invisible becoming visible, the incomprehensible being made comprehensible, the impassible become capable of suffering, and the Word being made man, thus summing up all things in Himself: so that as in super-celestial, spiritual and invisible things, the Word of God is supreme, so also in things visible and corporeal He might possess the supremacy, and, taking to Himself the pre-eminence as well as constituting Himself Head of the Church, He might draw all things to Himself at the proper time.[64]

Irenaeus, then, uses the key vocabulary of the Letter to the Ephesians: "mystery", "economy", "fulness", "recapitulation", but he does so in his own distinctive way.

So far as the word "economy" is concerned, his only real predecessor among the Fathers is Justin Martyr, who uses that word to express the typological relation between decisive acts of God described in the Old Testament and their fulfillment in the New, but fails to give it the comprehensive meaning we find in Irenaeus. Economy-thinking is Irenaeus' personal contribution to orthodox theology, triggered

---

[63] Jeremy Holmes, *Cur Deus Verba: Why the Word Became Words* (San Francisco: Ignatius Press, 2021), p. 130.

[64] Irenaeus, *Against the Heresies* III, 16, 6.

(I have suggested) by a realisation of how its use by Gnostics allowed them to set forth an impressive overall vision of the world.[65]

For Irenaeus, the phrase "the Incarnation" does not refer simply to the virginal Flesh-taking in Mary's womb. It encompasses the entire period from the Annunciation through the Baptism and public ministry[66] to the Death, the descent into hell, and the Resurrection, as well as the Pentecost sending of the Spirit to begin the time of the Church, where the Spirit is active for the salvation of individual persons, bringing about in them adoptive filiation as sons and daughters. Finally, the Incarnation also includes the time when Christ will reign with his elect, those configured to his image, in the presence of the Father, the knowledge of whom he mediates to the redeemed. This is the time, in other words, of the Kingdom, when human persons share as fully as possible in the life of God, participating in his glory, receiving not only immortality but incorruptibility, the immortality and incorruptibility which are otherwise, for Irenaeus, defining attributes of God himself.

In Irenaeus' writing, the creation is predominantly the precondition of the Incarnation so understood, just as is the Old Testament revelation, which, via patriarchs and prophets, makes its gradual approach to the Incarnation, God "accustoming" humanity to the shape of the divine plan.[67] The creation establishes man, in Adam, in an initial *imagehood* of the incarnate Son, the archetype of humanity. But only the progressive stages of the economy enable the Father to work through the Son and the Spirit to bring about in man the divine *likeness*, of which the Genesis creation account also spoke (1:26). The mode of the likeness is a new mode of existing, grafted onto the old mode of existing—the mode of the image, the mode of creation.[68]

Christ and Adam are thus the two key figures of Irenaeus' anthropology, marking in their continuity yet difference the two crucial stages

---

[65] Fantino, *La théologie d'Irénée*, p. 126.

[66] Here, on the life of Christ, Irenaeus stressed that the Mediator passed through every main stage of human living. Irenaeus, *Against the Heresies* III, 18, 7.

[67] Ibid., III, 20, 2.

[68] Jacques Fantino, *L'homme image de Dieu chez saint Irénée de Lyons* (Paris: Cerf, 1986). Irenaeus' many-sided but unsystematically expressed doctrine of the image and likeness involves both soul (rationality, freedom) and body (the latter shaped after the pattern of the incarnate God to be), distinguishing between origins, development, and ultimate outcome, all by way of the twofold mission of Son and Spirit.

into which the economy falls (Irenaeus is following Paul here in the Letter to the Romans [5:12–21]), even though the first pre-Incarnation stage itself consists of a series of economies, the "Covenants" of the Old Testament revelation, each of which is initiated by a fresh divine intervention in time.[69] The Incarnation Covenant, which will have no end, knows a gift of the Spirit that is fully stable, unlike previously. That is so even if this gift is as yet, in the time of the Church, only partial, unlike with the Parousia, when the gift will be not only stable but total. Nonetheless, the gift of the Spirit through the Son, even within its present limits, swings the economy onto a new level compared with anything that came before. "We do now receive a certain portion of the Spirit, tending towards perfection, and preparing us for incorruption, being little by little accustomed to receive and to bear God."[70] The Incarnation economy recapitulates the pre-Incarnation economy because in his obedience Christ relives the temptations and moral struggle that underlie the disobedience of Adam and his offspring—doing so triumphantly for human nature, while at the same time fulfilling the partial prefigurations of his own coming as experienced by patriarchs, prophets, and saints.[71] "For as it was not possible that the man who had once for all been conquered, and who had been destroyed through disobedience, could reform himself, and obtain the prize of victory, and as it was also impossible that he could attain to salvation who had fallen under the power of sin—the Son effected both these things, being the Word of God, descending from the Father, becoming incarnate, stooping low, even to death, and consummating the arranged plan of our salvation."[72]

If one wanted a single word to describe the structure of the economy for Irenaeus, the best word might, paradoxically, be one completely unknown to him: Trinitarian.[73] In the words of a French

---

[69] See J. T. Nielsen, *Adam and Christ in the Theology of Irenaeus of Lyons: An Examination of the Function of the Adam-Christ Typology in the Adversus Haereses of Irenaeus, against the Background of the Gnosticism of His Time* (Assen, Netherlands: Van Gorcum, 1968).

[70] Irenaeus, *Against the Heresies* V, 8, 1.

[71] Fantino, *La théologie d'Irénée*, pp. 242–58. Cf. Irenaeus, *Against the Heresies* IV, 11, 1 (on foreknowledge of Christ); IV, 20, 7–12, and IV, 23, 1–2 (on prefiguration not only in visions or words but in actions).

[72] Irenaeus, *Against the Heresies* II, 18, 2.

[73] "Although his contemporary Theophilus of Antioch had already employed the term *trias* ['Trinity'], Irenaeus does not make use of it in defining the one God in three persons." Quasten, *Patrology*, 1:294.

patrologist writing on Irenaeus' theology, "Salvation comes from the Father by the intermediacy of the Son who gives the Spirit, and the human being indwelt by the Spirit accedes by the Son to the Father."[74] What could be more full-bloodedly Trinitarian than that?

It would be difficult to dispute the importance of Irenaeus' place in the registering, exploration, and exposition of the biblical revelation, tasks which make up the proper role of a "Father" in the providentially guided history of the Church. Not less apparent is the inspirational potential of his teaching for the spiritual life of the faithful, the role of "singing-master", which gives this book its title. The reader can rightly expect the same to be true of all the Fathers to be studied in the pages that follow. This is why we should want to know the Fathers and to understand their aims.

[74] Fantino, *La théologie d'Irénée*, p. 208.

2

Pious Speculator: Origen

Origen was born in Alexandria in Egypt in 185 (or 186) and died in Caesarea in Palestine in 254 (or 255). From the time of its foundation by Alexander the Great in 331 B.C., Alexandria was the capital of Egypt for nearly a thousand years. With a mixed population—Greek, Jewish, and Egyptian—and library facilities unparalleled in antiquity, it was considered to be culturally and intellectually the centre of the Mediterranean world. Devastated by the Muslim invasion in the mid-seventh century, Alexandria reemerged in modern times as the fourth largest city of the Arab world. Caesarea, on Israel's Sharon Plain—its remains now part of an Israeli national park—could hardly compete. Yet this coastal town was the administrative capital of Palestine for both Romans and Byzantines. Not to be confused with its namesake city, also of patristic importance, in Cappadocia (in central Turkey), this Caesarea—that is, "Caesarea Palestinae" or "Caesarea Maritima" ("Caesarea-on-Sea")—was where Origen spent the last twenty years of his life. Along with Alexandria, Caesarea dominated his life story.

As befitted an Alexandrian Christian, Origen had the benefit of a thorough education in both the standard curriculum of Hellenistic paganism and the study of the Bible. The latter was owed to his father, Leonides, who died as a martyr when Origen was about eighteen (the story is recorded that Origen wanted to join him, but his mother frustrated this bid for martyrdom by hiding his clothes). The persecution under Septimius Severus in which Leonides died (cf. the case of Saint Irenaeus) appears to have been aimed chiefly at halting proselytism. From this it is conjectured that Leonides had contributed personally to the teaching of catechumens in the Church of Alexandria. Alexandria was famed for its high-level organisation of catechetical training. Leonides' death was not by lynching. It was an official act. This had immediate financial consequences for Origen's family. In cases of State execution, Roman law required the confiscation of the assets of a convicted criminal by the imperial exchequer. So Origen became the breadwinner of his family, teaching at first grammar, and then, as his reputation developed, philosophy, while simultaneously working in the catechetical school when the relatively short-lived persecution subsided.

Philosophy and the Bible are the twin pillars of Origen's theological edifice. The philosophy Origen knew was chiefly what is now called Middle Platonism—a development of Plato's thought which integrated with it Aristotelian logic and Stoic ethics and psychology, while also preparing the way for Neoplatonism by its confidence in the truth-attaining capacity of metaphysical speculation. Plotinus, the founder of Neoplatonism, was Origen's contemporary, and possibly a co-pupil under the same Platonist master. As to the Bible, Origen's enthusiasm for the Scriptures spurred his acquisition of what has been called an "extensive knowledge ... of Jewish traditions and customs, as well as of rabbinic interpretation",[1] and also a grasp of the Hebrew language, the extent of which, however, is debated.[2]

As an author he was a comparatively late starter, beginning to write when he was somewhere between thirty and thirty-five. Much of his writing has disappeared, either by accident in the historical process or because of deliberate suppression, thanks to the crisis in his reputation caused by disputes in the fourth, fifth, and sixth centuries. His output was colossal—not for nothing has he been called the "most prolific writer of the ancient world".[3] According to Saint Jerome, the Church historian Eusebius ascribed to him almost two thousand books; Jerome himself drew up an abbreviated list of about eight hundred titles. Origen's output was made possible by a single sustained benefaction. A former Valentinian Gnostic who converted to the Great Church (perhaps by the writings of Irenaeus, who knows?) put his fortune at Origen's disposal, financing a publishing house with a team of stenographers, calligraphers, copyists, and secretaries, as well as keeping up moral pressure on Origen to continue the work.

[1] Henri Crouzel, *Origen: The Life and Thought of the First Great Theologian* (Edinburgh: T&T Clark, 1989), p. 13.

[2] Nicholas de Lange, *Origen and the Jews* (Cambridge: Cambridge University Press, 1976).

[3] Crouzel, *Origen*, p. 37.

We are certainly reminded of Irenaeus when we hear Origen explaining the rationale of his writing in his *Commentary on the Gospel of John*:

> But even now the heterodox, with a pretext of knowledge, are rising up against the holy Church of Christ and are bringing compositions in many books, announcing an interpretation of the texts both of the Gospels and of the apostles. If we are silent and do not set the true and sound teachings down in opposition to them, they will prevail over inquisitive souls which, in the lack of saving nourishment, hasten to foods that are forbidden and are truly unclean and abominable.[4]

The passage continues: "It appears to me, therefore, necessary that one who is able to represent in a genuine manner the doctrine of the Church, and to refute those dealers in knowledge, falsely so-called, should take his stand against historical fictions, and oppose to them the true and lofty evangelical message in which the agreement of the doctrines, found both in the so-called Old Testament and in the so-called New, appears so plainly and fully."[5] In the same commentary, Origen frequently engages with a Gnostic commentator on John's Gospel called Heracleon, an obvious example of putting theory into practice. And in his treatise *On First Principles*, Origen writes: "We must be careful not to fall into the absurdities of those who picture to themselves certain emanations, so as to divide the divine nature into parts.... Rather, therefore, as an act of the will proceeds from the understanding, and neither cuts off any part nor is separated or divided from it, so after some such fashion is the Father supposed as having begotten the Son, his own image."[6] That, too, is clearly an anti-Valentinian comment. More generally, Origen seeks to give satisfying answers to questions posed by Christians with intellectual

---

[4] Origen, *Commentary on the Gospel of John* V, 8. Translation here is the present author's own. It has been suggested in the light of papyrology that Origen, when in Alexandria, gave priority to the Book of Genesis and Saint John's Gospel because these (along with the Psalms) were the books most read by Egyptian Gnostics; see Ronald Heine, *Origen: Scholarship in the Service of the Church* (Oxford: Oxford University Press, 2010), p. 85. This provides Heine with his perspective on the Alexandrian commentaries. Ibid., pp. 86–115.

[5] Origen, *Commentary on the Gospel of John* V, 8. Translation is the present author's own.

[6] Origen, *On First Principles* I, 2, 6, trans. Frederick Crombie, in *Ante-Nicene Fathers*, ed. Alexander Roberts, James Donaldson, and A. Cleveland Coxe, vol. 4 (Buffalo, NY: Christian Literature Publishing, 1885). Citations from *On First Principles* are from this translation.

difficulties, notably about what the Scriptures teach, so as to discourage them from having resource to such Gnostic sects.

Origen was in his late forties when he was pushed out of Alexandria by his bishop, Demetrius. Demetrius objected to the way that, without reference to himself, Origen had accepted priestly ordination at the hands of the bishop of Caesarea Palestinae—despite a plan to return and exercise a ministry in Alexandria. (Origen had stayed at this Caesarea Maritima once before. During a reprisal by the emperor Caracalla, who had been annoyed by a student protest during a visit to Alexandria, Origen took refuge in Caesarea and found he got on well with the bishop there, as well as with the neighbouring bishop in nearby Jerusalem.) What lay behind this expulsion from the Church of Alexandria is not entirely clear. In Demetrius' view, the most probable explanation is that priestly ordination was to the presbyterium of one's local church, rather than entry into a universal presbyteral college. But there may also have been a more explicitly doctrinal element, a harbinger of the difficulties Origen's reputation would undergo after his death. He had been misrepresented as teaching erroneous eschatological doctrines while on a visit to Athens (notably by claiming that the Devil would ultimately be saved), and felt obliged to issue a public denial in his *Letter to Friends in Alexandria.* Jerome, who in his early years was an enthusiastic devotee of Origen, thought jealousy was behind the whole thing. Writing to his wealthy Roman friend Paula, Jerome commented: "Men could not tolerate the incomparable eloquence and knowledge which, when he opened his lips, made others seem dumb."[7]

Origen took it all calmly and was soon reestablishing his book production at Caesarea, resuming his great *Commentary on the Gospel of John* from the point he had by then reached, the end of Book V. It is from the Caesarean period of his teaching that we have the informative *Address of Thanks* written by one of his students, the future Saint Gregory Thaumaturgus, a text also known as *The Panegyric on Origen.* From this we learn that the school Origen opened at Caesarea was more than a catechetical establishment. It was a missionary institute

---

[7]Jerome, *To Paula* (= *Letter* 33), 4, trans. W. Fremantle, G. Lewis, and W. G. Martley, in *Nicene and Post-Nicene Fathers*, ed. Philip Schaff and Henry Wace, 2nd series, vol. 6 (Buffalo, NY: Christian Literature Publishing, 1893).

aimed at young pagans interested in Christianity but not yet ready to ask for Baptism. Origen presented Christianity via a philosophy course emphasising those biblical doctrines that can be expressed in philosophical terms. If students asked for Baptism, only later would they receive catechesis in the full dogmatic sense, explaining the rule of faith as a whole. But in either phase, study was intended to serve spiritual development.

Gregory Thaumaturgus stresses the way Origen served as a true model of the virtues for his hearers, and above all, the virtue of piety—specifically piety towards the Logos, the Word of God. "And thus, like some spark lighting upon our inmost soul, love was kindled and burst into flame within us—a love at once to the Holy Word, the most lovely object of all, who attracts all irresistibly towards Himself by His unutterable beauty, and to this man [i.e., Origen], His friend and advocate."[8] Gregory surely has in mind Origen's reverence for the Bible. This is an accolade that reflects Origen's high view of Scripture as itself a kind of incarnation of the Logos, the Logos in a book.

Origen was arrested during the Decian persecution in 250. He was tortured but survived. Released when Decius was killed fighting the Goths in 251, he died a couple of years later, around 254. Not altogether surprisingly, a modern fresco I was shown in a Muscovite monastery portrays him as the holy Origen, with a halo around his head, though this is far from being the general view in the Eastern Church.[9]

Origen's Output

Origen would have said, and modern scholars agree with him, that the most important element in his output was his writings on Sacred Scripture. We have three hundred biblical homilies by Origen, a

---

[8] Gregory Thaumaturgus, *Address of Thanks* VI, 83, trans. S. D. F. Salmond, in *Ante-Nicene Fathers*, ed. Alexander Roberts, James Donaldson, and A. Cleveland Coxe, vol. 6 (Buffalo, NY: Christian Literature Publishing, 1886).

[9] There will not, I hazard, be many parallels in Orthodox iconography to the wall painting of Origen, standing among the holy Fathers, in the layfolk's refectory in the Visoko-Petrovskiy monastery in central Moscow, which I was shown in the winter of 2019–2020. It reflected the devotion of a married priest responsible for the catechetical work of the patriarchate who restored the building before the return of the monks.

fragment of the total, but still an amazing number when compared with the mere handful of ancient Christian homilies that are earlier than his. (English-language readers are well-supplied, as a glance at the Bibliography found at the end of this book shows.) Occasionally, new homilies are found. In 2012 the Bavarian State Library announced that an Italian scholar had identified twenty-nine previously unknown homilies in a twelfth-century Byzantine manuscript in the library's possession. Jerome's *Letter to Paula*, already mentioned, attempts a full list of his contributions to three genres of exegetical work: biblical commentaries, biblical homilies, and so-called scholia— short sets of comments on especially difficult or important extracts from Scripture.

Jerome's list does not include Origen's most ambitious biblical work, the Hexapla, a word that means "six columns": the text lays out side by side six different versions of the Old Testament. Though the Hexapla is lost (except for fragments), it is believed there were four columns for four different Greek translations, with two columns for the Hebrew text known to Origen, one column of which was written in Greek characters, and the other in Hebrew characters. Critical signs indicated where the texts in the various columns diverged from the Church's official version, the Septuagint, "the Bible of the earliest Christians", as it has been called.[10]

As to writings that are less exegetical in form, all include much interpretation of Scripture. If we leave aside two short spiritual classics, the *Exhortation to Martyrdom* and the *Treatise on Prayer*, and two minor works, only partly preserved, found in a stone quarry outside Cairo (the *Dialogue with Heraclides*, a debate with Arabian bishops about the Father and the Son and the human soul, and *On the Passover*, which, following Saint Paul in 1 Corinthians 5:7, identifies the true Passover as Christ himself), the most important of such nonexegetical writings are *On First Principles*, Origen's major theological work, and *Against Celsus* (Latin, *Contra Celsum*), a lengthy apologia for Christian claims.

First in time comes *On First Principles*, which describes the cosmos as coming forth from the Trinity and returning to it. While invoking

[10] Paul Lamarche, S.J., "The Septuagint: Bible of the Earliest Christians", in *The Bible in Greek Christian Antiquity*, ed. Paul M. Blowers (Notre Dame, IN: University of Notre Dame Press, 1997), pp. 15–33.

the contents of the rule of faith, it seeks to deal more especially with problems the rule of faith has left unresolved, using Scripture and reason. (The origin of the human soul is perhaps the most significant of these—certainly the most crucial for Origen's attempt at a Christian cosmology as a whole: for Origen, before the physical cosmos existed, our minds preexisted, but unfortunately they fell away from God.) Here is how Origen introduces this work in its Preface:

> Now it ought to be known that the holy apostles, in preaching the faith of Christ, delivered themselves with the utmost clearness on certain points which they believed to be necessary to everyone, even those [persons] who seemed somewhat dull in the investigation of divine knowledge; leaving, however, the grounds of their statements to be examined into by those who should deserve the excellent gifts of the Spirit, and who, especially by means of the Holy Spirit Himself, should obtain the gift of language, of wisdom, and of knowledge: while on other subjects they merely stated the fact that things are so, keeping silence as to the manner of origin of their existence; clearly in order that the more zealous of their successors, who should be lovers of wisdom, might have a subject of exercise on which to display the fruit of their talents—those persons, I mean, who should prepare themselves to be fit and worthy receivers of wisdom.[11]

After this, Origen lays out the rule of faith, noting that among the topics needing to be clarified are the status of the Holy Spirit, the origin of the soul, the mode of existence of the angels, and the question of what, if anything, existed before the present world, and what will exist after it.

So there you have in advance a list of the issues that later worried Origen's readers: his doctrine of the Trinity, his protology, his angelology (which is in fact included in his protology), and his eschatology—in other words, his account of the start of all things and their end.

---

[11] Origen, *On First Principles*, Preface, 3. Rowan Williams writes, "In his nearest approach to a full statement of his system, the treatise *On First Principles*, he distinguishes carefully [in I, 1, 1] between those matters that are part of the *ecclesiastica praedicatio*, the official proclamation of the Church, and those that are deliberately left uncertain, so that keener minds among believers may have the chance to display their love of wisdom by exploring the deeper meaning of Scripture." Rowan Williams, "Origen", in *The First Christian Theologians*, ed. G. R. Evans (Oxford: Blackwell, 2004), p. 132.

Sometimes described as the first-ever sketch of a Christian *Summa theologiae*, Origen's *On First Principles* is rather more tentative than that description would suggest. Not seldom, Origen lays out various opinions and invites the reader to select the one he thinks is best.[12] *On First Principles* is the source from which most of the later deviant Origenism took its rise. In introducing the work, G. W. Butterworth, translator of the Greek fragments and the Latin paraphrase, wrote: "The thoughts to which Origen's speculations led him proved strange and disturbing to Christians of later ages. But we need not doubt that they were natural enough to the age and intellectual environment in which they arose. It never occurred to Origen that he was anything but an orthodox defender of the faith. All he tried to do was to work out its implications for the educated world of his time."[13] The issues this involved will naturally need to be addressed in my account.

The other very important nonexegetical writing is *Against Celsus*, a treatise written to answer (posthumously) a Middle Platonist philosopher, Celsus, who had attacked Christianity. Celsus' onslaught, recorded in substantial citations by Origen, was to influence pagan and neo-pagan critiques of the Gospel from the fourth to the twentieth centuries. *Against Celsus* was Origen's last major effort, and, aside from Augustine's *City of God*, it is by common accord the greatest work of Christian apologetics antiquity produced.[14] It is the only substantial work by Origen preserved in its entirety in the original Greek as distinct from Latin translations. The renowned Oxbridge patristic scholar Henry Chadwick paid it the following compliment:

> In the *contra Celsum* Origen does not merely vindicate the character of Jesus and the credibility of the Christian tradition; he also shows that Christians can be so far from being irrational and credulous illiterates such as Celsus thinks them to be that they may know more about

[12] For example, see Origen, *On First Principles* III, 4, 5.

[13] G. W. Butterworth, Introduction to Origen, *On First Principles* (London: Society for Promoting Christian Knowledge, 1936; Gloucester, MA: Peter Smith Publishing, 1973), p. liii. Citations are from the 1973 edition.

[14] Crouzel, *Origen*, p. 47. The same evaluation is made by Henry Chadwick: "In the history of the intellectual struggle between the old and the new religion the *contra Celsum* is of the first importance, comparable only with Augustine's *City of God*." Henry Chadwick, Introduction to *Origen: Contra Celsum* (1953; repr., Cambridge: Cambridge University Press, 1980), p. xiii. Citations from *Contra Celsum* are from this translation.

Greek philosophy than the pagan Celsus himself, and can make intelligent use of it to interpret the doctrines of the Church. In the range of his learning he towers above his pagan adversary, handling the traditional arguments of Academy and Stoa [i.e., Platonists and Stoics] with masterly ease and fluency.[15]

The distinguishing feature of almost all Origen's writings is that it combines exegesis, spirituality, and speculative theology—a threesome often separated in Christian history with unfortunate results. In the words of a French patrologist, he "knows no distinction of the genres. They constantly interpenetrate, so that one of these aspects cannot be understood if abstracted from the other two."[16] Nevertheless, they must be to some degree abstracted by the student in order to present Origen's teaching in a manageable way. So I shall look now in turn at Origen's biblical interpretation, spirituality, and speculative theology on which his reputation foundered—at least until recently among Catholics but not the Orthodox, for whom, despite the discrete support given him at an early stage of their careers by two of the Cappadocian Fathers, Basil and Gregory Nazianzen, he remains irredeemably tarred with the brush of heresy, the modern Muscovite fresco notwithstanding.

Origen's Exegesis

Origen's exegesis has been enormously influential in the Christian tradition, even among authors who, owing to his apparent condemnation by the Church, did not want to mention his name. The upshot of his exegesis is found in his spirituality and speculative theology, but his method can be laid out in and for itself. He distinguished between the literal and the spiritual sense of Scripture, but not in the

---

[15] Chadwick, Introduction to *Contra Celsum*, p. xii. It is noteworthy, however, that Origen begins his work by disclaiming much value for an intellectual apologia for Christianity when compared with a moral defence: "Now Jesus is always being falsely accused, and there is never a time when he is not being accused so long as there is evil among men. He is still silent in face of this and does not answer with his voice; but he makes his defence in the lives of his genuine disciples, for their lives cry out the real facts and defeat all false charges, refuting and overthrowing the slanders and accusations." Origen, *Contra Celsum*, Preface, 2.

[16] Crouzel, *Origen*, p. 54.

way found in later authors, in the mediaeval and modern periods. For Origen, the literal sense does not mean, as it does for Saint Thomas, for instance, or for modern exegetes working in the Catholic tradition, the sense consciously intended by the human author of this or that biblical book. The literal sense for Origen is not what the biblical author was seeking to express; rather it is the *vehicle* for what he was seeking to express, the "raw material" found in a passage prior to all interpretation, of whatever kind.

In an example offered by Henri Crouzel, the literal sense of the parable of the prodigal son (Lk 15:11–32) is not at all for Origen a religious message; it is simply the dramatic situation set out in the parable, minus any interpretation that tries to establish the intention of the parable's author. Yet because the literal sense even in this minimalist construction of that phrase can still be worth investigating as a preamble to interpretation, Origen was keen on making use of any secular discipline that could throw light on it. This professional seriousness as a critic is compatible, then, with Origen's declaring from time to time that a particular instance of the literal sense is incoherent, absurd, impossible, or even scandalous. As he writes in *On First Principles*,

> Divine wisdom took care that certain stumbling-blocks, or interruptions, to the literal meaning should take place by the introduction into the midst of certain impossibilities and incongruities, that in this way the very interruption of the narrative might, as by the interposition of a bolt [as with a bolted door, he means], present an obstacle to the reader, whereby he might refuse to acknowledge the way which conducts to the ordinary meaning, and being thus excluded and debarred form it, he might be recalled to the beginning of another way, in order that, by entering upon a narrow path, and passing to a loftier and more sublime road, he might lay open the immense breadth of divine wisdom.[17]

One notes the words "another way", and it is a spiritual way. The principal aim of the divine author of Scripture is to "announce the

---

[17] Origen, *On First Principles* IV, 17. I have altered the Crombie translation by replacing "historical" with "literal". Origen's term *historia* can cover both, but in this context, the latter makes the greater sense.

spiritual connexion in those things that are done, and that ought to be done".[18] In more contemporary theological language, that means everything revelation contains in regard to God's action in history and in regard likewise to the desired human response to that action by Christian practice, with the two—action and response—seen as an interconnected whole.

Origen's single main reason for advocating spiritual—in his word, "allegorical"—exegesis of the Old Testament is that given down the ages under the general heading of "typology". Christians should practise such exegesis because they can see the New Testament authors doing so in the way they make use of the Old Testament. In Galatians, for example, Saint Paul treats Sarah and Hagar, the wife and concubine respectively of Abraham, as prefiguring a contrast between Christians and Jews (4:21–31). Sarah is a type of the New Covenant, which belongs to free men; Hagar of the Old, which is for those still slaves to the Law. Typology suited well Origen's overall strategy as a Christian apologist. As Henry Chadwick notes, "He needed to provide exegesis implicitly refuting Marcion's rejection of the Hebrew Scriptures but also disallowing rabbinic literalism."[19]

This typological version of spiritual or allegorical exegesis is paramount in Origen, who works with a three-level scheme: the Law, the Gospel, and the realities of the Age to Come—by which he means reality as apprehended in the perfect knowledge that belongs to the blessed in heaven. The Law is shadow; the Gospel is image; the *pragmata*, or realities, are the knowledge of the Age to Come. The main bifurcation here is between the shadow on the one hand, and the image and the *pragmata* on the other. The shadow, the Law, expresses only a hope or desire for the realities, a surmise or presentiment of their existence, whereas the image, the Gospel, is already a participation in the *pragmata*, albeit one that is finite and imperfect. Origen distinguishes between the temporal Gospel and the eternal Gospel. We might have assumed from the language used that shadow and image would be on one side, "the realities" on the other. But for Origen the image and the realities possess the same substance:

[18] Ibid., IV, 15.
[19] Henry Chadwick, *The Church in Ancient Society: From Galilee to Gregory the Great* (Oxford: Oxford University Press, 2001), p. 135.

they differ only aspectually, in the way human persons conceived them. Though the shadow remains of interest since the two Testaments together constitute a single word from God (they are both the expression of the Logos in human language enabled by the Holy Spirit), our chief task as interpreters of Scripture is to move from the temporal Gospel to the eternal Gospel: from the world of types, including New Testament types, to the world of the spiritual realities to come. As he writes in the *Commentary on the Gospel of John*: "What we have to do now is to transform the sensible Gospel into a spiritual one. For what would the narrative of the sensible Gospel amount to if it were not developed to a spiritual one? It would be of little account or none; anyone can read it and assure himself of the facts it tells—no more. But our whole energy is now to be directed to the effort to penetrate to the deep things of the meaning of the Gospel and to search out the truth that is in it when divested of types."[20]

In Origen's way of reading the Bible, there are also wider considerations relevant to the interpretation not just of the Old Testament, foreshadowing the image, but of the New Testament—the expression of the image—as well. Thus for instance, biblical authors may have had a didactic intention in writing their narratives, and for that, spiritual interpretation is required. They may have left conflicting historical accounts (for instance, Saint John's Gospel, so Origen points out, leaves no room for the forty days of the temptations of Christ[21]), and for that, spiritual interpretation is required. They may have used symbols, and for those, spiritual interpretation is required. They may—they did—speak anthropomorphically about God (they wrote "anthropopathically"—about God's hands, God's face, and even God's backside), and for that too spiritual interpretation is required. These exegetical strategies will recur in later writers and end up as commonplace.

But Origen has a further message for spiritual exegesis that is not commonplace at all. He wants to find in the Bible an extraordinary concentration of Christological meaning. As he explains in his

[20] Origen, *Commentary on the Gospel of John* I, 10, trans. and ed. Allan Menzies, in *Ante-Nicene Fathers*, vol. 9 (Buffalo, NY: Christian Literature Publishing, 1896). Citations from *Commentary on the Gospel of John* are from this translation.

[21] Ibid., X, 2.

Commentary on the Gospel of John, "What the Gospels say is to be regarded in the light of promises of good things; and we must say that the good things the Apostles announce in this Gospel are simply Jesus."[22] The many names Jesus receives in this Gospel[23] indicate for Origen the multitude of goods he contains in himself and offers to us, and to these goods spiritual interpretation holds the key. For Origen his single most important name in Saint John is Logos, the "Word" (1:1), and in this paramount example Origen explains what he means.

> He is also called the Logos, because He takes away from us all that is irrational, and makes us truly reasonable, so that we do all things, even to eating and drinking, to the glory of God, and discharge by the Logos to the glory of God both the commoner functions of life and those which belong to a more advanced stage. For if, by having part in Him, we are raised up and enlightened, herded also it may be and ruled over, then it is clear that we become in a divine manner reasonable, when He drives away from us what in us is irrational and dead, since He is the Logos and the Resurrection.[24]

Such spiritual interpretation is not necessarily easy. Origen emphasises the need for the Scriptures to be read in the same Spirit in which they were written. One can interpret the Gospel aright only if one has the mind of Christ, which the Spirit gives.[25] How does one acquire this mindset from the Spirit? Origen's answer runs, through living a life in conformity with the will of God there develops a resemblance, *homoiôsis*, to the divine in humans, humans who in any case are already made *kata ton eikona*, "according to the image [of God]". Such "resemblance" makes possible, according to Origen, an habitual attunement to the mind of Christ as disclosed in the Holy

---

[22] Ibid., I, 10.

[23] For example, "light of the world" (8:12), "the life" (11:25), "the way" (14:6), "the true vine" (15:1), "bread" (6:32), and "door" (10:1).

[24] Origen, *Commentary on the Gospel of John* I, 42.

[25] Cf. Origen's exegesis of the "many things" the disciples could not "bear" (Jn 16:12): "By 'many things' [Jesus] means the method of explanation and exegesis of the law according to the spiritual sense, and somehow the disciples could not bear them because they had been born and brought up among the Jews. I think also that it was because those ceremonies were a type, while the ultimate reality was that which the Holy Spirit was to teach them." Origen, *Contra Celsum* II, 2.

Scriptures. Origen can also offer a devotional explanation for how to get this mindset. In the *Commentary on the Gospel of John*, having declared that "the Gospels are the first-fruits of all the Scriptures, but that of the Gospels that of John is the first-fruits", he goes on: "No one can apprehend the meaning of it except he have lain on Jesus' breast and received from Jesus Mary to be his mother also."[26]

Origen as Spiritual Master

Turning now to Origen's spirituality, though Origen has things to say about asceticism—notably in the context of martyrdom, which was (at any rate periodically) an immediate possibility in his own period, and the two "lives" of marriage and virginity (the conjugal life, the virginal life)—his spirituality is principally taken up with the *via mystica*, the mystical way.[27] This is a way of union with God by knowledge and love that, for Origen, is not restricted to a spiritual elite, but is a matter of a general Christian calling. The Logos became flesh principally to give his faithful the liquor of spiritual joy. Commenting on Saint John's Gospel, he notes that whereas the Synoptics tell us that at the start of Jesus' ministry, the sick were healed at Capernaum (Mt 4:23; Mk 1:34; Lk 4:40), John chooses to make his first "sign" the miracle of turning water into wine at Cana (2:3–10). Origen comments: "The Word of God does not set forth His own beauty so much in healing the sick, as in His tendering the temperate draught to make glad those who are in good health and are able to join in the banquet"—"temperate draught" is what other Fathers speak of as the "sober intoxication" of spiritual joy.[28]

Origen's spirituality turns on his doctrine of the Image of God in man, which makes him representative of the patristic tradition at large—and yet his anthropology is distinctive and indeed controversial, though in his homilies, meant for public consumption as they were, he did not advertise the fact. At first sight, his account of man seems indistinguishable from that of Saint Paul's, whom he cites: we

---

[26] Origen, *Commentary on the Gospel of John* I, 6.

[27] I follow here the account in Crouzel, *Origen*, pp. 87–133.

[28] Origen, *Commentary on the Gospel of John* X, 10.

are made up of "spirit, soul, and body" (1 Thess 5:23).[29] But none of these terms are straightforward in Origen's use.

"Spirit" is in one sense the gift of the divine Spirit to man.[30] But Origen employs the term in his general anthropology, not simply for the human person under the impact of what the mediaeval and modern theologians call sanctifying grace.[31] By the "spirit" element in us, Origen appears to mean an opportunity, given with our overall constitution, for the Spirit of God to enter our lives in a new way.[32] In the language of twentieth-century Catholic theology, "spirit" for Origen is the locus of the openness of the natural to the supernatural.

As to the soul, that, for Origen, is bipartite. The higher soul he calls the intellect, and, for him, the soul in this sense preexists not only our personal life in the world but also the cosmic, or better, precosmic, Fall of God's rational creatures at the beginning of time as we know it. The intellect is the seat of the Image of God in us, or, in the phrase Origen prefers, the "according to the Image" in us, the *kata ton eikona*, for in his theology there is only one proper Image of God, the Father's uncreated Word, or Son.

There is, however, one unique example of a human mind that is perfectly "according to the Image". The created intellect of Jesus, Jesus' soul in the higher sense of the word, is the "image of the Image": a perfect—and in that way unique—created image of the uncreated Image, the Logos. Of all the minds that once existed in communion with God, only Jesus' mind never failed in charity and thus in likeness to the Word. At the Incarnation, this created image of the uncreated Image—and thereby the uncreated Image itself—was united with an instance of the lower soul of man, the element in us that carries our emotional life, as also, via that lower soul, with an earthly human body. Thus, the lower soul and body of a human being were united to the preexistent mind of Jesus and

---

[29] Origen can also operate with the rather simpler Platonic (and, before Plato, "Orphic") dichotomous scheme of material element and spiritual element, though this may be a matter only of "poles" which compete in attracting the soul—a decisive consideration in "spiritual warfare". Henri Crouzel, "L'anthropologie d'Origène dans la perspective du combat spirituel", *Revue d'ascétique et de mystique* 31 (1955): 364–85.

[30] Origen, *Commentary on the Gospel of John* II, 138.

[31] Origen, *Dialogue with Heraclides* 6.

[32] Origen, *On Prayer* 2, 4.

thereby to the divine Word himself, so producing what we call the "Word incarnate".

Just as the "spirit" is meant to guide the intellect, the higher "soul" in us, so the higher soul is meant in turn to guide the "lower" soul—which in Jesus' case it did, after the Incarnation, superlatively well. But in the case of all other souls—that is, the souls of the rest of the human race—the lower soul is turned towards the earthly body and expresses the condition described by Saint Paul as "flesh" (Gal 5:16–25), a disordered condition where the "according to the Image" in us is unable to reflect its ultimate archetype, the Word of God. The "flesh" for Origen is, then, as in Pauline theology, not the body; instead, it is the disordered condition in which the soul finds itself as a result of sin. But the body, entirely good in itself, is the excuse or occasion the soul makes its own in turning away from the spirit and falling into sin, into moral evil.

"Body", the last of the three anthropological components, is also a tricky term in Origen's writing. Not only our intellect as it now exists, united to a lower soul and an earthly body, but that same intellect in its preexistence, was or is in some ethereal sense "bodily". Origen has little difficulty about belief in the identity of the individual human body now and the individual human body as it will exist in the resurrection—precisely because he thinks our minds, even before their union with the body in its present form, had some sort of ("luminous") bodily aspect. (For Origen, only the divine Trinity is fully incorporeal.[33]) So the "spiritual body" with which Paul expects to be clothed at the Parousia, when human beings are raised to share the Resurrection life of the crucified divine Son, has already existed, albeit in a less exalted manner, before we were born. Even now that earlier version of a spiritual body underlies the earthly format of our body as we experience it in the present life. The earthly format is a "heavy" body which, owing to our common descent from Adam or our imitative following of his example, carries a tendency towards sin, or at any rate an impurity that baptismal regeneration, Gospel teaching, and ascetic practice serve to purge.[34]

---

[33] Origen, *On First Principles* II, 2, 2.

[34] Here Origen's *Commentary on the Letter to the Romans*, though available only in Rufinus' Latin translation, is key. See Caroline Bammel, "Adam in Origen", in *The Making of Orthodoxy: Essays in Honour of Henry Chadwick*, ed. Rowan Williams (Cambridge: Cambridge University Press, 1989), pp. 62–93.

We have been looking at these elements in Origen's anthropology under the heading of Origen as a spiritual master. I said that Origen's account of the mystical way turns on his doctrine of the Image of God in man—as is true of all the Fathers. The "according to the Image" in us, for Origen, is a dynamic reality that tends towards that assimilation to the divine which even pagan Hellenism thought necessary for the fulfillment of human nature. But the "according to the Image" in our higher soul cannot reach a condition of likeness with God— here is what pagans could not know—unless the incarnate Word, redeeming the human creation by his Passion and Death, forms it anew by the grace of the Holy Spirit. As Origen writes of the crucified yet triumphant Logos in the Apocalypse of Saint John (cf. Rev 19:11–16), "He is clothed with a garment sprinkled with blood.... For of that passion, even should it be our lot some day to come to that highest and supreme contemplation of the Logos, we shall not lose all memory, nor shall we forget the truth that our admission was brought about by His sojourning in our body."[35] Our remaking starts with Baptism. Then the active virtues come to be formed, and in due course there arises in us, to a greater or lesser degree, a contemplative knowing of the Father in the Son. This for Origen is the birth and growth in each human person of the presence of Jesus, that same Jesus whose created mind was eternally united to the Word by charity, and is now, in the time of the Incarnation, Easter, and Pentecost, united with an embodied soul-life exactly like ours, and empowered to bring all back to God through the Holy Spirit.

This is the mystery of our rebirth, our divinization, which, owing to its incomparable comprehensiveness, Origen calls not a mystery but "*the* Mystery". Like Irenaeus, he thinks that loving knowledge of the Mystery, obtained through spiritual exegesis of the Scriptures accompanied by prayer and asceticism, and lived out through the virtues (he stresses especially humility and charity), is what makes us holy, spiritual, and, ultimately, perfect. This loving knowledge makes possible, beginning now, the re-creation of the condition in which all minds were created, before the Fall, at the world's beginnings.

Origen created much of the enduring vocabulary of Christian mysticism, synthesizing biblical themes with language drawn from both philosophy and earlier Christian tradition. Examples are the dart

---

[35] Origen, *Commentary on the Gospel of John* II, 4.

or wound of love, and the mystical marriage of the bridal soul with the Bridegroom, the Word of God; the birth of Christ in the soul, already mentioned; and the theme of grace as light, life, and nourishment, which, while it has obvious sources in Johannine and Pauline thought, is enormously developed by him. More especially his own is the notion of the spiritual senses by which the mind under grace sees, hears, and touches the Word with the eyes of the soul, the ears of the heart, and a tact for his presence, and delights in so doing, which delight Origen links with the sense of taste and smell.

Origen as Doctrinal Theologian

After the councils of Nicaea (325) and Constantinople I (381), Origen's account of the Word and the Holy Spirit were justly criticised for "Subordinationism": an insufficient awareness of the equality of Son and Spirit with the Father when considered as possessors of the divine nature. Though Origen can speak, in the *Commentary on the Gospel of John*, of the "Only-begotten" as "by nature and from the beginning the Son", in the same commentary he also speaks of the Son as "not continuing to be God ... except by remaining always in uninterrupted contemplation of the depths of the Father".[36] And we saw how, in the Preface to *On First Principles*, Origen considers that the rule of faith has not made plain the status of the Holy Spirit. In the John commentary, Origen is inclined to consider the Spirit as called into existence by the Son without deciding absolutely firmly whether this is compatible with describing the Spirit as uncreated.[37] Yet Hans Urs von Balthasar, for his part, gives Origen the benefit of the doubt, stating,

> Origen is, even in this matter, the most orthodox of the pre-Nicene theologians. He clearly distinguishes the internal divine processions from the creation of the world. The Son is not, as he was for Arius and many before him, a "means" of creation but the eternal birth of love of the Father.... The way to salvation leads from the objective revelation of the Son, through the subjective appropriation in the

[36] Ibid., II, 2.
[37] Ibid., II, 6.

Spirit to perfect life in the Father.... Subordinationism in Origen has a stronger salvation-history aspect and thus can be better brought into harmony with Nicaean theology.... What is still lacking in Origen's inner-trinitarian theology he makes up for with his magnificent salvation-historical trinitarianism.[38]

The main problems with Origen's theology for later Christian orthodoxy concern his protology and eschatology—that is, his account of what happened at the beginning of creation and what will happen at the end of all things, the consummation of the world. In Origen's opinion, the rule of faith, Scripture read in the light of Tradition, contained no clear guidance on the question of the origin of the individual human intellect.[39] The solution he put forward to this protological question—namely, that minds "pre-existed"— influenced him in considering the eschatological question and, specifically, the possibility that, at the end, there will be a restoration of minds to the original condition in which they once existed. As he writes, "The end" is always "like the beginning."[40]

When thinking protologically of creation at large, Origen found it hard to credit that God's beneficent power could ever have been inert. But if that power were everlastingly active, this could be, in the face of biblical teaching on the world's origin in time, only in relation to an "ideal" existence—in the Logos, the Father's Wisdom—of things that were "prefigured" before they were "substantially" created.[41] This hypothesis had an additional advantage when the "things" in question were the minds of humans. If minds were, in this preliminary way, preexistent, perhaps they could have a moral history—for good or ill. If they were created from nothing, then they must have been mutable, and if they are, more especially, rational creatures, then they must have been capable of good and evil. Could they have

[38] Hans Urs von Balthasar, Introduction to *Origen: Spirit and Fire; A Thematic Anthology of His Writings*, trans. Robert J. Daly, S.J. (Washington, DC: Catholic University of America Press, 1984), p. 14.

[39] A gap that obviously worried him since he returns to it on a number of occasions, not only in the Preface to *On First Principles* but also in his commentary on Saint Paul's Letter to Titus (portions of which survive in the one extant book of an *Apology for Origen* by his pupil Pamphilus) and in his *Commentary on the Song of Songs*, II, 1, 8.

[40] Origen, *On First Principles* I, 6, 2.

[41] Ibid., I, 4, 3–5.

become—in various degrees, no doubt—negligent through compla-
cency, cooling in their intellectual love of God? Is their existence
in the physical cosmos a therapeutic treatment, in some cases mild, in
others harsh? This in turn suggested a possible theodicy: a justification
of God's overall activity vis-à-vis the world.

Origen was attracted to the notion of the precosmic "fall" of minds
imperfectly attached to God because he wanted to defend the justice
of God against pagan critics of Judaeo-Christianity.[42] If the condition in which individuals find themselves at birth—some handsome,
some ugly; some rich, some poor; some handicapped, some whole—
reflects their free choices in the so-called Church of the preexistence,
then the justice of God is vindicated. There is nothing unfair about
the unequal start different individuals have in life on earth.[43] Also
justified is God's election of the created mind (or "higher soul") of
Jesus to be uniquely the recipient of his grace. Christian orthodoxy,
after all, has accepted this idea of the crucial importance of precosmic
choice for one set of intellects—namely, the angels. Origen cautions,
however, that his hypothesis, whatever its seeming merits, requires
further examination and thought.[44]

As to Origen's eschatology, from the (admittedly incomplete) evidence we have at our disposal it seems unlikely that Origen ever
taught the ultimate salvation of the Devil—unlike the fourth-century
monk Evagrius of Pontus, who was deeply influenced by his teaching.[45] Yet the robust emphasis on human freedom, which drives his
protology, was continued in his eschatology. He did not see how
the exercise of freedom could ever be closed off for the individual
mind in the way the doctrine of everlasting punishment requires. Yet
there is reason to think that by the end of his life, when he wrote his
Commentary on the Gospel of Matthew, he began to think the restorative
power of God was not without all limitation. "It seems to me," wrote
the American Origen scholar Ronald Heine,

---

[42] He may have been thinking especially of Gnostics and *mathematici*, i.e., astrologers. So
much emerges from the First Origenist Controversy, at the end of the fourth century, triggered in the West by the translation into Latin of *On First Principles* in 397. See Elizabeth A.
Clark, *The Origenist Controversy: The Cultural Construction of an Early Christian Debate* (Princeton, NJ: Princeton University Press, 1992), p. 13.

[43] Cf. Origen, *On First Principles* II, 9, 5–8.

[44] Ibid., II, 8, 3–4.

[45] See Clark, *Origenist Controversy*, p. 101.

a defensible, but not an unquestionable, conclusion that in Caesarea Origen was in the process of rethinking his view of the ultimate salvation or restoration of all beings. If this is true, then we should proceed with caution when we encounter discussions of this subject in his late works and not immediately conclude that what he says in these works can be fleshed out with positions he held in Alexandria when he wrote the *On First Principles* and the early books of the *Commentary on John*.[46]

That is negative eschatology, but what of positive? Origen was clear that the blessed will never fall away again. In this regard the end *does* differ from the beginning. It will exclude any further possibility of deviation from the enjoyment of the divine Good, to which, by the saving economy of the Son and the Spirit, sent from the Father, they would by then be fully attached.[47] But eschatology, when concerned with human persons, has to consider not only souls but bodies. As to a new existence for the body in the Age to Come, in his (now lost) commentary on Psalm 1, Origen held that the bodily "form" (*eidos*) exists continuously in each person despite the flux of the body's elements, and it is this, not the elements, which will be raised in glory.[48] For some ancient writers, this proved the orthodoxy of Origen's account of the General Resurrection. For others, contrariwise, it proved his heterodoxy.

Successive revivals of Origenism understood as a set of distinctive theses about protology and eschatology meant that the issue of Origen's personal status as a Church teacher came onto the wider Church agenda, initially in the late fourth century—the so-called First Origenist Crisis.[49] Here the objection was to Origen's Subordinationism, what was deemed his excessive use of allegorical interpretation of the Bible, and his habit of proposing theses about Christian doctrine in a speculative manner, rather than dogmatically. Then in the mid-sixth century there followed the second, more serious, Origenist crisis, which centred on his protology and eschatology—more

---

[46] Heine, *Origen*, p. 256.

[47] Origen, *On First Principles* III, 6, 3.

[48] Clark, *Origenist Controversy*, p. 162.

[49] Emanuela Prinzivalli, *Magister ecclesiae: Il debattito su Origene fra III e IV secolo* (Rome: Institutum Patristicum Augustianum, 2002).

serious because it led to an imperial order that Origen's books should be burned. Posthumous condemnation of teachers who had the chance neither to explain themselves nor to recant was not popular in the patristic Church. But occasionally it happened. The condemnations of Origen were, on the one hand, from a local synod in Constantinople, and on the other, in the immediate aftermath of the general or ecumenical council held under the emperor Justinian in the same city in 553: the Fifth Ecumenical Council, Constantinople II.

It was, in part, owing to the local nature of the earlier synod and the absence of a condemnation from the sessions, strictly so defined, of the later council, that some figures associated with the *nouvelle théologie* of mid-twentieth-century Catholicism, notably Henri de Lubac and Jean Daniélou, hoped (or so it is said) to persuade Pope Paul VI, at the start of his pontificate, to rehabilitate Origen. There was also a shift at that time in the scholarly consensus. In the years 1961–1962, the French patrologist Antoine Guillaumont had pretty conclusively proved that the sixth-century condemnations concerned theses taken not from Origen's writings but from those of the aforementioned Evagrius (notably in the Syriac version of Evagrius' "Kephalaia Gnostica").[50] Rumblings of opposition from the Orthodox East are believed to have dissuaded the pope; yet it may not be coincidence that some passages from Origen's writings were incorporated into the patristic lectionary of Pope Paul's revised Liturgy of the Hours. In a series of 2007 addresses on the Church Fathers, Pope Benedict XVI called Origen "a figure crucial to the whole development of Christian thought", a true "maestro", and "not only a brilliant theologian but also an exemplary witness of the doctrine he passed on".[51] The pope, himself no mean theologian, invited his hearers to "welcome into your hearts the teaching of this great master of the faith".[52]

---

[50] Antoine Guillaumont, "Evagre et les anathématismes anti-origéniste de 553", in *Studia Patristica* 3, 1 (papers presented to the Third International Conference on Patristic Studies, Christ Church, Oxford, 1959), ed. F. L. Cross (Berlin: Akademie-Verlag, 1961), pp. 219–26; Antoine Guillaumont, *Les "Kephalaia Gnostica" d'Evagre le Pontique et l'histoire d'Origénisme chez les Grecs at chez les Syriens* (Paris: Seuil, 1962).

[51] Pope Benedict XVI, "Origen of Alexandria", in *Church Fathers: From Clement of Rome to Augustine* (San Francisco: Ignatius Press, 2008), p. 32.

[52] Ibid., p. 37. It is notable, however, that Benedict concentrates on Origen's hermeneutical theory and his teaching on the Christian life, steering clear of his proctology and eschatology.

The premier modern student of the Second Origenist Controversy, Elizabeth Clark, asks, pertinently, "Was the debate really over Origen?" And she replies, "In some ways, the answer is no: 'Origen' served as a code word for various theological concerns problematic to Christians."[53] Yet it can hardly be claimed that Origen's texts were nothing more than a pretext for later debates, that the condemned opinions had nothing whatever to do with his speculations. Nevertheless, Origen's spiritual presence in the patristic and subsequent tradition of both East and West is too pervasive for him simply to be unchurched.[54] As Balthasar put it, "While the jar was breaking into a thousand pieces and the name of the master was being overwhelmed and stoned, the fragrance of the ointment was coming forth and 'filling the whole house'."[55]

[53] Clark, *Origenist Controversy*, p. 6.

[54] For the profound influence of Origen's biblical exegesis on the monastic tradition of the Western Middle Ages, see Jean Leclerq, O.S.B., *The Love of Learning and the Desire for God: A Study of Monastic Culture*, trans. Catharine Misrahi (New York: Fordham University Press, 1961), pp. 100–103.

[55] Von Balthasar, Introduction to *Spirit and Fire*, p. 2.

3

Champion of the Lord's Divinity:
Saint Athanasius

Saint Athanasius was born at Alexandria, probably of pagan or mixed pagan-Christian parentage, in 295 or thereabouts.[1] His life, from the time he became bishop of Alexandria in 328, is an extremely complicated as well as turbulent story. That was owing to the contemporary use of synods in both East and West to deny, endorse, adjust, or mitigate (as the case may be) the teaching of the First Ecumenical Council, Nicaea I, in 325, in the face of changes of emperor or imperial policy on the one hand and the shifting balance of episcopal opinion on the other. Between Nicaea I, and the First Council of Constantinople in 381, counted by the Great Church as the Second Ecumenical Council, no less than twelve creeds were promulgated and then abandoned.[2]

Throughout his life as a bishop, Athanasius stood firm on the fundamentals of the Nicene doctrine, as taught by the Council he had attended as a deacon—though the often subtle and certainly tortuous debate on Christology that followed prompted him at times to nuance the terms of his assent. The Son, the One who became incarnate as Jesus Christ, so far from being a creature, as Arius, an Alexandrian presbyter, had claimed, is "consubstantial with"—of one being with—God the Father. Arius'

> subordinationist doctrine ran head-on into the principle stated by Irenaeus that only God can make God known, only the Creator can also be our redeemer, and one who is himself a part of the world

[1] For an overview of his life and writings, see David M. Gwynn, *Athanasius of Alexandria: Bishop, Theologian, Ascetic, Father* (Oxford: Oxford University Press, 2012), pp. 1–17.

[2] For the complex story see R. P. C. Hanson, *The Search for the Christian Doctrine of God: The Arian Controversy, 318–381* (Edinburgh: T&T Clark, 1988).

needing salvation cannot by definition save the world. In Athanasius of Alexandria the principles of Irenaeus would be reaffirmed; and any kind of Arian doctrine was treated not as a tolerable mistake but as heresy for which toleration is impossible, since it cut the lifeline of salvation.[3]

By the 350s, at any rate, he was crystal clear that only the full teaching could exclude the Arian heresy once and for all. It had been the teaching of his bishop, Alexander of Alexandria, found especially in the latter's letter to his name sake, Alexander of Thessalonica (some scholars call him "Alexander of Byzantium"). "His Sonship," wrote Alexander of Alexandria, is "according to the nature of the Godhead of the Father."[4] Alexander's aim in his letter was to express what a modern student of the Arian crisis has called the "eternal correlativity of Father and Son": "there could not be an eternal divine Father were there not an eternal divine Son."[5] In Alexander's own words, "The Father is always Father. And He is Father from the continual presence of the Son on account of whom He is called Father."[6]

Out of the forty-six years of his episcopate at Alexandria, Athanasius was in exile from his see, sometimes in hiding, for a total of seventeen years: from 335 to 337 at Trier in Germany, then from 339 to 346 at Rome, and, finally, on three occasions in the Egyptian desert, shielded by monks: that happened from 356 to 362, and again from 362 to 363, and lastly, the shortest of the five exiles, for some months in 365 and 366. The locations of these exiles tell us two things. At first Athanasius found far more support in the Western Church than in the East. But later his cause was supremely upheld by some of his own countrymen—namely, the Desert monastics— though he also had plenty of enemies close to home. It was unfortunate that, irrespective of the Arian controversy, he had inherited a local schism connected with the reconciliation—or otherwise—of

---

[3] Henry Chadwick, *The Church in Ancient Society: From Galilee to Gregory the Great* (Oxford: Oxford University Press, 2001), pp. 197–98.

[4] Alexander of Alexandria, *Letter to Alexander of Thessalonica* 7. Translation is the present author's.

[5] R. D. Williams, "The Logic of Arianism", *Journal of Theological Studies*, n.s., 34, no. 1 (1983): 58.

[6] Alexander of Alexandria, *Letter to Alexandria of Thessalonica* 7. Translation is the present author's.

those who had lapsed during the last, pre-Constantinian, persecution.[7] His own robust, and politically daring, temperament did not always ease the progress of his cause. (The first exile was prompted by his reported threat to initiate strike action, with a view to cutting off grain export to the East Roman capital.[8]) But in the end it was all worthwhile since, in the words of the American Capuchin theologian Thomas Weinandy, "he died knowing that the creed of the Council of Nicaea, for which he suffered all those years of exile because of his ardent defence, had triumphed."[9]

At his death in 373, the victory of the Nicene cause was assured in the Western Roman Empire. In the East, the "Neo-Nicene" theologians—preeminently the Cappadocian Fathers whom we shall study in the next chapter—were infusing fresh hope into its beleaguered partisans. Athanasius did not live long enough to see the accession of the pro-Nicene emperor Theodosius in the Eastern Roman Empire in 379 and the proscription of all Christologies incompatible with the decrees of Nicaea, which Theodosius promulgated in the following year. (The decrees were named only indirectly, by reference to their senior patriarchal supporters, the two "popes", Damasus of Rome and Peter II of Alexandria.) That decision was incorporated into the celebrated "Theodosian Code", the empire's fundamental law.

Athanasius' Early Works

In his early works, *Against the Gentiles* and *On the Incarnation*, which are really two wings of a diptych, Athanasius presents himself as someone who wishes to introduce others to the Christian religion by rehearsing its main lines. Yet in this bipartite work, we do not find

[7] "The persecution of Diocletian precipitated two serious and long-lived schisms, the Donatists at Carthage and North Africa and the followers of Melitius bishop of Lycopolis in Egypt. In both cases the argument turned on the question whether, when the state forbade Christian meetings for worship and required the surrender of Bibles and sacred vessels, one could quietly co-operate with the authorities, or if one was obliged in conscience to resist them as agents of Satan." Chadwick, *Church in Ancient Society*, p. 84. For a comparison with the better known Donatist schism in North Africa, see Gwynn, *Athanasius of Alexandria*, p. 23.

[8] The report is judged credible by Chadwick, *Church in Ancient Society*, p. 202.

[9] Thomas G. Weinandy, *Athanasius: A Theological Introduction* (Farnham: Ashgate, 2007), p. 7.

a complete commentary on the whole rule of faith. In these treatises, Athanasius is preoccupied only with what he considers the main
teachings of Christianity, and that vis-à-vis two groups. In the first
place, these were pagan Hellenes. This is the main concern of *Against
the Gentiles*, where he is confronting with the orthodox faith some
erroneous assertions of Greek philosophy about God and, more especially, the idolatry of Greco-Roman religiosity in its various forms:
polytheistic beliefs, image worship, superstitious rites extending even
to human sacrifice. Secondly, and this is uppermost in *On the Incarnation*, he is concerned with the Jews, who, lacking faith in the Gospel,
had an insufficient grasp of the Logos, the Father's Word, and also
rejected the Incarnation of that Word as Jesus Christ.

We can make some useful generalizations about Athanasius' thinking in *Against the Gentiles* and *On the Incarnation* when these treatises
are considered as a two-part whole. In those works, so the Indian-
born patrologist Khaled Anatolios has written, "emphasis on the
simultaneity of divine otherness and divine nearness to the world is
central" for the way Athanasius conceives the God-world relation.[10]
To Athanasius' mind, God's transcendence and God's immanence go
together. Contrastingly, in the Hellenistic world (not only pagan but
also Jewish—Anatolios is thinking here of Philo of Alexandria, the
Jewish sage who was an older contemporary of Jesus), the qualities
of "absolute transcendence" and "divine immanence" had typically
become separated. In Anatolios' term, they had been "assigned" to
"distinct entities", "higher and lower ... levels of divinity"—such as
"Primal Mind" and "Demiurgic Mind" among the Platonists, or "the
Lord" and "the Logos" or "the Powers" in Philo.[11] That same disjunction between a High God and a lower manifestation of divinity
would continue for the increasingly influential Neoplatonic school
in the form of a relation between the utterly transcendent "One",
on the one hand, and the Universal "Mind" or the "World-Soul", on
the other. But for the biblical perspective proper, so Athanasius
realised, God "paradoxically reveals his majestic greatness through
his liberating and beneficent involvement in the world".[12] On this

---

[10] Khaled Anatolios, *Athanasius: The Coherence of His Thought* (London: Routledge, 1998),
p. 6.

[11] Ibid., p. 10.

[12] Ibid., pp. 6–7.

view there is nothing incongruous about the highest divinity self-involving, without subordinate intermediaries, in the world it has made. Anatolios finds this pervasive feature of Athanasius' cosmology and soteriology to have an "Irenaean" flavor,[13] for Irenaeus too had to contend with those for whom the supreme Divinity, "The Abyss", was neither responsible for, nor in direct contact with, the created universe.[14]

Yet despite Athanasius' apologetic purposes, these two interconnected treatises give the overall impression that the author actually expects mainly Christian readers. On one theory, the books were a theological exercise Athanasius set himself so as to summarise what he had learned from his own teachers.[15] Certainly, Athanasius had learned well from the biblical theology of both Irenaeus and Origen. He reads the Bible (it has been said) as "from beginning to end ... the historical narrative of the economy of salvation: that is, of God's providential actions, beginning with the act of creation and culminating in the redemptive actions of the Son of God incarnate. The divinely established goal of this economy was to ensure that human beings would obtain eternal life and so [enjoy] everlasting communion with God."[16]

This hermeneutic explains Athanasius' almost obsessive concern with "incorruptibility", *aphtharsia*. For Athanasius, "incorruptibility" means not only continuing to lead an integral human life with body and soul. More than this, it means such a life lived in, precisely, "everlasting communion with God".

Against the Gentiles

The message of these crucial early works, with their focus on, above all, creation and Incarnation, runs, then, broadly as follows. First, in *Against the Gentiles* Athanasius claims that through the Father's Word,

---

[13] Ibid., p. 7.

[14] "In the context of the struggle against the Gnostics, with their elaborate system of mediations, Irenaeus emphasizes that the very notion of a God who is distant and uninvolved with creation compromises a fitting conception of the divine." Ibid., p. 21.

[15] F. L. Cross, *The Study of St. Athanasius* (Oxford: Clarendon Press, 1945), p. 14.

[16] Weinandy, *Theological Introduction*, p. 110.

whom he also calls God's "Image" and his "Offspring" or "Son", the Father not only created everything out of nothing. Through the Word the Father also conserves everything in being and order, since left to themselves creaturely things are subject to entropy, to decay and dissolution. As Athanasius writes,

> Seeing then all created nature, as far as its own laws were concerned, to be fleeting and subject to dissolution, lest it should come to this and lest the Universe should be broken up again into nothingness, for this cause He (the Father) made all things by His own eternal Word, and gave substantive existence to creation, and moreover did not leave it to be tossed in a tempest in the course of its own nature, lest it should run the risk once more of dropping out of existence; but because He is good He guides and settles the whole Creation by His own Word, who is Himself also God, that by the governance and providence and ordering action of the Word, Creation may have light, and be enabled to abide always securely.[17]

The act of creation distinguishes God ontologically from all other realities. By creation, God holds all things in being through his Word. But both ontologically and epistemologically, God has bonded the world to himself in mankind—united himself to our race—by virtue of that same Word. Uniquely, human persons are created in the image and likeness of the Word, the Father's Offspring, or Son. That is the ontological dimension. Through the Word, the Son, they can know the Father himself in his endless truth and life.[18] That is the epistemological dimension. A capacity to contemplate God is given with the rationality—the Logos-like character—of the human soul.[19]

And yet, as with all creatures, human persons are by nature inherently corruptible. Only so long as they stay united with the Word do they remain incorruptibly united with the Father, for the Father is immediate to them in his Word, who is his very own Wisdom and Power. Anatolios explains:

---

[17] Athanasius, *Against the Gentiles* 41, trans. Archibald Robertson, in *Nicene and Post-Nicene Fathers*, ed. Philip Schaff and Henry Wace, 2nd series, vol. 4 (Buffalo, NY: Christian Literature Publishing, 1892). Hereafter, this edition of the *Nicene and Post-Nicene Fathers* is cited as *NPNF*.

[18] Cf. ibid., 34.

[19] Ibid., 2.

Since humanity, like all creation, came to be from nothing, it belongs to its very nature to be predisposed to nothingness and corruption. If it is saved from that fate by divine mercy, then perseverance in its access to this mercy is the condition without which it must again lapse into a confirmation of its own predisposition to non-being. The essential principle is that there is no neutral mid-point in which humanity can "remain". The two fundamental ontological polarities are either Godward or toward non-being; salvation history is preconfigured by these ontological polarities.[20]

To Athanasius' mind a recognition of this "preconfiguring" is necessary if we are to understand the history of sin and salvation. Through the Word, human persons have by their creation, with its gift of rational—that is, Logos-like—intelligence, the vocation to grow in knowledge and love of the Father. But in the historical process, they have denied that vocation, turning away from God by a sinful, indeed idolatrous, concentration on creatures.[21] They replaced with a tendency towards nonbeing their own Word-given tendency towards plenary being, toward the fullness of being. The pleasures of sin run counter to reality: they are irrational, literally *alogikos*, "without the Word", entailing as they do a false deification—an idolatrous worship—of the creation. Ironically, that creation was itself brought into being in all its harmonious unity in order to testify to the existence and primacy of the Word.[22] Human persons have now separated themselves from the Word and lost their incorruptibility.

In this account of creation and the origin of evil in the *Against the Gentiles*, nothing is said about the Holy Spirit. Is that because in works of pagan philosophy, if not pagan religion, there is no notion of the Spirit, whereas there are notions of God and the Logos? Yet

[20] Anatolios, *Coherence of His Thought*, p. 36, with an internal allusion to *On the Incarnation* 4.

[21] The Latin tradition will make the same point via the notion of "creaturely defect"; cf. Augustine's assertion in *The City of God* 14, 13: "A nature cannot be degraded by a vice of the will unless it is made from nothing. That it is a nature is the result of its being made by God, but that it falls away from what it is is because it is made from nothing." Cited in Gerard O'Daly, *Augustine's "City of God": A Reader's Guide* (Oxford: Oxford University Press, 1999).

[22] Citing *Against the Gentiles* 40, Anatolios comments: "The world is a receptacle for the activity of the Word, and it is only in virtue of this radical receptivity that the cosmos is a harmonious order.... The intelligibility and reality of the universe is grounded in the reality of the Word." Anatolios, *Coherence of His Thought*, p. 51.

Athanasius will do no better in *On the Incarnation*, where Jewish interlocutors, as well as Greek, are in play, and certainly the Old Testament has things to say about the Spirit of God. Had we only these
two early works from his pen and nothing more, we would quite
reasonably conclude that Athanasius suffered from a "pneumatologi-
cal deficit" as the current phrase has it. But, as we shall see, this is by
no means the whole story.

On the Incarnation

In *On the Incarnation*, Athanasius opens by summarising what he had
said in *Against the Gentiles* about God the Father and the Father's
Word in their relation to a creation tending through man to return
to nonbeing. Now, in this second treatise, Athanasius moves on to
speak of the Gospel remedy. It would have been unfitting, he writes,
for the all-good Father to let this state of affairs persist. The Father
would have been allowing the ruination of his own work. "It were
unseemly that creatures once made rational and having partaken of
the Word, should go to ruin, and turn again towards non-existence
by the way of corruption."[23] His Word, through whom men were
made at the beginning, has an "inherent responsibility for humankind's well-being".[24]

This is the point at which the *On the Incarnation* turns to the biblical narrative, and specifically to the Fall from Paradise. "Our trans-
gression called forth the loving-kindness of the Word, that the Lord
should both make haste to help us and appear among men."[25] The
Son becomes man in order to re-create human persons into his own
image and thus restore in them the life incorruptible. The ruination
had to be reversed—yet this needed to be done in a way that respects
the judgment of God on human evil. In the Book of Genesis, God
had told the proto-parents that the introduction of sin into the world
spelt death for them. "For it were monstrous for God, the Father of

---

[23] Athanasius, *On the Incarnation* 6, trans. Archibald Robertson, in *NPNF*. Unless otherwise
indicated, citations from *On the Incarnation* are from this translation.

[24] Weinandy, *Theological Introduction*, p. 31.

[25] Athanasius, *On the Incarnation* 4.

truth, to appear a liar for our profit and preservation."[26] It fell to the Son, then, "once more both to bring the corruptible to incorruption, and to maintain intact the just claim of the Father upon us all. For being Word of the Father, and above all, he alone of natural fitness was both able to recreate everything, and worthy to suffer in behalf of all and to be an ambassador of all with the Father."[27] So the Word himself takes on our nature, marred as it is by sinful corruptibility. He does so in the womb of the Blessed Virgin, hallowing thereby the particular instance of our fallen nature that was taken into union with himself. "For being Himself mighty, and Artificer of everything, He prepares the body in the Virgin as a temple unto Himself, and makes it His very own as an instrument, in it manifested, and in it dwelling."[28]

By his Incarnation, which, says Athanasius, was prophesied in the Jewish Scriptures,[29] the Word is able to make known to people once again the truth of the Father, essential precondition as this is of their restoration to the divine image. By the events of his Passion, Death, and Resurrection, he then restores the condition of *aphtharsia*, the state of incorruption. By his saving Passion, the Word destroys death in the humanity, the "flesh" that he took on at the moment of the Incarnation. On the Cross he offered his "pure and stainless human life as a sacrifice in our stead and on our behalf", offsetting the "debt of death" that was "incurred" and therefore "owed" by sin.[30]

Sacrifice, payment of the debt: these "theories" of the atoning work of the Redeemer, though necessary for understanding that Atonement,[31] are subsidiary in Athanasius to what is sometimes called, after the Swedish historical theologian Gustaf Aulén, the "Christus victor" theory—namely, an understanding of the Passion of the Lord as the

---

[26] Ibid., 7.

[27] Ibid.

[28] Ibid., 8.

[29] Ibid., 33–39.

[30] Weinandy, *Theological Introduction*, p. 34; cf. Athanasius, *On the Incarnation* 8–9.

[31] It may be noted that Athanasius, like Origen, did not attempt to "unify his various strands of thought on the subject of the Atonement"—and of Origen, so it has been claimed in this regard, "it is hardly too much to say that [he] hints at almost every way of approach to the question of the Atonement that has been put forward since his day." Alan Richardson, *Creeds in the Making: A Short Introduction to the History of Christian Doctrine* (London: Student Christian Movement Press, 1935), p. 102.

death that destroys death.[32] The Word-made-flesh, writes Athanasius in *On the Incarnation*, did not lay aside his body by a "death of his own", a death (that is) to which he was inherently liable, "for he was Life and had no death to die". Instead, he "received that death which came from men, in order perfectly to do away with this when it met him in his own body".[33] His Death was the death of death. His Resurrection, which manifests the reality of his defeat of death, achieves in his own now risen flesh, his risen humanity, a new form of integral life in communion with the Father—that is, a new *aphtharsia*, a new incorruption comparable to (but different from) that offered to Adam by the creating Word at the beginning of human time.[34]

By sharing the incorruptibility of the risen Christ, sinners can themselves re-acquire incorruptibility in the fullest possible sense: namely, integral human life lived out in abiding—permanent—communion with the Father. Such incorruption is extended efficaciously to all who are united to the Son through faith in his saving Incarnation and his Paschal Mystery. As Athanasius writes by way of summary of all this:

> We have then now stated in part as far as it was possible and as we ourselves had been able to understand, the reason for his bodily appearing; it was in the power of none other to turn the corruptible to incorruption, none except the Saviour himself, he who at the beginning had also made all things out of nothing. No other could create anew the likeness of God's image for men, except the [uncreated] Image of the Father; no other could render the mortal immortal except our Lord Jesus Christ who is Very Life; no other could teach men of the Father, and destroy the worship of idols, except the Word, he who orders all things and is alone the Father's true, only-begotten Son.[35]

If, argues Athanasius, certain Greek philosophers agree that the Logos is united to the whole world, which is an extended cosmic

---

[32] Gustaf Aulén, *Christus Victor: An Historical Study of the Three Main Types of the Theory of the Atonement*, trans. A. G. Hebert (1931; repr., London: Society for Promoting Christian Knowledge, 2010).

[33] Athanasius, *On the Incarnation* 22.

[34] Ibid., 8.

[35] Ibid., 20.

body, why should the Logos not unite himself to a part of the whole, an individual body,[36] and become man, so as to achieve all these things?[37] For it is an achievement. Somewhat optimistically, Athanasius claims that, thanks to the coming of Christ, human persons have stopped worshipping idols and ceased to fear death. He also points to the witness of the courage of the martyrs, the continence of consecrated virgins and ascetics, the power of exorcism in Jesus' name.[38]

When Athanasius speaks of the Word as uniting to himself a body, we should not infer (though some patrologists have done so) that he has forgotten, neglected, or even denied the assumption by the Word of a human soul. In the words of Thomas Weinandy again, "The reason he employs the term *sôma* ['body'] so extensively is that 'the body', as physical and material, is now, for Athanasius, the visible means by which the Son humanly acts and so both discernibly reveals invisible divine truths and corporeally performs divine salvific deeds."[39] Athanasius refers as often as he does to the "flesh" or "body" taken by the Word so as to stress the visibility and tangibility of the Incarnation order—not because he doubts that Jesus had a human mind, a human soul.[40]

Later Writings

Contra Gentes and *De Incarnatione*, this two-part primer of Christian basics, would stand Athanasius in good stead for much of his later teaching, and in the first place for his defence, after 325, of the Nicene dogma.

---

[36] Cf. ibid., 17: "Even while present in a mortal body, and Himself quickening it, He was, without inconsistency, quickening the universe as well."

[37] Cf. ibid., 41.

[38] Cf. ibid., 48.

[39] Weinandy, *Theological Introduction*, p. 47.

[40] "Athanasius himself speaks of the 'instrument' of Christ's body not in order to emphasize that it is directly and physically moved by the Logos, but rather to characterize it as a privileged locus wherein the invisible God becomes knowable and visible.... The reference is to knowledge rather than locomotion and animation" (Anatolios, *Coherence of His Thought*, p. 72). There is also the question of emphasising the "extreme condescension" of the Word, the "extremes united in Christ". Ibid., p. 73.

In Defence of Nicaea

In *Contra Gentes* and *De Incarnatione*, he had insisted that the Word, while remaining unchangeably God, has now come to exist as man. So both divine and human attributes can be ascribed to one and the same Son—for this insistence is required by the soteriological thrust of the biblical narrative. To renew the image in us, the Image of the Father had to come among us and in that way restore the life incorruptible. It is what will lie at the heart of Athanasius' defence of the *homoousion*, the consubstantiality thesis. The Son who took flesh from us and for us is himself "of one substance (*ousia*) with the Father". For the soteriological narrative to be reality-based, the Son must be God as the Father is God. Otherwise, the Word's salvific actions cannot possess the divine effects ascribed to them. It was this conviction above all that he defended in his later writings, even when not mentioning the *homoousion* explicitly.[41] For the *homoousion* is simply one way, though it is the ecclesially approved or "concili-arly" accredited way, of expressing the truth that the Son is God as the Father is God.

Stimulated by Arius' erroneous teaching, Athanasius realised it was necessary to abandon the custom of speaking of the Father as the one God, for this custom led naturally (if perhaps inadvertently) to thinking of the Father's Word and Spirit as not only derived from the Father, which is true, but as somehow less divine than the Father, which is false. Origen's writing about God could and did give just this impression. For Athanasius, God is the Father eternally begetting the Son. We could if we wished complete that picture. For the full Christian definition of God, the Trinitarian conception of God, "God" is the Father eternally begetting the Son and spirating (breathing out) the Spirit. It is not possible to detach the Father from the Son (and the Spirit) as in and of himself "the one God".

---

[41] Daniel H. Williams states, "Not until the publication of the *De decretis* [*On the Decrees*] (c. 352/3) did Athanasius begin to champion publicly the terminology of the Nicene creed as a language uniquely necessary for the preservation of orthodoxy" (Daniel H. Williams, *Ambrose of Milan and the End of the Nicene-Arian Conflicts* [Oxford: Clarendon Press, 1995], p. 15). Henry Chadwick notes that in his *Letter to the Bishops of Egypt*, Athanasius was even willing at one point to countenance the description of the Son as "like in essence" to the Father. Chadwick, *Church in Ancient Society*, p. 260.

As Athanasius remarks in the first of his *Orations against the Arians*, "There is an eternal and one God in a Triad, and there is one Glory of the Holy Triad."[42]

Getting the rest of the bishops to grasp this point was what underlay the struggles of the half century that followed Nicaea. This is also what occupied Athanasius in writing his three *Orations against the Arians*; his two sets of analyses of the synodical ups and downs of that half century (entitled *On the Decrees* and *On the Synods*); his history of the whole affair, the *History of the Arians*; and, lastly, his justification of the Nicene definition by reference to what the greatest of his episcopal predecessors, Saint Dionysius of Alexandria ("Dionysius the Great"), revered confessor of the faith during the Decian persecution, had taught about Jesus Christ.

Defending Nicaea was no simple undertaking. Simple appeal to the authority of that assembly of the "318 Fathers" would have cut little ice. Experience of the tumultuous and confused decades after 325 had devalued the currency of synods. In *On the Synods*, Athanasius felt bound to agree that "not all those who questioned the authority of Nicaea must by definition be 'Arian'."[43] Even the use of non-homoousian language, employing such expressions as "of like essence" or "like in essence", might have an orthodox intent.

> Those ... who accept everything else that was defined at Nicaea, and doubt only about the Co-essential, must not be treated as enemies, nor do we here attack them as Ario-maniacs, nor as opponents of the Fathers, but we discuss the matter with them as brothers, who mean what we mean, and dispute only about the word. For, confessing that the Son is from the essence of the Father, and not from other subsistence, and that He is not a creature nor work, but His genuine and natural offspring, and that He is eternally with the Father as being His Word and Wisdom, they are not far from accepting even the phrase "Coessential".... Since they say that He is "of the essence" and "like in essence", what do they signify by these but "Coessential"?[44]

---

[42] Athanasius, *Orations against the Arians* I, 18, trans. John Henry Newman and Archibald Robertson, in *NPNF*.

[43] Gwynn, *Athanasius of Alexandria*, p. 15.

[44] Athanasius, *On the Synods* 41, trans. John Henry Newman and Archibald Robertson, in *NPNF*.

Nevertheless, only the full Nicene confession will really do. As Athanasius explains in *On the Decrees*, his study of the Council's teaching, "If the Son is Word, Wisdom, Image of the Father, Radiance, He must in all reason be One in essence. For unless it be proved that He is not from God, but an instrument different in nature and different in essence, surely the Council was sound in its doctrine and correct in its decree."[45] Athanasius did not have much time for the worry of his Western supporter Hilary of Poitiers that the single *ousia* could be misunderstood as a "prior substance in which the two persons Father and Son participate".[46]

Athanasius' strongest argument had always run, no Father, no Son. In the course of his appeal to the memory of Dionysius the Great, he reasoned thus: "The Father, as Father, is not separated from the Son, for the name ['Father'] speaks of the relationship [that is, the Father-Son relationship], nor is the Son expatriated from the Father, for the title 'Father' denotes the common bond [that is, the bond conjoining Father and Son]."[47] In the third of the *Orations against the Arians*, he makes the same point more concisely: "When we call God Father, at once with the Father we signify the Son's existence."[48] The Son must exist eternally with the Father, just as radiance exists with the sun, or the springing forth of water with a fountain, or a word with the thought that underlies it: favoured metaphors for the Son-Father relation in Athanasius' use. As a modern theologian has noted, if, as low Christologies, both ancient and modern, suggest, the Son merely "points to" the Father, rather than (also) being the Father's co-equal Offspring, then there is actually no "Father" to whom to point.[49] If the Father is by nature eternally Father, he must will eternally to beget the Son—though Athanasius avoids the language of "willing", fearing it might introduce a note of choice, and therefore of artifice or even caprice. That would be incompatible with the notion that God simply *is* the Father begetting the Son (and spirating the Holy

---

[45] Athanasius, *On the Decrees* 23, trans. John Henry Newman, in *NPNF*.

[46] Chadwick, *Church in Ancient Society*, with reference to Hilary in *On the Synods* 67.

[47] Athanasius, *On the Opinion of Dionysius* 17, trans. Archibald Robertson, in *NPNF*.

[48] Athanasius, *Orations against the Arians* III, 6, trans. John Henry Newman and Archibald Robertson, in *NPNF*. Unless otherwise indicated, citations from *Orations against the Arians* are from this translation.

[49] Weinandy, *Theological Introduction*, p. 68n61.

Spirit). Rowan Williams noted with his customary insight, "Athanasius and those who immediately followed him in effect proposed that 'God' should *not* be treated as a proper name: ['God'] is shorthand for that life or agency or process *constituted* by the inseparable, reciprocally definitory terms of Father, Son, and Spirit."[50]

Two Vital Corollaries

Athanasius was much concerned with two vital corollaries of the Nicene doctrine of the Father-Son relationship. The first of these is *co-inherence*.

When in the Gospel of Saint John Jesus addresses the question to the apostle Philip, "Do you not believe that I am in the Father and the Father is in me?" (14:10), the self-description is crucial for Athanasius' mature theology. The Father's communication of his substance to the Son—the "*homoousion* act" as we might call it—brings about their co-inherence, their reciprocal indwelling. They are "in" each other.

As the third *Oration against the Arians* has it,

> For the Son is in the Father ... because the whole being of the Son is proper to the Father's *ousia*, as radiance from light and a stream from a fountain; so that whoever sees the Son sees what is proper to the Father and knows that the Son's being, as from the Father, is the Father, and [that the Son] is therefore in the Father. [And likewise (so Athanasius continues)] the Father is in the Son, since the Son is what is from the Father and proper to him, as there is in the radiance the sun, and in the word the thought, and in the stream the fountain: whoever thus contemplates the Son, contemplates what is proper to the Father's *ousia*, and knows that the Father is in the Son.[51]

By elaborating in this manner the short text from Saint John's Gospel ("Do you not believe that I am in the Father and the Father in me?"), Athanasius opened for later theology a deeper entry into

[50] Williams, "Logic of Arianism", p. 81.
[51] Athanasius, *Orations against the Arians* III, 3.

the Father-Son relationship—into the paternal-filial intimacy that lies at the heart of Jesus' existence.

Another insight, comparable in importance to this perception of the co-inherence of Father and Son, had already occurred to Athanasius when writing the second of the *Orations against the Arians*. It is this: *the Father's fruitfulness is the explanation of creation*. The Father's eternal generation of the Son is the fundamental presupposition of God's temporal act of creating a world. The Father's fruitfulness in generating the Son is—in this sense—the explanation of God's activity as Creator. Citing Rowan Williams again:

> Once we accept that [God] is eternally engaged in generating the Son, we see that he is always producing what is other—first by nature [namely, the generation of the Son], then by free action relating to what is outside his own life [namely, by creating the world]. Creation would make no sense [Williams continues] without eternal begetting; they are two radically different categories, yet there is an analogy such that one [creation] is impossible and unintelligible without the other [generation].[52]

Or in Athanasius' own words, "If the divine essence is not fruitful in itself but barren, ... as a light that does not lighten or a dry fountain," then how is it possible for it to give being and life to others?[53]

Thomas Weinandy puts this in terms of the perennial metaphysical problem of the "One" and the "many". "If God is simply One, there could never be a many. However, if the One God himself is the oneness of the Father and the Son ([plural and in that sense] the many), then there could be a 'many' distinct from God which would be united to this one God of Father and Son through the persistent divine act of creation and conservation."[54] Athanasius had thought through a lesson he had long since learned from Origen: the "Father-Son relation [is] both prior to and ground for the God-world relation".[55]

---

[52] R. D. Williams, "Athanasius", in *The First Christian Theologians: An Introduction to Theology in the Early Church*, ed. G. R. Evans (Oxford: Blackwell, 2004), p. 163.

[53] Athanasius, *Orations against the Arians* II, 2, as cited in Weinandy, *Theological Introduction*, p. 79.

[54] Weinandy, *Theological Introduction*, p. 80n120.

[55] Anatolios, *Coherence of His Thought*, p. 24. On this, see Peter Widdicombe, *The Fatherhood of God from Origen to Athanasius* (Oxford: Clarendon Press, 2004).

Two Conflicting Soteriologies

In the wake of the Arian crisis, Athanasius found the affirmation of the *homoousion* indispensable if he was to sustain the account of divine agency he had given in his earlier writings (thinking especially of *On the Incarnation*), and the reason for this was soteriological—a matter of salvation. In order to save this manifold creation, the Son must be fully divine, not somewhat less than divine (as Origen had surmised), and certainly not a creature, even a superlative creature (as Arius maintained). Unless the Word is truly God, consubstantial with the Father, he cannot, in becoming man, save mankind, he cannot restore it to godliness, he cannot "deify" it.[56]

For their part, the Arians had been obliged to work out a different soteriology—for without soteriology, there is no practically useful Christian message. For Arians, the *creaturely obedience* of the Logos, the One created at the beginning of time, serves to fill the soteriological gap that opens up when Christ's divinity is denied. In other words, the obedience of the Logos—as the firstborn of creation as well as, when incarnate, the firstborn from the dead—provided for Arians the template for humanity's return to God.[57] The Son was obedient as we should be—and rightly so, in his footsteps, for the Son was never more than a creature, albeit the most wonderful of creatures, in a class of his own. Just as by his obedience Jesus merited to entered the bliss of the Father, so his disciples, by imitating the obedience of Christ, can do the same.

The Dispute over Proverbs 8

In that context, Arians made much of a text in the Book of Proverbs about the wisdom of God, identified by most early Fathers

---

[56] Athanasius, *Orations against the Arians* II, 70.

[57] Robert C. Gregg and Dennis E. Groh, *Early Arianism: A View of Salvation* (London: Student Christian Movement Press, 1981). Arius' "Son" is, however, unlike human persons, incapable of moral growth, since he is already perfect. Athanasius could not accept the coexistence of these two tenets: creatureliness is, to his mind, inseparable from mutability. See Gwynn, *Athanasius of Alexandria*, pp. 80–81.

(Irenaeus, so we saw, is an exception) with God the Son.[58] Proverbs 8:22 runs: "The LORD created me at the beginning of his work, the first of his acts of old." Yet three verses later, the Proverbs text goes on to say, "Before the mountains had been shaped, before the hills, I was *brought forth*" (v. 25; emphasis added). On Athanasius' reading in the second *Oration against the Arians*, verse 25 here speaks *absolutely* of the Son's being, speaks of it (that is) as it exists *in and of itself*. Contrastingly, verse 22 had spoken only *relatively* of the Son, only of him *in relation to one aspect of his identity*: specifically, of the predestined role that would in due course be his within the created order. First of all (cf. v. 25), the Son was generated, "brought forth", and then, subsequently in the fullness of time, anticipated in the eternal divine counsels (cf. v. 22), he was "created ... at the beginning of his work"; in other words, he was made flesh, made human, for the sake of our salvation. Not surprisingly, at the end of his life in the *Letter to Epictetus*, Athanasius anticipated the Christological discussion of the following century by insisting that "the divinity and humanity [in Christ] cannot be separated and yet [they] retain their independent identities."[59] "He it was Who suffered and yet suffered not. Suffered because His own Body suffered, and He was in it, Who thus suffered; suffered not, because the Word, being by Nature God, is impassible."[60]

Those who, by life in Christ, are simply creatures, if also redeemed creatures, experience the reverse of the process undergone by the Son that Athanasius had just described. In her summary of Book II of *Orations against the Arians*, the Methodist patristic scholar Frances Young writes: "God's Offspring [the divine Son] was [first] begotten then made, made flesh for our salvation in the economy, whereas creatures [redeemed human persons] were [first] made and then begotten through Christ, becoming sons by grace."[61] This is a more elaborate way of expounding what as early as *On the Incarnation* Athanasius

---

[58] In *Orations against the Arians* II, 16–22, Athanasius treats this text as the chief "proof-text" in the Arians' armoury (along with Philippians 2:9–10 and Psalm 45:7–8, discussed more briefly in the first of the *Orations*).

[59] Gwynn, *Athanasius of Alexandria*, pp. 101–2.

[60] Athanasius, *Letter* 59 (= *Letter to Epictetus*), 6, trans. Archibald Robertson, in *NPNF*.

[61] Frances Young, "The Interpretation of Scripture", in Evans, *First Christian Theologians*, p. 34.

had expressed in a pithy maxim: "He [the Logos] was humanized that we might be deified."[62] That controversy over Proverbs 8 was, to Young's mind, an excellent example of how for Athanasius "the reading of particular texts had to be subservient to the overarching sense of Scripture as a whole."[63]

Athanasius on the Holy Spirit

But we have still not heard from Athanasius on the Holy Spirit. In the decade and a half that separates the Council of Nicaea from the finalization of Orations against the Arians, what Athanasius has to say about the Spirit was largely confined to doxological expressions and comments relevant to the Sacrament of Baptism celebrated as this was in the threefold Name of Father, Son, and Holy Spirit. Undeniably he held that the terms "Holy Spirit", "Son", and "Father" convey what Weinandy calls "unique and irreducible identities".[64] Moreover, Athanasius was already clear that in the economy, Father, Son, and Spirit have distinct but interrelated roles to play. The Son, begotten by the Father, is made the source of the Spirit so that as man he can bestow the Spirit on his disciples, consecrating them for entry into the divine life he enjoys with his Father. In the third of the Orations against the Arians, Athanasius will remark, "We shall be accounted to have become one in Son and in Father because that Spirit is in us which is in the Word who is in the Father."[65] In that treatise there is already, in effect, an implicit confession of the divinity of the Spirit. The Spirit, in the Athanasian phrase, "receives from the Word" all that the Word has received from the Father.[66]

But it was not until towards 360, during his third exile, that Athanasius really turned his mind to the theology of the Holy Spirit in its

---

[62] Athanasius, On the Incarnation 54. Translation is the present author's.

[63] Young, "Interpretation of Scripture", p. 34.

[64] Weinandy, Theological Introduction, p. 104.

[65] Athanasius, Orations against the Arians III, 25.

[66] Ibid., III, 24. This might be taken to mean that the Spirit receives from the Son nothing less than the divine ousia. If so, for Athanasius the Spirit is not only from the Father but also from the Son—a contested point in Athanasian studies owing not least to the neuralgic role of the Filioque issue in later Latin-Byzantine (and so Catholic-Orthodox) relations.

own right. Athanasius had received a letter from an Egyptian bishop asking for advice about Christians who accepted the divinity of the Son but drew the line at affirming the Godhead of the Holy Spirit. "In Egypt, a group referred to as 'Tropici'—apparently because of their assumption that many biblical references to 'spirit' or 'wind' are 'tropes' or allegories for God's power—argued from a number of Old Testament passages that the Spirit mentioned in scripture is simply a mediating force, created by God to carry out his will."[67] The resultant *Letters to Serapion* are hardly less than a treatise on the Holy Spirit, the first such treatise in the history of the Church.[68]

In the *Letters to Serapion*, Athanasius' chief affirmation is that, since the Son gives himself in the Spirit, then if the Spirit is not God so neither is the Son, and if the Son is not God, then God is not the Father. If the One who transmits the life of the Son to us is not divine, then the life of the Son that he transmits is not divine life, and the Son is not God, and if there is no uncreated Son of God, then the divine One is only a Monad and not a Father at all. Here we see Athanasius seeking to integrate his doctrine of the Holy Spirit into the theology of the *homoousion* of Son with Father on which he had been working in the previous decades. In the first of his *Letters to Serapion* he wrote, "As the Son, who is in the Father and the Father in him, is not a creature but pertains to the essence of the Father, ... so also it is not lawful to rank with the creatures the Spirit who is in the Son, and the Son in him, nor to divide him from the Word and reduce the Triad to imperfection."[69] As with confession of the divinity of the Son, the underlying rationale here is soteriological. In the economy there is only one sanctificatory process, which, as he tells Serapion, is "derived from the Father, through the Son, in the Holy Spirit".[70] Thomas Aquinas will employ this same soteriological argument when dealing with the divinity of the Spirit and the Son

---

[67] Brian E. Daley, S.J., "The Fullness of the Saving God: Cyril of Alexandria on the Holy Spirit", in *The Theology of St. Cyril of Alexandria*, ed. Thomas G. Weinandy and Daniel A. Keating (London and New York: T&T Clark, 2003), p. 119.

[68] *The Letters of Saint Athanasius concerning the Holy Spirit*, trans. C.R.B. Shapland (New York: Philosophical Library, 1951). Citations from Athanasius' letters on the Holy Spirit are taken from this translation.

[69] Athanasius, *To Serapion* I, 21.

[70] Ibid., I, 20.

in his *Commentary on John*. Two Johannine passages are pertinent. In John 3:5 the Saviour tells Nicodemus, "Unless one is born of water and the Spirit, he cannot enter the kingdom of God." Thomas' comment runs: "He from whom men are spiritually reborn is God; but men are reborn through the Holy Spirit, as is stated here; therefore the Holy Spirit is God."[71] In the debate with the Jewish leaders in John 10:35 Jesus declares, "If he called them gods to whom the word of God came (and Scripture cannot be nullified), do you say of him whom the Father consecrated and sent into the world, 'You are blaspheming,' because I said, 'I am the Son of God'?" Thomas affirms on this saying of the Lord: "It is clear that a person by participating in the Word of God becomes 'god' by participation. But a thing does not become this or that by participation unless it participates in what this or that is by its essence.... Therefore, one does not become 'god' by participation unless he participates in what God is by essence. Therefore, the Word of God, that is the Son, by participation in whom we become 'gods', is God by essence."[72] That is a soteriological argument for the divinity of the Son, just as my previous citation of Thomas' commentary furnishes a soteriological argument for the divinity of the Spirit.

By and large Athanasius, unlike Thomas, is reserved on the question of the ultimate "place" of the Spirit within the Godhead—that is, on the question of the causal origin of the Spirit in relation to Father and Son. For the most part, he contents himself with two assertions: the Spirit proceeds from the Father, and he is the Spirit of the Son. He does not attempt to interconnect these claims in the systematic fashion that would later be characteristic of first Latin and then Greek theology.

Perhaps, in Weinandy's words, Athanasius thought it more profitable to consider how "human beings, through Christ, obtain the divinizing life of the Spirit and so come into a loving and everlasting communion with the Father"[73]—in other words, to persuade people

---

[71] Thomas Aquinas, *In Ioannem* 3, 5, section 444, in the English translation by James A. Weisheipl and Fabian R. Larcher, *Commentary on the Gospel of John*, part 1 (Albany, NY: Magi Books, 1980), and *Commentary on the Gospel of John*, part 2 (Petersham, MA: St. Bede's Publications, 1999).

[72] Aquinas, *In Ioannem* 10, 35, section 1460, in Weisheipl and Larcher, *Commentary on the Gospel of John*, part 1, and *Commentary on the Gospel of John*, part 2.

[73] Weinandy, *Theological Introduction*, p. 121.

not so much to look into the inner Trinitarian relations in the manner of the systematic theology of the late patristic, mediaeval, and modern periods, but, rather, to ask themselves how best they could live the Christian life.

In some ways this is a false dichotomy (we might reasonably ask, Why not do both?), but if there is to be an either/or, then, granted the limited time and energy of human persons, Athanasius' choice was no doubt the right one.

Athanasius on the Basic Christian Life

The best places to look for Athanasius' approach to questions of the basic Christian life are his *Festal Letters*, the letters he wrote annually, including from exile, to the Church of Alexandria announcing the date of Easter and, accordingly, the beginning of the great fast of Lent. Though in some editions they are termed "Paschal Homilies", they are really pastoral letters in which each year he could exhort the faithful—presbyters, monastics, layfolk—on the topic of holy living.

To these *Festal Letters* there should be added Athanasius' life of the Desert monk Saint Anthony of Egypt. In these texts we shall find his holiness programme with its key constituent elements of "praise, thanksgiving, prayer, fasting and suffering for the sake of the Gospel".[74] That programme will be in time a major stimulus to the ascetical doctrine of the later Church, in the Mediterranean world, notably through the *Life of Antony*, which was soon translated from Greek into Latin, and in Syria and Egypt itself through the *Festal Letters*, most of which survived only in Syriac and Coptic.[75] For Hellenistic Christian Egypt would soon by disrupted by two disasters: the Monophysite schism and, hot on its heels, the arrival of Islam.

---

[74] Ibid., p. 125.

[75] For a discussion of the *Life of Anthony* in conjunction with other, more minor, ascetical writings of Athanasius (a treatise on virginity and two letters to virgins), consult Gwynn, *Athanasius of Alexandria*, pp. 111–19, and for the role of asceticism in his pastoral theology in the *Festal Letters* (and a couple of more personal letters that survive), see ibid., pp. 146–52.

4

Trinitarian Devotees: The Cappadocian Fathers

The Cappadocian Fathers are a threesome: two Gregories and a Basil. One Gregory was a brother of Saint Basil the Great—that is, Saint Gregory of Nyssa, sometimes called "Nyssen" after his bishopric. The other, Saint Gregory of Nazianzus—often called "Nazianzen", after the bishopric he occupied for the longest period of his life—was, at least in early manhood, Basil's best friend. Understandably, then, in terms of "network theory", the three men are always grouped together. What is more surprising is that the iconographic tradition does not treat them thus, but substitutes John Chrysostom for Gregory of Nyssa—that is, in the icon-type called the "Three Holy Hierarchs": Basil, Nazianzen, Chrysostom (with Chrysostom, characteristically short-bearded, in the middle).[1] One inevitably wonders why Gregory of Nyssa was left out of the iconic trio. Perhaps the greater complexity of his prose reduced his popularity. Or maybe it was his tendency towards universalism—he thought that, through purification of the soul, all persons may eventually be saved.[2] This might well have been held against him, especially after the mid-sixth-century condemnations of radical Origenism.

---

[1] For what my Preface acknowledges as the principal omission in my set of "Singing-Masters", see J. N. D. Kelly, *Golden Mouth: The Story of John Chrysostom—Ascetic, Preacher, Bishop* (Ithaca, NY: Cornell University Press, 1995).

[2] Commenting on the Pauline text "God may be all in all" (1 Cor 15:28, ESV), Gregory of Nyssa wrote: "God becomes, to those who deserve it, locality and home, and clothing, and food, and drink, and light, and riches, and dominion and everything thinkable and nameable that goes to make our life happy. But He that becomes 'all' things will be 'in all' things too, and herein it appears to me that Scripture teaches the complete annihilation of evil.... The excepting of that one thing, evil, mars the comprehensiveness of the term 'all'." Gregory of Nyssa, *On the Soul and the Resurrection*, trans. William Moore and Henry Austin Wilson, in *Nicene and Post-Nicene Fathers* [*NPNF*], ed. Philip Schaff and Henry Wace, 2nd series, vol. 5 (Buffalo, NY: Christian Literature Publishing, 1893).

The Cappadocian Fathers had a common background. What was it? The two families from which they came were relatively wealthy landowners in a somewhat impoverished part of the Roman Empire. Cappadocia was a mountainous region, with limited natural resources. Its principal export was horses. Ancestral wealth and local influence was relevant to the election of Basil to the principal see of Cappadocia, Caesarea Cappadociae (not to be confused, as already mentioned, with the Caesarea Palestinae where Origen created his library). Nor were wealth and influence unrelated to Basil's appointment of his younger brother Gregory to the suffragan see of Nyssa, and his friend, the other Gregory, to two further such sees in turn: Sasima (briefly and under protest) and then Nazianzus (where his father had been bishop before him). These locations—Nyssa, Sasima, Nazianzus— were rather modest, not to say obscure, towns in western Cappadocia, but the appointments strengthened Basil's hand as metropolitan when dealing with other bishops. Nazianzen's father was a first-generation Christian, whereas Basil and Nyssen could boast that their paternal grandmother had been converted by no less a figure than Saint Gregory Thaumaturgus, pupil of Origen and apostle of Cappadocia. For all three of the Cappadocian Fathers, it was the mothers and sisters of the trio who seem to have been most directly responsible for the fervor of their Christianity.

They were almost exact contemporaries, born in the sequence Nazianzen, Basil, Nyssen, during the decade and a half between 325 and 340 (the precise dates are disputed). Their early training was similar. This is how the Eastern Orthodox patrologist John McGuckin describes Nazianzen's upbringing.

> After the formative years with the women in the villa, during which time Gregory had clearly absorbed his mother's deep-rooted and visionary form of Christianity, it was time for the children of the Roman upper classes to depart for a patriarchally dominated and male-oriented society, where the skills that would be necessary for their future careers would be absorbed.... Literature would be enough to form the basis of a total education, and rhetoric, the highest level of educational attainment, would not only allow a person to practice law and civic administration (perceived as the only fit occupations for a gentleman outside the supervision of his own estates) but would even equip him to embark on philosophical enquiries, of which a little, in

moderate measure, was always seen to be an ideal accompaniment to literary accomplishment in the archetypal figure of the Roman intellectual from the Augustan Age onwards.[3]

That makes the role of philosophy sound distinctly amateur, an upper-class hobby or pastime, and in that respect is probably misleading with regard to fourth-century attitudes, whatever might have been the case earlier. In Late Antiquity, philosophy was religiously serious.[4] There was a widespread tendency to appeal to philosophy in order to assist spiritual practice, first and foremost that of pagans.[5] "Philosophy" here meant especially the Pythagorean and, above all, the Platonic teachings. The patristic theologians would naturally wish to set aside conceptual errors in the different schools. Yet they could also welcome the broad current of metaphysical and ethical reflection found in Hellenic philosophy. Henry Chadwick can paraphrase a passage of the *Stromateis* (the "Miscellanies") of Clement of Alexandria by writing, "What the Old Testament law was to the Hebrews, philosophy has been to the Greeks, and now the two streams providentially have their confluence in the Gospel."[6]

Where philosophy is concerned, the outlook of all three Cappadocian Fathers has been brought under the general heading of "Christian Platonism". "Christian Platonism" is not an easy term to handle.[7]

---

[3] John Anthony McGuckin, *Saint Gregory of Nazianzus: An Intellectual Biography* (Crestwood, NY: Saint Vladimir's Seminary Press, 2001), p. 35. They would not have questioned the honourable place of rhetoric. "It is difficult for us to appreciate the degree of enthusiasm which the practice of eloquence inspired throughout the Late Roman world. Professors of rhetoric (called rhetors or sophists) held endowed chairs in the main cities, attracted students from a wide catchment area, gave public performances before huge audiences, were sent on embassies to plead local causes, and were honoured with statues. Along with famous philosophers, they were the only class of people, apart from ruler, whose biographies were written down before the same privilege was extended to Christian saints." Cyril Mango, "New Religion, Old Culture", in *The Oxford History of Byzantium* (New York: Oxford University Press, 2002), pp. 101–2.

[4] "Late Antiquity" was a profoundly religious epoch in the Greco-Roman world—the predominant theme in Peter Brown, *The World of Late Antiquity: From Marcus Aurelius to Muhammed* (London: Thames and Hudson, 1971).

[5] Martin Laird, *Gregory of Nyssa and the Grasp of Faith: Union, Knowledge, and Divine Presence* (Oxford: Oxford University Press, 2004), p. 7.

[6] Henry Chadwick, *The Church in Ancient Society: From Galilee to Gregory the Great* (Oxford: Oxford University Press, 2001), p. 127, commenting on *Stromateis* I, 29, 1.

[7] The classic study is Endre von Ivánka, *Plato christianus: Übernahme und Umgestaltung des Platonismus durch die Väter* (Einsiedeln: Johannesverlag, 1964).

The Platonist tradition underwent great changes, not least in the way it absorbed elements of Stoicism and Aristotelianism. In any case, one has to distinguish between, on the one hand, how the Cappadocian Fathers might have regarded particular Platonist teachers and texts, and, on the other hand, what one might call the general philosophical atmosphere generated by the predominance of some version of Platonism in their day. For instance, Gregory Nazianzen was quite hostile to the philosophical *systems* of antiquity, treating them in his first *Theological Oration* as worth studying mainly because they need refutation. Like Basil, in the latter's *Address to Young Men on the Value of Greek Literature*, it was the nonphilosophical classics such as the epic poet Homer that he really appreciated for their insights into human life and death, and admired for the linguistic refinement with which their authors expressed themselves.

From their experience of what we would call secondary and tertiary education, both Nazianzen and Basil had an acquaintance with the earlier Greek philosophers, from Pythagoras to the Stoics and Epicureans. Naturally enough, that historical sweep included Plato. But they had very little direct awareness, or so it seems, of Platonists closer in time to themselves such as Plotinus, the founder of Neoplatonism, and his disciple and biographer Porphyry.[8] Even Gregory of Nyssa, in whose writings Platonist vocabulary is most evident, refers rather rarely to contemporary philosophical debate. Yet there is no doubt Nyssen was soaked—saturated—in the general atmosphere created by the predominance of Platonism in the high culture of his day.

Indeed, an influential American classicist writing at the start of the 1930s, Harold Cherniss, claimed that "but for some few orthodox dogmas he could not circumvent, Gregory [of Nyssa] has merely applied Christian names to Plato's doctrine and called it Christian theology."[9] In sharp contrast, for two European Jesuits—Hans Urs von Balthasar, writing in 1942,[10] and Jean Daniélou, writing

---

[8] John M. Rist, "Basil's 'Neoplatonism': Its Background and Nature", in *Basil of Caesarea: Christian, Humanist, Ascetic*, ed. Paul Jonathan Fedwick (Toronto: Pontifical Institute of Mediaeval Studies, 1981), 1:137–220.

[9] Enrico Peroli, "Gregory of Nyssa and Platonism", in *Passionate Mind: Essays in Honor of John M. Rist*, ed. Barry David (Baden-Baden: Academia, 2019), p.214, citing Harold Cherniss, *The Platonism of Gregory of Nyssa* (Berkeley, CA: University of California Press, 1930), p. 62.

[10] Hans Urs von Balthasar, *Présence et pensée: Essai sur la philosophie religieuse de Grégoire de Nysse* (Paris: Beauchesne, 1942).

in 1944—the Platonism of Nyssen was only, in Daniélou's phrase, "exterior colouring", a matter of imagery or other terminology borrowed from the Platonist tradition so as to assist the transmission of a purely Christian content that itself owed nothing to Plato or Platonists.[11] More recent scholars have queried what seems to be an oversimplification on both sides of this dispute. They speak, rather, of an *acceptance*—which is simultaneously a *transformation*—of a number of the chief concepts of Greek metaphysics.

On this basis we can expect to find some general claims for the "Christian Platonism" of the Cappadocians to be verified. They would surely have agreed with the following proposition: "Christianity, possessing that complete revelation of the Logos of which the Greeks only possessed fragments, brought to fulfillment the efforts Greek philosophers had made in the search for truth."[12] So the Cappadocians tacitly took for granted that some form of Hellenic philosophy may have contained truths worth knowing. At the very least, as Nazianzen testifies in his encomium *In Praise of Basil*, the Cappadocian Doctors sought to take from the surrounding philosophical culture "principles of enquiry and speculation", while strenuously rejecting its idolatrous religion.[13] They would, moreover, have agreed with the later Platonist schools that "living according to the *logos*" (a phrase from Justin Martyr's first *Apology* intended as praise of pagan sages, notably Heraclitus and Socrates[14]) meant not just adopting a philosophical theory but taking up a way of life. In Late Antiquity, philosophy was spiritual exercise, entailing some form of asceticism. Knowledge was intrinsically linked to virtue since, as all Platonists were united in saying, human life had an "existential orientation towards the Good"— meaning by that the transcendent or divine Good.[15] Basil and the Gregories were committed to shaping a radicalized Christian version of a philosophical life, so understood. That entailed some version of

---

[11] Jean Daniélou, *Platonisme et théologie mystique: Essai sur la doctrine spirituelle de Grégoire de Nysse*, 2nd ed. (Paris: Aubier, 1954), pp. 9, 164.

[12] Peroli, "Gregory of Nyssa and Platonism", p. 218.

[13] Gregory Nazianzen, *In Praise of Basil* (= *Oration* 43), 11, trans. Charles Gordon Browne and James Edward Swallow, in *NPNF*, ed. Philip Schaff and Henry Wace, 2nd series, vol. 7 (Buffalo, NY: Christian Literature Publishing, 1894).

[14] Justin Martyr, *First Apology* 46.

[15] Peroli, "Gregory of Nyssa and Platonism", p. 219.

monastic life (or in Nyssen's case, since he was married, continent life) lived out in the service of the Church. An especially clear illustration is Gregory of Nyssa's biography of his (and therefore Basil's) sister, Macrina, which "fused Neoplatonic aspirations with Christian holiness and portrayed her as an ideal saint".[16]

Admittedly, the Cappadocians understood this "monastic" commitment in very different ways. Nazianzen understood it in primarily intellectual terms, as the working out of a more satisfactory doctrinal understanding, to be placed at the service of the Church. Nyssen saw it in primarily mystical terms as the making of a spirituality which would guide people towards the vision of God. As to Basil, after a first experience of a purely contemplative life, he made his lasting monastic contribution in primarily educational and organisational terms, writing a set of ascetical treatises for the use of monks and creating out of the wider ascetic movement a series of social welfare institutions.

But despite these temperamental or vocational differences, all the Cappadocian Fathers would have concurred with Platonists on three most important points. First, human life is essentially directed towards transcendence. Secondly, more than that, its aim is achieving likeness to the divine. Thirdly, this in turn means that its goal is a vision of spiritual beauty, which will reconnect the soul with its true homeland and bring about the salvation of the "intellectual substance" of the person—that is, his human mind.[17]

These assertions could readily be accommodated by finding a new context for them in the eschatological outlook of the Church. Such truth claims about the soul's nature and destiny, what we might call its "deification-direction", could be received in the Church community on one condition—namely, that they were recontextualized in the setting of what Irenaeus and Origen had called the "rule of faith". So, for example, Gregory of Nyssa's *On the Soul and Resurrection* is in one sense a Christian reading of Plato's dialogue *Phaedo*. But Plato was writing there about the soul only; he would never have written about resurrection, a theme that belongs to the Paschal proclamation of the Church—that is so even if Nyssen allows that philosophical speculation about the transmigration of souls into new bodies, while

[16] Chadwick, *Church in Ancient Society*, p. 331.
[17] Peroli, "Gregory of Nyssa and Platonism", p. 219.

erroneous, does touch on the question that Easter faith answers. On the one hand, such "acceptance" amounted to far more than adding a few superficial brush strokes in Platonic colours. But on the other hand, the "transformation" of what was received made it far less than the outright capitulation to pagan philosophy suggested by the severer critics such as Cherniss.

At the same time, it has to be remembered that the historical setting in which the Cappadocian Fathers pursued their aims was the ongoing Arian crisis concerning the divinity (and to a lesser extent the humanity) of the Son, soon spilling over as it did into a further crisis about the identity and status of the Holy Spirit. Inevitably, this meant directing a good part of their energies to the defence of basic Trinitarian and Christological doctrine. When studying the Cappadocian Fathers, this has to be given the primacy they themselves would have accorded it while not overlooking their other contributions.

Basil of Caesarea

First, then, let us look at Saint Basil, who is the only one of them to have attracted the sobriquet "The Great". Basil was born around 330. He came from an extremely devout family. His paternal grandparents had taken refuge in the Pontic Mountains to avoid pressure to apostatize during persecution. His parents were assiduous practitioners of self-discipline, almsgiving, and hospitality. The parental circle included a rather extreme ascetic figure, Eustathius of Sebaste, the son of a bishop in the neighbouring province of Armenia—it was probably Eustathius who aroused Basil's interest in monasticism.[18]

Basil's father—who was also (of course) the father of his blood brother, Gregory of Nyssa—made his living from the teaching of rhetoric. Basil and Gregory learned well. The rhetor's combination of the ability to analyse and argue as well as persuade were second nature to the son, as they were likewise to his younger sibling. Basil went on to study in two of the greatest cities of the Hellenistic world, Antioch and Athens. The aim was to acquire a comprehensive

---

[18] Stephen M. Hildebrand, *Basil of Caesarea* (Grand Rapids, MI: Baker Academic, 2014), pp. 3–7.

education, consisting of courses in grammar, dialectics, rhetoric, geometry, arithmetic, and astronomy, and sometimes music as well. (The contents of this *enkyklios paideia* may sound familiar—it would have a counterpart in the "liberal arts" of the Scholastic West.) But the classical system of education into which he had been dipped at home, and plunged at Antioch and Athens, was by no means an unmixed blessing for a Christian youth. Basil became highly ambitious, ambitious, that is, to succeed as a rhetor—to outshine, no doubt, his father, a provincial pedagogue. It looks as though it was family bereavement—the sudden deaths of his brother Naucratius and a future brother-in-law—that moved Basil's heart and made him want to adopt a more serious Christian life. (It was at this point that his sister Macrina, the dead man's fiancée, took vows as a consecrated virgin.) Basil embraced at one and the same time Baptism and the monastic way, establishing, with the family fortune, a homemade monastery on an inherited estate in Pontus, near the Black Sea coast. There he was accompanied by some friends who for a short while included Gregory Nazianzen.

At Athens he and Nazianzen had attended the same lectures, given by a mixture of pagans and Christians. They were studying just prior to the emperor Julian's "School Law" forbidding Christians to teach the Hellenic classics, a law quashed after Julian's unexpected death two years later in 364. What the Princeton historian G. W. Bowersock said of Nazianzen could equally well be applied to Basil: he "refused to accept the transmutation of the cultural Hellenism he cherished into a religion he could not tolerate".[19] As to the aims of the edict on teachers, Bowerstock remarked that "Julian knew perfectly well what he was doing. Within little more than a generation the educated élite of the empire would be pagan."[20] The law struck at the root of a common aim of the Cappadocians: to produce a high Christian culture to rival or surpass that of contemporary pagans. In that context, so Basil explained in his *Address to Young Men*, "we must use these books, following in all things the example of bees. They do not visit every flower without distinction or seek to remove all the nectar from the flowers on which they alight, but only draw from

---

[19] G. W. Bowersock, *Julian the Apostate* (Cambridge, MA: Harvard University Press, 1978), p. 5.

[20] Ibid., p. 84.

them what they need to make honey and leave the rest. And if we are wise, we will take from those writings what is appropriate for us and conforms to the truth, ignoring the rest."[21] Synthesising with the Gospel elements in pagan learning that cohered with the Church's faith was an apologetic imperative. As Gregory of Nyssa would put it: "The divine sanctuary of mystery must be beautified with the riches of reason," which desirable aim Basil (so Nyssen thought) had achieved in his life and work.[22]

That certainly throws light on Basil's first literary project. With the help of Nazianzen, he produced an anthology of texts from Origen intended to show how Christian faith and Hellenic rationality could profitably be harmonized, especially in three areas: firstly, how to conceive the nature of divine substance; secondly, how to interpret ancient texts, including the biblical writings; thirdly, how to understand the freedom of the will. Ancillary goals included the answering of objections to the Church's faith on the part of the Neoplatonist philosopher Porphyry and by the emperor Julian (both of whom can probably be regarded as former Christians) and deflecting criticisms of Origen.

Basil's energies in the late 350s and '60s were otherwise invested in two areas. First, he wanted to learn more about monasticism from the professionals. That explains his travels among the monastic settlements in Palestine and Egypt, where he arrived the year after Saint Anthony's death. Judging by the texts he produced for monks, and his own activity as a monastic founder, he was unimpressed by the hermits he met, but enthusiastic about the possibilities of "coenobitic" or communitarian monasticism—above all if it could be shaped in such a way as to meet wider human needs (using to this end manual labour, if need be: a shocking fate for a gentleman in the Late Antique world).

Basil's first experience of urban coenobitic monastic life was in Caesarea, his future episcopal see, where, five years after his Baptism, he was ordained priest in 362. In his own ascetic writings, Basil

[21] Basil, *Address to Young Men on the Value of Greek Literature* 4, trans. F. M. Padelford, in *Address to Young Men on Greek Literature* (New York: American Book, 1901).
[22] Gregory of Nyssa, *The Life of Moses* II, 115–16, trans. A. J. Malherbe and Everett Ferguson (New York: Paulist, 1979).

emphasised the practical love of neighbor. "In the solitary life the powers we have become useless: the power we lack cannot be supplied.... This is clearly contrary to the laws of love."[23] Basil wanted his monks to help the needy in education, healthcare, and the provision of accommodation for travellers, eventually creating in the neighbourhood of Caesarea, so the ecclesiastical historian Sozomen reports, a veritable city of charitable works (the "Basiliad") made up of monastic communities thus engaged.[24]

Such an exclusive option for coenobitism, for communal life, has been taken to illustrate Basil's desire to find openings in classical culture to evangelical faith—in this case, treating the Stoic belief that members of the same species have a natural attractiveness to one another as a sort of preliminary sketch for the *agape* command to the disciples in Saint John's Gospel: "Love one another" (13:34).[25] His first ascetic treatise, called simply *Morals*, is notable for its biblical quality. Like such later Church Doctors as Bonaventure, Basil regarded Sacred Scripture when taken together with the order of creation as the set of "books" God has written for all human enlightenment.[26]

After monasticism, Basil's other early, yet abiding, preoccupation was the doctrinal struggle for recognition of the Godhead of Jesus Christ. With an Arian Christian as emperor in the East and a multitude of Arian and Semi-Arian bishops in Oriental sees, Basil sought not only to defend the *homoousion* but, like Athanasius in the latter's more diplomatic moments, to show sympathetic understanding of those who had adopted the viewpoint called "homoiousianism", affirming the Son's "likeness of substance" to the Father. Shunning the original Arianism for which the Son could certainly not be (in Alexander of Alexandria's phrase) "proper" to the Father's being since "there was [a time] when he was not", and rejecting even more robustly the radical *Neo*-Arianism, which denied that the Son was like the Father in any way at all, some Christians could nevertheless not bring themselves to

---

[23] Basil, *The Longer Rules* 7, trans. W. K. Lowther Clarke, in *The Ascetic Works of Saint Basil* (London: Society for Promoting Christian Knowledge; New York: Macmillan, 1925).

[24] Sozomen, *Church History* VI, 34.

[25] Anthony Meredith, *The Cappadocians* (London: Geoffrey Chapman, 1995), p. 29.

[26] Hildebrand, *Basil of Caesarea*, p. 17. Those two "books" would be nicely brought together in one of his most-read works, his collected sermons on the six-day account of the creation in the Book of Genesis.

use the *homoousion* formula. Acknowledgement of the self-identical single substance of the Godhead, so they feared, would render Father, Son, and Holy Spirit simply modes of the divine substance rather than subsistent persons-in-relation—whether in relation to each other or to ourselves. This may indeed have characterised the background of the Asia Minor Church life from which Basil himself emerged.[27]

In his first doctrinal treatise, *Against Eunomius*, dated to 364, Basil argues that, if logic has any validity, only affirmation of the *homoousion* can guarantee the complete exclusion of any suggestion of unlikeness to the Father on the part of the Son. "Likeness", after all, may be in one or more respects—which logically implies that, in some other respect or respects, likeness may be countered by unlikeness, by dissimilarity. The *homoiousion* is powerless to exclude unlikeness.

Basil's chief target was the intellectual leader of the Neo-Arians, Eunomius of Cyzicus, for whom the essence of divine being could be captured in one word: "unoriginated". This term, said Eunomius, not only made the concept of God immediately intelligible to anyone who used it. It also ruled out, argued Eunomius, any claim that the "only-begotten Son"—*begotten*, and thus an originated one—could really himself be divine. In a rejoinder on Basil's behalf, Gregory of Nyssa would write:

> Since the meanings of "originate" vary and suggest many ideas, there are some of them in which the title "unoriginate" is not inapplicable to the Son. When, for instance, this word has the meaning of "deriving existence from no cause whatever" then we confess that it is peculiar to the Father, but when the question is about "origin" in its other meanings (since any creature or time or order has an origin) then we attribute the being superior to the origin to the Son as well, and we believe that that whereby all things were made is beyond the origin of creation, and the idea of time, and the sequence of order. He [the divine Son], who on the ground of His subsistence is not without an origin, possessed in every other view an undoubted *unoriginateness*, and while the Father is unoriginate and ungenerate, the Son is unoriginate in the way we have said, though not ungenerate.[28]

[27] Chadwick, *Church in Ancient Society*, p. 331.
[28] Gregory of Nyssa, *Against Eunomius* I, 33, trans. W. Moore, H. A. Wilson, and H. C. Ogle, in *NPNF*, 2nd series, vol. 5. Emphasis is that of the Victorian translators. Unless otherwise indicated, citations from Gregory of Nyssa's *Against Eunomius* are from this translation.

Replying to Eunomius' *Apologia* gave Basil an opportunity to remind readers that, so far from "unoriginatedness" constituting an adequate definition of the divine, God definitionally escapes all human comprehension—a typical claim of the orthodox Fathers since Irenaeus.[29] Once again, Nyssen, defending his brother's doctrine, has an especially fine formulation:

> The simplicity of the True Faith assumes God to be that which He is, viz. incapable of being grasped by any term, or any idea, or any other device of our apprehension, remaining beyond the reach not only of the human but of the angelic and of all supramundane intelligence, unthinkable, unutterable, above all expression in words, having but one name that can represent His proper nature, the single name of being "Above every name"; which is granted to the Only-begotten also because "all that the Father has is the Son's".[30]

In his own treatise *Against Eunomius*, Basil was keen to convince readers that calling God a Trinity of subsistent persons—*hypostases*—does not undermine faith in the unity of God. Some Nicenes were accustomed to speak of the Trinity as a single hypostasis. The orthodox among them were using the word "hypostasis" as synonymous with "substance", *ousia*, not with "person", *prosôpon*. That was true not least of Athanasius, who for that reason would never have spoken of three "hypostases".[31] There could also be a heterodox use of the hypostasis-*ousia* equation. "Sabellians" (followers of a third-century

---

[29] For the wider picture, see Georgios D. Martzelos, "Kataphasis and Apophasis in the Greek Orthodox Patristic Tradition", in *Naming and Thinking God in Europe Today*, ed. Norbert Hintersteiner (Leiden: Brill, 2007), pp. 247–63.

[30] Gregory of Nyssa, *Against Eunomius* I, 42.

[31] See, for instance, Athanasius, *Letter to the Africans* 4: "Of all the terms used of God after the Council of Nicaea, *hypostasis* was the only one about which application to God in the singular or plural was disputed. Hence this term, more than any other, became the focal point of theological controversy in the fourth century" (Joseph T. Lienhard, "*Ousia* and *Hypostasis*: The Cappadocian Settlement and the Theology of 'One *Hypostasis*' ", in *The Trinity*, ed. Stephen Davis, Daniel Kendall, S.J., and Gerald O'Collins, S.J. [Oxford: Oxford University Press, 1999], p. 120). Lienhard draws attention to G. L. Prestige's classic work *God in Patristic Thought*, 2nd ed. (London: Society for Promoting Christian Knowledge, 1952), pp. 162–78, where Prestige distinguishes between two senses of *hypostasis*: basis/foundation/substance, and positive, concrete, distinct existence—the first depending on the intransitive use (that will be the "middle voice") of the verb *hyphistêmi*, and the second on the same verb's transitive use (that will be the "active voice").

Roman priest about whom little is known) took it to mean that there is only one Person in God—namely, the Father. The Son and Spirit are but modes of the Father's being. "Sabellianism" was a bogey word that could be launched against any theologian who treated hypostasis and *ousia* as synonymous—here the main suspect, among the friends of Athanasius, was Bishop Marcellus of Ancyra, who "liked the formula of Neopythagorean mathematicians that the Monad contains the potential to engender the dyad and the triad ['one' can generate 'two' and 'three'], but is primary."[32] Meanwhile the Arians had seized on the phrase "three hypostases" for their own peculiar use. What Arians had in mind were three unequal Persons who certainly did not share one common substance.

For Basil, contrastingly, there are three personal hypostases who cannot be unequal precisely because they are consubstantial: they are one single being. He was so sensitive to the objection that three hypostases might be taken to mean three Gods that he rejected any notion of "counting" in relation to the Triune God. "When the Lord enjoined the use of the formula, 'Father, Son, and Holy Spirit', he did not add any numerical qualification."[33] The word "hypostasis" denotes what is particular to Father, Son, and Holy Spirit. It is not possible, therefore, to identify anything that is common to each hypostasis. There is nothing that would make it possible to count up Father, Son, and Holy Spirit, comparably to the way we count bananas, hummingbirds, or, for that matter, human persons. Anything common to the hypostases would have to be regarded as belonging to their shared substance, their common *ousia*. They can, therefore, only

---

[32] Chadwick, *Church in Ancient Society*, p. 234.

[33] Basil, *On the Holy Spirit* 44, trans. Blomfield Jackson, in *NPNF*, 2nd series, vol. 8, ed. Philip Schaff and Henry Wace (Buffalo, NY: Christian Literature Publishing, 1895). Citations from *On the Holy Spirit* are from this translation. Balthasar sees two strategies issuing from Basil's thought on number. Insofar as Basil offers a "quasi-permission" to speak of number in the Trinity, especially in connexion with the processions, Nyssa will follow him: for Gregory, number in the Trinity "means simply the *taxis* of the processions in the one, indivisible nature". Hans Urs von Balthasar, *Theo-Logic. Theological Logical Theory III: The Spirit of Truth*, translated Graham Harrison (San Francisco, CA: Ignatius Press, 2005), p. 123. Insofar as Basil is reticent on the topic, Nazianzen, Evagrius, and Maximus will follow him on a path that leads ultimately to Aquinas, for whom there is no "quantitative" number in the Trinity since the divine personal relations "pertain to the plurality of the divine Unity but refuse all separateness". Ibid., p. 124.

be "counted" singly—as 1, and 1, and 1—or, better still, using their proper names, "Father", "Son", and "Spirit", without further ado.[34] In practice, of course, it was not really possible to stop people speaking of "the Three".[35] Such linguistic restraint was asking too much of ordinary users of language.[36]

Such belief in "one substance, three persons" led in the East to distinguishing the *common attributes* of the single divine substance from the *individual properties* (otherwise called the "hypostatic particularities") of Father, Son, and Spirit—the 1, and 1, and 1 who personalize that substance. In *Against Eunomius*, Basil explained: "The divinity is common but the paternity and filiation are properties; and from the combination of these two elements, that is to say from the common and the proper, occurs in us the understanding of the truth."[37] Contrastingly, in the West, as embodied in Augustine, the formula "one substance, three persons" formed, rather, the starting point for developing the idea of the Persons as relations, relations within the one Godhead. That term "relation", as used in Trinitarian theology, was by no means unknown to the Cappadocians. In the

---

[34] After Basil's death, Nyssen would write, "In professing to expound the mystery of the Father, [Eunomius] corrects as it were the expressions in the Gospel, and will not make use of the words by which our Lord in perfecting our faith conveyed that mystery to us: he suppresses the names of Father, Son and Holy Ghost, and speaks of a 'Supreme and Absolute Being' instead of the Father, of 'another existing and through it, but after it' instead of the Son, and of 'a third ranking with neither of those two' instead of the Holy Ghost" (*Against Eunomius* I, 13). A modern theologian, interpreting Basil's *On the Holy Spirit* in defence of the revealed names, writes: "These names fix historical references, convey insights, and maintain the core of Christian identity. Alongside the name of 'Jesus', nothing else so expresses our continuity with the faith of the first Christians and their successors down through the ages." Gerald O'Collins, S.J., "The Holy Trinity: The State of the Questions", in Davis, Kendall, and O'Collins, *Trinity*, p. 17.

[35] Later in the West, Thomas will speak in this connexion of "transcendental multitude". The transcendental determination of being called "unity" has reference to being in its undividedness. A divine person, too, is undivided, just as the divine essence is undivided, but the revelation of the Trinity allows us to speak of each such person, distinct from another such person, and yet another—thus (on this Thomasian view) introducing a new transcendental determination of being, plurality, which has its origin in the processions of Son and Spirit in God. See Gilles Emery, O.P., *Trinity in Aquinas* (Ypsilanti, MI: Sapientia Press, 2003), pp. 30–31.

[36] The actual formula "three persons in one substance" seems, however, less frequent in Basil (and the other Cappadocians) than is often claimed: see Joseph T. Lienhard, S.J., "*Ousia* and *Hypostasis*: The Cappadocian Settlement and the Theology of 'One *Hypostasis*'", in Davis, Kendall, and O'Collins, *Trinity*, pp. 99–122.

[37] Basil, *Against Eunomius* II, 28. Translation is the present author's.

letter of Basil just quoted, he points out that only the "antithesis"—
the "relation of opposition"—between Unbegotten and Begotten
distinguishes the Father and the Son. Brought to the West by Augustine,[38] notably in Book V of his On the Trinity, the language of relationship would have to wait awhile to find in the Latin Church
its finest exponents—above all, in the thirteenth century, Thomas
Aquinas, for whom the Trinitarian Persons are, precisely, "subsistent
relations".[39] That would be, unfortunately, a source of difficulty for
"dialogue" between Byzantine and Latin theologians in the Middle Ages, and their Orthodox and Catholic successors today, since
the Cappadocian Fathers define the Trinitarian Persons as those who
possess the divine essence, whereas, beginning with Augustine, the
Latins see the Persons as first and foremost constituted by their rela-
tionships, as (in Aquinas' phrase) "subsistent relations".

To argue, as Basil did, for a triad of consubstantial hypostases
implies of course an acceptance of the divinity of the Spirit. In the last
of the (authentic) books of Against Eunomius, Basil went on to defend
the equality with the Father not only of the Son but also of the
Holy Spirit. He argues that, in matters of the enlightening of human
persons (through divine revelation) and their sanctification (through
the gift of salvation), the Spirit brings to perfection the work of the
Father and the Son. Such perfection activity is unthinkable unless
the Spirit is divine just as Father and Son are divine. Basil would
have found in Origen's writings the basic distinctive economic marks
of the Spirit—the Spirit is both the enlightener and the sanctifier—
and we have seen how Athanasius in the Letters to Serapion pursued
these themes. The Spirit, enlightener and sanctifier, bringing with
him in those ways the life of the Son, who himself has that life from
the Father, must be as uncreated as they—the Father and the Son—
are. Gregory of Nyssa took his cue from Basil here when he wrote,
"Every operation which extends from God to the Creation, and is
named according to our variable conceptions of it, has its origin from
the Father, and proceeds through the Son, and is perfected in the
Holy Spirit."[40]

[38] Irénée Chevalier, Saint Augustin et la pensée grecque: Les relations trinitaires (Fribourg: Libra-
rie de l'Université, 1940).

[39] Bernard Sesboüé, Saint Basile et la Trinité: Un acte théologique au IVe siècle (Paris: Desclée,
1998), pp. 14–15.

[40] Gregory of Nyssa, On Not Three Gods, trans. H. A. Wilson, in NPNF, 2nd series, vol. 5.

In his treatise *On the Holy Spirit*, written ten years after *Against Euno-mius*, Basil reaffirmed that teaching: "The first principle of all exist-ing things is One, creating through the Son and perfecting through the Spirit."[41] Father, Son, and Spirit are, he pointed out, inseparable in the New Testament doxologies.[42] Their equality is apparent, he noted, from Saint Matthew's baptismal formula. And here Basil draws his readers' attention to the significance of the unwritten apostolic tradition that Baptism is by *threefold* immersion.[43] So it should be plain to all Church teachers that the Spirit, like the Son, must enjoy the same honour as does the Father, owing to "His greatness, His dignity, and His operations".[44] To the annoyance of Nazianzen, Basil did not, however, favour introducing into the Creed an *explicit* pro-fession of the *homoousion* of the Spirit—anxious as he was not to re-ignite memories of the half century of debate over the imposition at Nicaea of the term "homoousios" for the Son. So the Creed of Nicaea-Constantinople recited at the Sunday Liturgy does not call the Spirit consubstantial with the Father and the Son but restricts itself to the confession that the Spirit receives the same glorification as Father and Son do. With them he is "worshipped and glorified", a statement about identity of honour.[45]

Basil's influence, which had been sealed by becoming metropolitan of Cappadocia in 370 and the voluminous correspondence whereby he sought to influence bishops and civic leaders, was also based on the reputation for asceticism, practical charity, and zeal for orthodoxy he had acquired over a lifetime of Church service.

Gregory Nazianzen

Nazianzen was probably born in 329, making him pretty well the exact contemporary of Basil. We have seen how Gregory Nazianzen's

---

[41] Basil, *On the Holy Spirit* 38.

[42] Despite the variety of propositions used to introduce their names—"with", "from", "through", and the rest. Basil devotes much of *On the Holy Spirit* (especially chapters 1–8 and 25–29) to such "close observation of syllables" as practised by his arch opponents, the Neo-Arians.

[43] Basil, *On the Holy Spirit* 35.

[44] Ibid., 23.

[45] It should be noted, however, that a post-conciliar synod of 382 sent a letter to Pope Damasus confessing the "uncreated, consubstantial (*homoousios*) and coeternal Trinity".

formation paralleled his friend's, which is not to say they were altogether uniform in what they took from the Hellenic heritage. Nazianzen was more attached than Basil to the literary aspects of a rhetor's training. Much of his output consists of poetry, both auto-biographical and theological.[46] One way to describe his theological method is to say he sought to synthesize the imagery of Scripture with the rational procedures of Hellenic philosophy. John McGuck-in calls this the bringing of order into biblical theology without los-ing the specific contributions of symbolism and mystical insight. McGuckin further remarks on the same topic—namely, theological method—that it was, in Nazianzen's case, "particularly characterized by ... the holding of apparent opposites in creative tension".[47] There is a good example in the Roman Office of Readings for the first week of Advent, taken from Gregory's *Oration* 45. "He who makes rich is made poor; he takes on the poverty of my flesh, that I may gain the riches of his divinity. He who is full is made empty; he is emptied for a brief space of his glory, that I may share in his fullness."[48] Mc-Guckin goes on to draw some wider conclusions:

> This aspect of antithetical method was a recognized form of Hellenis-tic rhetorical philosophy, and one which Gregory had learned to good effect in his time in Athens, but not since the time of Origen had any Christian intellectual so successfully combined philosophical method with theological speculation, thus rehabilitating his Alexandrian hero's vision of Christianity, and providing a paradigm for the whole future development of the Byzantine church.[49]

After local studies in grammar and rhetoric at Nazianzus and Cap-padocian Caesarea (this was probably the occasion of a first meet-ing with Basil), Gregory moved on to the other Caesarea, Caesarea Palestinae, or Caesarea-on-Sea, where the attraction lay in teachers of higher quality and the resources of Origen's great library. From

[46] For a selection, see *On God and Man: The Theological Poetry of Gregory Nazianzen*, trans. Peter Gilbert (Crestwood, NY: Saint Vladimir's Seminary Press, 2001).

[47] McGuckin, *Saint Gregory of Nazianzus*, p. 10.

[48] Gregory Nazianzen, *Orations* 45, 9, from the Second Reading for the first week of Advent, Office of Readings, *Liturgy of the Hours* (International Commission on English in the Liturgy Corporation, 1975).

[49] McGuckin, *Saint Gregory of Nazianzus*, p. 10.

Origen, whose memory remained green in that place, he learned, in the words of the Episcopalian patrologist Christopher Beeley, the "rudiments and the great heights of Christian theology", finding in Origen "a clear model of the spiritual and intellectual dimensions of his own life".[50] Alexandria, Origen's birthplace, was the next stop on his educational journey, after which Gregory set out across the Mediterranean for Athens. Off Cyprus, the ship was in danger of foundering in a storm, reminding him that he had not yet been baptised, so he might never be cleansed in what he called "those purifying waters by which we are made divine".[51] He appears to have asked for Baptism on arrival, committing himself at the same time to the ascetical practice that for serious Christians in the fourth century was the common accompaniment of baptismal initiation. That danger of shipwreck was thus the equivalent in Gregory Nazianzen's life to the family bereavements in Basil's.

His outstanding proficiency as a philosophically minded rhetor soon became apparent at Athens in the offer of a lectureship. But the call of Christian Cappadocia and his friendship with Basil was too strong. Returning home in increasingly unpropitious political and ecclesiastical circumstances, he found his father, a married bishop converted late in life to Catholic Christianity, rather insistent on his son's ordination to the priesthood—evidently with a view to keeping the episcopal succession in the family. Gregory's attempt to escape elevation to the episcopate by taking refuge in Basil's rural monastery in Pontus succeeded in the short term. But soon Basil would himself be both priest and bishop, in which latter capacity he proceeded to engineer the consecration of his friend to a see especially created for him at another Cappadocian locale, Sasima. Once again, Gregory was somewhat exploited: it served Basil's own purposes to have this brilliant man as his suffragan.

Unlike Basil, Nazianzen was not an obvious success in the office of bishop. He refused to take up residence at Sasima for a mixture of reasons, possibly realistic (it was a one-horse town) but not especially edifying. He may have been under the impression he was to be

---

[50] Christopher A. Beeley, *Gregory of Nazianzus on the Trinity and the Knowledge of God: In Your Light We Shall See Light* (New York and Oxford: Oxford University Press, 2008), p. 7.
[51] Cited in ibid., p. 8.

Basil's collaborator at Caesarea and a premier rank orator for special occasions.[52] (For Henry Chadwick, the problem was temperamental: "Gregory was one of those who like to be offered positions but withdraw in face of the practical obligations."[53]) Once consecrated, Gregory's father at last got his way with his son. Gregory moved on from Sasima to become bishop of Nazianzus—though by his own account he was merely a co-adjutor who, after his father's death, remained in place only because no "ruling" bishop had been chosen.

Though history would treat "Nazianzen" as synonymous with Gregory's name, here too was no lasting city. He was destined, albeit briefly, for higher things. In Constantinople, whither the orthodox party in the Church sought to transfer him, he turned out to lack the political adroitness required of an archbishop in the imperial capital—above all at the time of so crucial a council as the great assembly convened in 381. His enemies took advantage of his nominal position as bishop of Nazianzus to dethrone him. By accepting translation to another bishopric—so ran their complaint—he had transgressed the sixth canon of the Council of Nicaea, a canon more honoured (it must be said) in the breach than in the observance. So this was an excuse. It was wider currents that carried him off. In the matter of a disputed episcopal succession at Antioch, Gregory wanted the Roman- and Alexandrian-supported candidate Paulinus to be synodically approved. He was conscious of how the Church at Rome had abstained from sending delegates to the Council—later adjudged the Second Ecumenical Council—from a stance of steady antipathy to Paulinus' rival, Meletius, who had preceded Gregory as president of the gathering. Gregory's pro-Paulinus (and hence pro-Roman) policy was unpopular in the East. "Gregory's failure to persuade the council to make peace with the west by recognizing Paulinus at Antioch reflected a fairly general feeling of alienation in the Greek east that Rome and the west had not much helped in the elimination of 'Arianism'. Roman support for Marcellus [the 'Sabellian'], now being disowned by Pope Damasus, was not easily forgiven or forgotten."[54] The Roman Church paid a price for this

---

[52] Ibid., p. 14.
[53] Chadwick, *Church in Ancient Society*, p. 424.
[54] Ibid., p. 427.

débâcle: the passing of a canon that gave the see of Constantinople precedence over the other "Petrine" sees of Alexandria and Antioch "because it is the New Rome"—a claim to which "Old Rome" would never give its assent.[55]

Yet all was not lost. Gregory had used his short tenure in Constantinople to unify many of the disparate Christian groups in the capital under the neo-Nicene banner, and this in itself was a major achievement, the necessary condition for the holding of the true successor council to Nicaea.[56] "Constantinople I" was that "true successor", thanks to its explicit affirmation of the Nicene *homoousion* for the Son and its implicit affirmation of the further *homoousion*, left unmentioned at "Nicaea I", of the Holy Spirit. Nazianzen's speech of resignation has been described by Pope Benedict XVI as "heart-rending"—though, in all truth, had the Pope Emeritus left Rome he might have made Gregory's words his own.[57] "Farewell, great city, beloved by Christic.... My children, I beg you, jealously guard the deposit [of faith] that has been entrusted to you; remember my suffering."[58]

Subsequently, Gregory Nazianzen enjoyed a long retirement when, in McGuckin's words, he "took some well-deserved consolation in the beauty of Greek letters".[59] This should not be misconstrued as self-indulgence. He wanted to leave behind in the Church a body of Christian literature as fine as the pagan literature on which the education of his contemporaries rested. Nazianzen's version of monasticism, unlike Basil's, was neither communitarian nor socially oriented. Nor did it include manual labour—unless writing out and editing your own manuscripts counts as such. Gregory Nazianzen's notion of monasticism was that of a studious life lived mainly in solitude and dedicated to the production of books that would build up a Christian culture—and the single most indispensable aspect of such a culture, in his view, was safeguarding the truth of the Christian proclamation. Among the reasons he gives for writing poetry was its

---

[55] Council of Constantinople, canon 3.

[56] Beeley, *Gregory of Nazianzus*, p. 34.

[57] Pope Benedict XVI, *Church Fathers: From Clement of Rome to Augustine* (San Francisco: Ignatius Press, 2008), p. 80.

[58] Gregory Nazianzen, *Orations* 42, 27, in ibid.

[59] McGuckin, *Saint Gregory of Nazianzus*, p. xxvii.

possible value in making complex theology accessible and attractive to young people.[60]

There was, then, a doctrinal mission too urgent to yield to other aims. "As a servant of the Word, I adhere to the ministry of the Word; may I never agree to neglect this good. I appreciate this vocation and am thankful for it; I derive more joy from it than from all other things put together."[61] Christian posterity found his concentration of his energies justified by its fruits. Once Rufinus had translated into Latin the five "Theological Orations" Nazianzen gave at Constantinople on the eve of the Second Ecumenical Council, "Gregory was ever after regarded as a pillar of orthodox Trinitarian and Christological doctrine."[62]

Yet recent scholarship suggests that historical theologians have looked too exclusively to the "Theological Orations" for Gregory's doctrine.[63] Exposure to more of his writings, both the speeches and the poetry, indicates how he was not simply a continuator of Basil and, behind Basil, Athanasius. In particular, Nazianzen had his own "take" on the divine Trinity, which differed from Basil's by emphasising at all points the unity that holds good between, on the one hand, the "economy", God in his outreach to us, and, on the other hand, the "theology"—understood in the sense of that which God is in and of himself. "Just as Gregory normally assumes Christ's humanity and focuses instead on his divine identity, so too he begins with the divine economy and directs his attention to the identity of the triune God revealed in it.... When Gregory is regarded as 'the Theologian' par excellence of the patristic period, his title is best understood in this sense: as the one who most clearly showed the theological meaning of the divine economy, by which God is truly known."[64] For Nazianzen, if Christopher Beeley (here quoted) is correct, the theology is the meaning of the economy, not another realm to which the economy points—a formulation which, however, may reflect late twentieth-century discussion, allergic as much of the latter is to a fully realist theology of the Triune God in and for

[60] Gregory Nazianzen, *Poems* II, 1, 39.

[61] Gregory Nazianzen, *Orations* 6, 5, in Benedict XVI, *Church Fathers.*

[62] McGuckin, *Saint Gregory of Nazianzus,* p. xxviii. These speeches constitute Nazianzen's *Orations* 27–31.

[63] Beeley, *Gregory of Nazianzus,* p. 40.

[64] Ibid., p. 201.

himself.[65] As a student of the triadology of the "divine Thomas" has noted, "it is not in ascertaining God by his relations to the world that one realizes the profundity of the action of God (as a vast theological current today, issuing from Hegel, would have it), but inversely it is in the contemplation of the transcendent being of God the Trinity that one discovers the source of the divine economy: creation, man, grace, the mysteries of the incarnation, eschatology."[66]

If Beeley is correct, Gregory did not follow Athanasius in making the consubstantiality of the three Persons his key doctrinal concept where the Holy Trinity is concerned. The dominant idea in Gregory Nazianzen's theology of the Trinity is that of the "monarchy" of the Father—to be understood as how the Father is the "principle" or "source" of the Son and the Spirit.[67] That theological option enabled Nazianzen to recapture the feeling for the dynamism of the divine life that is found—albeit at the cost of an excessive subordinationism—in the writings of Origen. It is not simply that the Father shares his *ousia* with the Son (and the Spirit), as Athanasius would say. Nor is it simply that the *ousia* of God is particularized in the hypostases of Father, Son, and Spirit, as Basil would say. Rather, the Father is the spring from which the two rivers of the Son and the Spirit continually flow forth, in the unending begetting of the divine Son, the unending spiration of the divine Spirit. The outcome is a dependent egalitarianism that wholly confounds our contemporary expectations of interpersonal relations.

> The monarchy of the Father within the Trinity is thus the sort of causality that produces equality and shared being, rather than inequality; and the equality of the three persons is the sort of equality that derives from and involves a cause, source and first principle, not the sort that exists apart from any first principle. In the Trinity, then, dependence and equality are mutually involved in each other, however much the idea may run counter to certain ancient or modern sensibilities.[68]

---

[65] For an example of the latter, see Catherine LaCugna, *God for Us: The Trinity and Christian Life* (New York: HarperCollins, 1991); an antidote is provided by Francesca Aran Murphy, *God Is Not a Story: Realism Revisited* (Oxford: Oxford University Press, 2007).

[66] Emery, *Trinity in Aquinas*, pp. 163–64.

[67] Beeley, *Gregory of Nazianzus*, pp. 204–13.

[68] Ibid., p. 210.

In other words, the equality concerned (cf. *homoousion*), is sustained by the dependence itself (cf. *monarchia*).

Nazianzen did not, then, "centre-piece" consubstantiality. But he was far from forgetting it. Beeley makes plain that while for Gregory consubstantiality is only the "corollary" and "eternal result" of the Father's monarchy, yet within the Trinity "causality and consubstantiality, just as much as causality and personal distinctions ... necessarily belong together in the same theological principle".[69] Nazianzen was indeed insistent that the consubstantiality of the Spirit with the Father and the Son be confessed explicitly, without the diplomatic subterfuge of Basil's notion of a parity of honour. Distinctions of emphasis among the Cappadocians, while important,[70] should not be taken to overthrow the unity of their witness to the Triune Lord.[71]

Newmanians will wish to note how in the fourth of the "Theological Orations" Gregory offers a justification of his pneumatology in terms of what would later be called the development of doctrine. "The Old Testament," writes Nazianzen, "proclaimed the Father openly and the Son more obscurely. The New manifested the Son, and suggested the deity of the Holy Spirit. Now [meaning, presumably, since Pentecost] the Spirit dwells among us, and supplies us with a clearer demonstration of himself."[72] Time was needed, he explained, for this to sink in. "For this reason it was, I think, that [the Spirit] gradually came to dwell in the disciples, measuring himself out to them in accordance with their capacity to receive him." It was a justification of delay in affirming the *homoousion* of the Spirit reminiscent of Irenaeus' notion of how in salvation history God gradually "accustoms" human persons to himself.

---

[69] Ibid.

[70] They were not simply "Basilians". Not only Nazianzen, but also Nyssen had a distinctive triadological "take" of his own. For the differences see ibid., pp. 292–309.

[71] Arguably, Nyssen begins from the nature of the one God, not the Trinity of Persons; see Michel R. Barnes, *The Power of God: Dunamis in Gregory of Nyssa's Trinitarian Theology* (Washington, DC: Catholic University of America Press, 2001). Yet all three of the great Cappadocian Fathers are in view when André de Halleux remarks that the unity principle and the Trinitarian principle are equally important for these Fathers who "are at the same time, and totally, personalists and essentialists." André de Halleux, "Personalisme ou essentialisme trinitaire chez les Pères cappadociens?", in *Patrologie et oecuménisme* (Leuven: Leuven University Press/Peeters, 1990), pp. 265–66.

[72] Gregory Nazianzen, *Orations* 31, 26, trans. Charles Gordon Browne and James Edward Swallow, in *NPNF*, 2nd series, vol. 7.

A further advance on Basil's account of the Spirit should be noted, perhaps more for its implications for Nazianzen's soteriology and spirituality than for his pneumatology proper. Basil had argued that the Spirit must be God because the Spirit, in enlightening and sanctifying, perfects. Nazianzen preferred to say he must be God because he deifies. The language of *theôsis*, deification, as the preferred way of speaking about salvation and the goal of the spiritual life comes into its own in Gregory Nazianzen's teaching and preaching.[73] No Christian theologian before him had used the word "theosis" with anything like his frequency and consistency.[74] Echoed in occasional Latin Christian writers, including Augustine and Aquinas, it was to become on the whole the distinctive property of the Greek-speaking Church, a powerful marker of the reality of the communion between God and man set up by the Trinity in Christ, an indicator of how through grace we are to share the divine humanity in which Jesus, the God-man, existed by nature—by his two natures held together in one Person. This mark of his doctrine is unmistakable in the subject of the following chapter, Saint Cyril of Alexandria.

Nazianzen was one of the first people to recognise the threat to a soteriology of deification posed in the school of Antioch when Diodore of Tarsus began to teach about the "two Sons": the Son of God and the man Jesus to whom the Son of God was indissolubly united. In his *Letter to Cledonius* (that was the priest who had charge at Nazianzus after Gregory left the see), he suddenly saw a new enemy on the horizon. In the letter, Nazianzen was meant to be critiquing Apollinarius, contemporary and friend of Athanasius, for whom the divine Word takes the place of a human mind in Jesus. To speak of the Word becoming "flesh", as Athanasius customarily did, could give the false impression that the incarnate Word has no specifically human soul and therefore no created mind. Apollinarius had fallen into that trap, and Gregory had intended to deal with it. But instead Gregory breaks off to deal with this new aberration, stating, "If anyone introduces the notion of two Sons, one of God the

---

[73] For this crucial theme of Christian soteriology, see Norman Russell, *The Doctrine of Deification in the Greek Patristic Tradition* (Oxford: Oxford University Press, 2004).

[74] Donald F. Winslow, *The Dynamics of Salvation: A Study in Gregory of Nazianzus* (Cambridge, MA: Philadelphia Patristic Foundation, 1979), p. 179.

Father, the other of the mother, and discredits the unity and identity, may he lose his part in the adoption promised to those who
believe aright."[75] The tone is sharper than with the corresponding
anathema on the Apollinarians who, it is implied, are more idiotic
than impious. Gregory continues, "Anyone who has put his trust
in Him [Christ] as a man without a human mind, must be mindless
himself, and quite unworthy of salvation."[76] And so Nazianzen looks
ahead, from his retirement, to the work of Saint Cyril, who will be,
after these Cappadocians, our next topic. Only if One who is God
has taken our nature into personal union with himself can the way to
theosis really be open for human persons.

Gregory of Nyssa

Gregory of Nyssa—the youngest of these three Cappadocian figures, born in 340 and outliving the other two (Basil died before 380,
Nazianzen in 390, but Nyssen was still alive in 393)—had less of a role
to play than Basil or Nazianzen in the great ecclesiastical events of his
day. He also provides more enigmas for the biographer than do his
brother Basil or his reluctant episcopal colleague Gregory Nazianzen.
Nyssen lacked their university training, and yet he is more philosophically sophisticated than they are; he has attracted more interest than
they from twenty-first century writers.[77] (A comparison between his
treatise *Against Eunomius* and the work of the same name by Basil
would bring out Gregory of Nyssa's greater theological finesse.[78])
Another enigma: his treatise *On Virginity* offers a "philosophical
underpinning" to Basil's monastic theology, yet he himself was a

[75] Gregory Nazianzen, *Letter to Cledonius*, in *Saint Cyril of Alexandria and the Christological Controversy*, by John McGuckin (Crestwood, NY: Saint Vladimir's Seminary Press, 2004), Appendix 2, p. 391.

[76] Ibid., p. 393.

[77] Sarah Coakley, ed., *Re-thinking Gregory of Nyssa* (Oxford: Blackwell, 2003); David Bentley Hart, *The Beauty of the Infinite: The Aesthetics of Christian Truth* (Grand Rapids, MI: Eerdmans, 2003); Morwenna Ludlow, *Gregory of Nyssa: Ancient and (Post)Modern* (Oxford: Oxford University Press, 2007).

[78] Cf. Lucian Turcescu, *Gregory of Nyssa and the Concept of Divine Persons* (New York: Oxford University Press, 2005).

married man.[79] Again, he saw himself as the defender of his brother's preaching and teaching, writing treatises *On the Six Days of Creation* and *On the Making of Man*, which back up Basil's sermons on the same subjects, and composing his own *Against Eunomius*, to counter the Neo-Arian leader's riposte to Basil, by then dead.[80] Despite in that way playing second fiddle to his elder brother, Gregory of Nyssa struck out in a genre of writing not found in either Basil or Gregory Nazianzen—namely, treatises on mystical theology expressed in the form of biblical interpretation.

For that is what we find in his *Life of Moses*,[81] and in the *Homilies on the Song of Songs*, two spiritual classics with an influence on future Christian spirituality only comparable to Origen's own homilies and commentary on the Song of Songs written a century and a half before. The crucial differences from Origen lie, firstly, in Nyssen's doctrine of the infinity of God—Origen had denied God was infinite on the grounds that an unbounded God would be altogether unknowable— and secondly, in Gregory of Nyssa's related claim that the soul, by freedom and grace, only ever approaches God "asymptotically", that is, by drawing nearer to him but never attaining him in his fullness; whatever the soul comes to know and love in God increases its own desire and capacity to love and know more of him, and so it goes on in a process that has no end even in heaven.[82] For Platonism the

---

[79] Meredith, *Cappadocians*, p. 52.

[80] Eunomius had published his "An Apology for the Apology" after Basil's death. For the texts given as Gregory of Nyssa's *Against Eunomius* in the *NPNF* series, it should be noted that Book II is now regarded as Book IV (or a separate treatise for which different titles are suggested), while the "Answer to Eunomius' Second Book" is now regarded as Book II. Furthermore, Books III to XII in this edition are now regarded as simply constituting Book III (divided into sections as 1 to 100).

[81] Note, however, how Gregory Nazianzen, in the second of the "Theological Orations", anticipates the other Gregory when he speaks of going up Mount Sinai: "I both eagerly long, and at the same time am afraid (the one through my hope and the other through my weakness) to enter within the Cloud, and held converse with God, for so God commands." *Oration* 28, 2, trans. Charles Gordon Browne and James Edward Swallow, in *NPNF*, 2nd series, vol. 7.

[82] This theme of *epektasis* or "stretching forward" is foregrounded in *From Glory to Glory: Texts from Gregory of Nyssa's Mystical Writings*, ed. Herbert Musurillo, with an introduction by Jean Daniélou, S.J. (London: John Murray, 1962). In his *Homilies on Numbers*, however, Origen has a hint of the same notion; see Brian Daley, *The Hope of the Early Church: A Handbook of Patristic Eschatology* (Cambridge: Cambridge University Press, 1991), p. 50.

realm of the intelligible, as distinct from the sensuous, lies beyond time; it is without temporality. For Nyssen, a movement of what he calls "stretching out" towards God will continue even in eternity. There will be what Hans Urs von Balthasar calls "super-time" for human persons in the world to come.

Gregory's treatment of union with God, the heart of his spirituality, is perhaps the best topic on which to see that combination of the acceptance of broadly Platonist notions and their simultaneous transformation mentioned earlier under the rubric of "Christian Platonism". The characteristically Platonist goal of likeness to God is for Nyssen, as his commentary on the Our Father shows, the reacquisition of an original creation-based similarity lost through sin and recoverable now by spiritual progress through the imitation of Christ. Thus resituated in the biblical narrative, "assimilation to God" can be reconceived as the evangelical perfection commanded by Jesus in the Sermon on the Mount: "Be perfect as your heavenly Father is perfect" (Mt 5:48). Not for nothing does Gregory write a companion commentary on the Beatitudes, the first of a long line of writers (Augustine and Thomas come at once to mind) who will lay out the content of the Christian life, and Christian ethics, by reference to that Gospel text. Thus, Christian Platonism both accepts and transforms its own philosophical base—a base clearly apparent in Nyssen's *Catechetical Oration*, where he writes:

> It was necessary that man, who came into being to enjoy the good things of God, should have something in his nature akin to that which he is to share. Therefore he has been equipped with life and reason and wisdom and all the qualities appropriate to God, so that through each of those he might have a desire for what is congenial to him. Now since one of the good things pertaining to the divine nature is eternity, it was absolutely necessary that the organization of our nature should not be deprived of this attribute, but should contain an immortal element, so that by reason of his innate capacity man might recognize the transcendent and be seized with a desire for the divine eternity.[83]

---

[83] Gregory of Nyssa, *Great Catechism* 5, trans. William Moore and Henry Austin Wilson, in *Nicene and Post-Nicene Fathers*, ed. Philip Schaff and Henry Wace, 2nd. Series, vol. 5 (Buffalo, NY: Christian Literature Publishing, 1894).

Attaining that desire requires for Nyssen not only human striving but also, and even more fundamentally, divine grace. In his account, the soul experiences what has been called a "profound fracture between its own desire [for] the Infinite and the finite opportunities it has at its disposal".[84] Union with the Lord will mean taking this "fracture" with full seriousness—as entry into the "Cloud of Unknowing", the divine darkness that enveloped Moses on Mount Sinai, where the glory of God was too bright to be borne. This region, the region of the apophatic, literally without or beyond speech—beyond, then, both the images and concepts synthesized in his theology by Nazianzen—is the place where, for Gregory of Nyssa, faith is exercised in its most strenuous form. Functioning in this exalted way, faith is situated above knowledge, and not, as in Plato and the Christian tradition of Alexandria, beneath knowledge, inferior to knowledge.[85] Nyssen's theology of faith is based on Saint Paul's account of Abraham's faith in Romans, Galatians, and Hebrews, a letter which Gregory, like most of his contemporaries, took to be Pauline. In the words of a recent Italian student of Nyssen's thought, "Participation in God, which is the purpose of the created being, is always limited by the finiteness of the creature. However, it is always unlimited in virtue of God's creative action that continually broadens the capacity of the creature, enabling it to participate more and more in the divine goodness."[86] This is what faith apprehends.

Finally, faith's apophatic union with the Word beyond all concepts allows the Word to give the "bridal" soul, the soul uniting with God, a gift of new speech—the speech we typically find in the writings of the mystics. It enables the authentic mystics to become, in a word coined by a modern student of Gregory of Nyssa, "logophatic"— those who speak the Logos.[87] The Word can now speak through the

---

[84] Peroli, "Gregory of Nyssa and Platonism", p. 228.

[85] Laird, *Gregory of Nyssa*, pp. 63–107. It should be noted, however, that the early Alexandrian school did not render the role of faith superfluous on the negative way. Thus, Henry Chadwick writes of Christian gnosis in Clement of Alexandria, "We have to abstract all corporeal and even incorporeal ideas, images, casting ourselves upon the greatness of Christ for the final ascent", and of the same subject in Origen's writing: "The titles of Christ in the New Testament are rungs on a ladder of mystical ascent until, like Moses, one 'enters the darkness where God is'." Chadwick, *Church in Ancient Society*, pp. 128, 140.

[86] Peroli, "Gregory of Nyssa and Platonism", p. 231.

[87] Laird, *Gregory of Nyssa*, pp. 154–73.

mystics and by means of them exercise on others his attracting presence. This is what, for some, makes Gregory of Nyssa the foremost
figure among the Cappadocians, the one whose absence in the icon
of the Three Holy Hierarchs is so remarkably surprising.

5

Teacher of Deification: Saint Cyril of Alexandria

Saint Cyril was born in Roman Egypt in or around 376, in a town in the Nile Delta that is now, as El Mahalla, the area's largest city and a major centre of the textile industry. When he was a child, his maternal uncle Theophilus became patriarch of Alexandria. Cyril was educated in Theophilus' shadow, passing through the customary stages of grammatical and rhetorical studies before launching into Scripture and theology—that is, reading the texts of the earlier ecclesiastical writers. To what extent he was influenced by the growing monastic movement in fourth- and fifth-century Egypt is unclear, though he uses the title "father" for Isidore of Pelusium, a respected monastic superior who did not hesitate to chide Cyril (on various scores) in his correspondence. A plausible suggestion is that Cyril had spent some time in Isidore's monastery.[1] The Coptic monasteries, "then, as now, were the bastions of Egyptian Christianity".[2]

Cyril would become a voluminous commentator on the Bible while his doctrinal works gained for him the honorifics "Pillar of the Faith" and "Seal of the Fathers"—titles whose award also reflects his defence of Christological orthodoxy against Nestorius in the principal and defining Church controversy of his lifetime. His vigour and zeal, as well as family connexions, explain his meteoric rise.

In 412, when he was in his midthirties, Cyril succeeded his uncle as patriarch. He remained in office until his death in 444. His tenure

---

[1] Hubert du Manoir de Juaye, S.J., *Dogme et spiritualité chez saint Cyrille d'Alexandrie* (Paris: Vrin, 1944), p. 23.

[2] John McGuckin, *Saint Cyril of Alexandria and the Christological Controversy* (Crestwood, NY: Saint Vladimir's Seminary Press, 2004), p. 4.

of the see of Alexandria coincided with a great deal of civic unrest, notably between pagans, Christians, and Jews. His robust mode of leadership, learned from Theophilus, has not always endeared him to later historians—or indeed to contemporary opponents. Cyril's role in the closure of synagogues in Alexandria is better grounded historically than the claim that he inspired an urban mob to murder the Neoplatonist philosopher and mathematician Hypatia,[3] in modern times a feminist "icon" in the struggle against continuing Christian influence in society and the academy, not least in the United States.

The early period of Cyril's writing, the 420s, is dominated by his exegetical efforts. At the same time, in the wake of the Nicene crisis, he was working out a theology of the Triune God that rivals in sophistication and depth that produced by Augustine in the Latin West. Here the gems are his *Thesaurus* (a title that quite literally means a "treasure-house") and the seven dialogues *On the Holy and Consubstantial Trinity*. Hardly had he completed these works when in 429 the Nestorian crisis broke in the Church and necessitated the redirection of his attention to Christology. Cyril interspersed his correspondence with the bishop of the imperial city by writing treatises. From the 430s we have, first, *Against the Blasphemies of Nestorius*, an initial theological response to Nestorius' preaching. Then came the *Twelve Anathematisms against Nestorius*, which shocked those who, influenced by the prolific biblical commentator Theodore of Mopsuestia (to the Antiochene school, "*The* Interpreter"), thought of the union of natures in Jesus Christ as "one of moral will, determined by God's gracious love (*eudokia*)".[4] That reaction explains Cyril's subsequent composition of a trio of explanations or defences of the *Anathematisms*. There are also three texts with the title "On the Orthodox Faith", addressed either to the emperor, Theodosius II, or to women members of the imperial family; and a further trio of dogmatic treatises on the Incarnation: the *Scholia on the Incarnation of the Only-Begotten*; the dialogue *Christ Is One*;[5] and Cyril's final Christological

[3] Maria Dzielska, *Hypatia of Alexandria* (Cambridge, MA: Harvard University Press, 1995).

[4] Henry Chadwick, *The Church in Ancient Society: From Galilee to Gregory the Great* (Oxford: Oxford University Press, 2001), p. 522.

[5] Cyril of Alexandria, *On the Unity of Christ*, trans. J. A. McGuckin (Crestwood, NY: St. Vladimir's Seminary Press, 1995).

polemic, *Against Those Who Do Not Wish to Confess That the Holy Virgin Is Theotokos [the Mother of God].*[6]

The majority of the other documents ascribed to his authorship in the *Patrologia Graeca* are generally regarded as misassigned, while some of his authentic writings (but none of those listed above) have been lost among the accidents of time. One of these, his *Commentary on the Letter to the Hebrews*, was rediscovered in 2020 at the Institute of Ancient Manuscripts in the Armenian capital, Yerevan.

Cyril's Exegesis

Though Cyril wrote a commentary on the Gospel of John and a quasi-commentary on Luke (a set of 156 homilies, preserved in Syriac) and the former—a high point in patristic writing in any language, despite the loss of Books VII and VIII—is especially important for his Trinitarian theology,[7] nevertheless, in his role as an exegete he was mainly preoccupied with interpretation of the Greek Old Testament, the Septuagint. This was probably because the Jewish community in Alexandria, which also read the Septuagint, was large, influential, and had a different understanding of the Greek Old Testament, with no place for a Christian reading.[8] Two major works still extant in their entirety are commentaries on the Pentateuch, one of which proceeds via themes, the other via select passages as they occur. Cyril gave the first of this pair a title taken (more or less) from Saint John's Gospel, *On Worship and Cult in Spirit and Truth.* That may seem an odd choice for a title of a study of the Torah until one discovers the nature of his message. In the words of the American patristic scholar Robert Louis Wilken, an expert on this subject, "With the coming of Christ, the narratives in the Pentateuch as well as the institutions and laws of ancient Israel are to be understood in light of a higher, spiritual

---

[6] Cyril of Alexandria, *Against Those Who Are Unwilling to Confess That the Holy Virgin Is Theotokos*, trans. George Dragas (Rollinsford, NH: Orthodox Research Institute, 2004).

[7] Cyril of Alexandria, *Commentary on the Gospel of John*, trans. David Maxwell, 2 vols. (Downers Grove, IL: InterVarsity Press Academic, 2013–2015).

[8] For Cyril's "dialogue" with Judaism, see Robert Louis Wilken, *Judaism and the Early Christian Mind: A Study of Cyril of Alexandria's Exegesis and Theology* (New Haven, CT: Yale University Press, 1971).

meaning ..., a devotion to God that is bound neither to place nor to a certain people"—not of course an anonymous, nameless, faceless devotion but the distinctive devotion to God found within the mystery of Jesus Christ.[9] The other Pentateuch commentary, *Glaphyra*, a title sometimes put into English as "Elegant Comments", is more focussed on the detail of the texts it studies, but is no less Christological in its interpretative scheme.

Cyril also commented on all the Old Testament prophets, both major and minor.[10] He regarded Isaiah as by far the most important of the prophets, reflecting a widespread view in the ancient Church: the Book of Isaiah amounts to a "fifth Gospel".[11] Thus, Ambrose of Milan told the catechumen Augustine to go away and read the scrolls of Isaiah when preparing for Baptism—surely because, more clearly than any other biblical writer, Isaiah had foretold the Incarnation and the calling of the Gentiles of whom Augustine was one.[12] There were cues for this Christological and ecclesial interpretation in the use of Isaiah by the Gospels themselves, notably in regard to the Servant Songs from Isaiah 53 as these are echoed in the text of Saint Matthew, whose Gospel, according to tradition, was the first to be written. Cyril goes out of his way to underline the plausibility of the evangelist's application of these texts, drawing attention to the significance of the prophet's use of prepositions, prepositions that indicate the vicarious and substitutionary nature of the messianic figure's sufferings. Who on earth would *that* fit if not the Christ of the Church's proclamation? Without realising it, Cyril was anticipating the crucial role prepositions would play in the fifth century's Christological controversy, where it was asked (among other

[9] Robert Louis Wilken, "Cyril of Alexandria as Interpreter of the Old Testament", in *The Theology of St. Cyril of Alexandria: A Critical Appreciation*, ed. Thomas G. Weinandy, O.F.M. Cap., and Daniel A. Keating (London and New York: T&T Clark, 2003), p. 3.

[10] Only a very lengthy commentary on Isaiah and his commentary on the twelve minor prophets have survived in their entirety: *Commentary on Isaiah*, trans. Robert C. Hill (Brookline, MA: Holy Cross Press, 2008); *Commentary on the Twelve Prophets*, trans. Robert C. Hill, 3 vols. (Washington, DC: Catholic University of America Press, 2007–2012). There remain, however, fragments of lost commentaries on Ezekiel, Jeremiah (with Baruch), and Daniel, as well as bits and pieces from Cyril's commentaries on Proverbs, Job, and the Song of Songs, as well as the First and Second Books of Kings, and, rather more fully, the Psalms.

[11] John F. A. Sawyer, *The Fifth Gospel: Isaiah in the History of Christianity* (Cambridge: Cambridge University Press, 1996).

[12] Augustine, *Confessions* IX, 5, 12.

things), Was Christ only "from" two natures (divine and human) or was he, as the Word incarnate, both "from" them and also "in" them?

For Cyril, the Resurrection of Christ is the chief key to open the meaning of the Bible. As a Christian exegete, he saw himself as living in the last days, the "latter days" of Isaiah 2, which meant for him not simply the time after the Incarnation but, more specifically, the time after Easter and Pentecost. In the words of the opening verses of the Letter to the Hebrews, God spoke "to our fathers by the prophets; but in these last days he has spoken to us by a Son" (1:1–2). Cyril understood this claim in the light of Paul's teaching on how in the Son, Jesus Christ, there is a "new creation", issuing from his Resurrection and the gift of the Spirit.[13] This for Cyril is the reason why the interpretation of the Septuagint cannot now remain *simply* historical—that is to say, in effect, Jewish. The way in which such interpretation is carried out must be "new"—that is to say, in effect, Christian. But like his older contemporary Saint Jerome, Cyril does not pit against spiritual interpretation the historical dimension as such. In his Isaiah commentary, he writes:

> Those who, in the inspired Scriptures, reject the history as a frivolity, in a certain way deprive themselves of the understanding they need for what the Scriptures contain. Spiritual speculation, good and useful as it is, illumines the eye of understanding and creates no doubt highly enlightened minds. But when an historical event is presented to us by the sacred texts, it is appropriate to track down the utility of the history so that the inspired Scripture can save us and help us by all possible means.[14]

This might reflect sensibility or temperament and not just theological conviction. Some have noted in his works an "esteem for the sensuous", a "love for the concrete and human", finding here, in the words of a French Jesuit patrologist, "one of the reasons why the author of *On Worship and Cult in Spirit and Truth*, so severe on carnal false gods, and on a too narrow literalism, will nevertheless bow

---

[13] For the occurrence of the actual phrase, see Galatians 6:15 and 2 Corinthians 5:17.

[14] Cyril of Alexandria, *On Isaiah* I, 4, trans. Robert Louis Wilken, in "Interpreter of the Old Testament", in Weinandy and Keating, *Theology of St. Cyril of Alexandria*.

down so readily before the Mystery of a God made man, the Word made flesh."[15]

Cyril's Christology

It is on account of his Christology that in histories of doctrine Saint Cyril looms large. The conciliar history of the Church justifies the surveys or manuals, even though his Trinitarian theology, to which I shall turn in a moment, may be of greater importance still. Cyril's understanding of the Person of Christ, expressed in its most lapidary form in his Second Letter to Nestorius, was accepted by the Third Ecumenical Council, Ephesus (431), as the basis for its own profession of faith. There is only one Son, born eternally of the Father and born in time through taking flesh of Mary, the Godbearer, the *Theotokos*. More than simply the individual case of Nestorius was at stake here. The entire direction of thought of one influential strain of patristic Christology—namely, that of the school of Antioch—was, in Cyril's opinion, wrongly conceived. According to Henry Chadwick, "Cyril was concerned about his duty to repress heresies. He meditated deeply on the Christology presupposed by the Gospel of Saint John, and felt its incompatibility with the language used by Theodore of Mopsuestia."[16] In the year of Theodore's death, 427, his disciple Nestorius, a presbyter of Antioch, was enthroned at Constantinople. His own theological zeal took him in precisely the opposite direction to Cyril's. He sought to outlaw the *Theotokos* title—seen as the shibboleth of a defective Christology for which God became passible and the humanity of Jesus minimal. Chadwick continues, "The enthronement at New Rome of a bishop consciously averse to language and understandings of salvation which were native to the tradition of Alexandria was to inject a heady mixture into the already existing rivalry between these two great sees."[17] The unfolding of events at the 431 Council of Ephesus—a cliff-hanging moment for Cyril since elements in the imperial court and the influential theologians of the school of Antioch opposed both him and

---

[15] Juaye, *Dogme et spiritualité*, p. 79.
[16] Chadwick, *Church in Ancient Society*, p. 526.
[17] Ibid., p. 529.

his doctrine—is one of the most dramatic stories in the history of the ancient Church.[18] The proceedings, taken as a whole, were chaotic, since the late arrival of the bishops of the Antiochene patriarchate, delayed by bad weather, meant there were in effect two subsynods, whose conclusions had subsequently to be fused in a "Formulary of Reunion", dated 433. Though Cyril's more enthusiastic supporters regretted any accommodation with Antiochenes, the crucial point was that the title *Theotokos*—with its distinctive implications—was reaffirmed. Christ is one, albeit from two natures.

At Ephesus the issue at stake was, then, the single subjectivity of God-made-man—the all-important sign of which was Mary of Nazareth's status as *Theotokos*. John McGuckin explains that "the phrase 'Mother of God' for Cyril was a quintessential synopsis of his doctrine that the divine Word was the direct and sole personal subject of all the incarnate acts (including that of his own birth in the flesh)."[19] Cyril found in Jesus Christ only "mia phusis": one "reality" or one "entity" of the Word incarnate. As Thomas Weinandy explains, this expression should not be misunderstood as "one quiddity": a tertium quid or "third thing", something between God and a human person and actually consisting of neither of them.[20] What Cyril was asserting was that the union of divinity and humanity "takes place within the [single] person of the Word".[21] Involved is one sole "phusis-person", one real person—and thus no question can arise of two Sons: the Word and the man Jesus who was morally united to the Word. It was, readers of the last chapter may recall, the notion of "two Sons" that had alerted Gregory Nazianzen to the dangers of Antiochene Christology in his *Letter to Cledonius*.

By contrast, Nestorius' account of the unity of Christ was pitifully weak. McGuckin explains why. Nestorius found there to be "two prosopa in Christ, the divine Logos and the human Jesus", while admitting that the "the church's experience of Christ is as a single prosopon", a single subject.[22] But, continues McGuckin, Nestorius approached that "concept of subjectivity largely in semantic terms,

---

[18] McGuckin, *Christological Controversy*, pp. 53–107.
[19] Ibid., p. 154.
[20] Thomas Weinandy, "Cyril and the Mystery of the Incarnation", in Weinandy and Keating, *Theology of St. Cyril of Alexandria*, p. 35.
[21] Ibid., p. 41.
[22] McGuckin, *Christological Controversy*, p. 159.

as the grammatical subject of reference in discourse, whereas Cyril tended to understand the subject primarily as the initiator of actions, especially the spiritually dynamic action of redemptive restoration of communion."[23] It was the latter understanding that would come to prevail in Christian thought; indeed, it is a soteriological requirement if Christians really are on the way to theosis. Our theosis is possible because One of the Trinity has made human nature his own. There could be no concessions on this point: Nestorius' attempts to back-pedal on the Antiochene "two Sons" were just not good enough.[24]

In the view of many scholars, the Christological Definition of Chalcedon, the Fourth Ecumenical Council, held twenty years after Ephesus in 451, can itself be correctly understood only in the light of Cyrilline teaching—even though that "Definition" was produced after Cyril's death and, owing to its statement that "after the union" there still remain two "natures" (also *phusis*, hence *duo physeis*), incurred the dislike of his most fervent followers.[25] Like Cyril, Chalcedon would emphasise how it was one and the same Son who was generated by the Father and lived on earth, his divine and human natures united indivisibly and inseparably if also unconfusedly and unchangeably from the moment of the Incarnation onwards.

The Durham patrologist Andrew Louth points out that these "four adverbs [indivisibly, inseparably, unconfusedly, unchangeably] were drawn from Cyril of Alexandria and used by him to express the closeness of the union and the reality of the natures thus united", and he comments:

> In using these terms, Cyril, though no professional philosopher him-self, was drawing on the developing philosophical terminology of the late Platonists, such as Proclus who was fond of adding such adverbs

[23] Ibid.

[24] McGuckin cites with approval the judgment of an Anglican patrologist of an earlier generation, H. E. W. Turner: "Nestorius's failure did not lie in positing a double personality in Christ, but rather in being unable to offer a convincing explanation, on his logical terms, of why there should *not* have been one." Ibid., p. 173.

[25] In "his Christological writings the penetrating thought of the bishop of Alexandria ... attains full serenity after the 433 accord with the Orientals, with John of Antioch and the great Theodoret, anticipating already the expressions of Pope Saint Leo whose Christological formula was to impose itself with an extraordinary authority in the churches, in the East as in the West." Juaye, *Dogme et spiritualité*, p. 6.

as "inseparably and indivisibly" when saying that two identical things were nevertheless distinct, and "unconfusedly and unchangeably" when saying that distinguishable things are ultimately identical. Such philosophical terminology helped Cyril to affirm the mysterious unity of God and man that effected human salvation.[26]

Understandably, then, Cyril preferred to say that the incarnate Word is "from"—meaning "from out of"—two natures, rather than "in" them, though he would occasionally concede the second of these prepositions for the sake of peace and harmony in the Church. His disciples would not always be so accommodating. The peace made with the moderate Antiochenes two years after Ephesus, in 433, would not outlast Cyril's death. From the collapse of that consensus spring the Nestorian and Monophysite churches of ancient, mediaeval, and modern times.

Suggestions that for Cyril the Christological controversy was merely an instrument for reasserting Alexandrian primacy in the East are far from the mark. Cyril had set in stone the foundations of his Christology well before the Nestorian crisis broke. His biblical commentaries, and above all his commentary on Saint John's Gospel, lay out the criteria he would bring to bear on the issues Nestorius and other Antiochenes raised. He had already emphasised the unity of the incarnate Word, a unity which inevitably entails a "kenotic" or self-emptying character for the Incarnation so far as concerns the person or hypostasis of the Word—but not, however, for the Word's divine nature with its unchanging attributes.[27] (Not for nothing did Cyril resume his uncle Theophilus' suspended struggle against the anthropomorphic view of divine substance widespread among the Desert monastics.[28]) Cyril can call the Incarnation, quite simply, "the Kenosis".[29]

Cyril's assertion that an unchanging divine nature was possessed by a hypostasis who, on assuming flesh, could consequently suffer, made possible the most distinctive and moving of Christian claims.

---

[26] Andrew Louth, *Denys the Areopagite* (London: Geoffrey Chapman, 1989), p. 11.

[27] Cyril confesses the immutability of the divine nature of the Word in *On the Orthodox Faith, to the Empresses* 1.

[28] Juaye, *Dogme et spiritualité*, pp. 72–73.

[29] McGuckin, *Christological Controversy*, p. 189.

It runs: One of the Holy Trinity was crucified for us. In Weinandy's words, the "unchangeable impassibility of the Son of God as God" guarantees it is "actually the divine Son of God who truly suffers as man. Only if the Son remains immutably God in becoming man, and equally, only if the Son remains impassible and so truly God within his incarnate state can one guarantee that it is actually that same impassible divine Son who is passible as man."[30]

Among the different expressions Cyril tried out to convey his sense of the unity of Christ,[31] the most enduringly valuable was when he declared the union to be *kata hypostasin*, a "hypostatic" union, a union in the very Person of the Word, he the eternal Son and no other. The hypostatic union makes it possible for us to ascribe to the Person of the Word the properties not only of his divine nature in which he has existed since before time began but also of the human nature he took from Mary—in other words, what theologians came to call "the communication of idioms". A somewhat more collo-quial translation of the original Greek phrase, "antidosis idiomatôn", would run "the exchange of attributes". Our language embodies that "exchange of attributes" when we say, for instance, "One who is eternal God suffered for our sake," or, "One who is in our human nature upholds the universe by his power." Origen had sketched out the notion. Athanasius and Nyssen and other Greek Fathers were aware of it. But it took the Nestorian crisis to give it the full weight it receives from Cyril, especially in the "Anathematisms" where the communication of idioms is, in McGuckin's words, "a statement full of power, that by its inherent paradox forces the hearer to reflect on the fact that a single subject christology means a dynamic and inti-mate union of different conditions in the one life of God".[32]

Over against his opponents in the school of Antioch, Cyril denied that his own rigorous affirmation of the unity of the Word incarnate

---

[30] Weinandy, "Mystery of the Incarnation", p. 52. See more widely, Paul Gavrilyuk, *The Suffering of the Impassible God: The Dialectics of Patristic Thought* (Oxford: Oxford University Press, 2004).

[31] There is a full discussion of this lack of uniformity, already noted by the seventeenth-century Petavius, in Juaye, *Dogme et spiritualité*, pp. 124–34, the conclusion of which is that "he never varied as to his basic doctrine; if his vocabulary lacks fixity that is because he holds onto ideas and not at all to words." Ibid., p. 132.

[32] McGuckin, *Christological Controversy*, p. 192.

had the effect of minimizing the significance of Jesus' humanity.[33] On the contrary, it was as human that the Word redeemed us and transformed our nature, becoming "the pattern for *our* humanity, for how we receive the Spirit and how we live a life pleasing to God".[34] Admittedly, on Cyril's view, the humanity of Christ *when considered as agent of our salvation* is unique and unlike ours. Yet *when considered as recipient of salvation* that same humanity is the pattern as well as the firstfruits of the new human vocation to live as those redeemed by the divine Word. That distinction can also be made in terms of the two essential stages of the incarnate economy: the Logos assumed our humanity so as to restore and deify it, "first in the divine transformation of his own authentically human life, and then (as he was the paradigm of salvation in his resurrection) in the transformation of Christians".[35] Or again: "What Christ has naturally deified in his own flesh he 'gratuitously' deifies in the human race at large."[36]

Modern students have wondered how the Christ of Saint Cyril could have increased not only in "stature" but in "wisdom", as is claimed by Saint Luke in his Gospel (2:52), and have sometimes concluded that any ignorance on the part of Christ was for Cyril merely apparent or indeed feigned. Once again, Cyril's answer would have been in terms of the saving economy. The ignorance of Jesus as man was real but "economic". It belonged to the abasement of his earthly life in its salvifically necessary kenotic phase, ending with his Resurrection. And in any case it ought not to be confused with the knowledge he had in his eternal life and being.[37] As with the other limiting experiences Jesus underwent, "the human limitations are genuinely assumed, but do not absolutely condition the life of the Saviour in the way they do the life of a normal human being who has no choice but to acquiesce in the limitations his nature imposes."[38]

---

[33] Antiochenes worried that Cyril's Christology was covertly Apollinarian, or even Arian in its implications; Cyril sought to calm their anxieties by accepting the 433 "Formulary of Reunion", though his more zealous disciples feared he was diluting his doctrine; see Graham Gould, "Cyril of Alexandria and the Formula of Reunion", *Downside Review* 106 (1988): 235–52.

[34] Daniel A. Keating, "Divinization in Cyril: The Appropriation of Divine Life", in Weinandy and Keating, *Theology of St. Cyril of Alexandria*, p. 174.

[35] McGuckin, *Christological Controversy*, p. 184.

[36] Ibid., p. 187.

[37] Juaye, *Dogme et spiritualité*, p. 157.

[38] McGuckin, *Christological Controversy*, p. 220.

Cyril's Trinitarian Theology

For Cyril, belief in the Trinity is the primary article of Christian faith. In one of his *Festal Letters* (he continued the Alexandrian practice of writing such letters for the pre-Paschal and Paschal seasons), Cyril declared: "We say that the kerygma of the Church is simple. We have been baptized in the Father, the Son and the Holy Spirit; and believing that the Holy Trinity is consubstantial, we worship in the Trinity one sole Divinity."[39] Using the preferred vocabulary of the French Cyrilline scholar Marie-Odile Boulnois, in the discourse of orthodox Christians the Godhead is "deployed" in three hypostases but it is also "recapitulated" in its unity since the three are consubstantial. As she understands Cyril, this is the correct way in which to think through, and speak of, the Church's Lord. It follows that Christian faith is a true monotheism. Separating one hypostasis from the rest—a prerequisite for ditheism or tritheism—is impossible if this formula is followed faithfully. In an anthropological aside, one might comment on an implication of this account of the Holy Trinity: it is surely why Cyril departs from the early Greek Christian tradition that the Image of God in man concerns only the Logos, the Son, and affirms that the divine image in human nature is, rather, fully Trinitarian.[40] The Son is always the Trinitarian Son, never separable from Father and Spirit; hence, the image in us is always both Christological (or "Logological") and Trinitarian. By a different route Augustine would arrive at the same conclusion.[41]

Cyril agrees that in theology there can be, alas, a hubristic and therefore of course misplaced desire to comprehend fully the mystery of God. Yet, in Boulnois' words, "in order to worship properly [and 'orthodoxy' means in the first place right worship], we must have

[39] Cyril of Alexandria, *Festal Letter* 12, trans. John McGuckin, in *Christological Controversy*.

[40] Walter J. Burghardt, *The Image of God in Man, according to Cyril of Alexandria* (Washington, DC: Catholic University of America Press, 1957).

[41] Cf. Augustine, *On the Trinity* XII, 6 (7), trans. Arthur West Haddan, in *Nicene and Post-Nicene Fathers*, First Series, vol. 3, ed. Philip Schaff (Buffalo, NY: Christian Literature Publishing, 1887). Citations from *On the Trinity* are from this translation. Augustine begins from the Genesis author's "Let us make man in our image, to our likeness", with its plural form. Ignoring the plural form and confining of divine imagehood in man to imaging the Son would play into the hands of semi-Arians: "For if the Faher made man after the image of the Son, so that he is not the image of the Father, but of the Son, then the Son is unlike the Father."

a correct understanding of the relationship of the Trinity to divine unity, and that is what the Cyrillian view tries to establish."[42] Cyril's terms "deployment" (*diastolê*, literally "expanding") and "recapitulation" (*anakephalaiôsis* [but not in the Irenaean sense], which he also calls "contracting", *systolê*) are meant to rule out two opposed errors. Deployment—meaning, of the one God as three Persons— rules out a monadic or bare monotheism such as Judaism (or, later, Islam) professes. Recapitulation—meaning of the three Persons as a single consubstantial Divinity—rules out tritheism, the affirmation that there are three Gods. Cyril thinks this procedure—deployment, recapitulation—is already there in embryo, at any rate for the first two Persons, at the start of Saint John's Gospel. "The Word was with God" (1:1) implies deployment, while "The Word was God" implies recapitulation, attesting the consubstantiality and therefore the unity of the Son and the Father.

Though for Cyril the revelation of God as triad is essentially a New Testament affair, the Alexandrian patriarch finds hints of it in the Old Testament, especially in the episode of Abraham's visitors at the Oaks of Mamre in Genesis 18. (Was there one of them or were there three of them?) Some readers may have seen reproductions of Saint Andrei Rublev's famous icon of that scene—or even the original, now found in the Tretyakov Gallery in Moscow. The icon is often called, significantly, "The Old Testament Trinity".[43] And, furthermore, so Cyril points out, an élite of Greek philosophers (he was thinking of Plotinus and his disciple Porphyry) had affirmed that transcendent reality consists of three principal hypostases: the One, the Mind, and the Soul. All three, since they transcend the world, should be given initial capital letters in English (and other languages that make the uppercase-lowercase distinction) even though those who acknowledged them considered the One, the Mind, and the Soul unequal in ontological importance. Unfortunately, the pagan philosophers proved unable to recapitulate the three as a unity, and

[42] Marie-Odile Boulnois, "The Mystery of the Trinity", in Weinandy and Keating, *Theology of St. Cyril of Alexandria*, p. 80. For her full study, see Marie-Odile Boulnois, *Le Paradoxe trinitaire chez Cyrille d'Alexandrie: Herméneutique, analyses philosophiques et argumentation théologique* (Paris: Collection des Etudes Augustiniennes, 1994).

[43] Gabriel Bunge, *Rublev's Trinity: The Icon of the Trinity by the Monk-Painter Andrei Rublev* (Crestwood, NY: Saint Vladimir's Seminary Press, 2007).

thus unwittingly paved the way for Arius and his supporters to treat Father, Son, and Spirit similarly—namely, as an unequal hierarchy, with descending qualities of transcendence. That is the message of Cyril's treatise "Against Julian, the emperor",[44] where the range of his acquaintance with pagan authors is at its most apparent.[45] Not that Cyril argues to the Trinity from either Old Testament anticipation or Hellenistic metaphysics. Rather, he argues to the Trinity from the Lord's baptismal command, to initiate in the Triune Name, as recorded at the end of Saint Matthew's Gospel (28:19–20). Basil the Great had done the same before him.

That divine Name is itself made up of three names. It is through their particular names that the properties of the three hypostases are disclosed. That is easy enough for Father and Son: the Father's distinctive hypostatic property is Fatherhood, the Son's is Sonship, and these two terms are correlative. The case of the Holy Spirit is trickier, since Father and Son are themselves both spirit and holy. Building on the initial, not very satisfactory, efforts of Athanasius and Basil, Cyril can take a step beyond them to give theological thought a helping hand in this regard. Saint Athanasius held that the role of the Spirit in human salvation is to complete the sanctifying process begun in the Father and achieved through the Son. Saint Basil had spelt that out in terms of the Spirit's work in the economy as a whole—the Spirit "perfects" the action of Father and Son. Cyril now seizes on the idea of completing or perfecting and develops it. Completing or perfecting does not only tell us what the distinctive hypostatic property of the Spirit is *in the economy*. More than this, it also tells us what his distinctive hypostatic property is *within the Godhead itself*. What, then, is it? It is to be the completer of the deployment— the expansion—which begins in the Father and passes through the Son. The Holy Spirit is the "completion", *symplêrôma*, of the Trinity.[46] This removed from Greek patristic thought the handicap of

---

[44] Cyril of Alexandria, *Against the Emperor Julian* 8. This was Cyril's response to the now lost imperial treatise *Against the Galilaeans*; see G. W. Bowersock, *Julian the Apostate* (Cambridge, MA: Harvard University Press, 1978), p. 102.

[45] Juaye, *Dogme et spiritualité*, p. 17.

[46] Attested by both Cyril's *Commentary on John*, expounding John 14:23, where the evangelist records the words of Christ, "We will come to him and make our home with him," and his treatise on the Trinity, the *Thesaurus* 34.

describing the hypostatic particularity of the Spirit in terms that only make sense when we are thinking of his activity in regard to creatures in space and time, not in regard to the eternal Father and the eternal Son in the Godhead itself.

Such emphasis on the threeness of God must then be reintegrated, by "recapitulation", into a fresh statement of the unity of God. Cyril's way of doing this is to speak as often as he can about the "Holy and Consubstantial Trinity": what the Spirit perfects is a new form of existence for the unity of God, a new form that follows on the hypostatic deployment taking place within God. The unity of God is perfected as the unity of a consubstantial Trinity.

When looking at Athanasius we saw that the Son and the Spirit are not only *from* God the Father—by the principle of consubstantiality as the Father shares his being with them. They are also *in* him—by a principle of co-inherence or mutual indwelling. The three Persons become distinct in the expansion phase without, as Boulnois puts it, "withdrawing into their own individuality" since they "remain united in dwelling within each other".[47] But the fact that the Son and Spirit are "in" the Father does not cancel out their origin "from" the Father. So the mutual indwelling is itself founded in a relationship of origin. Once again prepositions are crucial here. The Son is in the Father as his source; the Father is in the Son as his perfect expression; the Spirit is in the Father and the Son as the one who expresses the perfected unity of the divinity Father and Son share. It is noteworthy that Cyril speaks of the Spirit not only as from the Father *through* the Son, but also as *from* the Father and the Son—he could be quoted both by the Eastern Orthodox and by Catholics in the longstanding and still unfinished *Filioque* controversy. Granted that Athanasius' *Letters to Serapion* also have possible "openings" of this sort, it is sometimes suggested that Alexandrian and Latin theology share an affinity in this regard.[48]

---

[47] Boulnois, "Mystery of the Trinity", p. 99.

[48] "Without wishing to exaggerate the implications of the texts written by Athanasius and Cyril, we can at least recognize that their thinking remains open to the affirmation of the procession of the Spirit *a Filio*" (Gilles Emery, O.P., *Trinity in Aquinas* [Ypsilanti, MI: Sapientia Press, 2003], p. 238). Emery also draws attention to Bertrand de Margerie, "Vers une relecture du concile de Florence grâce à la reconsidération de l'Ecriture et des Pères grecs et latins", *Revue Thomiste* 86 (1986): 31–81.

The sophistication of Cyril's discussion has prompted Boulnois to call his theology of the Trinity "a point of junction between patristics and Scholasticism".[49] It could also be called a point of junction between patristics and Balthasarianism, for her Cyril sounds remarkably like von Balthasar's, with the Trinitarian relations set out as "movements of mutual giving", since the Son and the Spirit "receive everything from the one of whom they are the image and in return glorify their archetype", the Father.[50]

Cyril's Soteriology

If for Cyril the Image of God in human persons is the Image of the Trinity, then the unity of the Trinity, combining difference and identity, will be for him the model for human solidarity in God. But there is no way in which that model can be realised in the world except through the sanctifying activity of the Father and the Son, as brought to bear on us by the Holy Spirit. When his *Commentary on the Gospel of John* reaches John 17:21 ("That they may all be one; even as you, Father, are in me, and I in you, that they also may be in us"), Cyril remarks that "the Mystery of Christ has come into being as a kind of beginning, a way for us to share in the Holy Spirit and in unity with God."[51] Cyril sees that unity as mediated by the Spirit in a dual fashion: it is mediated to our "spirits" in the Sacrament of Baptism, which makes Christians one people; it is mediated by the Son to our "flesh" in the Sacrament of the Eucharist, which makes the baptised one body.[52] Obviously enough, the Church of baptised and "eucharistized" individuals is not a social people like other communities or any sort of natural body, for the unity Cyril has in mind is *unity in God*.

Cyril has been called the great Doctor of *theôsis*, divinization—even if he tends to avoid the word itself, perhaps because Nestorius had

---

[49] Boulnois, *Le Paradoxe trinitaire*, p. 16. Perhaps surprisingly, Balthasar's book on contemplative prayer is the best place to find this Trinitarian theology laid out in brief compass. See Hans Urs von Balthasar, *Prayer* (San Francisco: Ignatius Press, 1986).

[50] Boulnois, "Mystery of the Trinity", p. 100.

[51] Cited in Brian E. Daley, S.J., "The Fullness of the Saving God: Cyril of Alexandria on the Holy Spirit", in Weinandy and Keating, *Theology of St. Cyril of Alexandria*, p. 143.

[52] There is a good discussion in Keating, "Divinization in Cyril", notably pp. 160–82.

accused him of treating Christians, or indeed the humanity of Jesus, as undergoing apotheosis—with all the frankly pagan associations of that term. Most typically, Cyril speaks of how Christians, united in spirit and flesh with the Spirit and the Son and thus brought to the Father, share the divine life. Writing in his Johannine commentary on words of Christ in John 14:20 ("In that day you will know that I am in my Father, and you in me, and I in you"), Cyril concludes that since "we have all become partakers in [the Son], and have him in ourselves through the Spirit, for this reason we have become partakers of the divine nature." In the words "partakers [or 'sharers'] of the divine nature", he appeals to the same celebrated text in Second Peter 1:4, which is often regarded as the charter of mysticism in the Church (and treated accordingly with some caution by Lutherans and other Evangelicals).[53] In Cyril's corpus taken overall, one finds alongside the language of *methexis*, "participation", the vocabulary of *mimêsis*, "imitation", and *koinônia*, "communion"—also quasi-synonyms for *theôsis*—together with a wide range of metaphors, all employed in the expression of a "theology of individual deification operated by the incarnate Logos and his Spirit"[54].

Cyril would have agreed with the nineteenth-century Russian hermit saint Serafim of Sarov: the aim of the Christian life is the acquisition (thanks to the redemptive Incarnation) of the Holy Spirit.[55] But Cyril would probably have wanted to adjust Serafim's formulation: not so much "acquisition" as "*re*acquisition". Once, in Adam, our species *had* the Spirit, albeit briefly, a reference to the second of the two creation accounts in the Book of Genesis when God breathes the "breath of life" into man (2:7). The reacquisition of that same Holy Spirit is the essential precondition for any recovery of the "archetypal beauty" in which the human creature was moulded, a moulding which began when the Creator impressed the Spirit on the first human—"like a seal of his own nature", remarks

[53] The perceived danger is that mysticism might come to displace faith rather than crown it.

[54] Jules Gross, *La divinisation du chrétien d'après les Pères grecs: Contribution historique à la doctrine de la grâce* (Paris: Lecoffre-Gabalda, 1938), p. 297, cited in Juaye, *Dogme et spiritualité*, p. 50.

[55] Constantine Cavarnos and Mary-Barbara Zeldin, *St. Seraphim of Sarov: Widely Beloved Mystic, Healer, Comforter and Spiritual Guide; An Account of His Life, Character and Message, Together with a Very Edifying Conversation with His Disciple Motovilov on the Acquisition of the Grace of the Holy Spirit and the Saint's Spiritual Counsels* (Belmont, MA: Institute of Byzantine and Modern Greek Studies, 1980).

Cyril in his *Commentary on the Gospel of John*.[56] But that primordial moulding could not be completed, for the Fall intervened. The
Image of God in man as based on human nature's rationality and
attraction to the good survived, but not the higher-power image that
exemplified the divine Archetype in its spiritual beauty.[57] The Spirit,
writes Cyril, flew away from Adam—but then alighted on Christ at
his Baptism, signifying that the re-creation of the human race was to
take place "through the re-acquisition of the Spirit in and through
the Incarnate Word".[58] The American Cyrilline scholar Daniel Keating stresses how, for Cyril, Christ at the Baptism is in his humanity
the recipient of salvation before he is the appointed agent of its transmission to others. As the Only Begotten Son who always has the
Spirit from the Father, he gives that Spirit to himself as man,[59] but
since his humanity is precisely that of the New Adam, the representative of us all, the matter does not stop there. Comparing, on the
one hand, how Cyril treats the Baptism of Christ and, on the other,
how he deals with the risen Christ's gift of the Spirit to the disciples, Keating remarks: "As Christ at his baptism is the firstfruits
of our sanctification, this select number of apostles on Easter day
become the firstfruits of the reception of the Spirit."[60] The apostles
become that new "firstfruits", that initial down payment, because the
goal of refashioning in the Spirit is intended not just for the Eleven
but for the entire human race. Christ's Ascension and Session (his
"Enthronement") make possible the Pentecostal outpouring of the
Spirit intended as it is for speakers of all tongues—that is, for all human

---

[56] Cyril, *Commentary on John* at John 14:20, to which parallel texts exist in *Glaphyra* 1 and
On the Holy and Consubstantial Trinity, dialogue 4. If that breathing of the breath of life was
in or onto a being already composed of body *and* soul, then "Cyril distinguishes the order of
created nature 'necessarily subject to corruption' [*Festal Letter* 15] and due to return to its origin which is nothingness [cf. *Commentary on John* at 1:4], and a participation of created nature
in that nature which is uncreated—incorruptible and indestructible by essence," in effect the
aphtharsia of Athanasius [cf. *Commentary on John* at 1:14]. Juaye, *Dogme et spiritualité*, p. 94.

[57] Juaye, *Dogme et spiritualité*, p. 94.

[58] Keating, "Divinization in Cyril", p. 157.

[59] As an historian of Thomas' use of the Greek Fathers has commented, "Because Christ is
the Son of God in person, when he is sent as man into the world he comes breathing forth
Love [the Holy Spirit] to own his sacred humanity." Dominic Legge, O.P., "Christ and the
Trinity at the Transfiguration", in *Thomas Aquinas and the Greek Fathers*, ed. Michael Dauph-
inais, Andrew Hofer, O.P., and Roger Nutt (Ave Maria, FL: Sapientia Press, 2019), p. 26.

[60] Keating, "Divinization in Cyril", p. 158.

persons. A share in divine life will be passed on to Christians through Baptism and the Eucharist, or as Cyril says, *pneumatikôs* and *sômatikôs*, spiritually (more connected with Baptism) and somatically or bodily (more connected with the Eucharist). As long ago as 1944, Hubert du Manoir prefaced his classic study "Dogma and Spirituality in Saint Cyril of Alexandria" by writing, "Despite appearances to the contrary, [Cyril] never wandered off into an 'abstract dogmatism', into discussions that have no relation to the spiritual life. Quite the opposite: he was preoccupied with maintaining the link between, on the one hand, thought and its formulations, and, on the other, the piety and life of Christians in the Church of God."[61]

The connexion has often been made (and Cyril makes it himself) between Cyril's Christology of the Word-made-flesh and his strongly realist Eucharistic doctrine; here is the flesh of the Word again in another, now sacramental mode.[62] But for Cyril the indwelling of the Spirit is *the* mark of the New Covenant. Keating succeeds admirably in balancing the two: Christ and the Spirit; the Eucharist and Holy Baptism. He writes: "As the eucharistic manner of indwelling most aptly and fully expresses the enfleshment of Christ and our union with him according to the flesh, so the indwelling of the Holy Spirit most aptly and fully exhibits God's purpose for the human race and the restoration which brings us to our final goal."[63] That goal is "the full spiritualization of our nature, accomplished in Christ first through his reception of the Spirit, and encompassing the whole of our nature, spiritual and corporeal".[64]

---

[61] Juaye, *Dogme et spiritualité*, p. 6.

[62] See the classic essay by Henry Chadwick, "Eucharist and Christology in the Nestorian Controversy", *Journal of Theological Studies*, n.s., 2 (1951): 145–64. This was the teaching, passionately reiterated by the Anglican "Tractarian" Dr. Pusey in his sermon "The Holy Eucharist a comfort for the Penitent" (May 14, 1843), which led Oxford's professor of Hebrew to be suspended from preaching before the university; citing St. Cyril, Pusey had spoken of "the Life which [the eternal Word] is ... first giving its own vitality to that sinless Flesh which He united indissolubly with Himself and in it encircling and vivifying our whole nature, and then, through that bread which is His Flesh, finding an entrance into us individually, penetrating us soul and body, and spirit, and irradiating and transforming into His own light and life." E.B. Pusey, *The Holy Eucharist a Comfort for the Penitent: A Sermon Preached before the University of Oxford on the Fourth Sunday after Easter* (Oxford: J.H. Parker; London: Rivington, 1843), pp. 11–12.

[63] Keating, "Divinization in Cyril", p. 170.

[64] Ibid.

Conclusion

John McGuckin remarks:

> In antiquity Cyril was called the "Seal of all the Fathers" and he certainly summated the east Christian tradition of Christology, Trinitarianism, and mystical allegorical interpretation. From the early medieval period onwards his exegetical work was progressively neglected in the West, though his general impact on Latin theology in key areas remained strong, if perhaps not as dominant as it was in the Byzantine world where, despite the fraught post-Chalcedonian controversies, his star remained in the ascendant.[65]

A survey in the journal *Medieval Studies* of Cyril's influence in Latin theology from the mid-fifth century to 1260 goes some way to bear out this claim.[66] Though Latin translations of Cyril's writings consisted mainly of extracts in anthologies, Carolingian theologians made good use of these materials when faced with the reemergence of Adoptionism—the theory that the Father adopted a man and united him to his Word—in ninth-century Spain. In the eleventh century, early Scholastics in France appealed to Cyril's realist view of the Eucharistic presence during controversies about that sacrament.

But it was not till Saint Thomas set himself to study the Greek Fathers more thoroughly around 1260 that Cyril's Christology made a major reappearance in the West—after which the West never looked back, not at least until Neo-Nestorian tendencies began to appear in Catholic theology in the later twentieth century. Notable high points in Cyril's influence are the seventeenth-century assembler of patristic texts Denys Pétau ("Petavius"), sometimes called the father of positive theology, and in the nineteenth century the widely influential if interestingly idiosyncratic neo-Scholastic Matthias Joseph Scheeben. In his essay "Cyrillus" in the original edition of the well-known German language theological encyclopaedia *Lexikon für Theologie und Kirche*, Scheeben undertakes a comparison between Cyril and

---

[65] John A. McGuckin, "Cyril of Alexandria: Bishop and Pastor", in Weinandy and Keating, *Theology of St. Cyril of Alexandria*, pp. 208–9.

[66] N. M. Haring, "The Character and Range of the Influence of St. Cyril of Alexandria on Latin Theology (430–1260)", *Medieval Studies* 12 (1950): 1–19.

Aquinas. Cyril did for the Greek Fathers who preceded him what Aquinas did for the Latin Fathers as a whole. In each case a capacity to synthesize the teaching of predecessors (what Cyril termed "the orthodox *didaskaloi* [teachers]") was married with a powerful and rigorous dialectical intelligence, in the service of divine revelation.[67] But more than one writer has played the game of spotting the Greek Aquinas. Both Maximus the Confessor and John of Damascus have been entered for this competition. It is, I suppose, a mark of respect of patrologists both for Saint Thomas' knowledge of the Fathers and his ability to find for them a better constructed intellectual dwelling than their own.

---

[67] See Juaye, *Dogme et spiritualité*, pp. 35–37.

6

Mystical Metaphysician: Denys the Areopagite

There is a simple answer to the question, What do we know about Denys in any personal sense? It runs: Almost nothing. This writer, uniformly dated in twentieth-century scholarship to the turn of the fifth and sixth centuries, achieved anonymity by making himself a mouthpiece for Saint Paul's pagan convert Dionysius, who was a fruit of Paul's preaching in Athens according to the Book of Acts 17:34. Denys' letters, and the treatises he left, prop up this façade by name-dropping references to apostles and early Christian figures he claims to have known, and, not least, pretending he was present at the deathbed of the Mother of God. Doubts about Denys' identity began to surface at the Renaissance. Discussion continued for much of the next four centuries. The last scholar to have assumed, or defended, Denys' location in history as a contemporary of Saint Paul was, so far as I can discover, John Parker, the English (I assume High Anglican) translator of Denys' two books on the "hierarchies", celestial and ecclesiastical, a translation published in London in 1894.[1] One year after Parker's introduction to the hierarchies was printed, two German scholars discovered independently of each other that Denys had quoted liberally from the fifth-century Neoplatonist philosopher Proclus, whom we encountered as the possible source of the four celebrated adverbs in the Chalcedonian Definition. Ever

---

[1] John Parker, *The Celestial and Ecclesiastical Hierarchy of Dionysius the Areopagite* (London: Skeffington, 1894), pp. 1–14. Parker's translation, with its introduction and notes, is available online at Roger Pearse's website of additional texts by early Church Fathers at https://www.tertullian.org/fathers/. See also John Parker, *Are the Writings of Dionysius the Areopagite Genuine?* (Oxford and London: James Parker, 1897). Parker might have known better, if Henry Chadwick is to be trusted: "Dionysius' indebtedness to Proclus was seen by the English Platonist Thomas Taylor in the 1830s." Henry Chadwick, *The Church in Ancient Society: From Galilee to Gregory the Great* (Oxford: Oxford University Press, 2001), p. 313.

since that time, "Dionysius Areopagitica" has become the "Pseudo-Denys", except for students who, without necessarily challenging the reassignment of his dates to around 500, find the "Pseudo-" prefix unfitting to the dignity of this influential ecclesiastical teacher. After all, he believed that what he was teaching was the perennial truth of both metaphysics and Christianity and should therefore be considered morally speaking simultaneous with the first promulgation of the Gospel. Pope Benedict XVI puts it like this: "He wanted to do what [the original] Dionysius had intended, that is, to make Greek thought converge with Saint Paul's proclamation; being a Greek, he wanted to become a disciple of Saint Paul, hence a disciple of Christ."[2]

There is also the question of the so-called "missing" treatises—other writings to which Denys refers as attempts by him to fill out his overall presentation of theological doctrine. Scholars who think these treatises never actually existed would surely have to agree that Denys' conviction of the unchangeableness of divine truth was matched by a highly developed taste for literary invention. However, perhaps it can all be brought under the rubric suggested by, again, Benedict XVI: Denys "did not want to glorify his own name; he wanted, not to build a monument to himself with his work, but rather truly to serve the Gospel, to create an ecclesial theology, neither individual nor based on himself."[3]

In modern scholarship, Denys is frequently described as "Syrian"—not that he shows any knowledge of Syriac, but then Western Syria was Greek-speaking. Syria has been selected as his likely home base for two main reasons. The first is that when he takes his readers through the structure of the Eucharistic Liturgy, he includes the reciting of the Creed—which was introduced in the Greek-speaking Syrian Church in the 470s;[4] more widely, the rites he describes in *The Ecclesiastical Hierarchy* fit best with what is known of the ancient Syrian liturgical tradition. The second reason for calling Denys "Syrian" is that some of his references to Christ seem to place him on the borderline between Chalcedonian Christology and the Christology

[2] Pope Benedict XVI, *Church Fathers and Teachers: From Saint Leo the Great to Peter Lombard* (San Francisco: Ignatius Press, 2010), pp. 25–26.

[3] Ibid., p. 26.

[4] Andrew Louth, *Denys the Areopagite* (1989; repr., London and New York: Continuum, 2001), p. 9.

of the Monophysites—extreme Cyrillians who refused to acknowledge two distinct natures in Christ after the Incarnation.[5] This is a
further possible indicator of Syrian provenance since the West Syrian
Church was divided along just those lines. The first commentators on
Denys' corpus—known as "scholiasts" because they concentrated
on a close reading of short extracts from his writings (a commentary
form called "scholia" was already practised by Origen)—were themselves strongly Chalcedonian, and they made great efforts to ensure
Denys was *not* read as a Monophysite Christian.[6]

Denys' Writings

Apart from ten letters, which in effect introduce the main themes
of Denys' work, the *corpus Dionysiacum* consists of the two treatises
on hierarchies, together with a book on the God-world relationship, *On the Divine Names*, and a final book (if the word can be used
for so short a text) on the relation between God and the individual
God seeker, the *Mystical Theology*. All four of these texts have been
enormously influential in Christian East and Christian West, above
all in the West once they were translated into Latin, which they
were at different times between the ninth and the twelfth centuries.
The Celestial Hierarchy influenced angelology; the *Ecclesiastical Hierarchy* influenced commentaries on the Liturgy and the understanding

---

[5] *Letter 4*, notes Andrew Louth, "contains the key phrase quoted by the Monenergists—
'one divine-human (or theandric) activity'. According to all the manuscripts of the Corpus
Areopagiticum that we possess, this letter in fact refers to 'a new theandric activity', and this
is the reading Maximus knows and uses as the basis for his exposition. But since all the Greek
manuscripts of the Dionysian writings go back to the edition proposed by John of Scythopolis
in the middle of the sixth century, and John was himself anxious to present Denys as an orthodox Cyrilline Chalcedonian, the authenticity of the Monophysite/Monenergist/Monothelite
reading 'one theandric activity' cannot be ruled out." Andrew Louth, *Maximus the Confessor*
(London: Routledge, 1996), p. 53.

[6] The better known of these scholiasts was Saint Maximus Confessor (mentioned above),
a complex figure whom we shall be looking in the succeeding chapter. The more prolific of
them is less well known, a so-called "Neo-Chalcedonian" Palestinian, John of Scythopolis
(also mentioned in the above note). Neo-Chalcedonians read Chalcedon through Saint Cyril's spectacles, which partly explains why John might have been attracted to Denys' unusual
output in the first place. "[Denys'] idea that what is beyond being (namely, God) takes on
being in the person of Jesus [cf. Denys' *Letter* 4], seems to express in his own peculiar language, a Cyrilline way of speaking of the incarnation." Louth, *Denys the Areopagite*, p. 14.

of sacramental causality; the *Divine Names* influenced philosophical theology; and the *Mystical Theology* influenced spirituality, especially in the West.[7] And all of them influenced hermeneutics: how to interpret biblical language (which was also the exclusive topic of one of Denys' letters, *Letter* 9). To the matter of biblical interpretation we might add, for the *Ecclesiastical Hierarchy*, liturgical interpretation: what to make of the ritual gestures of Christian worship. That is why Denys is important enough to be included among the Greek Fathers, though some modern Orthodox do not agree that he merits the right to this place in the sun.

The Celestial Hierarchy

The Celestial Hierarchy is where some, not all, of the manuscript collections of Denys' writings begin. These manuscript collections begin there for a good reason. The opening chapters of *The Celestial Hierarchy* are a helpful introduction to Denys' view of the world as a whole. Those who are at all familiar with the *Summa theologiae* of Saint Thomas Aquinas will know that the most commonly met with interpretation of this work is that it follows a so-called "*exitus-reditus*" scheme. All things go out from God—that's the *Prima Pars*, which looks at the Triune Creator and what he has made. And what has gone out from God returns to him—that's the *Secunda Pars* and the *Tertia Pars*, which show how rational creatures return to God through a combination of their own freedom and God's grace (*Secunda Pars*), and how this return is made possible by the salvific work of Jesus Christ (*Tertia Pars*). The opening chapter of *The Celestial Hierarchy* begins by sounding that *exitus-reditus* theme, and quite possibly this is where Thomas first encountered it if indeed it really is the ground plan of the *Summa theologiae*. Though Thomas never wrote a commentary on *The Celestial Hierarchy*, only on *The Divine Names*, he was perfectly familiar with it, as his lengthy treatise on the angels in the *Summa theologiae* demonstrates. "Each procession of the Light [cf. *exitus*],"

[7] Dom David Knowles, "The Influence of Pseudo-Dionysius on Western Mysticism, in *Christian Spirituality: Essays in Honour of Gordon Rupp*, ed. Peter Newman Brooks (London: SCM, 1975), pp. 79–94.

writes Denys, "spreads itself generously towards us, and in its power to unify, it stirs us by lifting us up. It returns us back [cf. *reditus*] to the oneness and deifying simplicity of the Father who gathers us in."[8] Denys is able to cite in this connexion two New Testament authorities: Saint James, whose letter declares in its own opening chapter, "Every perfect gift is from above, coming down from the Father of lights" (1:17), and St. Paul in the Letter to the Romans: "From him [cf. procession] ... and to him [cf. return] are all things" (11:36). Denys borrowed the terms "procession" and "return" from Proclus.[9] They are a duo that really belongs with a trio, both philosophically for Proclus and theologically for Denys. The trio runs: "remaining" or "rest", procession and return—in other words, as Paul Rorem of Princeton Theological Seminary explains in his commentary on the Dionysian treatises, "the divine remains immanent in itself, yet it also proceeds outward or downward, and then reverts or returns back to itself."[10] Proclus, in his treatise *The Elements of Theology* (by "theology" was meant here metaphysical philosophy), had taught that every effect remains in its cause, proceeds from its cause, and returns to its cause. So originally, this is an analysis of transcendent causality. To know that helps us to avoid the trap of assuming that Denys must be talking about a movement that happens spatially, or indeed for that matter, temporally, in the sense of in historic or otherwise measurable time. Saint Thomas, for his part, uses this same causality language to speak of how the being of God finds objective expression in the creation, as well as in the economy of grace in Incarnation and salvation. While this could also be said of Denys, his emphasis does not lie there. His emphasis lies less on these objective structures of divine action, as we might call them, and more on what Rorem terms the "subjective or cognitive processes of revelation and spiritual knowledge".[11] In

[8] Denys, *The Celestial Hierarchy* I, 1, trans. Colm Luibheid, in *The Complete Works*, by Pseudo-Dionysius (Mahwah, NJ: Paulist, 1987). Translated citations from Denys' works are from this translation.

[9] Proclus was the successor of Plato as head of the Athenian Academy. "The pseudonym expressed the author's belief that the truths that Plato grasped belong to Christ, and are not abandoned by embracing faith in Christ.... Just as Denys saw no anachronism in speaking with the voice of a first century Christian, so Proclus saw no anachronism in counting his elaborate speculations no more than elucidations of Plato." Louth, *Denys the Areopagite*, p. 11.

[10] Paul Rorem, *Pseudo-Dionysius: A Commentary on the Texts and an Introduction to Their Influence* (New York: Oxford University Press, 1993), p. 51.

[11] Ibid., p. 52.

other words, Denys is concerned with how a sacred ordering (that is what is meant by the word "hierarchy", which he invented) enables us to receive into our minds illumination from God, the Father of lights, and, once we have received it, make use of it to return to him, to enter into union with him. This is not a spatial process, and it may not even be in any measurable sense temporal either. Denys' concern is with revelation and spiritual knowledge, for the word "subjective" here does not of course mean vague, impressionistic, arbitrary, or made up by the individual. The word "subjective", as Rorem uses it, means what has to do with the human subject, the person who comes to know and to make use of knowledge.

In this same opening chapter of *The Celestial Hierarchy*, Denys also introduces the theme of how symbolism, whether biblical or liturgical, plays a crucial role in this illuminating divine activity and the illuminated human activity that is a response to it. As he writes of the divine Light as proceeding in our direction, "This divine ray can only enlighten us by being upliftingly concealed in a variety of sacred veils which the Providence of the Father adapts to our nature as human beings."[12] By "sacred veils" Denys means sensuous symbols that are humanly accessible and function "anagogically", by lifting up minds and hearts towards the immaterial Light. As he was well aware, Scripture and the Liturgy are full of such symbols. The second chapter of *The Celestial Hierarchy* is devoted to this area.

One clue that suggests *The Celestial Hierarchy* was always meant to be the opening treatise in Denys' corpus is that his discussion of the value of symbols in this second chapter is not restricted to angels, as one might expect, but extends also to imagery for God. The principles involved are the same, whether it is angels or God we are talking about. Sensuous symbolism helps us in two ways. First, it identifies vehicles through which the imaginative mind can move up towards a transcendent realm. Secondly, by making use of vehicles that cannot possibly be taken as literal descriptions of that realm, such symbolism draws attention to the difference between that realm and our own. Thus, the symbolism helps in both ways, encouraging us and discouraging us in diverse respects. So on the one hand, Denys states the positive rationale for symbols: "We need our own upliftings that come naturally to us and which can raise before us the permitted forms of the

---

[12] Denys, *The Celestial Hierarchy* I, 2.

marvellous and unformed sights,"[13] that is, that which is "unformed" because it—angelic reality or divine reality—has no "shape" we can perceive. And on the other hand, Denys states the negative rationale for symbols, specifically here for the angels: "Scriptural writings, far from demeaning the ranks of heaven, actually pay them honour by describing them with dissimilar shapes so completely at variance with what they really are that we come to discover how those ranks, so far removed from us, transcend all materiality."[14] There is also a further, more than just incidental, advantage: the cryptic or riddling character of biblical and liturgical symbolism shields divine revelation from the common gaze of people who have not been initiated—not been properly instructed and baptised.

The dialectic of the positive and the negative is even more radical when we come to think of God, whose transcendence does not consist simply in his immateriality, as with the angels, but in his mode of existence, or as Denys would say, superexistence or even (daringly) nonexistence. For to distinguish God from finite existing things by saying God is the Source of beings is not by itself enough to do justice to God's difference from beings[15]—hence Denys' remarking "the way of negation appears to be more suitable to the divine".[16] Not that the way of affirmation is altogether unsuitable, since insofar as things are effects of God, they do enjoy some similarity with him that can be deployed in language about God. Yet the negative way is superior, just because things are more dissimilar to God than they are similar. This will be explained more fully in the treatise *The Divine Names*, which builds on Denys' opening remarks in *The Celestial Hierarchy*.

Yet as we shall see when we come to look at *The Mystical Theology*, the last of the Dionysian treatises, this conclusion from the opening chapters of *The Celestial Hierarchy*—more fully set out, so far as God

[13] Ibid., II, 2.

[14] Ibid., II, 3.

[15] This was a claim easier to make in Greek than in Latin. Explaining why for fear of being misunderstood Augustine avoids the expression "beyond being", preferring to say that God is being itself, or true being, or *idipsum*, John Rist writes, "The Latin 'beyond *esse*' might in any case convey a different sense (or no sense) from the Greek 'beyond *einai*' ('beyond finite being')." John M. Rist, *Augustine: Ancient Thought Baptized* (Cambridge: Cambridge University Press, 1994), p. 157.

[16] Denys, *The Celestial Hierarchy* II, 3.

is concerned, in *The Divine Names*—does not quite hit off Denys' theological epistemology. Authentic knowledge of God for Denys is not only beyond positive statements about him. Such knowledge is *beyond negative statements as well*.

But this is for the future. Denys' last task in introducing *The Celestial Hierarchy* is to explain the word "hierarchy" itself, which, as I said, he appears to have invented. I also said that "hierarchy" means "sacred order", which is true; but in Denys' own definition, he adds two further key characteristics: hierarchy is an order that transmits some kind of understanding from a higher source to a lower and does so by an activity which itself has three phases: it purifies, it illuminates, and it perfects. In later spiritual theology, this would be understood—in both East and West, but especially the latter—as consisting of, firstly, a moral purification, through disabling the vices and promoting the virtues, and so, secondly, an enlightenment of the mind made possible by that moral purification, and thus, thirdly, an entry into union with God based on that enlightenment and therefore purification. The purgative way, the illuminative way, the unitive way: a very popular spiritual schema still used in books on prayer and growth in holiness written today. But for Denys, these are essentially three phases in the receiving of revelation and the consequent acquisition of spiritual knowledge.

Ultimately, it is God, the all-highest, who purifies, illuminates, and perfects; but he does so hierarchically, and in the first place, then, through the ranks of angels. Only secondly will that procession and return take place through the ecclesiastical hierarchy or what Denys calls "our hierarchy", the earthly one (the word "ecclesiastical" was probably added to the title of that further treatise by a later editor). It is thought likely that Denys took the three key terms "purification", "illumination", and "perfection" from Gregory of Nyssa. Before Gregory some version of them had appeared in Origen. But of course Denys can hardly admit this since he claims to be the contemporary of the apostles. For Denys the three key terms mean the dispelling of relative ignorance (that is, purification), and two modes of understanding: contemplative understanding (that is, illumination) and perfected understanding (that is, perfection).

In the rest of *The Celestial Hierarchy*, Denys will group the biblical names for angels into three triads, indicating three sets of angelic choirs, each choir containing three ranks of angels (that takes up chapters 4 to 10), and then (in chapters 11 to 15) discuss some issues raised for angelology by the biblical narrative.

The Ecclesiastical Hierarchy

Revelatory understanding cascades into human minds through the mediation of divine light by the bodiless powers, the immaterial angels. The situation is very different once the context becomes earthly rather than heavenly. The further transmission of understanding within the human context, from one person or group of persons to another, implies materiality, not immateriality. Suitably for human animals, it entails sense perception and thus an awareness of extension in space and sequence in time.[17] Specifically, in the Christian context of teaching humanly the divine truth conveyed angelically, these dimensions—sensorial, spatial, temporal—suggest the need for a sacramental life, a life that operates through signs of the sacred, sensuous signs enacted in space and time, that is, in the form of rite. Denys' *The Ecclesiastical Hierarchy* is the first full exposition of the liturgical rites to come from the pen of a Father of the Church.

Naturally enough, what Denys has already said in *The Celestial Hierarchy* about "sacred veils", the desirability and even necessity of symbols in Scripture and Liturgy, immediately comes into its own. The purpose of the ecclesiastical hierarchy is the same as that of the celestial hierarchy—to convey revelation and make possible growth in the kind of spiritual knowledge that unites others with God. Denys explains as much in the opening chapter of this new work.

As to the rest of *The Ecclesiastical Hierarchy*, chapters 2 to 4 are devoted to Baptism, the Holy Eucharist, and the consecration of chrism. Chapter 5 looks at the threefold ministry of bishops, priests, and deacons with particular reference to their ordination rites. Chapter 6 considers the laity whom Denys divides up into monastics (here he signals the importance of the rite of monastic profession), Eucharistic communicants, and those still being purified (catechumens, penitents, and the demonically possessed). Bishops, priests, deacons,

[17] Rorem, *Pseudo-Dionysius*, p. 94.

monastics, and communicant laity, and those who though within the Christian assembly are excluded from Eucharistic communion, form together, in descending order, the overall hierarchy of the Church. Divine activity, aimed at purifying, that is, removing ignorance; illuminating, that is, conveying contemplative understanding; and perfecting, that is, bringing to perfection the contemplative understanding of those illuminated—all take place through the celebration of the rites as interpreted in the preaching and teaching that comes from the bishop. It passes through priests and deacons to monastics who will, then, presumably guide as spiritual fathers (or, possibly mothers) the communicants of the Church who themselves will be called on to lead on the right path the catechumens, the penitents, and those possessed. That is the overall picture that emerges from Denys' second great work, which concludes with a discussion of the rites for the departed.

The Divine Names

Denys' third treatise, *The Divine Names*, is, as its name suggests, a teaching about God. It is an example, then, of the kind of teaching that, angelically prompted, should come from the mouth of the bishop in expounding the Scriptures, and find its ongoing resonance—or as Denys would say, its continuing downflow—in and through the other ranks of the ecclesiastical hierarchy as just described.

In 1897, John Parker, whom we have already encountered as possibly the last true believer in the apostolic rather than patristic Denys, followed up his work on the hierarchies by translating this third Dionysian treatise into English.[18] In his introduction he gave an unusual explanation. The work, he thought, would be useful in British India for converting to Christianity educated Brahmins who found their view of the Deity superior to that of Christian missionaries from the West. Parker speculated that Denys' treatise had been taken from Alexandria to India in early patristic times (there were indeed early connexions between Christian Egypt and India), and

---

[18]John Parker, *The Works of Dionysius the Areopagite* (London and Oxford: James Parker, 1897), pp. 1–127.

that it had influenced the eighth-century Hindu philosopher Śankara, and his distant successor the thirteenth-century Ramanuja. It was the Proclean element in Denys—manifested in Neoplatonic-style language about the "rest, proceeding and return" that typify the relation between God and the world—which gave Parker this impression. For Hindu philosophers of a certain stamp, the relation between God and the rest of reality is seamless or "non-dual"—hence the title of the school of Indian philosophy called "Advaita (Non-dual) Hinduism". If the God who is immanent in himself proceeds from himself by creating in such a way as through the creation to return to himself, then all reality is indeed a seamless web.

No reading of Denys could be more different from this than that of Hans Urs von Balthasar, who wrote in his study *Cosmic Liturgy*,

> Dionysius pointed to the indissoluble autonomy of the finite world, as a whole and in its individual members, in relation to the infinite reality of God. Nothing could be more Western [continued Balthasar], nothing points more clearly back, beyond Proclus and Plotinus, to decisively Greek, non-Asiatic sources.... The salvation, the preservation, the confirmation of finitude by God himself: these are the Areopagite's basic intellectual models.[19]

How it was possible to come to two such diametrically opposed views of Denys' intentions I shall explain later.

Perhaps the first thing to be said about *The Divine Names* is that, despite the Neoplatonist vocabulary, the author is largely justified in his claim that he will represent as revelation only what is given in the Scriptures. Though the Bible teaches that the Deity is "unsearchable and inscrutable" (Denys quotes Saint Paul at Romans 11:33) as well as invisible and incomprehensible, nevertheless, the same Scriptures illuminate human persons through the revelation of certain "names" of God, names that imply what Denys calls God's "beneficent processions".[20] Here, at the outset of the treatise, he issues a warning

---

[19] Hans Urs von Balthasar, *Cosmic Liturgy: The Universe according to Maximus the Confessor* (San Francisco: Ignatius Press, 2003), p. 49. However, Balthasar noted that Maximus the Confessor in effect recognised a need to guard against interpreting Denys in an emanationist fashion (ibid., pp. 115–26). This implies that the "Parker view" was not without its merits.

[20] Denys, *The Divine Names* I, 1.

against going beyond the limits of this scriptural disclosure: "We must not dare to resort to words or conceptions concerning that hidden divinity which transcends being, apart from what the sacred Scriptures have divinely revealed."[21] Still, as he explains, that leaves us considerable latitude, since the names of God in the Bible are many and various. "The theologians"—Denys' name for the biblical authors—give God many names such as "being", "life", "light", "truth", "good", "beautiful", and "wise", and indeed for that matter, "sun", "star", "fire", "water", "dew", "cloud", "stone", and "rock". Denys stresses that these names should be taken to apply to the entire Godhead, the only exceptions, among biblical names, being those of Father, Son, and Spirit, which are reserved exclusively for the Trinitarian hypostases.

God's causation of all things justifies, says Denys, the use of these concepts and images, all of which are taken from the creation and exemplify positive epistemology, the affirmative way. Yet the same theologians, the hagiographs—that is, the authors of Scripture—also declare God to be the One who has the "name which is above every name" (Phil 2:9), a Name which is therefore no name at all: the supreme example, this, of negative epistemology, the negative way. The divine transcendence requires that as soon as names for God are posited they must be denied, the Trinitarian names alone excepted. This turns on the fact, to which the reader was alerted at the start of *The Celestial Hierarchy*, that God is not only the Source of beings, which therefore enjoy a resemblance, a similarity, to him, but is also so dissimilar to beings as to be rightly called superexistent, and in that sense nonexistent—meaning not existing in the way any existent thing in creation exists.

The author of *The Divine Names* explains that he intends to consider the significance of names for God based on sense perception, what we would call metaphors for divine being, in a subsequent treatise, *The Symbolic Theology*. This is one of the "missing" treatises that many scholars believe were never actually written. In *The Divine Names*, Denys goes on, he will confine himself instead to names of God drawn from concepts—from what in the Thomist tradition would be called the "pure perfections": concepts formed

---

[21] Ibid., I, 2.

to express aspects of being, which though belonging to the finite realm are not in any obvious way limited to that realm since of their nature they identify "perfections" of being that in principle are limitless. Unity, goodness, truth, and beauty are obvious examples, for Denys as much as for mediaeval Scholastics. God is the Source of these perfections found in finite things: while remaining or resting in himself he proceeds into a plural creation, which, essentially differentiated not only from him but within itself, in its own multiplicity God calls back into unity with himself. This is the point at which John Parker and von Balthasar part company, Balthasar stressing the differentiation of the "procession" as it creates finite things in their relative autonomy, Parker emphasising the identity of the God who always, in his presence in creation, "remains" and to whom creation everlastingly "returns". The importance of this discussion for both Saint Thomas and his teacher Saint Albert accounts for the fact that in recent scholarship both men (Thomas and Albert) have been seen as Christian Neoplatonists quite as much as they are Christian Aristotelians.

The Mystical Theology

So finally, we come to *The Mystical Theology*. For the Denys of *The Divine Names*, the most important divine Name was "Good", since *this* name, as he put it, "shows forth all the processions of God".[22] To that name, however, he had yoked the name of "Beauty", which in effect he identifies with the Good. It is the Good grasped as Beauty which attracts and gathers and so, in that crucial Proclean-Dionysian term, "returns" things to their ultimate Source in God. In a Greek pun that cannot be reproduced in English, the beautiful "calls" to us to move on to our true destiny, our true home. As Denys had written in *The Divine Names*, "All things must desire, must yearn for, must love, the Beautiful and the Good."[23]

Denys does not contrast *erôs*, "yearning", with *agapê*, "charity", but sees them as twin expressions of a movement of love that exists

---

[22] Denys, *The Divine Names* IV, 1.
[23] Ibid., IV, 7.

archetypally in God himself.[24] Pope Benedict XVI refers explicitly to this claim of Denys in *The Divine Names* in his 2005 encyclical *Deus caritas est*, writing: "God's *eros* for man is also totally *agape*."[25] Thus, God does not need our love, yet he desires it (*erôs*) and moreover wills to give us his own love (*agapê*); we are needy (*erôs*) for his love, but when we receive it (*agapê*) we can also become its transmitters (*agapê* again).

The "erotic" dimension of yearning for God finds expression as soon as *The Mystical Theology*, the final Dionysian treatise, opens, which it does, alone of the four treatises, with a prayer:

> Trinity! Higher than any being, any divinity, any goodness! Guide of Christians in the wisdom of heaven! Lead us up beyond unknowing and light, up to the farthest, highest peak of mystic scripture, where the mysteries of God's Word lie simple, absolute and unchangeable in the brilliant darkness of a hidden silence. Amid the deepest shadow they pour overwhelming light on what is most manifest. Amid the wholly unsensed and unseen they completely fill our sightless minds with treasures beyond all beauty. For this I pray ...[26]

Notice that Denys asks to be lifted up—that is, raised up anagogically by the symbols of Scripture and the Liturgy—"beyond unknowing and light". This is his way of intimating to the reader as his corpus comes to its close; *The Mystical Theology* is both its climax and a summary of the earlier treatises[27]—that union with God, which is the aim of the processions of God outside himself, will lie beyond both affirmation and negation, beyond both "light" and "unknowing".

Denys could perhaps have taken this from the mystical theology of Gregory of Nyssa, whose spiritual exegesis of the Song of Songs conveys a light mysticism, whereas in the *Life of Moses*, spiritual exegesis of the Book of Exodus, Nyssen puts forward a mysticism of darkness.

---

[24] Ibid., IV, 12–14. This was feasible because in the Platonic tradition, eros has selfless as well as self-interested elements; see Catherine Osborne, *Plato and the God of Love* (Oxford: Oxford University Press, 1994).

[25] Pope Benedict XVI, *Deus caritas est* (December 25, 2005), no. 10, https://www.vatican.va/content/benedict-xvi/en/encyclicals/documents/hf_ben-xvi_enc_20051225_deus-caritas-est.html.

[26] Denys, *The Mystical Theology* I, 1.

[27] Rorem, *Pseudo-Dionysius*, p. 183.

The mystic at the stage of union experiences the uncreated Light, but then that Light becomes so superradiant that subsequently it is experienced as Darkness, a "Cloud of Unknowing". But in Denys' case, there are two differences from the Cappadocian Father at least as the latter is generally understood. Firstly, according to this prayer, it's not that we go through light into darkness. It's that we go beyond both light and darkness. And secondly, Denys' urging us to go beyond both knowing and unknowing, both affirmation and negation, is not simply spiritual advice. It belongs with his theological epistemology as a whole, his entire account of both metaphysics and the biblical revelation. As he writes when this very short treatise is coming to its close: "Darkness and light . . .—it is none of these. It is beyond assertion and denial. . . . It is both beyond every assertion, being the perfect and unique cause of all things, and, by virtue of its preeminently simple and absolute nature, free of every limitation, beyond every limitation, it is also beyond every denial."[28] Here Benedict XVI came—all unwittingly, I feel sure—upon a point of agreement with the long-forgotten John Parker: "Today Dionysius the Areopagite has a new relevance: he appears as a great mediator in the modern dialogue between Christianity and the mystical theologies of Asia."[29]

[28] Denys, *The Mystical Theology* V.

[29] Benedict XVI, *Church Fathers and Teachers*, p. 30. By way of example, the English-born Benedictine monk Bede Griffiths echoed Parker's "Denys for Brahmins" idea, in a context less of evangelization than of "inculturation", finding Denys and Gregory of Nyssa, in their use of Neoplatonism, to be "the nearest equivalent in the West to the Vedantic tradition of Hinduism in the East"; see his "Towards an Indian Christian Spirituality", in *Prayer and Contemplation*, ed. C. M. Vadakkekara (Bangalore: Asirvanam Benedictine Monastery, 1980), p. 385. Whether Pope Benedict would underwrite Griffiths' theology of religions—all religions issue from primordial experiences of the Spirit but can meet on the grounds of Advaita—is quite another matter. Benedict does not explain how he would reconcile his "Asiatic" description of Denys' theology with his own acceptance of a Bonaventurian reading of the *corpus Dionysiacum* as a theology of love, centred on Christ and the Cross. Benedict XVI, *Church Fathers and Teachers*, pp. 29–30.

7

Cosmic Theologian:
Saint Maximus the Confessor

We know, with what historians would deem adequate security, a good deal about the second half of the career of Saint Maximus—this influential seventh-century monk, whose combination of doctrinal precision and spiritual flair has generated comparisons, at least among Catholics, with Saint Thomas Aquinas.[1] The doctrinal controversy that dominated the latter part of his life—the issue of Monothelitism, or whether there is only one will, the divine will, in the Word incarnate—is especially well documented. Here there are texts written by Maximus himself, such as the "Theological and Polemical *Opuscula*" ("little works"), of which the most important for this issue are the six that take as subject Jesus' Agony in the Garden.[2] And there are also texts from other hands that describe Maximus' involvement in contemporary Church affairs, like the record of a debate in 645 with a Monothelite patriarch of Constantinople, when the two of them were in exile in North Africa, the "Disputation with Pyrrhus".[3] Equally well documented is the trial (actually two trials) of Maximus for treason before the imperial authorities in Constantinople in 655 and the subsequent sufferings and death in 656, which gave

[1] Mari-Joseph Le Guillou, O.P., Préface to *Le monde et l'Église selon Maxime le Confesseur*, by Alain Riou (Paris: Beauchesne, 1973); Antoine Lévy, O.P., *Le créé et l'Incréé: Maxime le Confesseur et Thomas d'Aquin* (Paris: Vrin, 2006); Gilles Emery, O.P., "A Note on St. Thomas and the Eastern Fathers", in *Trinity, Church and the Human Person: Thomistic Essays* (Naples, FL: Sapientia, 2007).

[2] Numbers 3, 6, 7, 15, 16, 24, highlighted by F.-M. Léthel, *Théologie de l'agonie du Christ: La liberté humaine du Fils de Dieu et son importance sotériologique mises en lumière par S. Maxime Confesseur* (Paris: Beauchesne, 1979).

[3] St. Maximus the Confessor, *The Disputation with Pyrrhus of Our Father among the Saints Maximus the Confessor*, trans. Joseph P. Farrell (South Canaan, PA: St. Tikhon's Monastery Press, 1990).

him his title "The Confessor".[4] He died in prison at a place on the eastern shore of the Black Sea, currently in Georgia, which was the first region to develop a cult of his holiness. The gruesome character of his judicial mutilation (the removal of a hand and his tongue) is attested in the Acts of his quasi-martyrdom.

Contrastingly, about the first half of his life there is not much of a consensus. There can be no certainty about the date of his birth, but a time around 580 is conjectured. That at least is a start. The general conditions of life in Byzantium in this period can be reconstructed, up to a point, with the aid of chroniclers and some rare nonchronicle sources.[5] Maximus lived in a period of great turbulence as a consequence of the westward ambitions of the Persians, whose army reached the shores of the Bosphorus in 615, and then, much more devastatingly, the rise of Islam—by the time of Maximus' death just over twenty years later, the Byzantine provinces of Syria, Palestine, and Egypt had all fallen victim to the seemingly unstoppable Muslim advance.[6] But just how Maximus spent the first part of his life, up to and including his middle manhood, is much disputed.[7]

How so? A very hostile life in Syriac, from the hand of a Monothelite author—so, a sworn enemy—has the advantage of being written shortly after the events it describes. So far as can be ascertained, the Greek life of Maximus—which, in contrast, is highly favourable to the saint—was not written before the tenth century. For the Syriac life, Maximus is a Palestinian of humble birth (and illegitimate), a monk in a Judaean monastery that was strongly inclined to Origenism. According to this author, Maximus gained an unhealthy influence over the then patriarch of Jerusalem, Sophronius, who became the whistleblower for the supposed doctrinal crisis (originally framed as a matter of the single "operation" or "energy" of Jesus Christ rather than his "will", hence the name "Monoenergism",

[4] Pauline Allen and Bronwen Neil, eds. and trans., *Maximus the Confessor and His Companions: Documents from Exile* (Oxford: Oxford University Press, 2002).

[5] On the relative poverty of Byzantine sources compared with what is available to historians of the mediaeval West, see Introduction to *The Oxford History of Byzantium*, ed. Cyril Mango (New York: Oxford University Press, 2002), pp. 1–16, especially pp. 6–8.

[6] Phil Booth, *Crisis of Empire: Doctrine and Dissent at the End of Late Antiquity* (Berkeley, CA: University of California Press, 2014).

[7] For discussion of the biographical issues, see Andrew Louth, *Maximus the Confessor* (London and New York: Routledge, 1996), pp. 3–18.

rather than "Monothelitism"). Sophronius undertook to warn Chalcedonian Christians that their belief in the two natures of the Word incarnate was under threat.

For the Greek life, Maximus is a high-born citizen of the imperial capital who worked as a court official—secretary to the emperor Heraclius, no less—before becoming a monk in first one then another monastery on the Asiatic side of the waterways separating Europe from Asia. That will be, then, in the wider environs of Constantinople. Accepting the Greek life would explain how Maximus came to have a correspondence with highly placed civil servants. Accepting the Syriac life would explain how he came to be thrown together with Sophronius of Jerusalem.

The Greek life has Maximus and Sophronius meeting up in Carthage, in North Africa, some time around 630. A monastery at Carthage did indeed act as a safe haven for Eastern monks fleeing from the Arab invasions. Taking refuge in the West gave Maximus the opportunity to forge an alliance with the popes of the time, one of whom, Martin I, was arrested by imperial agents in 653 and shared Maximus' exile if not all his punishments. So there is something to be said for each of these incompatible biographies.

What everyone can agree on is that Maximus' writing is copious. It exists in a wide variety of literary genres, and some of it is written in extremely complicated Greek—complained of even by Byzantine intellectuals living only two centuries later. It is not always possible to date it, but it would seem that his simplest and most straightforward work, which would come under the heading of spiritual theology, and more especially monastic theology, dates from his earliest period when he was living the life of an ordinary monk either in the area of Constantinople or in Judaea, depending on which of the biographical traditions one has decided to follow. So I begin with Maximus' spiritual, monastic, or—perhaps the best word—*ascetical* theology.

Ascetical Theology

Maximus' *Dialogue on the Ascetical Life* is, in literary genre, much like the instructions for monks recorded in Greek in the *Sayings of the Fathers*—the Desert Fathers, that is—or in Latin by Saint John Cassian in his *Conferences*, a book that transmitted Oriental monastic wisdom to the West.[8] Maximus' *Four Centuries on Charity*,[9] and his *Centuries on Knowledge*,[10] take the form of sets of maxims or at any rate relatively short statements called "chapters" (a hundred of them at a time, hence "centuries") on issues raised by the spiritual life. It was a kind of treatise that Maximus was not the first to write, nor the last. Selections from these writings fitted easily enough into the *Philokalia*, the anthology of ascetical and mystical teaching produced by two Greek monks at the end of the eighteenth century, and now increasingly recognised as the preeminent classic of Eastern Orthodox spirituality.[11] (This late eighteenth-century *Philokalia* should not be confused with the original *Philokalia*, the anthology of texts from Origen made by Basil and Gregory Nazianzen.) Maximus works with a very popular scheme. The individual moves through ascetic practice, aimed at rooting out the vices, via the contemplation of God in creation to, finally, the theological contemplation of God—that is, the contemplation of God *in himself*.

Yet even in these works more is going on than meets the eye. Maximus is seeking to enlarge the tradition of spirituality, and doing so in two respects. In the first place he is drawing together rather different subtraditions, subtraditions which, presumably, he had encountered personally in monastic circles. The principal subtraditions involved come from two major figures: Evagrius and Macarius.

Evagrius is Evagrius of Pontus, the disciple of Origen, often called the first Christian psychologist. Writing in the fourth century, Evagrius' focus was on the ascent to God of the mind, once freed from the distractions caused by the passions.[12] Macarius, sometimes called

---

[8] St. Maximus the Confessor, *The Ascetic Life and the Four Centuries on Charity*, trans. Polycarp Sherwood, O.S.B. (Westminster, MD: Newman Press, 1957).

[9] Two English translations exist, one by Sherwood (see the note above), the other by George C. Berthold (see the note below).

[10] More fully, "Two Hundred Chapters of Our Holy Father Maximus the Confessor on Theology and the Economy in the Flesh of the Son of God"; see Maximus the Confessor, *Selected Writings*, trans. George C. Berthold (London: Society for Promoting Christian Knowledge, 1985), pp. 127–80.

[11] St. Nikodimos of the Holy Mountain and St. Markarios of Corinth, comps., *The Philokalia: The Complete Text*, trans. G. E. H. Palmer, Philip Sherrard, and Kallistos Ware, 4 vols. (London: Faber and Faber, 1979–1999). A fifth and final volume is not yet published.

[12] On the Evagrian heritage, see Andrew Louth, *Wisdom of the Byzantine Church: Evagrios of Pontos and Maximos the Confessor* (Columbia, MO: University of Missouri Press, 1998).

"Pseudo-Macarius", is a fifth-century or early sixth-century Meso-potamian author who took the name of an early Egyptian monastic saint. For Macarius what is crucial is the presence of God in the heart, based ultimately on baptismal regeneration.[13] In particular, by allow-ing the Macarian tradition to complement or correct the Evagrian tradition, Maximus is warning against too intellectualist an approach to union with God, and one that may be disinclined to give much weight to the role of the sacraments. These were, perhaps, typical temptations for monks (and other people) who took Origen of Alex-andria for their one and only spiritual master.

The other thing that is going on in these early (or putatively early[14]) ascetical writings is that Maximus is seeking to contextualize spiritual effort in the wider setting of dogmatic Christianity, above all in regard to the doctrines of creation and Incarnation. Evagrius had started this trend, Gregory of Nyssa continued it, but Maximus took it further still.[15] The two doctrines of creation and Incarnation are for Maximus closely connected. He sees the Incarnation as the goal of the creation, the end or purpose God had eternally in view in creating the world and, within the world, mankind. It is only through the Incarnation that "divinisation"—which for Maximus means (in the title of a French monograph on his thought) the reign of charity, "the divine future of man"—can be brought about.[16] The importance of doctrine for spirituality is underlined when in the *Dialogue on the Ascetical Life* the very first question the novice asks his spiritual father runs, "What was the purpose of God becom-ing man?"

---

[13] Marcus Plested, *The Macarian Legacy: The Place of Macarius-Symeon in the Eastern Christian Tradition* (Oxford: Oxford University Press, 2004).

[14] Hans Urs von Balthasar, in his capacity as patrologist, thought the *Centuries on Knowledge* was from Maximus' middle period. See Hans Urs von Balthasar, *Cosmic Liturgy: The Universe according to Maximus the Confessor* (San Francisco: Ignatius Press, 2003), p. 78.

[15] Maximus makes it clear that "there can be no natural contemplation independent of the Incarnation by bracketing together 'His most wise providence, which binds all things together, and His economy for our sake, which is passing marvellous and transcendently ineffable',... an understanding of natural contemplation as embracing both a true understand-ing of the created cosmic order through beholding its *logoi* and a grasp of the economy of salvation, especially in the Incarnation." Louth, *Maximus the Confessor*, p. 69, with an internal quotation of Maximus, *Ambigua* 10.

[16] Juan Miguel Garrigues, *La Charité, avenir divin de l'homme* (Paris: Beauchesne, 1976).

Dogmatic Synthesis

These two concerns—correcting an overreliance on Origen's teaching while nonetheless profiting by that teaching, and relocating spirituality within the total dogmatic framework of Christian revelation—are also evidenced in the two substantial treatises Maximus wrote for, in the first place, individuals he sought to help by his writing.

The treatise called *The Ambigua* consists of two sets of discussions: one set, *Ambigua to John*, is addressed to a bishop on the northwest coast of Asia Minor (at Cyzicus, the little town on the Sea of Marmara where the Greek "Life" placed Maximus' second monastery); the other, *Ambigua to Thomas*, to an abbot who, unhelpfully, Maximus does not locate for us geographically, though he does describe him as his own spiritual teacher. The *Ambigua* takes as its subject certain passages in the writings of Gregory Nazianzen: "Gregory the Theologian" as he was becoming known. In the works of this preeminent figure, there were passages ambiguous enough to cause problems in the interpretation of Scripture and the construction of a Christian metaphysics—and Christian doctrine more widely—not least if those passages were taken in a defectively Origenist sense.

A good example is *Ambiguum* 7, where Maximus clears Nazianzen of the claim that the Cappadocian Father accepted Origen's controversial account of the mind, *nous*, as passing out of a stationary condition in God, *stasis*, through entry into movement, *kinêsis*, so as to instantiate becoming, *genesis*—that is, embodiment in the material world, into which the preexistent mind falls by union with the body. Maximus offers instead a sequence: becoming (on the basis of creation), then movement, and finally rest in God, in this way neatly inverting the Origenist scheme. I should mention that the Latin word *ambiguum* translates the Greek *aporia*, a difficulty or problem, so Maximus was not necessarily saying Gregory had written unclearly. He could be—and was—saying that Gregory had left some problems unresolved.

The other major treatise, *Questions for Thalassius* or *Questions and Responses for Thalassius*, was written for a Libyan abbot; it looks at issues of biblical interpretation through the lens of some particularly tricky sections of Scripture. Maximus evidently agreed with Origen that the Holy Spirit has lodged in the Scriptures some *skandala* (if not outright "scandals" then at least "obstacles") in order to goad students into a deeper exploration of the mysteries. In effect, *Questions for Thalassius* is a set of *scholia*—which, as already mentioned in connexion with Origen's work, is a kind of highly focussed exegetical enquiry, confining itself to short extracts from the Bible. (The *Ambigua* might also be called "*scholia*" if we are willing to allow that *scholia* can take as their subject patristic texts and not just verses from the Bible—and why not? Contemporaries wrote *scholia* on Denys—who, however, they took to be the companion of the apostles and so enjoying, after the biblical writers, a unique authority.)

The *Questions for Thalassius* show that, however much he may have agreed with critics of Origenism, not least in his *Ambigua to John*, Maximus was very keen to continue Origen's method of spiritual exegesis, which was at once allegorical and anagogical: treating the biblical texts as a rich and thought-provoking set of symbols (hence "allegorical"), a set of symbols that, when read aright, help the mind and heart to rise up to God (hence "anagogical").[17]

We can be fairly confident that these two books (with the possible exception of the *Ambigua to Thomas*) come from the first half of Maximus' adult life. The reason for saying so is that they show little concern for, or anxiety about, the Christological problem of the one will or two wills of the Word incarnate, the issue that occupied Maximus during the latter part of his life and took him to his death. If, with regard to these two treatises, we can generalize to the point of finding one issue that is uppermost in their author's mind, one promising candidate would be human freedom and its implications. The Cappadocian Fathers had inherited from Origen the latter's profound conviction of the existence of interior freedom in every human person. That was especially notable in Gregory of Nyssa, who regarded the freedom of the intelligent soul as constitutive of the Image of God in man.[18] Maximus felt a need to emphasise that our freedom, though real and even indispensable for human salvation, does not mean that we live in a totally undetermined and thus potentially anarchic

---

[17] See Paul M. Blowers, *Exegesis and Spiritual Pedagogy in Maximus the Confessor: An Investigation of the "Quaestiones ad Thalassium"* (Notre Dame, IN: University of Notre Dame Press, 1991).

[18] Roger Leys, S.J., *L'image de Dieu chez saint Grégoire de Nysse: Esquisse d'une doctrine* (Brussels: Editions universelles; Paris: Desclée de Brouwer, 1951).

universe where, for instance, minds could become either devils or angels, in dependence on free choice.

Here Maximus could put to good effect his reading of Denys, for whom the world is stably founded on the divine energies or operations. There is nothing chaotic, therefore, about existence, despite the broad latitude that through freedom is ours. A structured process of procession and return, *exitus-reditus*, founds the world's creation and destiny on the God who, despite his multifarious activity in taking forward creation and salvation, remains unchangeable in his own indescribable "rest", his immanence within himself. There is nothing chaotic, therefore, about existence, despite the broad latitude that is ours through freedom.

The man who wrote these two key works was already, we can say, a theological master. In the developed tradition of Christian thinking, a theological master will always be someone who can synthesize earlier Christian sources, and that is what we find Maximus doing. Maximus combines Denys' account of the God-world relation,[19] the Trinitarian doctrine of Gregory Nazianzen,[20] the teaching of Origen, Evagrius, and Macarius on asceticism and mysticism—along with the speculations of Origen and Evagrius, which required his correcting touch, on protology and eschatology, the beginning and the end.[21] There was, furthermore, another ingredient in this mix, not mentioned yet either in this lecture or in this course: the anthropology of a Greek-speaking Syrian bishop called Nemesius, to which topic I shall return.

In Christian theology a genuine synthesis must not simply integrate the particular contributions of earlier theologies. It must also place them in a single overall perspective or setting. Here the best description for Maximus' work is probably "Neo-Irenaean". That is argued by the American patristic scholar Paul Blowers, who, unusually for patrologists, is a member of the "Disciples" or "Churches of Christ", a Revivalist denomination founded by three nineteenth-century Protestant reformers in the United States.[22] Maximus sees the

[19] See Torstein Theodor Tollefsen, *The Christocentric Cosmology of St. Maximus the Confessor* (Oxford: Oxford University Press, 2008), pp. 65–66; 74–76, 162–63.

[20] See Lars Thunberg, *Man and the Cosmos: The Vision of St. Maximus the Confessor* (Crestwood, NY: St. Vladimir's Seminary Press, 1985), pp. 37–39, 45.

[21] Von Balthasar, *Cosmic Liturgy*, pp. 127–36.

[22] Paul M. Blowers, *Maximus the Confessor: Jesus Christ and the Transfiguration of the World* (Oxford: Oxford University Press, 2016), pp. 102–5.

"economy", that key Irenaean term, as embracing everything from the creation to the Parousia, just as Irenaeus had done. But he consistently centres that economy on the mystery of Christ. In this sense, Maximus' teaching is a version of Irenaeus' theology, at once more expanded and more concentrated, and freed from the distractions Irenaeus' feud with the Gnostics entailed.

Maximus has two special emphases when dealing with the economy. First, as already signaled, he takes Jesus Christ in his Incarnation and Paschal Mystery to be the goal of creation. As he writes in an often quoted passage from the *Centuries on Knowledge*, "The mystery of the incarnation of the Word (*Logos*) bears the power of all the hidden meanings (*logoi*) and figures of Scripture as well as the knowledge of visible and intelligible creatures. The one who knows the mystery of the cross and the tomb knows the principles (*logoi*) of these creatures. And the one who has been initiated into the ineffable power of the Resurrection knows the purpose for which God originally made all things."[23] That purpose was to sum up all things in Jesus Christ, their divine-human Head. The *logoi* of creatures, the meaning or purpose of their natures, cannot be grasped, then, without some reference to the Incarnation, Death, and Resurrection of the humanised Word of God, Jesus Christ. An excellent formulation by Blowers, writing together with the Catholic patrologist Robert Louis Wilken, sums this up. They comment, compendiously enough: "In Maximus's vision of the world, the incarnation of the Second Person of the Holy Trinity in Jesus of Nazareth holds the secret to the foundations—the architectural *logoi*—of the created cosmos, its destiny after the fall of created beings (the mystery of *redemption*), and the transcendent end (*telos*) of creation (the mystery of *deification*) wherein the prospect of ever more intimate communion with the Trinity is opened up."[24]

This stupendous claim is aided by Maximus' view that man is a microcosm of the entire cosmos, which therefore can be called itself the macrocosm of man. Man is the microcosm of the macrocosm

---

[23] Maximus, *Capita theologica et oeconomica* 1, 66, cited in Berthold, *Selected Writings*, pp. 139–40.

[24] Paul M. Blowers and Robert Louis Wilken, Introduction to *On the Cosmic Mystery of Jesus Christ: Selected Writings from St. Maximus the Confessor* (Yonkers, NY: St. Vladimir's Seminary Press, 2003), p. 20.

in such a way that he—originally Adam but then, with Adam's failure, the New Adam, Jesus Christ—is called by God to mediate the
tensions that follow from the co-existence of different dimensions
of the cosmic macrocosm. That could be anything from the tension between male and female to the tension between heaven and
earth. "Mediating" these tensions ("divisions" Maximus terms them)
means, in effect, reconciling them in a reunified creation. "Human
beings are found on both sides of each division. They belong in paradise but inhabit the inhabited world, they are earthly and yet destined
for heaven, they have both mind and senses, and though created they
are destined to share in the uncreated nature by deification."[25] The
most stupendous division of all is that between God and the world.
Who would have thought that the abyss between the Uncreated and
created could ever be bridged?

Bridging divisions is the theme of a great study by the Swedish
Lutheran patrologist Lars Thunberg. In *Microcosm and Mediator: The
Theological Anthropology of Maximus the Confessor*,[26] Thunberg showed
how Maximus took the kernel of this microcosm idea from the late
fourth-century Greek Christian philosopher Nemesius, the Syrian
bishop to whose place in the Maximian scheme of things I promised
to return. Maximus, however, adds a dimension that did not occur to
Nemesius. In Thunberg's words, "Man's microcosmic constitution
[is] an anticipatory sign of God's Incarnation."[27] The complexity of
our manifold being together with our vocation to deification make
it congruent—suitable, fitting—that the uniting to God of the entire
creation comes about through a member of our species.

That, then, is Maximus' first distinctive take on the economy, distinguishing him from Irenaeus. But secondly, Maximus treats Jesus

---

[25] Louth, *Maximus the Confessor*, p. 70, commenting on *Ambigua* 41.

[26] Lars Thunberg, *Microcosm and Mediator: The Theological Anthropology of Maximus the Confessor*, 2nd ed. (Chicago: Open Court, 1995). See also the summary offered of the first edition
in Thunberg, *Man and the Cosmos*, pp. 80–91. Balthasar anticipated the microcosm idea in
Cosmic Liturgy, pp. 173–77, though his notion of "mediation" was "synthesizing", a theme he
expounds in different ways—"The Syntheses of the Cosmos", "Christ the Synthesis", "The
Spiritual Syntheses" (ibid., pp. 137–78). "All things, for [Maximus], had become organic parts
of ever more comprehensive syntheses, had become themselves syntheses pointing to the final
synthesis of Christ, who explained them all.... For Maximus ... a synthetic understanding of
Christ became a theodicy for the world: a justification not simply of its existence but of the
whole range of its structure of being." Ibid., p. 66.

[27] Thunberg, *Man and the Cosmos*, p. 75.

Christ in his divinity, as distinct from humanity, as the Trinitarian Son (a convenient Balthasarian expression) who is always inseparable from the Father and the Holy Spirit. That means in the first place that Maximus understands the Incarnation as at all points the work of the Trinity as a whole. As he wrote in *Questions for Thalassius*,

> The Father and the Holy Spirit were not ignorant of the incarnation of the Son because the whole Father is by essence in the whole Son who himself carried out the mystery of our salvation through the incarnation. The Father himself did not become incarnate but rather approved the incarnation of the Son. Moreover, the whole Holy Spirit exists by essence in the whole Son, but he too did not become incarnate but rather cooperated in the Son's ineffable incarnation for our sake.[28]

And so in the second place, the self-revelation of the One who as man is Jesus is the revelation of the entire Godhead in its utterly essential tri-unity. "In becoming incarnate, the Word of God teaches us the mystical knowledge of God because he shows us in himself the Father and the Holy Spirit."[29]

That further statement, this time from Maximus' *Commentary on the Our Father*, gives the leitmotif of his entire exposition of the Lord's Prayer. The prayer is a mystagogical initiation into the Triune life. The Name of the Father ("hallowed be thy Name") is the Son; the Father's reign ("thy kingdom come") is the Holy Spirit.[30] In comparison with the fruitful Triune God of love, Maximus in this commentary can call the Jewish Image of God, somewhat scandalously, an approximation to atheism.[31] If we compare Maximus with Irenaeus, it will readily be apparent that Maximus' Trinitarian doctrine is much more richly developed, thanks not least to the work of Athanasius and the Cappadocians.

Blowers and Wilken sum up very well Maximus' overall view of the economy and its divinizing purpose. Discussing what for Maximus

---

[28] Maximus, *Questions for Thalassius* 60, cited in Blowers and Wilken, *On the Cosmic Mystery of Jesus Christ*, p. 127.

[29] Maximus, *Commentary on the Our Father* 2, in *Selected Writings* [of Maximus Confessor], trans. George C. Berthold (London: Society for Promoting Christian Knowledge, 1985).

[30] Ibid., 4.

[31] Von Balthasar, *Cosmic Liturgy*, pp. 103–4.

the word "theology" implies, they have this to say: "*Theologia*—
as the aspiration to intimate knowledge of the Holy Trinity that must
always remain grounded in, and integrated with, the contemplative
and ascetic life of the Christian—entails for [Maximus] an intensive,
ongoing, multifaceted, 'intellectual quest' into the foundations and
future of the world created by God, recreated through the work
of Jesus Christ, sanctified by the Holy Spirit, and summoned to an
unprecedented and glorious deification."[32]

There is much there that is Irenaean. Yet to call Maximus' thought
"Neo-Irenaean" may overlook at least one important structural difference between Irenaeus and Maximus. Though there are elements
of philosophical analysis or discussion in Irenaeus' work, they are not
by any means as prominent as in the subsequent Greek Fathers from
Origen to Denys. And Maximus continues that tradition of using
philosophical tools theologically, doing so in an especially intense and
systematic way. Unlike Irenaeus, Maximus brought to bear a very
rigorous metaphysical mind when he thought about the economy.

Here he was assisted by the increasing application of such philosophical tools to Christology in the course of the complex and often
tortuous discussions that followed the Council of Chalcedon, and,
notably, in the resistance aroused among Cyrillines by that Council's
definition of the two natures and single Personhood of Christ. In this
respect Maximus can be called a "proto-Scholastic".[33] That is what
causes much of the difficulty of his prose. It is not difficult because
it is rhetorically overrich, using excessive adornment in figures of
speech, as might be the case with a self-consciously literary writer
like Gregory Nazianzen. It is difficult because it is quasi-Scholastic,
making constant use of fine distinctions, and distinctions within those
distinctions. His sentences have been compared to Chinese boxes,
where within a box is contained a smaller box, and in that second box
a further box smaller still, and so on.[34]

Perhaps the most important of Maximus' philosophical tools is the
distinction between *logos* and *tropos*—the distinction between, on the

---

[32] Blowers and Wilken, Introduction to *On the Cosmic Mystery of Jesus Christ*, pp. 16–17.

[33] See Brian E. Daley, "Boethius' Theological Tracts and Early Byzantine Scholasticism",
Medieval Studies 46 (1984): 158–91.

[34] Thunberg, *Man and the Cosmos*, p. 29.

one hand, the nature of something, and, on the other, its condition of being or mode of acting.[35] The same something can exist in a variety of conditions and come to active expression in a variety of modes.[36] This basic metaphysical distinction enabled Maximus to speak of the crucial changes that creation undergoes in the history of salvation, where human nature finds itself engaged or deployed in different manners. These range from fallen humanity (the same *logos* but a different *tropos* from humanity as humanity was originally created) to deified humanity (the same *logos* but a different *tropos* from the *tropos* of fallen humanity) with, at the midpoint of time itself, the humanity assumed by the Word, Jesus Christ (the same *logos*, our own human nature, but with a unique *tropos*), which replicates the filial "mode of existing" of the Trinitarian Son, now living and acting on earth, living and acting within history.[37] The *tropos* changes, but it is the same human nature, the same *logos*, that endures throughout.

Maximian Christology

This brings us fairly neatly to the question of Maximus' Christology. It is sometimes said that the key to Maximus' entire worldview, and not just his Christology, lies in the Christological Definition of the Council of Chalcedon, with its celebrated four adverbs, which we examined in connexion with Cyril of Alexandria.[38] That quartet

[35] See Riou, *Le monde et l'Eglise*, where Riou makes much of this for anthropology and soteriology; for Christology, see Felix Heinzer, *Gottes Sohn als Mensch: Die Struktur des Menschseins Christi bei Maximus Confessor* (Fribourg: Universitätsverlag, 1980).

[36] The remote origin lies in the Cappadocian theology of the Trinity where the one *ousia* or "substance"—compare *logos*, meaning in this context "the intelligible [though not to us!] nature" of God—finds expression in the three "subsistent modes" (*tropoi [tes] hyparxeos*) that are the Persons.

[37] Louth states, "Whatever we share with others, we are: it belongs to our nature. But what it is to be a person is not some thing, some quality, that we do *not* share with others—as if there were an irreducible somewhat within each of us that makes us the unique person we are. What is unique about each one of us is what we have made of the nature that we have, our own unique mode of existence, which is a matter of our experience in the past, our hopes for the future, the way we live out the nature that we have. What makes the Son of God the unique person he is the eternal life of love in the Trinity in which he shares in a filial way." Louth, *Maximus the Confessor*, pp. 57–58.

[38] Von Balthasar, *Cosmic Liturgy*, pp. 63–64.

of adverbs amounts to saying that the divine and human natures of the Word are united in his single Personhood without either fusion (which would mean confusion) or disjunction (which would mean separation). That things can be united without being absorbed or obliterated is, on this view, the main metaphysical insight that governs Maximus' cosmology.

Yet his more particular background is not standard Chalcedonianism. It is, rather, neo-Chalcedonianism—the attempt of theologians after Chalcedon to rally to the Definition the supporters of the now deceased Saint Cyril.[39] Neo-Chalcedonianism takes a step beyond Chalcedon by making it crystal clear that the single Person in whom the two natures are united is not a novelty, not a new Person who is brought into existence by the union of the natures. No, he is the same eternal Word who was begotten by the Father before time was. This claim was dogmatised by the Fifth Ecumenical Council, Constantinople II, in 552.

In point of fact, both Chalcedon and Constantinople II serve as Maximus' Christological benchmarks. Making use of Cyril's notion of the union of natures in the Word as "hypostatic"—that is, made in the *hypostasis*, the Person—Lars Thunberg wrote: "The hypostatic relationship between human and divine in Christ, as [Maximus] understands it in his personal faithfulness to both Chalcedon and Constantinople [II], is alone able to manifest and safeguard the purpose for which man was created, deification, while preserving man himself unchanged in his natural make-up. It alone establishes man in an unchangeable union with God forever, if only he is willing, by divine grace, to receive the deifying powers as effective within himself."[40]

For the neo-Chalcedonians who followed Constantinople II, then, the human nature of Jesus is rendered personal, the nature of "a someone", precisely because the eternal Word personalizes that nature in making it his own, leaving its own essentially human characteristics intact as he does so. To express this claim, neo-Chalcedonians used the phrase the "composite person" of the Word.

[39] For these theologians, see Alois Grillmeier, S.J., "Der Neo-Chalkedonismus: Um die Berechtigung eines Kapitels in der Dogmengeschichte", in *Mit Ihm und in Ihm: Christologische Forschungen und Perspektiven* (Freiburg: Herder, 1975), pp. 371–95.

[40] Thunberg, *Microcosm and Mediator*, p. 433.

"The composite person"—that sounded attractive to Cyrillians, since it drew attention to the unity of the Word incarnate, his *mia phusis* or single reality, Cyril's overriding preoccupation. Indeed, some scholars call neo-Chalcedonianism "Cyrilline Chalcedonianism".[41] The "composite person" is the Person who personalises not only the divine nature but the continuing human nature of Christ as well. Unfortunately, as subsequent Church history showed, neo-Chalcedonianism was insufficient to win round extreme Cyrillians. The consequent schism from the Great Church of those we now call Monophysites, or, in more recent usage, Miaphysites, meant eventually the loss to the Christian State, Byzantium or East Rome, of most of Syria and all of Egypt.

It was understandable, then, that successive emperors, aided and abetted by the patriarchs of the imperial capital, should look for ways and means by which further concessions might be made. Monothelitism was simply the last of these: the last of a series, and the last attempt at reunion until the ecumenical movement of modern times. Naturally, this explains the odium in which Maximus and his papal supporter Martin I were held by many Byzantines, from the emperor down. They were frustrating a policy designed to hold Christians within one empire, one imperial Church.

Maximus would hardly have gone the whole hog as a Dyothelite had he not been convinced that vital truths were at stake. That the same composite Person energizes in both divine and human natures does not cancel out the reality of the finite, created will of the humanity assumed. That a human person has a finite, created will is a truth that must hold good in any example of human nature, and the humanized Word is such an example. The reason we should want to say so is not just metaphysical. More than that, it is soteriological. Unless the human nature of the incarnate Word had its own willing, its own agency, the humanity of Christ could not enjoy that *tropos*, that mode of existing and acting, which replicated the Son's eternal mode of existing and acting. And without that particular *tropos*, the Son could not change the condition of our humanity from within in the way that is required by the foundational principle of Christian

[41] Andrew Louth, *St. John Damascene: Tradition and Originality in Byzantine Theology* (Oxford: Oxford University Press, 2002), p. 152.

soteriology, which states, in Gregory Nazianzen's words, "What has not been assumed has not been healed."[42]

Here Maximus could look to Rome for support. The Roman Church was already disposed towards Dyothelitism, thanks to its corporate memory of the Tome of Leo, the letter Pope Leo had sent to the Council of Chalcedon in which he spoke of the distinctive activity of the two natures of Christ after the union. Maximus' teaching was upheld in his lifetime by the Lateran Synod of 649, attended by many exiled Greek monks; one lone Greek bishop took his seat among a number of his Latin colleagues. At his trial Maximus would be asked, "Why do you love the Romans and hate the Greeks?"

Maximus' teaching was finally vindicated throughout the empire by the Sixth Ecumenical Council, 681, which, however, for diplomatic reasons, to save the court embarrassment, did not mention Maximus' name.

Maximian Ethics

Maximus took from Origen the notion that the Logos has multiple embodiments. Not that Origen, or Maximus, for that matter, was thinking of multiple incarnations in the way the Northern Irish literary historian, fantasy writer, and lay theologian C. S. Lewis did in the twentieth century. Lewis speculated that, if in other solar systems there are planets inhabited by rational species, the Word might conceivably—it is a possible hypothesis—become incarnate in many different worlds.[43] Origen and Maximus had in mind not a succession of "incarnations", *ensarkôseis*, but a diversity of modes of embodiment, *ensômatôsis*. Thus, the Logos is embodied in the *logoi* or intelligible natures of created things; he is embodied in the Holy Scriptures; he is embodied, or more correctly incarnated, in Jesus Christ, the supreme and unique embodiment; and moreover, in a theme especially stressed by Maximus, he, the Logos incarnate, is further embodied in the virtuous lives of the Church's faithful. Through the virtues, of which charity is both summit and the supreme integrating factor, Christ is formed in the Christian who thereby comes to live not only in the

---

[42] Gregory Nazianzen, *Letter* 101. Translation is the present author's own.

[43] Paul Brazier, "C. S. Lewis: The Question of Multiple Incarnations", *Heythrop Journal* 55 (2014): 391–408.

divine image, given everyone by creation, but in the divine likeness. The various "embodiments" are not, of course, called so in the same sense. Their relation is analogical, and the embodiment of the Logos in human virtues is not the least of the analogues in question.

That the Word is incarnate in the virtues is Maximus' chief gift to Christian ethics, his personal contribution to virtue theory.[44] It was, one might say, a predictable consequence of his Dyothelitism. The Incarnation was meant to bring about a communion between energies or activities, the energies or activities of divine nature and human nature. In the first instance, this took place in Jesus of Nazareth, to utterly stunning effect. But from there it flows out to others, when the grace of the Head redounds on the members of the Body, fruiting in the virtues as it does so. Thunberg noted how, for Maximus, "Christian perfection" is "a life which consists in the total sanctification of all the possibilities inherent in human nature".[45] But each and every virtue must be seen in the light of the Mediator's synthesizing work. The work of the Redeemer has as its goal—just as it took as its means—reciprocity between the natures of God and man. As Thunberg wrote, for Maximus "Christian perfection" was "a life which consists in the total sanctification of all the possibilities inherent in human nature".[46] Hence the virtues and hence the two wills of the Redeemer, Maximus' accompanying and inseparable gift to Christian dogmatics. In the words of Pope Benedict XVI, "Values that are justly defended today, such as tolerance, freedom, and dialogue ... can remain true values only if they have the point of reference that unites them and gives them true authenticity. This reference point is the synthesis between God and the cosmos, the figure of Christ in which we learn the truth about ourselves and thus where to rank all other values, because we discover their authentic meaning."[47]

[44] For Maximus on the virtues, see Thunberg, *Man and the Cosmos*, pp. 93–112; also, Blowers, *Maximus the Confessor*, pp. 254–83. A rare example of Orthodox interest in comparing Maximus with Thomas Aquinas on this issue is found in Andrew Louth, "Virtue Ethics: St. Maximos the Confessor and Aquinas compared", *Studies in Christian Ethics* 26 (2013): 351–63.

[45] Thunberg, *Man and the Cosmos*, p. 24.

[46] Ibid.

[47] Pope Benedict XVI, *Church Fathers and Teachers: From Saint Leo the Great to Peter Lombard* (San Francisco: Ignatius Press, 2010), p. 65. The quotation can also be found in the pope's discussion of St. Maximus in his General Audience, Wednesday, June 25, 2008, https://www.vatican.va/content/benedict-xvi/en/audiences/2008/documents/hf_ben-xvi_aud_20080625.html.

8

Inspired Compiler: Saint John Damascene

Saint John was born in Damascus at a date now impossible to ascertain with any exactitude. The principal Anglophone student of his life and thought, Andrew Louth, is unwilling to say more than that it must have been at some time in the second half of the seventh century—an inference from the approximate date of John's death, which is 750. That approximate death date is based on the fact that the iconoclast synod of Hieria, meeting in 754 in Constantinople, declared of John and two other leading or representative iconophile figures, figures the synod was in the process of anathematizing, "The Trinity has deposed them": a rather nasty way of saying they had already died.

John Damascene is the only one of the figures we have encountered in these patristic investigations (so far) who did not live in the Greek-speaking Roman Empire—the *Byzantine* Empire as by this period it is customary to call it in Western and, for that matter, in modern Greek and Russian scholarship. In the course of the lifetime of Maximus Confessor, the empire's eastern provinces were lost to Islamic rule, initially to the Umayyad Caliphate whose capital Damascus was. The new Arab rulers functioned at first as a military elite, superimposed on top of civil society. Already existing administrative and educational cadres were left in place. Thus, John's father was able to maintain his position as a senior civil servant in the tax office, a post he had inherited from his own father; John himself, after the kind of education based on grammar, rhetoric, and philosophy traditional among Greek-speaking Romans (so much is plain from his theological writings), was also able to gain a civil service job, no doubt of a more modest kind. It is at this point, however, when John is in early manhood, that such biographical sources as we have for his life begin to diverge, if not as dramatically as with Maximus, then at any rate to a significant extent.

From passing references in the eighth-century historian Theophanes the Chronicler and equally rare allusions in John's own writings, it can be inferred that he became a hieromonk, a monk in priest's orders, in a monastery in the environs of Jerusalem, and that he was accorded a ministry, probably as a preacher, in the Church of the Anastasis, better known in the West as the Church of the Holy Sepulchre. That is as far as Andrew Louth is willing to go.

A tenth-century or possibly eleventh-century Greek life of John, which claims to be translated from the Arabic, has struck some Continental European scholars as not implausible, apart from its miraculous elements (scholars nowadays have to present themselves as Deists). If that additional source is credited, it is possible to add some further elements. Those include John's education with an adopted brother, Cosmas, who accompanied him into the monastic life, and rivalled him in writing Greek Christian hymnography (this is Saint Cosmas of Maiuma, who often appears paired with John in iconography); the identity of their monastery, Saint Sabas or Mar Saba, in the gorge of the Jordan opposite Jerusalem; the occasion of John's resignation from the civil service—a mendacious message sent to the Caliph by the Byzantine emperor Leo III, whom John had annoyed by his theological defence of icons (the letter accused John of offering to give away State secrets about the fortifications of Damascus); and, finally, an account of how John started writing religious poetry, and, after a period when this was prohibited by his spiritual father, how he resumed writing, thanks to a timely dream where the said spiritual father was chastized by the Mother of God. Louth, sufficiently charmed by this narrative to lower his guard rather on the matter of historicity, compares John's experience to that of the late nineteenth-century English Jesuit Gerard Manley Hopkins, who also resumed versifying only when specifically commanded to do so by his religious superiors.

John's Writings

The high profile of the poetry in the Greek life is important because John would be remembered in the Byzantine tradition primarily as a liturgical poet and only secondly as a theologian. For the most part indeed he was not an original theological mind. Much of his material incorporates either verbatim or by paraphrase earlier patristic sources, thus constituting, to some extent at least, a kind of elaborate anthology or "florilegium"—literally, a bunch of flowers. Lionel Wickham, one of the last of the great line of scholarly Church of England parsons working on the Fathers, was moved to comment that "patristic theology may be said to aspire to the condition of the florilegium and in its last representative John of Damascus whose *de Fide Orthodoxa* [*On the Orthodox Faith*] is a mosaic of quotations, attains its goal."[1]

But of course matters are not quite as simple as that. Louth may wittily remark that John anticipates the post-Modern critic's notion of the "death of the author" because he was never really born as an author in the first place; but actually John's decisions in regard to his theological works, decisions about who to quote, and who to follow, on what subject, for how long, and in what way, are all properly authorial decisions that give a perfectly clear idea of where John stands on matters of doctrine. The "idea" thus arrived at might then be confirmed by reference to the texts of his surviving homilies and indeed of his liturgical hymns whenever these can safely be ascribed to him as author.

In his classic study *Saint John Damascene: Tradition and Originality in Byzantine Theology*, Louth implies he would really have liked to have followed Byzantine tradition and expounded John's poetry first before going on, by way of a sequel, to look into John's prose. Unfortunately, the lack of critical texts for the poetry prevents this, whereas for the prose there is a magnificent critical edition, a lifetime's work by a monk of the abbey of Scheyern, just north of Munich, Dom Bonifatius Kotter.[2] Since Kotter's death in 1987, collaborators have been taking the project further by bringing out editions of some minor works traditionally ascribed to John's authorship: a strange piece of hagiography, the "story of Barlaam and Josaphat", which seems to be a Christianized version of the life of the Buddha; a commentary

---

[1] Cited in Andrew Louth, *St. John Damascene: Tradition and Originality in Byzantine Theology* (Oxford: Oxford University Press, 2002), p. 228.

[2] Bonifatius Kotter, ed., *Die Schriften des Johannes von Damaskus, I–V* (Berlin: de Gruyter, 1969–1988).

on the letters of Saint Paul, much of it drawn from the homilies of the fourth-century archbishop of Constantinople John Chrysostom; and a florilegium of biblical and patristic citations relevant to ethics. Called the *Sacra Parallela*, this falls into three parts: on God as the end of human life, on human nature as the basic precondition of that life, and on the virtues and vices by which we orient our nature to or away from its goal in God—broadly speaking, then, an equivalent to the *Secunda Pars* of Aquinas' *Summa theologiae*, which begins with a question about God as the beatitude that gives human nature its fulfillment and otherwise continues after the fashion of the Damascene florilegium though doubtless in ignorance of it.[3]

Wickham, aware of what Western readers would expect on the subject, referred to John's best-known treatise as *De fide orthodoxa* (*On the Orthodox Faith*). But in the Greek, the work is actually called *Pêgê gnôseôs* (*The Fountain of Knowledge*), and the section—the set of chapters—translated into Latin in the eleventh century under the title *On the Orthodox Faith* is only one part, if the most important part, of the whole. Study of the manuscripts in which John's masterwork, the *Fountain of Knowledge*, has come down to us in the original Greek indicates that John produced two editions, the second of which he meant to be a rearrangement of the first. In a dedicatory letter to Cosmas of Maiuma, which Louth, following Kotter, believes to have been written for the second edition, John explains that his work will fall into three parts. The three parts can be summed up as logic, heresy, and orthodoxy.

So what are they about? That question is easy to answer in broad terms. In the first part, the *Dialectica*, John will set out the philosophical tools the theologian needs so as to debunk heresy and establish orthodoxy. In the second part, *On Heresies*, he will outline the principal heresies that have afflicted the Church in her history, ending with those most widespread in his own day (the last to be treated is Islam). In the third part, *The Exact Exposition of the Orthodox Faith*, he will expound that faith for members of the Great Church, the Church that accepted the six ecumenical councils as the criteria of

---

[3] Two Munich-based editors, Robert Volk and Tobias Thum, were joined for these further works by José Declerck of Ghent, in Belgium: *Die Schriften des Johannes von Damaskus, VI–VIII* (Berlin: de Gruyter, 2006–2019).

orthodoxy. Set up by itself in a Latin translation and divided, at some point in the twelfth century, into four distinct books, mediaeval and later theologians in the West will know *The Exact Exposition of the Orthodox Faith* as *De fide orthodoxa*, the title given it by the translator Burgundio of Pisa.

From the manuscript tradition, however, it can be seen that all copies except one of the *Fountain of Knowledge* consist only of the *Dialectica* and the *Exact Exposition* (so logic plus dogmatic theology), a kind of book certainly known in John's day since an anonymous work of his period, with precisely that structure, has been found in the Bodleian Library at Oxford. Hence the conviction of Byzantinists that John's dedicatory letter, introducing a tripartite work—logic, heresy, and orthodoxy—was meant for a second edition in which John incorporated his notes on a variety of heresies, an edition not completed by his death, which explains why so few copies seem to have been made.

The assumption is, then, that John revised his work, adding the section on heresies because he had a new audience for whom heresiology was crucial. Who might they have been? Perhaps monastic teachers or catechists rather than simply students of theology: people who would need to know what could go wrong with the entire process of teaching others logic and dogmatics.

Logic

I now look in turn at each of the three parts of the *Fountain of Knowledge*, in what we are calling its "second edition". Taking my cue from Louth (and in dependence on his study), I include where it seems worth doing so side references to Damascene's other more minor theological writings. We begin, then, with logic. All Church students in the modern Catholic tradition, conveniently defined as starting with the Council of Trent, have to study philosophy before they begin theology. At least with future priests this tends to be the part of the course they most resent, on the ground that its relevance to what they will be doing and saying after ordination is unclear to them.

One main reason for doing philosophy before theology is to sharpen the mind; the other chief reason is to equip the student with concepts that can helpfully be deployed theologically in teaching the faith. To what extent Church institutions succeed nowadays in this latter respect may not unreasonably be questioned. That is because the secular context of such studies, a radical philosophical pluralism where people easily talk past each other rather than to each other, makes modern philosophy, when globally surveyed, inherently problematic. But in his situation John is very clear, and very plain. What needs to be studied under the heading "logic" are the basic ontological concepts drawn upon by the Fathers in setting forth their Trinitarian and Christological doctrine: everything from essence or nature to activity and will.

John was himself drawing on logical handbooks that aimed to set out such key philosophical concepts. These had become common in Church use in the course of the fifth, sixth, and seventh centuries, especially in the context of debates with Monophysites, and subsequently with Monothelites as well. There was, however, one key concept where the handbooks could not find much in their usual sources, which were Aristotle's *Categories* and the *Isagogê* or "Introduction" (to *Categories*) of the Neoplatonist philosopher Porphyry. As a consequence, philosophy teachers in the Church were obliged to turn to Christian writers.

In John's day the idea of *hypostasis* was deemed the great breakthrough concept of Christian philosophy. That concept was unknown in its developed form to any of the classical philosophical schools. It was a concept that enabled the same discourse to be applied consistently to both Christology and the theology of the Triune God.[4] In Louth's words, "Because of the key position that *hypostasis* occupied in theological discourse, it came to be conceded a key role in matters ontological", but here "John and the tradition he inherited were obliged to look to the Fathers", for nothing else would serve.[5]

To state John's key concept in its fullest version—this would draw on the *Exact Exposition* as well as the *Dialectica*—is something John does not explicitly do, but twentieth-century Greek Orthodox theology will do it for him. "Hypostasis" is the concrete embodiment of being, in a form of existence endowed with individually distinctive

[4] Louth, *St. John Damascene*, pp. 47–53.
[5] Ibid., p. 48.

properties, where nature is made to be a subject, made to be a unique person.[6] In modern Greek Christian thought, this notion is central not only to Trinitarian theology and Christology but to theological anthropology as well.

Heresy

Next, heresy. John's work as a heresiologist combines compilation work on the one hand with original reportage on the other—the latter in regard to heresies he could encounter in the Caliphate in his own day. The *Heresies* section of *The Fountain of Knowledge* looks at one hundred heresies in all, some dealt with so briefly that the prose becomes that of a catalogue; but it was important to John that his list be, so far as possible, comprehensive and complete—hence the symbolic number of one hundred chapters. The first eighty chapters, dealing with ancient heresies, mostly long extinct, summarise the accounts of the fourth-century bishop Epiphanius of Salamis, whose book *Panarion* or "The Medicine Chest" (Epiphanius had compared the heresies to poisonous beasts—one needs a supply of antidotes) was the first attempt to review between two covers all the errors the early patristic Church had faced.[7] In the following chapters, John brought Epiphanius up to date by adding heresies that had appeared in the fifth century and thereafter. Some of these are well known to historians of doctrine, like Nestorianism. Others are too bizarre or at least marginal to make an appearance on the agenda of any council; examples might be the Heliotropites, who, John says, believed sunflowers to be possessed of occult properties, and the Agonyklitai, who opposed all kneeling for prayer. Some of the latter, however, are occasionally met with in modern Roman Catholicism.

---

[6] According to Hans Urs von Balthasar, "The notion of existing 'without confusion' (*asunchutos*) will allow the Greek genius for clarity, precisely in this kind of reflection, to achieve a final triumph, while the notion of 'individual being' (hypostasis), as the contribution of Christian theology, will become, in its intellectually highest form, the necessary condition of that triumph. In the sphere of a Christian philosophy of person and existence, the clarity of the Greek grasp of the world of being was to find its final fulfilment." Hans Urs von Balthasar, *Cosmic Liturgy: The Universe according to Maximus the Confessor* (San Francisco: Ignatius Press, 2003), p. 65.

[7] Epiphanius of Salamis, *The Panarion*, trans. Frank Williams, 2 vols. (Leiden: Brill, 1987–1993).

The three heresies that John deals with at greatest length occupy the last three chapters of the work: Manichaenism, rather brief, but John also produced as a separate treatise a dialogue with a Manichee that is more substantial; Messalianism, a full account, and the only one of these three topics that would strike a modern student of world religions as genuinely a Christian deviation; and lastly Islam—again, this is a meaty chapter, though John also wrote a separate dialogue with a Muslim to parallel his dialogue with a Manichee.[8]

The dialogue with a Manichee enabled John to discuss such issues as the ultimate principle of reality, which he describes as one but more specifically triune: the nature of evil, the problem of free will and determinism, and the role of Providence in human affairs. It has been suggested that this is an early work, written in Damascus, and that John uses the comments of the Manichee in order to present what is really a coded case to Muslims, answering typically Muslim objections to Christian belief and intervening in philosophical disputes already lively among Muslim thinkers themselves.[9]

The treatment of Messalianism, a fourth-century movement, mainly monastic, already known to Epiphanius, may also be code— since proper Messalians, who regarded spiritual experience as far more important than continuing participation in the sacraments, had more or less died out by John's day. Louth takes the view that John was actually addressing a persistent crypto-Messalian tendency in the Byzantine Church that would find expression in, for instance, the eleventh-century figure Symeon the New Theologian—acclaimed by his disciples as the new Nazianzen for his wonderful poetry, but also inclined, unlike Nazianzen, to downplay the sacramental rites vis-à-vis the free play of the Holy Spirit.[10] Homilies passed down under the name "Macarius" express a Messalian-type desire for direct experience of the Spirit's "sweetness", which attracted early Christians (including Gregory of Nyssa),[11] and continued to be appreciated by later readers, from the Byzantine archbishop Gregory Palamas to John Wesley, the founder of Methodism.

[8] Daniel J. Sahas, ed., *John of Damascus on Islam: The Heresy of the "Ishmaelites"* (Leiden: Brill, 1972).

[9] Louth, *St. John Damascene*, p. 71.

[10] Ibid., pp. 75–76.

[11] Columba Stewart, *"Working the Earth of the Heart": The Messalian Controversy in History, Texts and Language to AD 451* (Oxford: Oxford University Press, 1991).

That leaves Islam. These are the earliest discussion of Islam by a Christian theologian; there is no Epiphanius to come to John's aid here.[12] What is John going to say about Islam, given the obvious delicacy of his position as a Christian monk in an Islamic polity? He is far less reticent and courteous than, say, Pope Benedict XVI in the latter's nevertheless controversial 2006 Regensburg address "Faith, Reason and the University: Memories and Reflections".[13] In the closing chapter of *Heresies*, John accords a low credibility value to the revelations made to Muhammad. Indeed, he calls them "laughable": revelations made to someone asleep must inevitably be suspect.

More widely, John appears to be answering a two-pronged Muslim critique of Christianity. One prong is well known from the Koran: Christians "associate" Christ with God, blasphemously compromising the uniqueness of God by treating Christ as divine. And yet, John points out, in the Koran Christ is called a word of God, expressive of God's breath or spirit—and surely, then, to deny the divinity of Christ is to deny the divinity of God's word and his breath or spirit. It sounds rather like the argument Athanasius had used against the Arians: Could God ever be without his Word or his Spirit?

The other prong in the two-pronged critique concerns Christians worshipping the Cross, an objection found not in the Koran but in the *hadith*, the oral traditions about Muhammad and his teaching. John replies that Christian veneration of the Cross makes more sense than Muslim veneration of the black stone contained in the Kaaba, the centrepiece of the Grand Mosque at Mecca. In the opinion of modern Western students, the stone belongs to pre-Islamic paganism when the Kaaba contained a collection of idols of the local Meccan gods. According to Muslim tradition, it fell from heaven as a guide to Adam and Eve where to build an altar. It may be a meteorite or a "pseudo-meteorite"—a recognised geological category.

In the *Dispute between a Saracen and a Christian*, John's dialogue text, expanding what he has to say in *Heresies*, he is once again acting

---

[12] Unsurprisingly, this topic has aroused much recent interest; see Daniel J. Janosik, *John of Damascus: First Apologist to the Muslims* (Eugene, OR: Pickwick, 2016); Peter Schadler, *John of Damascus and Islam: Christian Heresiology and the Intellectual Background to Earliest Christian-Muslim Relations* (Leiden: Brill, 2017).

[13] For the text of the lecture and commentary, see James V. Schall, *The Regensburg Lecture* (South Bend, IN: St. Augustine's Press, 2007).

the apologist, notably on the key issue as to whether incarnation is possible for a transcendent God. But he is also seeking to intervene in intra-Muslim debates, as he had in the dialogue with a Manichee if the "coded" interpretation of that text be correct. Here he argues for a distinction between God's positive will and God's permissive will. One group of Muslim thinkers was inclined to say that human persons have complete power over their own actions, some even going so far as to deny to God any foreknowledge of what those actions might be; other Muslim thinkers claimed that God is the cause of everything, both good and evil. The existence of the latter group throws some light on how in 2019 the Grand Imam of Al-Azhar could have signed, with Pope Francis, the Abu Dhabi declaration on God's willing a plurality of religions, including (by the standards of Islam) highly erroneous ones.[14]

Orthodoxy

I turn finally to what John has to say about Orthodoxy in *The Exact Exposition of the Orthodox Faith*, which occupies the remainder of *The Fountain of Knowledge*. It was above all through the *De fide orthodoxa* that a developed understanding of the Greek Fathers entered the mainstream of Latin Christianity.

As the Latins realised by dividing *De fide orthodoxa* into four books, its one hundred chapters have essentially four topics: God; creation (with mankind at its heart); the Incarnation or the incarnate dispensation, that is, the economy; and lastly a ragbag of topics that, on one view, have it in common that all of them are practices by which Christians differed from their neighbours, whether Muslims or Jews. Alternatively, John may simply have been following the order of the Creed, which also ends, after naming the Holy Spirit, in what looks like another ragbag of assorted issues—although in the case of the Creed, we are probably meant to take the concluding set of *credenda*,

[14] Pope Francis and the Grand Imam of Al-Azhar Ahmad Al-Tayyeb, *Document on Human Fraternity for World Peace and Living Together* (February 4, 2019), https://www.vatican.va /content/francesco/en/travels/2019/outside/documents/papa-francesco_20190204 _documento-fratellanza-umana.html.

articles to be believed, as listing outcomes of the Spirit's mission—from the Church to the life everlasting.

John's theology of God one and three makes use of a number of his predecessors, including Gregory Nazianzen, Cyril of Alexandria, and Denys; but he is especially indebted to Gregory of Nyssa in the latter's most wide-ranging doctrinal treatise, the *Great Catechism* or *Great Catechetical Oration*—a text much too demanding for catechumens and intended, surely, for their teachers, the catechists. Following Nyssen means that John will emphasise certain themes: the witness of creation that a Deity exists; the incomprehensibility of God; the choice dictated by God's goodness whereby nonetheless God chose to make himself known in history, in the Incarnation; how God is never without his Word and his Spirit, by whom he communicates that knowledge of himself—in creation, in the prophets, and above all in the sending of his Son.

On the divine incomprehensibility, and the need it creates for close attention to the language in which we attempt God description, John is able to accept what Gregory of Nyssa has to say about the usefulness of negative adjectives such as "without beginning" as well as adjectives expressing God's transcendent causality like "all-creative", and to add to this repertoire of "God-talk" the distinctive Dionysian language of God's "hyper" status, what we might call God's "beyondness". Denys had been very fond of saying God is "beyond" being, "beyond" the good, "beyond" fullness. On naming God, John concludes that "all we can affirm concerning God does not show forth God's nature but only the qualities of his nature", the properties or attributes of that nature.[15] He will, however, go on to admit a major exception. Like Thomas, John considers that, in his own words, the "most proper of all names given to God is 'He that is' as He Himself said in answer to Moses on the mountain: 'Say to the sons of Israel, He that is has sent me'. For He keeps all being in His own embrace, like a sea of essence infinite and unseen." John immediately adds: "Or as the holy Dionysius [i.e., Denys] says, 'He that is good', for one cannot say of God that He has being in the

---

[15] John of Damascus, *On the Orthodox Faith* I, 4, trans. E. W. Watson and L. Pullan, in *Nicene and Post-Nicene Fathers* [*NPNF*], 2nd series, vol. 9, ed. Philip Schaff and Henry Wace (Buffalo, NY: Christian Literature Publishing, 1899). Citations of *On the Orthodox Faith* are from this translation.

first place and goodness in the second."[16] Thomas will pick up these statements in his own treatise on the divine names in the "First Part" of the *Summa theologiae*.

Two major reasons why John may have been especially attracted to Gregory's *Great Catechetical Oration* are, firstly, its stress on the unity of God,[17] and, secondly, its framing of a theology of the second and third divine hypostases in the Old Testament language of "word" and "breath",[18] which, long after Gregory's time, would also be found, as already mentioned under *Heresies*, in the Koran. Both these emphases could be regarded as gestures towards potential Jewish and Muslim readers. It is notable that John omits a passage in the *Oration* where Gregory called Trinitarianism a middle way between pure monotheism and sheer polytheism, a typical argument of the Cappadocians. That would not have gone down so well among those constituencies, jealous defenders as they were of the absolute oneness of God.

Importantly for the history of doctrine, John is the first to apply to the relations of the Trinitarian Persons the set of adverbs applied at Chalcedon to the union of the natures in the single Person of Christ. The Trinitarian Persons are united without confusion but also without any possibility of separation. As he writes, "The subsistences dwell and are established firmly in one another for they are inseparable and cannot part from one another but keep to their separate course within one another, without coalescing or mingling, but cleaving [adhering] to one another. For the Son is in the Father and the Spirit: and the Spirit in the Father and the Son: and the Father in the Son and the Spirit, but there is no coalescence or commingling or confusion."[19] In his favourite metaphor for such inseparable yet unconfused union, they "rest" or "abide" in one another.[20] John's suggestion that the Spirit, on his proceeding from the Father, "rests" on the Son (a claim for which there were already hints in the Cappadocian Fathers[21]) was taken by some later Byzantine theologians,

---

[16] Ibid., I, 12.

[17] Ibid., I, 5.

[18] Ibid., I, 6–7.

[19] Ibid., I, 14.

[20] Ibid.

[21] Boris Bobrinskoy, "Le repos de l'Esprit sur le Fils chez les Cappadociens", in *La Pensée orthodoxe: Travaux de Institut de théologie orthodoxe Saint-Serge* 4 (Lausanne: L'Âge d'homme, 1987), pp. 24–39.

as well as some modern Orthodox, to be a sort of halfway house to the Western doctrine of the procession of the Spirit from or through the Son.

John of Damascus is also the first Church Doctor to apply to the Trinitarian Persons the term *perichôrêsis*, or "interpenetration". Earlier Fathers like Athanasius and Cyril had got hold of the idea, but not the word. The word, when used earlier, notably by Maximus, was reserved for the relations between the divine and human natures in the Christ of the economy. In Andrew Louth's explanation,

> Now, with John ... the term is transferred [from the economy] to the realm of *theologia* [the theology]. It describes something that is uniquely true of the uncreated reality of the Godhead, where the distinction of *hypostaseis* [hypostases] does not detract from the unity of the Godhead: the *hypostaseis* [hypostases] can be discerned to be distinct in their several "modes of existence", but in reality they are wholly at one, and that unity between the *hypostaseis* [hypostases] is manifest in their interpenetration or coinherence, *perichôrêsis*.[22]

That notion of "mode of existence"—the hypostasis as personal subsistence, subsistence of a unique kind, an idea that emerges with the Cappadocians, and is taken further by Maximus—will be vital also for John's Christology. The divine Word or Son can become hominized, can become incarnate, because the same filial "mode of existence" he enjoys eternally as God can be replicated, re-created in time, by application to an instance of human nature in the womb of his Mother.

But like the Western Scholastics Peter Lombard and Thomas Aquinas, John does not wish to turn to the topic of Christology until he has spoken about the creation, both invisible (in the angels and demons) and visible (in the physical cosmos). Here he relies heavily on Basil and Gregory of Nyssa in their writing on the six-day work of creation, as well as Gregory's *On the Making of Man* and Nemesius' *On Human Nature*. As with these authors, John makes a synthesis of Greek philosophy and what in his day passed for natural science, seen in the light of the creation narratives in the Book of Genesis. He treats man as the mediator between the visible and

---

[22] Louth, *St. John Damascene*, p. 113.

invisible realms, "a sort of second microcosm set within the great world, surveying the visible creation and initiated into the mysteries of the realm of thought", which might be an echo of the cosmology of Saint Maximus, or otherwise of his source for "microcosm" thinking, Bishop Nemesius.[23]

The Christological section of *On the Orthodox Faith* calls for amplification from the treatises John wrote for Nestorians, Monophysites, and Monothelites—distinct treatises far fuller than the short accounts in the *Heresies* section of *The Fountain of Knowledge*. He is writing as someone who has profited from, and integrated into his thinking, the texts of the earlier Fathers and, not least, the six ecumenical councils held by his time, just prior as it was to the seventh and last of the ecumenical councils of the patristic epoch: Nicaea II, 787, the "icon" council, to which, as we shall see in a moment, he had a major contribution to make. We register, for instance, John's debt to Cyril when he writes that "the divine Word was not made one with flesh that had an independent pre-existence, but taking up His abode in the womb of the Holy Virgin, He unreservedly in His own subsistence [hypostasis] took upon Himself the first-fruits of man's compound [i.e., body-soul] nature, Himself, the Word, having become a subsistence in the flesh."[24] And he echoes the Council of Chalcedon when he writes that it was "without confusion or change or division" that the Word became one in subsistence with the flesh", insisting against the Monophysites that there was no "compound nature ... produced out of the two"; rather, Christ "consists of two natures and exists in two natures".[25] He affirms the communication of idioms as a consequence of not only the singleness of the hypostasis but the "inter-penetration", *perichôrêsis*, of the two natures, using that very term and thereby reflecting the influence of Maximus the Confessor.[26] That influence, and the teaching of the Sixth Ecumenical Council that Maximus inspired, is most apparent when John says of Christ that "He has, corresponding to the two natures, the two sets of natural qualities belonging to the two natures": "two

---

[23] John of Damascus, *On the Orthodox Faith* II, 12.
[24] Ibid., III, 2.
[25] Ibid., III, 3.
[26] Ibid., III, 4–5.

natural volitions, one divine and one human, two natural energies, one divine and one human, two natural free wills, one divine and one human, and two kinds of wisdom and knowledge, one divine and one human. For being of like essence with God and the Father, he wills and energizes freely as God, and being also of like essence with us He likewise wills and energizes freely as man."[27] There is an echo of the Tome of Leo the Great, a papal letter read out at Chalcedon, when he remarks that Christ "wills and energizes in either form in close communion with the other", since it "is one and the same person who wills and energizes naturally in both natures";[28] Leo's notion of the two "forms" of the incarnate Word working always in communion with each other gives John the key to how to understand Denys' phrase about the "novel theandric [divine-human] energy" in Jesus Christ—a claim which could otherwise be held to favour "Monoenergism", a halfway house to Monophysitism.

Perhaps the most important theme in John Damascene's Christology is one already mentioned while looking at his theology of the Trinity. Most fully developed in *On the Jacobites*, his treatise on Monophysitism,[29] the theme goes like this: in the Incarnation, the second Trinitarian Person's property of divine Sonship must really be preserved when the Word begins to exist in human nature because in Jesus Christ the "filial mode of existence is maintained".[30] The filial manner of being that is his as the eternal Son is reproduced in his humanity, so there is no need to worry that the unity of Christ will be imperilled by saying that, after the union, he is "in" two natures (and not just "from" them, Cyril's preferred usage). That was John's message to Monophysites. Louth thinks that John was more indulgent with Monophysites than with Monothelites, despite the fact that most Chalcedonian Christians would regard Monothelitism as less substantial an error. According to Louth, for John, Monophysites were basically just confused thinkers, whereas Monothelites, by denying that there was in any sense a specifically human will in Jesus Christ, undermined all understanding of the whole economy

[27] Ibid., III, 13.
[28] Ibid., III, 14.
[29] The nickname "Jacobites" refers to James or Jacob of Serugh, the first Monophysite bishop actively to go around consecrating alternative bishops for sees held by Diophysites.
[30] Cited in Louth, *St. John Damascene*, p. 162.

of salvation. Still, we can hardly help noticing that in Book III of *On the Orthodox Faith* John calls Dioscorus of Alexandria and Severus of Antioch, the two founders of Monophysitism, "God-accursed"— even if he balances things by speaking of Nestorius, their diametrical opposite in matters Christological, as "hated of God". There was nothing mealymouthed about doctrinal controversy in the age of the Fathers.

Perhaps that will suffice for John Damascene's account of the being of the Word incarnate. To find out what John thought of the saving work of Jesus Christ—as distinct from the ontological composition of the Saviour—one would have to look more to his sermons and liturgical poetry, with all the problems the latter raises for establishing authorship and texts. There is, however, a succinct statement of what Christ has achieved not long after the opening of Book IV of *On the Orthodox Faith*, a book which, when the Latins subdivided the contents of the *Exact Exposition of the Orthodox Faith*, begins with the condition of Christ after the Resurrection. Here John states for us the purpose of the economy of the Son. Everything he did and underwent was so that

> through Himself and in Himself He might renew that which was made after His image and likeness, and might teach us, too, the conduct of a virtuous life, making through Himself the way there easy for us, and might by the communion of life deliver us from corruption, becoming Himself the firstfruits of our resurrection, and might renovate the useless and worn vessel [of our old humanity] calling us to the kingdom of God that He might redeem us from the tyranny of the devil, and might strengthen and teach us how to overthrow the tyrant through patience and humility.[31]

Here we can catch echoes of, among others, Irenaeus and Athanasius, as well as the ascetical tradition, with its emphasis on acquiring the virtues in spiritual warfare, as exemplified in Maximus. In Book IV, John ties together in this way some loose ends of his Christology, what I called (rather irreverently) the "ragbag" of assorted topics that concludes *On the Orthodox Faith* and runs from faith and

[31] John of Damascus, *On the Orthodox Faith* IV, 4.

Baptism to the coming of the Antichrist and the General Resurrection. Halfway through, in his chapter on the Holy Eucharist, "Concerning the Holy and Immaculate Mysteries of the Lord", he provides a further description of the work of Christ as the context for this sacrament. He adds to what he already said on the work of Christ some mention of *theôsis*, adoptive divine filiation, and counterposing to our birth from Adam, which makes us "heirs of the curse and corruption", our second birth, which makes us "heirs of His [Christ's] incorruption and blessing and glory".[32]

Book IV's most intriguing chapter is surely that on icons.[33] John will be known to Byzantine posterity, along with Germanus of Constantinople, as the first of the iconophile Doctors. It is, in effect, a condensation of the three treatises he wrote in defence of the holy icons that were exceptionally influential.[34] John was aware of the wave of iconoclasm breaking over the Byzantine Empire in the last two decades of his life, and aware too, in the contrast he knew at firsthand between Christian iconophilia and Jewish and Islamic aniconicism, that something essential to the essence of Christianity was at stake.

For John, the defence of images was necessary to the truth of the Incarnation. In the Old Testament, God had not appeared as a man among men, so a ban on images was appropriate then, since "who can make an imitation of the invisible, incorporeal, uncircumscribed, formless God?"[35] Jewish revulsion from pagan statues that claimed to represent gods and goddesses was fully warranted. But now, with the Incarnation, things are different—now icons are made of the Incarnate One, and "we fall down and worship not the material but that which is imaged", the honour passing in words of Saint Basil, from the image to the archetype. The making and venerating of images is for John, as he explains, "an unwritten tradition, just as is also the worshipping towards the East and the worship of the Cross, and [he adds, rather vaguely], very many other similar things".[36]

---

[32] Ibid., IV, 14.

[33] Ibid., IV, 16.

[34] John of Damascus, *Three Treatises on the Divine Images*, trans. Andrew Louth (Crestwood, NY: St. Vladimir's Seminary Press, 2013).

[35] John of Damascus, *On the Orthodox Faith* IV, 16.

[36] Ibid.

For Andrew Louth, interpreting John's central insight in the theology of the icon, the Incarnation itself implies that different levels of reality are interrelated through imaging each other, such that truths otherwise unavailable are communicated by signs. By gesturing from one realm to another, visible to invisible, material to spiritual, signs are what bridge the gaps. In becoming incarnate the Word entered fully that realm of signs. The signs—and therefore the icons—in Louth's words, "bridged the border between the uncreated and the created, thus opening up to men and women the destiny of deification—thereby restoring to human kind the role of microcosm, bond of the cosmos, that they have failed to fulfil".[37] The cult of icons may be "one of the most distinctive aspects of Eastern spirituality, up to the present day", yet it constitutes "a form of cult which belongs simply to the Christian faith, to the faith in that God who became flesh and was made visible".[38]

---

[37] Louth, *St. John Damascene*, p. 218.

[38] Pope Benedict XVI, *Church Fathers and Teachers: From Saint Leo the Great to Peter Lombard* (San Francisco: Ignatius Press, 2010), pp. 101–2.

9

Patron of Apologists: Tertullian

It is time now to move to the other principal cultural tradition of
the Fathers: to the world of the Western Mediterranean, where men
used the Latin tongue. We begin in what was for the earliest Christian centuries the second city of the West: Carthage. Indeed, "there
are grounds for regarding that city as the cradle of a Latin-speaking
Christianity in the West rather than Rome, where Christians worshipped in Greek until at least the third century."[1]

Tertullian was born around the year 155 into a pagan family at
this great metropolis of North Africa, at that time a constituent part
of the Roman Empire. Twentieth-century scholarship called into
question the claims made by fourth-century sources, specifically Saint
Jerome and the Church historian Eusebius, to the effect that Tertullian was the son of a high-ranking military officer[2] and, after his Baptism, a presbyter of the Catholic Church (he himself seems to imply
he belonged among the laity). Tertullian was well informed about
ancient philosophy, Roman jurisprudence, and contemporary medicine. On the basis of his legal knowledge, which he invokes at times
for theological purposes, he has often been regarded as a professional
jurist. But does his knowledge go beyond that to be expected of an
educated Roman citizen of his epoch?[3]

At some point after the year 207, Tertullian became involved with
the so-called New Prophecy, the work of a trio of charismatics in
Asia Minor who claimed that, in ecstasy, they were speaking with

---

[1] Christopher Page, *The Christian West and Its Singers: The First Thousand Years* (London and
New Haven, CT: Yale University Press, 2010), pp. 16–17.

[2] The rank in question does not appear to have existed in the Roman army.

[3] For these issues, see T. D. Barnes, *Tertullian: A Historical and Literary Study* (Oxford: Clarendon Press, 1971).

the voice of the Holy Spirit, calling the Church back to a new purity in morals and ascetical living.[4] Possibly their movement was fanatical rather than heretical, yet it became schismatical. It has generally been held that Tertullian indeed became a "Montanist", as followers of the New Prophecy were called. No doubt this is why he was never numbered among the canonized Church Fathers. Unquestionably he became more acerbic in his criticisms of the moral and spiritual level of the average Catholic Christians of his time, and of the policies of the bishops in matters of sacramental discipline. But a widespread view today is that his teaching would never have been as influential as it was on the great theologian-martyr of the Church in North Africa in the following generation, Saint Cyprian, had Tertullian in fact died as a schismatic, rather than a member of the Great Church.[5] Cyprian was devastating on the topic of schismatics; yet, if we can trust Saint Jerome's account, he called Tertullian his "master".[6] A late twentieth-century study entitled quite specifically *Tertullian and the Church* declares roundly, indeed, "Tertullian was no schismatic. Reports of a breach with the Catholic church have been exaggerated."[7]

So it seems we know less about Tertullian than we thought we did—unless of course the pendulum of scholarship swings back again. Meanwhile, however, Tertullian has left an enormous corpus of writings that justify the titles he has been given: father of Latin Christian literature and the first theologian of the West.

If we may credit the view of the French Jesuit patrologist and theologian Jean Daniélou, Tertullian was writing against the background of a Latin-speaking Christianity that, not least in Africa, was still profoundly Jewish in its self-expression. The way it presented itself was imagistic, rather than argumentative; it was indebted, in fact, to the often exotic inter-Testamental literature and to a rabbinic-style exegesis whose use of Old Testament texts was remarkably free.

---

[4] Pierre de Labriolle, *Les sources de l'histoire du Montanisme* (Fribourg: Librairie de l'Université—Paris: Leroux, 1913); Pierre de Labriolle, *La Crise montaniste* (Paris: Leroux, 1913).

[5] Barnes goes so far as to say that "Tertullian helped to rescue the catholic church from theological heresy precisely because he was a Montanist" (Barnes, *Tertullian*, p. 142); Tertullian's conviction that he was led by the Holy Spirit energized his defence of the doctrine of the Trinity.

[6] Jerome, *On Famous Men* 53, 3.

[7] David Rankin, *Tertullian and the Church* (Cambridge: Cambridge University Press, 1995), p. 3. Rankin marshals the evidence that supports his claim at pp. 27–51.

The technical term is "midrashic". "Midrash" paraphrased the biblical text, saw it as prophesying things happening or about to happen in the present day, and treated it as having deeper—possibly mystical, certainly imaginative—meanings than appeared on the surface. Tertullian's aims, as Daniélou sees them, were ambitious. "In the first place, he wanted to disassociate the Christian message from its Jewish trappings in order to give it a truly Latin expression. Secondly, he was anxious to overcome the criticism common among pagans that Christian faith was unacceptable because of the mythical elements contained in the Judaeo-Christian expression of Christianity."[8] That might alert us to the consequent likelihood that Tertullian will specialize in two areas of theology as defined by early modern Western Catholicism: apologetics and dogmatics.

Tertullian's Writings

Though not everything has survived, and some of the minor treatises are of marginal relevance to Christian theology and spirituality at large, the work is impressive. Tertullian wrote with enormous verve, making good use of humor and, especially, paradox that might remind the modern Anglophone reader of G. K. Chesterton. If you are wondering whether, given his associations with the—admittedly or at any rate arguably heterodox—New Prophecy, Tertullian should be included among the Latin Fathers at all, it may be reassuring to hear that out of thirty-three extant treatises, possibly as few as five are explicitly Montanist—though those five include one of the most important, *Against Praxeas*, Tertullian's principal writing on the Holy Trinity, a text that counts as a major source for the early Christian doctrine of God. Tertullian's quarrel with the Catholic Church was "fought only on the narrow front of penitential discipline",[9] on

---

[8] Jean Daniélou, *The Origins of Latin Christianity*, vol. 3 of *A History of Early Christian Doctrine before Nicaea* (London: Darton, Longman and Todd, 1977), p. 139. Daniélou admits, however, that Tertullian was not entirely consistent in his rejection of the Jewish apocrypha, admitting some on the ground of what he considered their antiquity, or (in the case of First Enoch) because they had received a mention in acknowledged Scripture (the Letter of Jude). Ibid., pp. 161–76.

[9] Rankin, *Tertullian and the Church*, p. 29.

which issue he considered himself qualified to criticize the bishops by reference to Christian prophecy (or in his own term, "ecstasy").[10] According to David Rankin,

> Nowhere, not even when he repudiates particular Catholic bishops— as he does on occasion—as being unworthy pastors of the people of God (despite, or perhaps because of, what one commentator calls his "grand respect for the hierarchy") does he actually repudiate or even challenge the notion of a Catholic hierarchy as such. Indeed, there are a number of passages from his later works—his "Montanist" period—which will support a contention contrary to that traditionally adopted; namely, that Tertullian never left the Catholic church, but rather continued his fight for a more vigorous and disciplined Christian discipleship from within the Catholic church itself; and further, that the so-called "Psychici", whom Tertullian so maligns, are not to be identified with the Catholic church and its hierarchy in toto, but rather with a particular element within that church.[11]

Not a few orthodox Roman Catholics in the early twenty-first century will have considerable sympathy for Tertullian on this point. The words of a Reformed theologian will resonate with them: "Tertullian's disagreement in his later period is not with the church as such—for he retains throughout a 'high' ecclesiology—but rather with those who threaten her dignity and integrity."[12]

Tertullian's Apologetics

Tertullian was especially remembered in the West as an apologist, someone arguing for the truth of the Christian religion. If he were a canonized saint, instead of a figure with a question mark against his

[10] Tertullian, *Against Marcion* IV, 22, 2. Unfortunately, his treatise *De ecstasi* has not survived, or we should be better informed as to how he understood this more intense or concentrated expression of the *sensus fidei*.

[11] Rankin, *Tertullian and the Church*, p. 28, with an internal citation of Paul Monceaux, *Histoire littéraire de l'Afrique chrétienne depuis les origines jusqu'à l'invasion arabe* (Paris: Ernest Leroux, 1901–1923), 1:394.

[12] Rankin, *Tertullian and the Church*, p. 85. "It is not that the church should be or could be holy; it is holy. It is already, in the present-time, the virgin Bride of Christ. It can seek only to conform to its own inherent nature." Ibid., p. 114.

name, he might well be regarded as the patron of apologetics, a discipline especially important in ancient Christianity, vis-à-vis pagans and Jews, and subsequently, in the wake of the eighteenth-century Enlightenment, vis-à-vis rationalists or, more generally, "Post-Christians". In Catholicism, the first half of the twentieth century was especially rich in apologetics (Chesterton's name could well be mentioned once again here); but for a variety of reasons the discipline became marginalized after the Second Vatican Council until a revival took place, beginning in the United States, in the pontificate of John Paul II.

Thus, two of Tertullian's earliest treatises, written before 200, are *The Apology*—an open letter addressed to "the magistrates of the Roman empire", with a self-explanatory title—and *On the Testimony of the Soul*, which provides arguments for the existence of one God. Rather later come *Against Marcion*, *Against the Jews*, and *Against the Valentinians*. This trio, seeking to defend against a variety of adversaries the entirety of the saving revelation, Old and New Testament together, moves in much the same ambience as Saint Irenaeus had done when writing *Against the Heresies*.[13] Accordingly, all three can be qualified as apologetic works. Finally, Tertullian's *On the Prescription of Heretics*, which seeks to de-legitimise Christian heretics in advance by appealing to the way the Great Church is the moral owner of the Scriptures, also has something in common with Irenaeus' approach—insofar as Irenaeus had appealed to the witness of the presbyter-bishops as the accredited guardians of the biblical revelation passed down in Tradition. The Gnostics were simply outside the household. They had no right to use the Bible at all.

Tertullian's aim in his apologetics, as with all apologetics, is to demonstrate that the claim of Christianity to have a divine origin is acceptable to the reasonable person. He was not without philosophical knowledge, in the manner of an educated Roman of his period, but

[13] It has been pointed out that "many treatises of great authors, which have outlived their literal occasion, retain a value from their collateral arguments which is not inferior to that effected by their primary subject.... If Marcionitism is in the letter obsolete, there is its spirit still left in the church.... [This heresy] gave Tertullian his opportunity of proving the essential coherence of the Old and the New Testaments and of exhibiting both his great knowledge of the details of Holy Scripture, and his fine intelligence of the progress of God's revelation as a whole. This constitutes the charm of the present volume, which might almost be designated a Treatise on the Connexion between the Jewish and the Christian Scriptures." Peter Holmes, Preface to *Five Books against Marcion*, in *Ante-Nicene Christian Library* (Edinburgh: T&T Clark, 1868), 7: vii–viii.

remained unimpressed by professional philosophers—these "animals of glory" and "patriarchs of the heresies" as he called them,[14] noting how many of the errors the Church had to deal with took their origin from philosophical mistakes. (Tertullian did not notice, it seems, that his own view that the soul is material—Augustine would consider this opinion demented[15]—derived from the Stoic philosophers.) He was not, however, the irrationalist that some frequently quoted or misquoted sayings of his have made him seem. The often quoted statement "credo quia absurdum" ("I believe it because it is absurd") is actually a misquotation, but there are in his writings authentic quotations that resemble it, notably in his treatise *On the Flesh of Christ*, a study of the Incarnation. There he writes of the Crucifixion, understood as the Death of the Son of God, "credibile est, quia ineptum est"—"it is credible because it is silly"—and of the burial and Resurrection of Christ, "certum est quia impossibile"—"it is certain because it is impossible."[16]

The Australian patrologist Eric Osborn describes for his readers the contrasting interpretations of these sayings among modern scholars. He himself in no way concedes that Tertullian is in general a fideist, much less an extreme example of the genre. On "credibile quia ineptum", he writes that Tertullian "finds a credible ineptitude in the incarnation and not elsewhere".[17] That is because for Tertullian, the "shame of the incarnation was a test of its reality".[18] In Osborn's words, paraphrasing *On the Flesh of Christ*, "What ... for the worldly [is] morally and intellectually inappropriate" is quite likely to be "good and profitable in the presence of God", in the eyes of God.[19] Tertullian's "irrationalism" is, says Osborn, in reality a rationality that "takes account of a wider, eschatological range of factors" than do most commentators,[20] just as Saint Paul does in First Corinthians when praising the wise folly of God: "The foolishness of God is wiser than men" (1:25). The very idea of the death

[14] Tertullian, *On the Soul* 1 and 3.

[15] Augustine, *Letter* 190. It would give him a headache: Tertullian's notion that we inherit guilty souls by propagation from Adam was a tempting, but philosophically unsustainable, solution to the problem of original sin.

[16] Tertullian, *On the Flesh of Christ* 5.

[17] Eric Osborn, *Tertullian, First Theologian of the West* (Cambridge: Cambridge University Press, 1997), p. 50.

[18] Ibid., p. 51.

[19] Ibid., p. 55.

[20] Ibid.

of God is, of course, "inept" when the divinely revealed direction and goal of human history (eschatology) is denied. But if the entire course of the economy is borne in mind, the "silliness" of divine self-surrender on the Cross makes excellent sense: this is how human pride in its arrogant strength will be overthrown in the End.[21] So far from being the "apostle of unreason", Tertullian's general view of the relation between reason and faith, says Osborn, anticipates that of Saint Bonaventure in the thirteenth century: the innate light of reason is "consummated"—completed, rounded off, fulfilled—by the infused light of divine revelation.[22]

On the Resurrection of the buried Christ, which Tertullian declared "certain because impossible", Osborn notes how the claim that if an incredible event is held to have occurred, then at any rate *something like* that event must have taken place, was anticipated by Aristotle in his treatise on rhetoric.[23] Whatever one might make of this argument, no historian of philosophy is likely to regard Aristotle as an irrationalist.

In fact Tertullian ascribes a rational character to Christian faith, even if (as he thinks) that faith surpasses the resources of reason when reason is separated from revelation. Tertullian's argument for the existence of God, specifically for monotheism, is an unusual one. At the beginning of *The Apology*, he sets out an argument for the existence of one God that is developed at greater length in his book *On the Testimony of the Soul*.[24] It runs as follows. In all parts of the world (those parts known to Tertullian, of course), ordinary people make use of interjections such as "My God!" and "Good God!", as well as other formulae whereby even the atheists among them gave involuntary testimony to monotheism in times of stress or at any rate when seriously surprised. These exclamations, writes Tertullian, are not odd, since if the soul comes from God, then naturally it knows the author of its own being—hence his maxim *anima naturaliter christiana*, "the soul is naturally Christian",[25]

---

[21] Ibid., p. 55.

[22] Ibid., p. 53.

[23] Ibid.

[24] Tertullian, *Apologeticus* 17; Tertullian, *On the Testimony of the Soul* 2.

[25] For a suggestion that this is the "seed" of the "branch of apologetics" called in the early twentieth century the apologetics "of immanence", see Adhémar d'Alès, *La Théologie de Tertullien* (Paris: Beauchesne, 1905), p. 1n2.

meaning "beneath the encrusting prejudices imposed by the customs and habits of society" lies a natural openness to supernatural revelation.[26] After J.L. Austin and the later Ludwig Wittgenstein, doyens of ordinary language philosophy in Oxford and Cambridge, respectively, this appeal to unreflective language use might seem more potentially philosophical than it did to earlier generations. But the prominence Tertullian gives this "ordinary language" argument for God's existence—over against arguments he might have used from the Platonist, Aristotelian, or Stoic traditions of thought, arguments drawn on by many of the Fathers—is symptomatic of his reaction to the "excesses of reason" he found in professional works of philosophy at large.[27]

Yet the witness of the soul to a latent theism half-buried in human consciousness is by itself hardly enough to establish the claims of the Christian religion in its totality. More widely, Tertullian's case for Christianity consists in three elements that will recur in Catholic apologetics (and not only there) right up to modern times. His arguments for the divine origin of the faith consist in, firstly, an appeal to the fulfillment of prophecy; secondly, an appeal to the evidential value of Christ's miracles; thirdly, an appeal to the moral effects of the New Testament revelation as shown in the life of the primitive Church—that is, the Church of his own day.

On prophecy, Tertullian has noticed the two kinds of eschatological expectation in the Jewish Scriptures: one based on the emergence of a supreme human mediator with God (a Messiah figure), the other based on a direct manifestation of the divine (often in the "Day of the Lord" passages of prophets and apocalypticists); he links these two forms of expectation to the two comings of Jesus Christ—in lowliness, which has already happened, in glory, which is still awaited. On the miracles of Christ, Tertullian stresses how, like other events in his incarnate life, they exemplify the fulfillment of prophecy, giving them an additional cachet that is unavailable to other miracle workers—putative or real, past or future. These claims were pertinent to Tertullian's Jewish interlocutors in *Against the Jews*, to pagans

---

[26] Henry Chadwick, *Early Christian Thought and the Classical Tradition* (Oxford: Oxford University Press, 1966), pp. 2–3.

[27] D'Alès, *La Théologie de Tertullien*, p. 2. Tertullian is less persuasive when he seeks to add to the credenda thus known by the soul; see ibid., p. 49.

in the *The Apology*, and in *Against Marcion* to Marcionites who posited a "disconnect" between the God of the Old Testament and the God of the New. The Book of Isaiah and the Psalms were Tertullian's chief sources here, though when he spoke of prophecies of the calling of the Gentiles and the reprobation of the Jews, he extended his range to Deuteronomy, Ezekiel, and Daniel.

Tertullian's Church was overwhelmingly a Gentile Church, but, so far from being at home in its native environment, it was hated in Roman society and its members denigrated for their imagined vices. So the third element in his overall apologetics, the appeal to the virtues of Christians, was definitely countercultural. Tertullian emphasised the demandingness of the law of Christ, which extends not only to actions but to words and even thoughts. He stressed its superiority over other versions of moral law, a superiority seen above all in its primary precept, the love of all human persons without exception, expecting a recompense from God alone.[28] In the course of his account of the moral behavior of Christians, Tertullian describes how the Liturgy unfolds. With its exclusion of unbelievers and catechumens at the Anaphora (the Eucharistic Prayer), the Liturgy had become the focus of pagan suspicion: the scene of alleged acts of infanticide, cannibalism, and incest. Tertullian emphasises that pagans do not read the Judaeo-Christian Scriptures; thus, if they are to be brought to faith it must be by the practice of Christians. So Christians have to be absolutely vigilant about never giving scandal.

Tertullian's idea of what that moral practice should be was highly demanding, indeed rigorist, and it opened him to the influence of Montanism. In the words of a French student of his theology, "African Montanism was not yet a sect; it was, in the bosom of Catholicism, an extreme current that had the reputation of being orthodox."[29] The manner in which it was "extreme", yet at the same time seemingly "orthodox", appealed effortlessly to Tertullian's combination of spiritual enthusiasm and moral rigorism. The followers of the Paraclete spoke of a new outpouring of the Holy Spirit to perfect discipline in the Church by way of preparation for the return of Christ. Features

---

[28] Tertullian, *The Apology* 36.
[29] D'Alès, *La Théologie de Tertullien*, p. 445.

of such perfected discipline included the duty not to flee persecution; a prohibition on second marriages (that means after the natural death of a spouse); and a more severe regime of fasting and abstinence. Furthermore, Tertullian disputed the claim of bishops to be able to absolve from the most serious post-baptismal sins, such as apostasy, idolatry, blasphemy, homicide, and adultery; he opposed the emergent episcopal practice of mitigating public penances by invoking on behalf of penitents the merits of martyrs and confessors who had previously suffered for the faith (later to be called the granting of "indulgences"). These, he thought, were yet more recipes for laxity. Elsewhere in the Western Church, notably at Rome and in Spain, there were people who, without undergoing influence from the New Prophecy, would have agreed with him on some if not all of these points.

One thing appears to have been more personal or at least more especially North African. Tertullian's theology of Baptism had always made much of charismatic graces. Increasingly he would emphasise the role of such extraordinary charisms as visions, ecstasies, and dreams as normal features of the Christian life. The acts of the martyrdom of saints Perpetua and Felicity, who died in the amphitheatre at Carthage in 203 or thereabouts (in Tertullian's lifetime, then), seem to echo this conviction. Visions, ecstasies, and dreams abound in the Perpetua-Felicity narrative. To describe Catholics who lacked such supernatural experiences, Tertullian drew on the vocabulary of the Gnostics whom he had long fought. Such Catholics were only "psychics". Though the Church herself is the Church of the Holy Spirit, they did not deserve the title "pneumatics". They had closed themselves against the message of the Paraclete and his heightening demands as the End of the Ages approached. What counts in the Church is the number of pneumatics, spiritual men, not the "number of bishops".[30] Yet Tertullian continued to identify with the psychics whenever there was a common enemy. That is especially true in his greatest doctrinal treatise, *Against Praxeas*, the principal source for his theology of the Triune God, dating from the last years of his life. This brings us conveniently to Tertullian's dogmatics.

[30] Tertullian, *On Modesty* 21.

Tertullian's Dogmatics

Tertullian's dogmatics are amazingly mature when compared with the immediately post-apostolic writers who join the New Testament epoch to that of the great Fathers and ecclesiastical writers. Whatever the temperamental excesses that inclined him towards Montanism, he was and remained a theological genius of the first order, able to clarify and reformulate the key doctrinal claims of Scripture in a Latin prose that is both robust and ardent. Some of his formulations anticipate by two or three centuries the dogmatic conclusions arrived at by a painfully slow and tortuous process in the Greek-speaking Church farther East.

Tertullian's starting point is the unity of God, which is for him the content of an act of intuition on the part of the soul (as source of the ejaculation "My God!" and similar expressions), an act that is then confirmed by the divinely inspired Scriptures. One might well think in this regard of Osborn's claim that Tertullian's view of the reason-revelation relation is Bonaventurian: innate light of reason confirmed by infused light of revelation. His understanding of how belief in one God is attained neatly illustrates that overall view.

Tertullian developed his account of the unity of God over against three kinds of opponent: pagan polytheists; the Valentinian Gnostics with their "pleroma" of multiple divine emanations; and Christian heretics, notably the artist-cum-philosopher Hermogenes, who posited over against the Deity the eternal existence of matter, and the better known Marcion with his dual divinities, the Creator God of the Old Testament and the Redeemer God of the New.

Tertullian's polemic against polytheism is amusing rather than philosophically serious. The bizarre variety of the gods of the Greco-Roman pantheon especially when lumped together with the native divinities in the provinces of the empire gives him plenty of scope for satire. His treatment of Valentinus, borrowed from Irenaeus' *Against the Heresies*, also takes the form of parody.[31]

Tertullian's critique of Hermogenes, by contrast, is a genuine exercise in argumentative theology. Hermogenes had proposed that God

---

[31] Tertullian's humor in his *Against the Valentinians* is explored in Osborn, *Tertullian*, pp. 191–208.

could not have created the world either out of his own being—that would contradict divine immutability—or from nothing, for then the world would be entirely good, which it is not. So God must have made the world from preexisting matter functioning within creation as the source of the evils the world contains. That for Scripture God is the everlasting Lord, *Dominus*, in Hermogenes' judgment corroborates this account: God could not be eternally Lord without an eternal counterpart over whom or over which he everlastingly claims sovereignty, and there is no other candidate than preexisting materiality. Tertullian counters that to ascribe eternity to matter is to divinize it, for eternity is a divine attribute, and the attributes of God are inseparable one from another. All that is in God *is* God—an early statement of what will later be called the "divine simplicity".[32] From eternity Tertullian would infer what the Scholastics termed "aseity", absolute independence, and from "aseity", infinity, and from infinity, perfection. Matter could hardly be as Hermogenes had asserted, the origin of evil, if its attributes included perfection. Moreover, if God is constrained by the force of matter, so understood, then matter must surely be invincible—yet the Scriptures tell us to fight what is evil. In any case, observation indicates that matter is changeable, yet mutability is incompatible with eternity. Hermogenes had interpreted the opening verse of the Bible—"In the beginning God created the heavens and the earth"—to mean that God created heaven and earth "in" eternal matter, effectively identifying eternal matter with "the beginning", the primordial principle. For Tertullian the only possible "principle" of divine creative action is *sapientia*, Wisdom (see Proverbs 8), and Wisdom is not a material principle.

Marcion's errors resembled those of Hermogenes in that they too sprang from a desire to solve the problem of evil. But Marcion's alternative principle at work in the world is not matter but a Creator God to be distinguished from, and contrasted with, the all-loving Father of the Son, Jesus. Tertullian's *Against Marcion* is his longest and dogmatically most meaty work. Tertullian argues that a rightly framed concept of God can allow for only one, unique instantiation of that concept. The incomparability of God implies God's unicity, an attribute that combines the uniqueness of God with his unity. Tertullian

---

[32] Cf. Tertullian, *Against Hermogenes* 4.

puts forward another philosophical-style argument if Marcionites are unsatisfied with the first. Either Marcion's two Gods differ—in which case one is greater than the other, and thus the other not God, since God is definitionally that which is greatest in reality—or they do not differ, in which case "they" are only one God, for no ground is left on which to justify dividing up the sovereignty of God.

Tertullian further appeals to the consensus of humanity. The disdain with which Marcionites regard the created order arouses a protest from all humanity: it does not take a philosopher to see the wisdom manifest in the works that God has made. Though the world is not, as philosophers have claimed, divine, it is nevertheless worthy of God. Tertullian asks rhetorically, "Will one tiny flower from a hedge (I do not say the meadow), one tiny shell from whatever sea (I do not say the Red Sea), one tiny wing from a moorfowl (I do not speak of a peacock), pronounce for you the meanness of the creator's skill?"[33] This is an informal argument from normal human reaction to the wonder and beauty of the material world, analogous to the argument for the existence of God in *The Apology* and *On the Testimony of the Soul*.

As to the biblical presentation of the divine, Tertullian admits that the God of the Old Testament is severe. Anger, zeal, and rigour are accessories of his severity. But this is no more justified a reproach to the divine Judge than would be a complaint to a surgeon for using instruments that cut and cauterize in order to heal. The God of the Old Testament is also, after all, depicted as good: patience and mercy are the accessories of his goodness. There is no conflict here, says Tertullian: the righteousness of God is at the service of the reign of his goodness.

But perhaps it is not necessary to field particular arguments, whether philosophical, broadly human, or specifically scriptural. For the churches founded by the apostles and those in communion with them are unanimous in honouring the Creator God, the God of the Old Testament, in Jesus Christ. This exemplifies Tertullian's a priori legal argument from "prescription": the orthodox own the Bible, and that should be the end of the matter.

But was Tertullian himself entirely orthodox in his view of God? Without being aware of the fact, his language was strongly affected

---

[33] Tertullian, *Against Marcion* I, 13, 5, cited in Osborn, *Tertullian*.

by Stoicism, which explains how he can describe the one God as *corpus*, literally "body"—a word that for him sometimes means simply substance, reality, but on other occasions has a grosser meaning. Tertullian found it difficult to think of the divine essence in nonmaterial terms, a difficulty shared by Augustine two centuries later. "Popular Stoicism ... as such allows no final distinction between matter and spirit."[34] The metaphysician in Tertullian, wrote one patrologist, was not at the same high level as the dialectician in him.[35]

At the other extreme from the polytheists and Valentinus, and even from Marcion, was another heretical thinker, Praxeas (like Irenaeus, he came from Asia Minor), who so insisted on the unity of God as to deny the Trinity. For Praxeas, a Roman theologian and a strong opponent of Montanism, the distinction of Persons in the Trinity is simply a question of modality. In Praxeas' view, there is ultimately no real distinction between Father, Son, and Holy Spirit—a heresy better known as "Sabellianism" (we have encountered it in the Eastern context in the age of Athanasius), the term coined from the name of Sabellius, a presbyter, possibly Libyan, who taught at Rome.

Tertullian's own emphasis on the divine unity lay on the unity of substance in God, not as with Praxeas on a unity of person. According to Tertullian, Praxeas had two diabolic achievements to his discredit: he had driven the New Prophecy out of the Roman Church and in its place he had introduced Trinitarian heresy there. In Tertullian's words, Praxeas first put the Paraclete to flight and then crucified the Father.[36] Praxeas took the Son, as indeed the Holy Spirit, to be a mode, simply, of the Father's Person. Though, Tertullian told Praxeas, the evangelical tradition certainly affirms the unity of the divine being, the economy as understood by that same tradition makes plain the Trinity of Persons. Once again, prescription—appeal to the exclusive rights of the apostolic churches—should suffice but, says Tertullian in *Against Praxeas*, he would not want to give the impression of not listening to his opponents' arguments. He

---

[34] Allen Brent, *Cyprian and Roman Carthage* (Cambridge: Cambridge University Press, 2010), p. 27; cf. ibid., p. 87: "God and the world are, like soul and foresight in the individual, ultimately material and one in the Stoic monism that will admit no final distinction between matter and spirit."

[35] D'Alès, *La Théologie de Tertullien*, p. 65.

[36] Tertullian, *Against Praxeas* 1.

denies their claim that the Son and the Spirit by sharing in the same substance as the Father serve to undermine the unity of God. So far from destroying the Father's monarchy they are, to the contrary, its essential instruments.

As with the Greek-speaking "Apologists" in the subapostolic period, Tertullian writes of the Word as immanent in God until such time as he is manifested—manifested by carrying through the creative work of the Father, which then morphs into the Word's revealing activity in the "economy",[37] assisted in both regards— creative work, saving work—by the Holy Spirit. For Tertullian, the Spirit is "in" the Word, *Spiritus in Sermone*, just as the Word had been "in" the Father.[38] The Spirit is made manifest in the Word's work in the world.

Tertullian's language for the Trinitarian processions and relations is rudimentary. Yet with hindsight, his can be recognised as a first sketch in the Latin language of the developed patristic doctrine of the Triune God. In the words of Eric Osborn, "Praxeas argues that monarchy [the single divine principle of all reality] requires the identity of Father, Son and Spirit. Tertullian claims that the economy distributes unity into trinity so that the three are one in quality, substance and power (*status, substantia, potestas*), but distinct in sequence, aspect and manifestation (*gradus, forma, species*)."[39] There are here inspired if partial anticipations of both Nazianzen (the "monarchy") and Cyril (the "distribution"). One of his linguistic innovations was going to last. Importantly for the future, Tertullian hit on the term "persona", as suited to Father, Son, and Spirit

Eric Osborn answers his own question, "What did Tertullian achieve?", by saying he "handed on a form of discourse, which opened the way to further development, and above all a formula for the Trinity, 'one substance in three persons'."[40] Tertullian arrived in one fell swoop at the conclusion that in the Greek East the old Nicene and neo-Nicene parties took the best part of another two hundred years to achieve. Tertullian's Christology makes use of

[37] Ibid., 2.

[38] Ibid., 12. Notice how Tertullian, using a Latin Bible now lost to us, translates the word *Logos* from the Prologue to Saint John's Gospel not by the familiar term *Verbum* but as *Sermo*.

[39] Osborn, *Tertullian*, p. 121, citing *Against Praxeas*, 2, 4.

[40] Osborn, *Tertullian*, p. 138.

the same term: Jesus Christ, the Word incarnate, is one Person in two substances. Tertullian speaks of a "twofold status, not confused but conjoined".[41] This too anticipated the future. The unconfused union points on to Chalcedon, while the employment of the same vocabulary, the language of "persona", for Christology and the doctrine of the Trinity, uniting the two realms of discourse, points further ahead still, to the early Byzantine Doctors, Maximus and John of Damascus, in the seventh and eighth centuries. In their case, that key term would be, of course, "hypostasis"—by their time, the recognised Greek equivalent of "persona". Tertullian was in fact extraordinarily adept at anticipating, not least in Christology, the later judgments of the universal Church. As the Australian Jesuit Gerald O'Collins rightly pointed out, "Tertullian can be seen to have ruled out in advance four aberrations to come: Arianism by maintaining that the Son is truly God ('Light from Light'), Apollinarianism by defending Christ's integral humanity, Nestorianism by insisting on the unity of Christ's one person, and Eutychianism by excluding any mixture of divinity and humanity to form some *tertium quid.*"[42]

Just how much Trinitarianism meant to Tertullian is apparent when he tells Praxeas that he, Praxeas, a would-be Christian, has in effect reverted to Judaism. Separating Jews and Christians there is only this dogma: the God who already under the Old Law had announced himself in obscure ways as Son and Holy Spirit kept for these latest times, Christian times, the great light that is now shed on his own being.[43] The Trinity *is* the true doctrine of God.

---

[41] *Against Praxeas* 27, 11.

[42] Gerald O'Collins, S.J., *Christology: A Biblical, Historical and Systematic Study of Jesus* (Oxford: Oxford University Press, 1995), pp. 174–75.

[43] Ibid., p. 31.

10

Doctor of the Episcopate: Saint Cyprian

Saint Cyprian was born into a pagan family in Carthage in the early third century at a date that can only be very approximately inferred.[1] His ordination to the presbyterate, quickly followed by his consecration as bishop of Carthage in 248, came about within a few years of his conversion to Christianity. An element in his rapid promotion may have been his wealth, and the local influence wealth gave in a society where rich men acted not only as patrons of aspirational individuals (a role shared between pagans and Christians) but also as benefactors of the poor, a specifically Christian duty (it is known that Cyprian sold his family estate in Carthage to provide for needy Church members).[2] Nevertheless, it seems unlikely he could have been entrusted with ecclesial responsibilities had he been a very young man. He was probably, therefore, in Late Antique terms, middle-aged, a stage of life regarded as beginning earlier then than in the twenty-first-century West now. Reckoning in this way, scholars hazard that Cyprian was born around 200. He is described as not only a teacher

[1] For modern studies, see Michael M. Sage, *Cyprian* (Philadelphia: Philadelphia Patristic Foundation, 1975), and J. Patout Burns, *Cyprian the Bishop* (London: Routledge, 2002). The older work of a late Victorian archbishop of Canterbury remains the most detailed account: Edward White Benson, *Cyprian: His Life, His Times, His Work* (London: Macmillan, 1897). It is, however, a characteristically Anglican account: "The influence of Bishop [Christopher] Wordsworth [of Lincoln], a noted opponent of the spirit and teaching of Rome, had greatly influenced him in his formative years, and his own historical studies, especially the life of Cyprian, served to confirm the total absence of foundation of the Roman claim." Geoffrey Palmer and Noel Lloyd, *Father of the Bensons: The Life of Edward White Benson, Sometime Archbishop of Canterbury* (Harpenden: Lennard, 1998), p. 185.

[2] Henry Chadwick explains how "by the mid third century the laity were coming to expect their bishop to perform a social role, not only in hospitality but also in advising and defending their secular interests if they were in difficulty with tax authorities or with the law or if they needed a bridging loan for their interests." Henry Chadwick, *The Church in Ancient Society: From Galilee to Gregory the Great* (Oxford: Oxford University Press, 2001), p. 147.

of rhetoric but a "pleader in the courts", a job description which has given rise to debate as to whether he may have been a professional advocate, or what in English common law is termed a "barrister". Cyprian's letters—filled with argument about the nature and limits of the Church, the character of schism and heresy, and the conditions of sacramental validity—certainly read like the work of one who is used to addressing judges or other lawyers.

Cyprian became a Christian in the aftermath of an especially turbulent time in Roman North Africa. The province of Africa Proconsularis had been the epicentre of a failed revolt against the emperor of the time. This was the age of the "soldier-emperors", when between the end of the Severan dynasty in 235 and the accession of Diocletian in 284, the imperial office changed hands over twenty times as different legions of the Roman army jostled for power. In his *Letter to Donatus*, he describes his conversion as fuelled by pessimism about contemporary life that only acceptance of the Gospel could dispel. But he would not have an easy time as a bishop of the Church. The years that span the period between his consecration and his martyrdom in 258 were filled with both persecution and intraecclesial controversy, where Cyprian's enemies consisted not only of pagan bureaucrats but those of his own church-household as two simultaneous schisms broke up the unity of the Church in Carthage and threatened its communion with other churches, notably the Church of Rome. This explains the fact that Cyprian's two great theological treatises are entitled respectively *On the Lapsed* (or *On the Fallen*) and *On the Unity of the Catholic Church*.

On the Fallen

What was the context of the treatise *On the Fallen* or *On the Lapsed*? Cyprian's first great test as bishop was the persecution launched by the emperor Decius in 250. Most modern scholars hold that Decius' target was not Christians as such. It just so happened that Christians, at least in North Africa, were the most common dissenters from the religion of the State. The background thinking of the decree was a combination of traditional Roman civic religion and Stoic philosophy. For the former, a time of decline and chaos, such as the age of the soldier-emperors, was the consequence of the anger of the gods. The ancient gods required propitiation if peace were once again to prevail. For the latter, according to Stoic cosmology, history consists in a series of cycles where a golden age is followed by ever less fortunate ages of silver, bronze, and iron, until such time as a new golden age can be introduced. Decius (or his advisers) devised a ceremony of rededication to the gods in which all Roman citizens—and since the Severan emperor Caracalla, that meant virtually the entire population—must take their part. As the Cambridge patrologist Allen Brent explains:

> Decius' legislation aimed at achieving a universal sacrifice, in which all such citizens participated, that was at once a thanksgiving for his accession, and an apotropaic rite banishing the forces of disorder and chaos both in nature and in society. Thus he proposed a universal cult, now organized by his edict, centrally and not locally, superintending a rite whose purpose was to avert the forces of metaphysical chaos and to re-establish the *pax deorum* [the peace of the gods], in a returning *saeculum aureum* [golden age].... [The] universalistic and individualizing tendency ... [of] Decius' policy ... is but an index of the extent of the metaphysical decline, and the drastic measures needed to remedy it.... Every individual must be shown positively in participation in the supplication to be co-operating in the act of achieving the *pax deorum*.[3]

In the early years of his episcopate, many of Cyprian's problems were connected with the terms of the Decian decree and the different ways in which Christians in Carthage had reacted to the imperial demands. Some Christians had formally refused to make the acts of worship of the gods the decree required, and as a consequence had undergone punishments amounting in individual cases to death whether as a result of torture or from starvation while in prison. These were the martyrs, or, if they had survived their trials, the "confessors". Other Christians had chosen to abandon their property and flee. As it happened, one of these was Cyprian himself.

Cyprian defended his conduct on several grounds. First, it was his responsibility as bishop to continue to shepherd the Church, which

---

[3] Allen Brent, *Cyprian and Roman Carthage* (Cambridge: Cambridge University Press, 2010), p. 191.

he was able to do from his hiding place through emissaries. Secondly, as the Christian with the highest profile in the city (this probably refers to his being not only bishop but a member of the patrician class), his presence, had he stayed, would have focussed attention on the Church community as such, to its disadvantage. It does seem to have been true that many Christians of lower social status were able to evade attendance at the ceremonies by keeping their heads below the parapet. Thirdly, the loss of property in flight, so Cyprian claims in *Letter* 58, was itself a form of martyrdom or at any rate of confession of the faith. In Cyprian's view, furthermore, death from natural causes, if it was brought on by stress and anxiety during times of persecution, could count as martyrdom. That was why he regarded his contemporary Pope Cornelius as a true martyr, who died in just such circumstances. Needless to say, there were critics of Cyprian who found these arguments unconvincing, and Cyprian's flight unedifying—hence in part the difficulties he encountered when the persecution stopped on Decius' death.

But in addition to the martyrs, confessors, and fugitives, there were those of the baptised, and in no small number, who had attended the rededication ceremonies—taking part in the formal acts of worship of the gods the Decian decree required, doing so either unwillingly or, if Cyprian's account can be trusted, in some cases eagerly. Presumably the eager citizens were Christians holding inconsistently to two belief systems simultaneously—people who, without intending to abandon the Church's worship, hoped that the favour of the ancient gods might indeed help the State in its time of need. Those who had thus sacrificed to the gods, in whatever state of mind, were called the *sacrificati*.

Then again, there were Christians who had managed to evade the obligatory act of sacrificing animals to the gods but not the obligation to offer incense to the genius or spirit of the emperor. These were the *thurificati*, a term obviously cognate with our English word "thurifer".

Finally, there were those who escaped both obligations, either by bribing officials to issue falsified certificates attesting the participation of citizens who had not in fact participated or, alternatively, by paying other people to stand proxy for them or even coercing them into doing so (coercing was a possibility in, for instance, the case of those who owned domestic slaves). These holders of false certificates were the *libellatici*, from the Latin word for a little book, a *libellus*.[4] The *sacrificati*, *thurificati*, and *libellatici* constituted the three forms of the *lapsi*, the "fallen", which is probably a better translation here than "lapsed".

It will readily be seen that, once persecution stopped, this spectrum of reactions, and the controversies it aroused, would constitute a threat to the inner cohesion and harmony of the Carthaginian church. No one who claimed to speak for that church, whether the bishop himself or other clerics who intervened in the debate, or the confessors on their emergence from prison, considered that compliance with the Decian decree was anything other than an act of apostasy or at the very least an act of idolatry. There were no Pachamama apologists. Nor was anyone found to argue that *sacrificati*, *thurificati*, and *libellatici* could simply resume the practice of the Christian life, and above all of Eucharistic Communion, as though nothing whatever had happened. What had happened, it was generally agreed, was evangelically disastrous.

On his return from hiding, Cyprian was faced with two sets of—let us call them, conscious of the partisanship involved in this phrase— "ecclesial extremists". On the one hand, there were those who considered that the sins of apostasy and idolatry had put people beyond the pale of Church life. The Church had neither the formal mandate nor the sacramental resources to absolve those who had denied their own Baptism in this fashion. That appears to have been numerically the smaller of Cyprian's problems, but it was, though, an international problem because exactly the same case was being mounted within the Church at Rome.

On the other hand, there were those who claimed that the confessors, whether when still in prison or on emergence from prison, by appealing to the salvific value of the sufferings of the martyrs and indeed of their own sufferings, could in their own right declare the forgiveness and thus reconciliation of members of some or all of the categories concerned (*libellatici*, *thurificati*, *sacrificati*). By "in their

[4] Brent states, "The strict wording of a *libellus* ruled out the possibility of the purging of the past offence of not worshipping the gods of the state. Yet present compliance and that with a sacrifice of incense alone, were permitted locally, and thus testify to the impression left on local officials that the procedure which they were administering was highly like that of a tax return, and could be administered in a similar way, with surrogates also admitted." Ibid., p. 223.

own right" is meant without reference to the bishop or the wider Church. This was the numerically larger and the more immediately pressing of Cyprian's problems. In Brent's words, "Unyielding and surviving Christian martyr-confessors now formed a group that asserted a sacramental authority distinct from that of the bishop, claiming fellowship with the departed martyrs by virtue of their common suffering. By virtue of the suffering Christ whose image they collectively wore, they could absolve those weaker than themselves."[5] So such "martyr-confessors issued from their prison a 'certificate of peace' (or reconciliation)—*libellus pacis* on behalf of their corporate body."[6] This, they said, was the Church certificate needed to "restore and reconcile" offenders who had accepted the State certificate which registered their lapse.

Cyprian replied that the supposed right of a martyr or confessor by virtue of his suffering to give absolution to the fallen had never existed. "We do not call in question," he wrote in *De lapsis*, "the power which the merits of the martyrs and the works of the just have with the Judge, but that will be when the day of judgment comes, when after the passing of this present world, Christ's flock stands before His tribunal."[7] In his version of the dispute, the *libellus pacis*, the certificate of reconciliation or "little book of peace", was "simply a request to a bishop to reconcile the person named therein".[8] As he wrote in *Letter* 15, it was an *honorificata petitio*, an "honorific petition". Such a *libellus* could not, he insisted, substitute for episcopal absolution. "Let each one, I entreat you, brethren, confess his sin while he who has sinned is still in this world, while his confession can still be heard, while satisfaction and forgiveness granted through the priests [*sacerdotes*, i.e., the bishops] are pleasing to God."[9] The bishops, not the confessors, were the successors of the apostles, to whom the Lord had declared (in Saint John's Resurrection narrative), "If you forgive the sins of any, they are forgiven; if you retain the sins of any, they are

[5] Ibid., p. 251.

[6] Ibid.

[7] Cyprian, *De lapsis* 17, trans. Maurice Bévenot, S.J., in Cyprian, *De Lapsis and De Ecclesiae Catholicae Unitate* (Oxford: Clarendon Press, 1971), p. 29. Citations of *De lapsis* are from this translation.

[8] Brent, *Cyprian and Roman Carthage*, p. 251.

[9] Cyprian, *De lapsis* 29, p. 45.

retained" (20:23), and (in the famous promise to Peter in Saint Matthew's Gospel), "I will give you the keys of the kingdom of heaven, and whatever you bind on earth shall be bound in heaven, and whatever you loose on earth shall be loosed in heaven" (16:19). As Cyprian writes in *Letter* 13, it is a matter of *lex divina*, the divine law.

For proponents of any catholic-style ecclesiology—whether this be Roman Catholic, Eastern Orthodox, or High Anglican—Cyprian's case will not seem surprising. Surely only the ministerial priesthood, of which the episcopate is the highest grade, can absolve mortal sins committed after Baptism? A rather substantial issue is, accordingly, at stake.[10] The case has been made that it was not an innovation to say there could be for the presbyterate (and diaconate) such a thing as ordination *per confessionem*, ordination "through confession of the faith"—in the context, specifically, of persecution. Holy Orders, including in the presbyteral grade and therefore in the ministerial priesthood (albeit not in its higher episcopal form), could be acquired through a confession of faith made in the course of suffering for that faith. Compare the way Baptism in blood has been regarded as a proxy for Baptism in water—something Cyprian himself certainly accepted (for instance, in *Letters* 13 and 73).

According to Allen Brent, for presbyters and deacons (including those tacitly ordained *per confessionem*) to give Communion to the lapsed was already known to the Church from former persecutions where it had been understood as precisely the act of reconciliation needed by the *lapsi*. In a letter from the churches of Lyons and Vienne delivered by Saint Irenaeus to Pope Eleutherius and preserved in Eusebius' *Church History* (or *Ecclesiastical History*),[11] the anonymous authors had spoken of how the martyrs "gave grace" to those who were not martyrs, which Brent takes to mean those who suffered in the cities of Gaul during that previous persecution granted Christian apostates renewed access to the sacraments. A text called the *Apostolic Tradition*, which is a major witness to the early Liturgy[12], is also pertinent here. There we read: "If a confessor has been in chains on

---

[10] Maurice Bévenot, S.J., "The Sacrament of Penance and St. Cyprian's *De Lapsis*", *Theological Studies*, n.s., 16 (1955): 175–213.

[11] Eusebius, *Ecclesiastical History* V, 1, 45.

[12] Arguably reflecting life in the Roman community during the second decade of the third century, the early Liturgy is the origin of Eucharistic Prayer II in the modern Roman Missal.

account of the Lord's name, hands shall not be laid on him for the diaconate or presbyterate. For he has the honour of the presbyterate through his confession [i.e., his confession of faith under persecution]. If however he is to be ordained bishop, hands shall be laid on him."[13] On an alternative view, what is envisaged in this text is simply that those who have confessed the faith are to be seated in church alongside the episcopally ordained presbyters as a mark of respect. The author of a fourth-century Syrian text, the *Apostolic Constitutions* (in which, in fact, the text called the *Apostolic Tradition* is embedded), seems to share Brent's opinion while making it clear that it disapproves of such claims to ordained status—and that for the same reason as Cyprian. Such alleged ordinations deny what Christ himself instituted when he established the apostolic ministry. That ministry continues exclusively through the episcopal laying on of hands.

In Cyprian's view, it did not help matters that, often enough, the confessors failed to inquire into either the circumstances of the idolatrous act or the subsequent state of mind of the *lapsi* (were they genuinely repentant?), sometimes even issuing blank certificates where other names, not known at all to the confessors, could be added.

In his treatise *De lapsis*, while never accepting that the *libelli pacis* of the confessors were a sufficient basis for the reconciliation of the fallen, Cyprian sought to satisfy the conflicting demands of justice and mercy by distinguishing between *sacrificati* on the one hand and *thurificati* and *libellatici* on the other.

On the *sacrificati*, he began at least by agreeing with the rigorists. There was no way the Church could absolve those who had committed formal acts of apostasy. They could be commended only to the mercy of God in the hour of their deaths. As to the *thurificati* and *libellatici*, they, by contrast, could be absolved but must do ecclesiastical penance for a period of time—longer for *thurificati*, shorter for *libellatici*—before being reconciled by the bishop's laying on of hands.

But many anomalies soon came to light. There were *sacrificati* who had undergone dreadful tortures before yielding. There were *libellatici* who had gained their certificates by forcing junior members of their households to make the offering of incense to the emperors. In other words, the penitential system Cyprian introduced proved

---

[13] *Apostolic Tradition* 9, cited in Brent, *Cyprian and Roman Carthage*, p. 262.

unworkable, and five years before Cyprian's own martyrdom, a council meeting in Carthage abandoned it. In its place, Cyprian and the bishops gathered round him issued the sort of pronouncement of general absolution that earlier on they had condemned the laxist party for supporting when they gave credence to the confessors' powers to reconcile all and sundry. But by now the chief representatives of the laxists, including the bishop they had consecrated as an alternative leader of the Church in Carthage in Cyprian's place, had themselves been excommunicated and were outside the visible unity of the Church. The situation obviously required attention to ecclesiology—and it is to Cyprian's other treatise, *On the Unity of the Church*, that I now turn.

On the Unity of the Catholic Church

By this point (when the Carthaginian Council just described met in 253) the rigorists too had undergone excommunication. The process of expulsion commenced when their theological leader in Rome, Novatian, allowed himself to be consecrated as an antipope two years earlier, in 251. He thus laid down his challenge to Pope Cornelius, who was willing to accept the reconciliation of all classes of the fallen, granting suitable repentance and acceptance of penances. Cyprian now sought to assist the Roman see by taking the opportunity of the Novatianist schism to put forward a wider ecclesiological theory of his own. Just as in any one city of the empire, within a space defined by marking out a territorial boundary, there can be only one magistrate's chair, one *sella curulis*;[14] so in any one local church, defined as a geographical territory, there could be only one *cathedra*, occupied by a single bishop, who was not only teacher but pastor or governor as well. Here Cyprian's background, his "pagan formation in jurisprudence", served his purposes well.[15] Each such bishop, in order to exercise his office legitimately, must be in peace and concord with other bishops similarly placed—just as the magistrates of the cities of

[14] The "curule chair", the emblem of governance (*imperium*), was supposedly brought to Rome by the first of the Etruscan kings, Tarquinius Priscus; see J. Wells, *A Short History of Rome to the Death of Augustus* (1896; repr., London: Methuen, 1963), p. 7.

[15] Allen Brent, *A Political History of Early Christianity* (London: T&T Clark, 2009), p. 269.

the empire had to be. "According to [Cyprian's] model of Church Order, ordination was to be solely through the imposition of hands of a territorially located bishop, whose jurisdiction over a defined geographical space was acknowledged by a network of bishops spread throughout the imperial world."[16] There was a satisfying cosmological ring to this conception. "For Cyprian, the unity of the Church as the body of Christ who is the Logos reflects the unity of the cosmos. If that unity of the body consist of parts, of members that now configure into dioceses whose agreement is the 'bond (*vinculum*)' holding together the whole, then it reflects how the material cosmos is held together."[17] Athanasius, for whom the universe inheres and thus has its unity in the Logos, would have seen the point.

The Cyprianic vision did not entirely sweep the board. In the Celtic churches on or beyond the northwest fringe of the empire, territorial bishoprics were unknown (the "system" was effectively tribal—kinship-based). In the mediaeval and post-mediaeval periods, the eparchies of the Oriental Catholic churches often overlapped with those of Latin bishops, while the emergent claims of the Roman bishop to universal jurisdiction, ultimately conceded in 1870, required the wholesale reconstruction of Cyprian's scheme.[18] Nevertheless, Cyprianic ecclesiology had a huge impact on the later Church. "No longer was it sufficient to establish a teaching succession between a bishop and his predecessor going back to the apostles guaranteeing the authenticity of true Christian doctrine, as Irenaeus had taught"[19] and Tertullian had echoed. As Brent puts it, Cyprian's "was a quest for absolute episcopal control distributed throughout

---

[16] Brent, *Cyprian and Roman Carthage*, pp. 286–87.

[17] Brent, *Political History of Early Christianity*, p. 273.

[18] Such "universal jurisdiction" made possible the creation, in the later twentieth century, of episcopally governed "Ordinariates", largely or even entirely nonterritorial in character, for specialized categories of laity and their clergy. Such creatures as titular bishops and auxiliary bishops (in the East "chorepiscopi") were long-standing anomalies in Cyprianic terms, while in modern Orthodoxy the tolerance of plural jurisdictions in the diasporas of autocephalous churches implies the effective abandonment of the Cyprian picture. English Anglicans, though venerating Cyprian as an icon of nonpapal Catholicism, muddied the waters by introducing assistant ("suffragan") bishops, initially by an Act of Parliament of 1534. Dying out in the early seventeenth century, they were summoned back to life by administrative action in 1870. The Provincial Episcopal Visitors (or "flying bishops"), appointed in the early 1990s for parishes unwilling to receive the ministry of women priests, are a subspecies of this class.

[19] Brent, *Cyprian and Roman Carthage*, p. 287.

a worldwide organization, and an ecclesiastical jurisprudence that
would justify such a foundation".[20] In the words of another Cyprian
scholar, "The unity of the episcopate and its indivisible authority to
judge and sanctify became the foundation of the unity and unicity
[meaning the uniqueness] of the church."[21]

The way Cyprian interpreted his own ecclesiology was harsh.
Thus, even prescinding from Novatian's views on the condition
of the *lapsi* (which, in part, Cyprian himself had once shared), the
mere fact of Novatian's acceptance of episcopal orders in a city
where a bishop already sat in the *cathedra* not only convicted Novatian of schism but (in Cyprian's opinion) removed from him all
ministerial status such that those Novatian claimed to have baptised,
confirmed, and, in some cases, ordained were and would remain
from a sacramental point of view simply pagans, in every sense outside the Church, *extra Ecclesiam*. As Cyprian wrote to a Numidian
bishop, Antonianus by name, "There is no call for us to investigate
what [Novatian] may be teaching, because he is teaching *outside*.
Whoever he may be, and whatever may be his endowments, that
man is no Christian who is not in the Church of Christ."[22] Thus,
in Henry Chadwick's words, "The principle stated in Tertullian's
polemic against heresies that once they have left the one Church
their opinions are of no relevance or consequence became sharply
reformulated by Cyprian."[23]

Cyprian perceived that this network of bishops—the interlocking
web of local episcopal jurisdictions—required some kind of centre, a
centre by reference to which it was possible to judge the authenticity
of one such network over against others.[24] After all, Novatian did not
remain alone, but sought to bring into communion with him bishops
in other sees, or, subsequently, supported the consecration of new
bishops in other places—including in Carthage. Novatian was creating

[20] Ibid., pp. 288–89.

[21] Burns, *Cyprian the Bishop*, p. 164.

[22] Cyprian, *Letter* 55, 24, trans. Maurice Bévenot, S.J., "Appendix: Extracts from Letters 55
and 59", in Cyprian, *De Lapsis and De Ecclesiae Catholicae Unitate*, p. 108.

[23] Chadwick, *Church in Ancient Society*, p. 154.

[24] Adrien Demoustier, "Episcopat et union à Rome selon S. Cyprien", *Recherches de science
religieuse* LII (1964): 337–69; Adrien Demoustier, "L'ontologie de l'Eglise selon S. Cyprien",
in ibid., pp. 544–88.

in fact an alternative episcopal web of communion. How would it be possible to distinguish theologically one "web" from the other?

This question led Cyprian in the first edition of his *On the Unity of the Catholic Church* to accord a special prerogative to the see of Rome. The first edition is thus the so-called Primacy Text of the *De ecclesiae catholicae unitate*, defined as such over against the Received Text, Cyprian's second version of his treatise. "If a man deserts the throne of Peter, on whom the Church is founded, is he confident that he is in the Church?"[25] Cyprian would produce the second version of his book, adjusted from the first, in the light of his quarrel with a new pope, Stephen I. Stephen had succeeded Cornelius with, in between, the one-year pontificate of Lucius I.

To his dismay, Cyprian found that Stephen could not accept the thesis that, outside the Roman-defined network of episcopal churches, there was no genuine Church life of any kind, no sacramental life, and above all, no baptismal life, no presence of baptismal regeneration and thus of the most foundational element in the being of the Church. Outside the visible unity of the churches governed by the bishops in union with the Roman see, there was for Cyprian no possibility of Baptism. One Church, one faith, one Baptism. Cyprian soon discovered that, in this matter, he and Stephen did not have one faith, in the sense of one shared doctrinal position.

The tradition of the Roman Church had been to acknowledge the baptismal acts of schismatics so long as they were carried out in the Triune Name, and to receive baptised schismatics into communion purely by the laying on of hands together with a signing in oil—in other words, by chrismation or Confirmation, not Baptism. For Cyprian this was impossible. He wrote: "Cut off one of the sun's rays—the unity of its light permits of no division; break off a branch from the tree, it can bud no more; dam off a stream from its source, it dries up below the cut."[26]

Cyprian's decisive rejection of Pope Stephen's view, a rejection still found among many Eastern Orthodox Christians today, finds expression

---

[25] Cyprian, *De ecclesiae catholicae unitate* 4, trans. Maurice Bévenot, S.J., in Cyprian, *De Lapsis and De Ecclesiae Catholicae Unitate*. Citations of *De ecclesiae catholicae unitate* are from this translation. I am grateful to Dominic White, O.P., of Blackfriars, Cambridge, for the provision of pagination for citations from this work.

[26] Ibid., 5, p. 67.

in his letters.[27] Stephen's arguments can be reconstructed not only from Cyprian's negative references in the same letters but also from a text called the *De rebaptismate* (*On Re-Baptism*), which if not from Stephen's own hand at any rate reflects his views. The power of the Holy Spirit through the invoking of the divine Name during the immersion of the candidate in the baptismal waters makes the sacramental act what it is—and no deficiency in the status, actions, or attitudes of the minister of the sacrament can annul it. In later, Scholastic language, sacramental validity works *ex opere operato*, not *ex opere operantis*. In Stephen's eyes, to re-baptise Novatianist converts in Rome, or to require bishops with whom he was in communion to re-baptise Novatianist converts in their own churches, as Cyprian insisted he must, was to deny the power of the Name. It was a blasphemous act.

Two councils of African bishops held at Carthage in 254 and 255 supported Cyprian. No one can be baptised outside the Church. Baptism requires an affirmation answer to the question "Do you believe in everlasting life and the forgiveness of sins through the Holy Church?" Heretics and schismatics cannot give this answer since for them there isn't just one "Holy Church". Baptism involves an anointing that implies receiving the Holy Spirit and thus corporate participation in the one Church-Body of Jesus Christ. Heretics and schismatics cannot claim such participation; they cannot, therefore, validly baptise. Cyprian had earlier held that "The see of St. Peter, representing the *origo* [source] and *exordium* [beginning, i.e., of the Church], is necessary to sustain the unity of the web of autonomous and reciprocal intercommunion: the web itself must have a centre to secure its unity."[28] But now he had to alter his view. In Brent's words, Cyprian was "gravely affronted when Stephen had not acted in accordance with his theory by communicating with bishops who were not part of the web of episcopal interrelationships, and [furthermore] requiring submission from bishops generally regarding his [Stephen's] baptismal practice [at Rome]."[29] The Primacy Text was

---

[27] It would not be forgotten that Cyprian had been supported by major Eastern sees, notably Caesarea, the metropolis of Cappadocian, under its bishop Firmilian, and Alexandria, under a predecessor of Athanasius, Dionysius. See Chadwick, *Church in Ancient Society*, pp. 158, 160, 165.

[28] Brent, *Cyprian and Roman Carthage*, p. 312.

[29] Ibid., p. 314.

dropped; the Received Text took its place. The English Jesuit Maurice Bévenot, while taking the view that in the Primacy Text the phrases "primacy" and "Chair of Peter" need not have the maximalist connotations they possessed in later ecclesiology,[30] agrees that, in consequence of the disagreement with Pope Stephen, Cyprian at any rate "removed the phrases which could bear too 'Roman' a sense".[31]

So how does the teaching of the treatise run now? Cyprian retains the notion of a special connexion between the Church of Rome and the *exordium* or starting point of the Church at large. But the connexion now is simply that Peter is the one who began at Rome the series of proliferating episcopal churches all, hopefully, in communion with each other. The Church of Peter is no longer for Cyprian the centre of the web. Once Stephen had excommunicated entire provinces over the re-baptism issue, Cyprian could no longer maintain that the rest should hold to the *unitas Petri*, the "unity of Peter". Yes, the Roman see is uniquely Petrine, says Cyprian in *Letter* 71, written about the time of the second edition of *De ecclesiae catholicae unitate*. But, adds Cyprian, Saint Peter did not require obedience from Saint Paul when they had their fallout over circumcision and the Jewish Law. Peter only proposed concord and forbearance. The implication was clear. Rome had no right to demand obedience from Carthage.

The dissension between the two primatial sees—Carthage, the primatial see of Africa, and Rome, the primatial see of Italy—led to two further Carthaginian councils held in 256. At the first of these, Cyprian urged to the necessity for Africans to appeal to "reason" rather than "custom", the rather cool term he now used for Tradition in its sacramental aspect. Yes, the African practice of re-baptising schismatics had been of quite recent date, while the Roman practice of not re-baptising schismatics was much older. So Cyprian, the loyal teacher of Tradition, had to argue against Stephen that custom (which might be thought a synonym of Tradition) is not enough. Reason—that is, theological reason, and more especially, ecclesiological reason—outweighs custom. No doubt Cyprian, if challenged on the point,

---

[30] "*Primatus*, in those days, could imply no more than a certain priority, usually in time", while "as for the 'Chair of Peter', though it could, naturally, be used of the see of Rome, it stood primarily for the episcopal office which derived, wherever it was, from Peter." Maurice Bévenot, Introduction to Cyprian, *De Lapsis and De Ecclesiae Catholicae Unitate*, p. xiv.

[31] Ibid., p. xv.

would have appealed to Tertullian, for whom "custom", *consuetudo*, can mean "unthinking fashion". "Our Lord Christ surnamed Himself Truth, not Custom."[32] These last councils of Cyprian's life rejected the enforcing of judgment by the pope, whom Cyprian described witheringly in *Letter* 74 as a self-appointed *episcopus episcoporum*, the "bishop of bishops", a superbishop or, in later parlance, a "universal bishop". Cyprian's horror of schism and heresy led him to assert that these crimes were worse than apostasy itself.

> This crime is a greater one than that which the lapsed ... have committed; [the lapsed], becoming penitents for their crime, are at least calling upon God's mercy by making satisfaction for it to the full. In their case the Church is being sought and appealed to [for absolution and the setting of ecclesiastical penance], in the other [schism and heresy] the Church [in and for herself] is repudiated; in the first [apostasy] likely enough there was coercion, in the second the will persists in its guilt; in the first the man who fell hurt only himself, in the second the instigator of heresy and schism has deceived many by dragging them after him; in the first case harm is done to a single soul, in the second many are imperiled.... Lastly, the lapsed can by subsequent martyrdom obtain the promises of the kingdom; but the other, if he be put to death outside the Church, cannot come to the rewards which are prepared for the Church.[33]

Stephen's death and Cyprian's martyrdom in renewed persecution under the emperor Valerian (for this time Cyprian did not seek to escape) meant that the controversy between Carthage and Rome was left unsettled. But as Brent remarks, "The Roman Church's narrative of unity was nevertheless to forget the conflict with Stephen and to honour Cyprian's contribution to the theology of papal power in his support for Cornelius as well as his definition of the unity of the

---

[32] Tertullian, *On the Veiling of Virgins* I, 1, trans. S. Thelwall, in *Ante-Nicene Fathers*, ed. Alexander Roberts, James Donaldson, and A. Cleveland Coxe, vol. 4 (Buffalo, NY: Christian Literature Publishing, 1885). Augustine would continue to draw the same distinction after Cyprian, and, moreover, in the same context of schismatic or heretical Baptism: "In the Gospel the Lord says, 'I am truth'. He does not say, I am custom. When the truth is made manifest, custom must give way to truth." Augustine, *On Baptism, against the Donatists* III, 6, 9, trans. J. R. King and Chester D. Hartranft, in *Nicene and Post-Nicene Fathers*, ed. Philip Schaff, 1st series, vol. 4 (Buffalo, NY: Christian Literature Publishing, 1887).

[33] Cyprian, *De ecclesiae catholicae unitate* 19, p. 89.

Catholic Church."[34] So Cornelius and Cyprian stand side by side in the Roman canon and share the same feast day in the Roman calendar (September 16).

Yet the unresolved nature of the clash meant trouble in Africa in the future. Cyprian's insistence that the ecclesial integrity of the bishops was essential to the being of the Church, such that where such integrity was lacking (for instance, if a bishop had collaborated with pagan authorities over against the Church), the Church of that bishop (and bishops in communion with him) ceased to exist as holy Church and became a mere conventicle, would give Saint Augustine his main headache in the early years of his own episcopate. The headache is known to history as "The Donatist Crisis".[35]

[34] Brent, *Cyprian and Roman Carthage*, p. 321.

[35] "The division between Catholics and Donatists had occurred, not because of any profound disagreement in doctrine, but, rather, because of the rival claims of two groups of bishops to have lived up to the ideal of a bishop's office as exemplified by S. Cyprian." Peter Brown, *Augustine of Hippo: A Biography* (London: Faber and Faber, 1967), p. 203; cf. Sage, *Cyprian*, pp. 361–62.

11

Bulwark of Orthodoxy: Saint Ambrose

Saint Ambrose was born in (probably) 339, at Trier, now in Germany,[1] a city founded just after the end of the Roman republic by Augustus Caesar. By the fourth century, owing to its strategic position at the junction of both roads and waterways, Trier had come to replace Lyons, the city of Irenaeus, as the capital of Roman Gaul. Ambrose's father, also named Ambrosius, held a major administrative office either as prefect of the Gauls or at least in some high position in that prefecture.[2] (In the Late Antique period, "praetorian prefectures", a unit of government, were the top-level administrative divisions of the Roman Empire.) The family appear to have been native Romans, since from the source that furnishes information on the elder Ambrose—a life of Saint Ambrose that Augustine commissioned from the Milanese deacon Paulinus—we know how Ambrose's mother, brother, and sister (the latter a consecrated virgin) lived at Rome after his father's demise, if not also before.

The younger Ambrose had been trained as rhetor and lawyer, and received a good grasp of the Greek language, something by no means to be taken for granted in the fourth-century West (Augustine, for instance, lacked such a grasp, and so probably did Jerome until he moved to the East). Later on, after his Baptism and ordination, these linguistic skills enabled Ambrose to access the writings of the Greek Fathers, especially Alexandrian and Cappadocian texts, before they were translated into Latin. Ambrose was plainly destined for a career in the imperial civil service, and by his early thirties was considerably

[1] For the date, which is disputed, see Boniface Ramsey, O.P., *Ambrose* (London and New York: Routledge, 1997), p. 16.

[2] Angelo Paredi, *St. Ambrose: His Life and Times* (Notre Dame, IN: University of Notre Dame Press, 1964), p. 2, and see p. 380n5.

advanced along that road. Around 374, having served for five years in the office of the praetorian prefect of Illyria at Sirmium (now Sremska Mitrovica in Serbia), he was promoted to the governorship of the provinces of Liguria and Emilia, covering the northwest of the Italian peninsula. This was at the time an important part of the world. "Almost all of the cities and towns of any importance in fourth and fifth century Italy lay in the great plain between the Alps and the Apennines, the province of Liguria and Aemilia."[3] If his birthdate has been calculated correctly,[4] he was at the time about thirty-five years of age. He had hardly begun his tasks when, still a catechumen, he was chosen by popular acclaim to be bishop of Milan at one of several climactic moments in the struggle between Catholics and Homoians in that city.[5] This sudden elevation was not without criticism. Saint Jerome, with his customary acerbity, declared himself disgusted that "a catechumen today becomes a bishop tomorrow; yesterday at the amphitheatre, today in the church; in the evening at the circus, in the morning at the altar; a little time ago patron of actors, now dedicator of virgins."[6] At least Ambrose made a good start so far as the people were concerned, by giving away the lion's share of his property. His brother Satyrus resigned his own office as a prefect so as to move to Milan and help Ambrose with the temporal affairs of the Church (the touching homily Ambrose would give at Satyrus' funeral has entered the Roman Liturgy for the Office of Readings on All Souls' Day).

Episcopate and Politics

"Struggle between Catholics and Homoians": I might have spoken there, as older writers do, of "the struggle between Catholics *and Arians*" in the Milanese church; but this would be to leave out of account Athanasius' propaganda triumph in his *History of the Arians*

[3] Bernard Green, *The Soteriology of Leo the Great* (Oxford: Oxford University Press, 2008), p. 13.

[4] Ambrose's principal Italian-language biographer, sometime historian of the Ambrosian Library in Milan, Angelo Paredi, would place it five years earlier; see Paredi, *St. Ambrose*, p. 2.

[5] For the Latin Homoians, see Michel Meslin, *Les Ariens d'Occident, 335–430* (Paris: Editions du Seuil, 1967).

[6] Jerome, *Letter 69*, 9, cited by Henry Chadwick, *The Church in Ancient Society: From Galilee to Gregory the Great* (Oxford: Oxford University Press, 2001), p. 434.

when he managed to homogenise all opponents of the Council of Nicaea—all critics of the "consubstantiality thesis" for the Son's relation to the Father—by tarring opponents and critics with the same brush. In reality, as modern Church historians have come to realise, the word "Arianism" can be shorthand for a variety of Christologically defective movements.[7] "Homoians"—the word *homoios* means "alike"—held that the Son was "like" the Father (normally adding "in all things"), but abstained from teaching, with Arius, that in this likeness he was simply the most wonderful of all creatures. Homoianism was the most characteristic form of Western Arianism. In the West it took its cue from the creed of the 359 Council of Ariminum (the modern city of Rimini on the Adriatic coast of Italy), though a peculiarity of that particular creed was the way the bishops permitted the addition of a rider capable of interpretation—though not positively requiring interpretation—in a *properly* Arian sense. The extra clause ran, if anyone says that the Son is "a creature like other creatures", let him be anathema. This formula was undoubtedly ambiguous. The original Arians did indeed hold that the Son was "not a creature, like other creatures", not because the Son is uncreated (they denied that he *was* uncreated) but because he is too wonderful a creature to be just like the rest. It was after this Rimini Council, and its simultaneous Eastern equivalent, held at Seleucia Isauriae (now Silifke on the southwest coast of Turkey), that Jerome made his famous comment, "The whole world groaned, and was astonished to find itself Arian."[8]

But in 361 (so two years later) the strongly anti-Nicene emperor Constantius II, Constantine's last surviving son, died of fever in the course of a war with Persia. His cousin, the neo-pagan Julian the Apostate, succeeded him. Julian's policy was to weaken Christianity by playing off Christian factions against each other, which meant that pro-Nicene forces could now revive, not least in northern Italy.[9] A

[7] See M. R. Barnes and D. H. Williams, eds., *Arianism after Arius: Essays on the Development of the Fourth Century Conflicts* (Edinburgh: T&T Clark, 1993).

[8] Jerome, *Dialogue against the Luciferians* 19, trans. W. Fremantle, G. Lewis, and W. G. Martley, in *Nicene and Post-Nicene Fathers*, ed. Philip Schaff and Henry Wace, 2nd series, vol. 6 (Buffalo, NY: Christian Literature Publishing, 1893).

[9] Daniel H. Williams, *Ambrose of Milan and the End of the Nicene-Arian Conflicts* (Oxford: Clarendon Press, 1995), pp. 69–103. Williams notes the evident need for continuing anti-Homoian polemic in this region as evidenced in Filastrius of Brixia (Brescia), Zeno of Verona, the anonymous author of the *Commentary on the Nicene Symbol* (thought to be north Italian) and the *Twelve Books on the Trinity* ascribed by some to Eusebius of Vercelli.

tussle with Homoian Christianity dominated the first twelve years of Ambrose's episcopate. At first the election of Ambrose was supported by Catholics and Homoians alike: both because of his reputation as an even-handed civil official and because each side was hoping he might opt for them. Though Nicenes (i.e., Catholics) are usually regarded by modern scholars as the more numerous party, there were plenty of convinced Homoians among the Milanese.[10] But Ambrose's mind was already made up in favour of the Nicene teaching. He thus acquired enemies, not least through the political machinations of the imperial court in the West, periodically resident in Milan as that court was.

In his book *Ambrose of Milan and the End of the Nicene-Arian Conflicts*, the Canadian Baptist scholar Daniel Williams sought to show how "many modern analyses of the Trinitarian conflicts in the late fourth century" are coloured by a common misconception of "a uniform, essentially pro-Nicene west and a religiously lifeless, politically manipulative Arianism".[11] Yet Williams, who seems more sympathetic to Homoianism than to the Nicene faith, would not disagree that, at the time of Ambrose's Baptism and ordination, it was in political life that anti-Nicenes held most of the cards.

How so? Like Constantius II, Julian the Apostate died on the Persian frontier. His short-lived successor, Jovian, an army commander, reigned long enough to restore Christianity as the State religion before he too died and was followed by another military man, Valentinian I—who is sometimes called "Valentinian the Great" since he was the last really successful Western Roman emperor. During his reign, which ran from 364 to 375, Valentinian I stayed neutral in the Christological debates, while his brother Valens, whom he made co-emperor in the East, was openly pro-Homoian. Under Valentinian I, no Homoian bishop could be legally deposed; the Catholics had, at best, to wait for death to take its course.[12] The predecessor of Ambrose, Auxentius, had been a Homoian, appointed when a previous Catholic bishop had been forced into exile. In 371 a Roman synod, presided over by the pope, asked the emperor to remove Auxentius from office; he refused.

[10] Enrico Cattaneo, *La religione a Milano nell'éta di sant'Ambrogio* (Milan: Archivio ambrosiano, 1974), pp. 34–35.

[11] Williams, *Ambrose of Milan*, p. 5.

[12] Ibid., p. 71.

There was certainly no guarantee that a Nicene Christian was going to succeed on Auxentius' death. The Nicene transition would hardly have been as smooth as initially it was if people had not believed Ambrose would follow Valentinian's nonalignment policy. And though ensuring he was baptised by a Nicene, Ambrose appears to have begun by behaving tactfully towards the Homoian clergy. Yet his earliest writings after his elevation—these were his ascetic treatises—already provide, in Williams' words, "clear evidence of Ambrose's own doctrinal orientation toward Nicene catholicism".[13]

A degree of tact must have seemed well-advised. When Valentinian I died in 375, he was succeeded in the West by his son Gratian, who at first continued his father's neutralist policy in matters religious. But there was also the question of the "second" or "junior" *augustus*, the heir-in-waiting, then resident in Sirmium. This was Gratian's four-year-old half-brother, Valentinian II, in whose name a regent had been appointed, the child's mother Justina. Justina was a fervent anti-Nicene who gave strong support to the Homoian party. In 378, owing to the Gothic invasions, the empress, taking the boy with her, fled to Milan, where they established their court. In their wake came numerous Homoian refugees, prompting Gratian to take away from the Catholic party one of the Milanese basilicas for Homoian use.

Meanwhile a campaign was orchestrated against Ambrose, centring on his sale of Church vessels to benefit a fund for ransoming prisoners in the hands of barbarians. Daniel Williams speculates that these were vessels given in memory of Christians who had supported Auxentius—a church plate inscribed with their names. Inevitably such donors would have been Homoians. In the campaign Ambrose found himself delated for his heretical—"tritheistic"—homoousianism. These complaints are likely to have been the cause of Gratian's asking Ambrose for a reasoned explanation of his "faith"—that is, his doctrinal beliefs.

The result was the first two books of Ambrose's principal dogmatic work, his treatise *On Faith*. Often called *The Exposition of the Christian Faith*, it was written in the autumn of 378. In it Ambrose attacked Western Arianism in all its forms. The root error lay in its affirmation of the dissimilarity of the Son to the Father. Thus, Ambrose lumps in

[13] Ibid., pp. 128–29.

the Homoians, who held the Son was like the Father, with the Ano-
moeans, who held the Son was unlike the Father. Ambrose was not
without logical justification, however: likeness excludes identity and
therefore implies otherness, which in turn entails dissimilarity. Basil
had made the selfsame point.

More positively, Ambrose explained his faith in terms of the essential unity of Father and Son. "While there is fullness of Godhead in
the Father there is also fullness of Godhead in the Son: not diverse,
but one. The Godhead is nothing confused, for it is a unity; nothing
manifold, for in it there is no difference"—meaning, no difference of
nature, of *ousia*.[14] Father and Son are so much one that "no possible
wedge of inequality can be driven between them."[15]

Gratian's favourable reception of the first two books of *On the Faith*
emboldened Ambrose to compose three more books, largely drawn,
it seems, from preexisting material he had to hand in his liturgical
sermons. After clarifying Christological issues raised by Homoian
rejoinders to *On the Faith* I and II, in *On the Faith* III, IV, and V,
Ambrose also sketched out a pneumatology, a theology of the Spirit.
He would continue to write Christology, notably in his 382 *On the
Sacrament of the Divine Incarnation*. His Christology can be regarded as
anticipating that of the Council of Chalcedon, since both in *On Faith*
and in *On the Sacrament of the Divine Incarnation* Ambrose "devoted a
good deal of space to distinguishing the natures, and to asseting the
fullness of Christ's humanity", as well "rejecting any suggestion that
the natures act separately [since] it is Christ who is the *unus* [the single
subject] who is not one thing from the Father and another thing from
the Virgin, but [is] from the Father in one way and from the Virgin
in another".[16] Ambrose also continued the investigations into pneumatology begun in the treatise *On Faith*, notably in his *On the Holy
Spirit* published in 381, the year when the Second Ecumenical Council, Constantinople I, added to the Creed of Nicaea a clause on the

---

[14] Ambrose, *On Faith* I, 16, trans. H. de Romestin, E. de Romestin, and H. T. F. Duck-
worth, in *Nicene and Post-Nicene Fathers*, ed. Philip Schaff and Henry Wace, 2nd series, vol. 10
(Buffalo, NY: Christian Literature Publishing, 1896). Hereafter, this edition of the *Nicene and
Post-Nicene Fathers* is cited as *NPNF*.

[15] Williams, *Ambrose of Milan and the End of the Nicene-Arian Conflicts*, p. 145.

[16] Green, *Soteriology of Leo the Great*, pp. 46–47, citing Ambrose, *On the Sacrament of the
Divine Incarnation* V, 35, in his own (Green's) translation.

equal worship owed the Third Trinitarian Person. As we saw when looking at the Cappadocians, that was in effect the dogmatization of the Spirit's divinity. A crucial text that set the tone for *On the Holy Spirit* was 1 Corinthians 2:10, "The Spirit searches everything, even the depths of God"—How, asked Ambrose, can one of whom that is said not be divine?[17] In this treatise more widely, Ambrose argues that faith implies the acceptance of the rule of faith (he actually uses Irenaeus' alternative expression, "the rule of truth") and the rule of faith is essentially Trinitarian. That means for Ambrose that, whenever one divine Person is named, the entire Holy Trinity is signified. As he writes, "If you name Christ, you imply both God the Father by whom the Son was anointed, and the Son himself who was anointed, and the Holy Spirit with whom he was anointed. And if you name the Father, you denote equally his Son and the Spirit of his mouth.... And if you speak of the Spirit, you name also God the Father from whom the Spirit proceeds, and the Son inasmuch as he is also the Spirit of the Son."[18]

The year 381 was also the year when Gratian's equivalent in the eastern portion of the empire, Theodosius the Great, whom Gratian had made co-emperor on the death of his uncle Valens, issued a decree banning the teaching of any Christological doctrine incompatible with what was taught by Nicene bishops at Rome and Alexandria. This 381 decree marked the triumph of orthodoxy in the East and the political defeat of Homoianism (and other versions of Arianism) there. And this in turn triggered in the West a significant change in Gratian's own approach. Fortified by the decisions of a Western council meeting at Aquileia, near what is now Venice, in that same momentous year, Ambrose was able with Gratian's help to recover the basilica given to the Homoians and in due course to expel the remaining Homoian bishops from the north Italian sees.

This did not transpire without a struggle with the imperial court. In 383 Gratian was murdered at Lyons in a revolt led by the grandiloquently named Magnus Maximus, the commander of the Roman field army in Britain, whereupon Valentinian II and Justina took

---

[17] Ambrose, *On the Holy Spirit* I, 1, 23.

[18] Ibid., I, 3, 44, trans. H. de Romestin, E. de Romestin, and H. T. F. Duckworth, in *NPNF*.

power locally in Milan. Their aims included the restoration of legality to Homoian Christians and the recovery of a basilica for their own use. Their weapons were the removal of legal impediments to "Homoian activities",[19] the invitation to a Homoian bishop to take up residence in competition with Ambrose, and the imposition of fines and terms of imprisonment on wealthy pro-Nicenes. The aim, plainly enough, was the replacement of Nicene Christianity at Milan by their form of Arianism. Justina may have calculated that, with Goths pressing ever farther southward, imperial policy makers would eventually recommit to some version of Arianism, the form of Christianity most acceptable to Gothic soldiers and settlers.

Ambrose's spirited resistance to court demands for the Portian Basilica (now the Basilica of San Lorenzo) is deservedly a prominent feature of his biography. With the church surrounded by soldiers, he led the embattled Catholics inside the building in hymn singing— "after the manner of the Eastern church", explained Augustine,[20] but the hymns were anti-Homoian.[21] The simultaneous rediscovery of the bodies of the martyrs Protase and Gervase (the cultus of the Church in Milan had hitherto lacked martyrs' remains), and the miracles that accompanied their solemn reinterment in a newly built "Basilica of the Martyrs" (now called the Ambrosian Basilica, in honour of Ambrose), also helped the Nicene cause. Augustine recorded in his *Confessions*, addressing God: "You revealed them at the right moment to repress the fury of a woman, even a queen [namely, the regent Justina]. Thereafter the mind of that enemy, even if not turned to healing belief, was checked nevertheless from the rage of persecution."[22] Through their relics the saints were present. In *Letter* 77, Ambrose himself called them "my bodyguards". Possibly a threat from the pro-Nicene Magnus Maximus, now in firm control of Gaul and Spain, that he would intervene in Italy if the Milanese court persisted in its policy (Ambrose had travelled to Maximus' base at Trier to keep him informed), was even more effective in the Nicene

---

[19] Williams, *Ambrose of Milan*, p. 212.

[20] Augustine, *Confessions* IX, 7, trans. R.S. Pine-Coffin (London: Penguin, 1961). Citations of the *Confessions* are from this translation.

[21] For the suggestion that there were two sieges, only one of which Ambrose attended in person, see Williams, *Ambrose of Milan*, pp. 214–15.

[22] Augustine, *Confessions* IX, 16.

interest. Intervene Maximus eventually did, whereupon Valentinian II and Justina fled to the protection of Theodosius at Thessalonica, the capital of Macedonia. That meant they sought the protection of a firmly, not to say rigorously, Nicene Christian.

Valentinian II soon abandoned Homoianism—it was the price to be paid for Theodosius' support against Maximus, though de facto Theodosius was now the sole ruler in West as well as East. The still youthful Valentinian was given a sinecure, an office with little or no work attached, in Gaul. Theodosius took up residence in Milan in 388, remaining there until 391. The following year he became sole emperor de jure, for Valentinian died at Vienne, near Lyons, ostensibly by suicide but probably at the hands of barbarian soldiers in his nominal employ.

So Ambrose's remaining years would have Theodosius as their constant companion, for good or ill, almost to the end. Theodosius died two years before Ambrose, leaving his son Arcadius, who was eighteen, as emperor in the East, and another son, Honorius, who was only eleven, as emperor in the West, with as their guardian the Vandal general Stilicho, a barbarian but a Catholic Christian faithful to the policies of Theodosius.

Ambrose admired Theodosius for his Nicene zeal, for the courageous way he had accepted a normalization of large-scale Gothic invasion/immigration in the East, and the clemency he had shown at the time of serious rioting against his rule at Antioch, where John Chrysostom had also intervened in a request for mercy. Their mutual respect was tempered by awareness that they differed over the ideal of Church-State relations, Ambrose standing for the independence of the episcopate vis-à-vis the ruler, Theodosius for the "symphonic" idea familiar since Constantine by which the bishops and the emperor rule the imperial Church together.

That mutual respect was tested by events surrounding a second riot, this time at Thessalonica, where the emperor ordered a massacre of citizens prior to cancelling his order—but cancelling it too late. Ambrose wrote to him privately, asking in courteous but unmistakable terms that Theodosius should make an act of public repentance and request reconciliation with the Church, which he did at Milan at Christmas 390. The episode was regarded in the Christian West as an especially clear demonstration of the subordination of the emperor to the Church as moral teacher ("mater et magistra", "mother and teacher"), despite the autonomy of the two in civil matters. It would be a marker of a significant difference in the attitudes of the *sacerdotium*, the episcopate, to the *regnum*, kingship, in the Latin West as over against the Greek East.

Asceticism and the Mysteries

When writing the life of Ambrose, the deacon Paulinus claimed to be following in the steps of Jerome's life of the hermit Paul of Thebes, Athanasius' life of Anthony, and Sulpicius Severus' life of the monastic founder Martin of Tours, three great ascetic saints. Paulinus was signalling to readers that this grouping—the ascetic saints—indicated the category of holy man with which Ambrose belonged. As we have seen, Ambrose had begun his episcopate by giving away his goods, both lands and mobile property, to the benefit of the Church of Milan and the poor of the city. It was a kind of vow of poverty. For a member of a senatorial family, this would have been a considerable sacrifice.[23] In his adaptation of Cicero's treatise *On the Duties*, written for the better instruction of the Milanese clergy in the virtues they needed for the ministerial life, Ambrose wryly observed: "Riches are hardly to be found among the saints of the Lord so as to become objects of contempt to them."[24]

By fourth-century standards, Ambrose was not a monk. But he was nevertheless a celibate ascetic, which by third-century standards amounted to much the same thing. "Paulinus tells us that Ambrose spent many hours of the night in prayer, study, and writing, and that he fasted every day with the exception of Saturdays, Sundays and the more solemn feasts of the martyrs."[25] "Fasting" would mean not eating until after the hour of None—that is, after three in the afternoon. Such fasting was of course a major feature of ascetic practice.

[23] Senatorial positions, which required wealth in land and buildings for their upkeep, were by this date more or less hereditary, making the senatorial class the equivalent of what would later be termed a (landed, and otherwise propertied) "nobility".

[24] Ambrose, *On the Duties of Ministers* II, 128, trans. H. de Romestin, E. de Romestin, and H. T. F. Duckworth, in *NPNF*. The civic virtue Cicero had praised was to be realised in the Gospel and its ministers; for the significance of this work as a template for clerical conduct, see John Moorhead, *Ambrose: Church and Society in the Late Roman World* (London: Routledge, 1999), pp. 157–69.

[25] Paredi, *Saint Ambrose*, p. 125.

So was the pursuit of *lectio divina* (divine reading). Paulinus' account of Ambrose's practice of *lectio divina* concurs with Augustine's report in the *Confessions* from his own time in Milan, where Augustine lived from 384 to 387.[26] What Augustine observed Ambrose reading (and noted how, contrary to the norm, when he read no sound could be heard) was likely to have been the Scriptures. Ambrose transferred to the Latin environment the meditation on the Scriptures that Origen had begun, introducing in the West the practice of *lectio divina.* "The method of *lectio* served to guide all of Ambrose's preaching and writings, which stemmed precisely from *prayerful listening* to the Word of God."[27] Ambrose saw Scripture as, in his own preferred metaphors, a source of spiritual "refreshment", a form of spiritual "nourishment", and a spiritual exercise to strengthen the "limbs" of the soul.[28] It certainly fed his preaching where, unusually, to judge by what has come down to us, he was more concerned to explain for the people the Old Testament than the New—probably because, like most modern congregations, they found its content less easy to assimilate.

But his reading matter, as observed by Augustine, might also have been a text from the Greek divines. Ambrose's spirituality is conspicuous for its Oriental caste. He drew on the Cappadocians, especially Basil (with whom he corresponded), and the early Alexandrian theologians—not only Athanasius but above all Origen, and Origen's pupil Didymus the Blind, and on the Alexandrians' Jewish model in exegesis, Philo. It has been said that Ambrose's "keen sense of orthodoxy enabled him to correct the excessively Jewish interpretations of Philo and the extreme allegorical interpretations of Origen".[29] This was just as well insofar as it is Philo and Origen who are the principal influences on Ambrose's interpretation of the Old Testament—which explains that predominantly allegorical character of his exegesis.

Despite his often expressed disdain for Greco-Roman paganism (not for nothing had he faced down two attempts by pagan senators to restore the "altar of victory", symbol of continuity with Roman

---

[26] *Confessions* VI, 3, 3.

[27] Pope Benedict XVI, *Church Fathers: From Clement of Rome to Augustine* (San Francisco: Ignatius Press, 2008), p. 123. Italics in original.

[28] For texts using these metaphors, see Paredi, *Saint Ambrose*, pp. 130–31.

[29] Ibid., p. 133.

civil religion, in the Senate House at Rome),[30] he was deeply influenced by the classical literary tradition, notably by the long-standing practice of treating the poets as allegorists—purveyors of "profound teachings on the nature of the world and the human soul behind the mask of fable and fiction".[31] That would explain his attraction to Philo and Origen, who used the same method. Echoes of later Platonists—Plotinus and Porphyry—have also been detected in his sermons, especially (on his own account) when his congregation included pagans.[32] Some have considered that the Church in Milan deliberately used Neoplatonism as a preparation for the Gospel.

If Ambrose's readings of the Old Testament have a distinctive character in any more thoroughgoing way, it would probably lie in the overwhelmingly *moral* nature of his practice of allegory. Thus, in *On Cain and Abel*, he interprets the brothers not only in terms of two groups in salvation history: the Synagogue, which like Cain is fratricidal, killing one who, through the childbearing of the Virgin Mary, was their brother, and the Church, which, like Abel, cleaves to God. He also thinks of the contrast between Cain and Abel in terms of two schools of metaphysical thought, each with clear implications for ethics. Cain, who sought to gain all for himself, and Abel, who ascribed to his Creator all he received from God, correspond to two great streams of thought, with huge implications for moral existence. As Ambrose writes, "There are two schools of thought, therefore, totally in opposition one to the other, implied in the story of the two brothers. One of these schools attributes to the mind itself the original creative source of all our thoughts, sensations, and emotions. In a word, it ascribes all our productions to man's own mind. The other school is that which recognises God to be the Artificer and Creator of all things and submits everything to His guidance and direction. Cain is a pattern for the first school and Abel of the second."[33]

[30] For attempts belonging to a reassertion of traditional Roman religion at this period, see Herbert Bloch, "The Pagan Revival in the West at the End of the Fourth Century", in *The Conflict between Paganism and Christianity in the Fourth Century*, ed. Arnaldo Momigliano (Oxford: Clarendon Press, 1963), pp. 193–218.

[31] Paredi, *Saint Ambrose*, p. 260.

[32] Chadwick, *Church in Ancient Society*, p. 356, drawing attention to Ambrose's own remarks to that effect in a homily on Psalm 36.

[33] Ambrose, *On Cain and Abel* I, 1, trans. John J. Savage, in St. Ambrose, *Hexameron, Paradise, and Cain and Abel* (New York: Fathers of the Church, 1961), p. 360.

One is a Godless ethics, where man is the measure of all things; the other is a Godly ethics, where that measure is God himself.

An important exception to the generalizing statement that Ambrose's exegesis is chiefly by way of moral allegory will be found, however, in his homilies on the *Hexaemeron*, the "Six Days" of the biblical creation narrative. These addresses largely confine themselves to the literal sense of Genesis, in effect reproducing in Latin Basil the Great's commentary on the same text—so much so that Jerome had to defend Ambrose, very halfheartedly, against the charge of plagiarism. Still, Ambrose's version of a *Hexaemeron* commentary consists of homilies and homilists are not normally expected to acknowledge their sources. And at least the echoes from the greatest of Roman poets, Virgil, are Ambrose's own. In the words of the English translator of *The Six Days of Creation*:

> Following in the footsteps of his great model [Basil], Ambrose has made these sermons into a series of Christian and humanistic observations on nature and man in their relations to their Creator, who formed them out of no pre-existing material. In elaborating this thought from the manifold body of evidence presented by the Scriptures, Ambrose has in addition resorted to over a hundred reminiscences from his beloved Latin poet [Virgil].... Ambrose has something of the spirit of the Roman poet who also marvelled at the wonders of the created world in language that is often full of charm.[34]

In the *Confessions*, Augustine commented on the "sweetness", *suavitas*, of Ambrose's pulpit eloquence.[35] A modern historian remarks, "The *suavitas* that informed the rhythms of Ambrose's sermons (and likewise his hymns) is far more elusive for the modern reader than his erudition, which can be confirmed through indices and concordances; but it is perhaps more fundamental to the spell his preaching cast over his audience."[36]

In his preaching, Ambrose was especially concerned for the consecrated virgins. A major presence in the Roman Church since

---

[34] John J. Savage, Introduction, in ibid., p. vii.

[35] Augustine, *Confessions* V, 13, 23.

[36] Neil B. McLynn, *Ambrose of Milan: Church and Court in a Christian Capital* (Berkeley, CA: University of California Press, 1999), p. 243.

Athanasius' years of exile there, groups of such women, whether living in the family home or in the predecessors of "convents", also existed at Milan. Ambrose saw them as pioneers, heroines of the ascetic movement. In 377 he brought together various homilies and exhortations he had given on the topic of their way of life, under the distinctly unoriginal title, *On the Virgins*. A year later he responded to criticisms by the girls' parents and relatives (why are you stealing our girls?) in a short treatise—really a sermon for the feast day of the apostles Peter and Paul—entitled *On Virginity*. In the words of Neil McLynn, author of a predominantly political biography of Ambrose,[37] "Ambrose's talents as advocate and exegete harmonized perfectly, dissolving the serious charge of interference in the affairs of family and property into a sustained display of biblical imagery which drenched his audience in the dizzy perfumes of the spiritual life."[38] Actually, the heart of Ambrose's *On Virginity* is Christological. "Christ is all things to us. Art thou wounded and wouldst be healed, He is the physician; dost thou burn with fever, He is the refreshing fountain; art thou pressed down with iniquity, He is righteousness; needest thou help, He is the power of God; fearest thou death, He is life; desirest thou Heaven, He is the way; fliest thou from darkness, He is light; seekest thou food, He is the bread that came down from Heaven."[39]

In the 390s Ambrose would return twice to the same theme: in *On the Education of a Virgin* for the veiling of a niece of his brother-bishop in Bologna in 392 and then in 394 in an *Encouragement to Virginity* delivered at Florence. The destination of these texts (Bologna, Florence) shows Ambrose's determination to make his influence felt more widely—beyond Milan—where proto-monasticism for women was concerned. The movement was too potentially important to be confined to his own see.[40]

[37] McLynn explains that "we should not unduly regret the lack of a key to Ambrose's inner life. What matters is his performance upon the public stage, enfolded in the dignity of his priestly office." Ibid., p. 377.

[38] Ibid., pp. 63–64.

[39] Ambrose, *On Virginity* 16, 99, trans. Albany J. Christie, *On Holy Virginity with a Brief Account of the Life of St. Ambrose from Whom the Tract Is Derived* (Oxford: John Henry Parker, 1843), p. 46

[40] See Philip Rousseau, *Ascetics, Authority, and the Church in the Age of Jerome and Cassian* (Oxford: Oxford University Press, 1978).

Ambrose's teaching activity, and, in the perspective of ecclesiology, his activity as bishop as a whole, found its summit in the
Liturgy. We know his approach to the latter from his hymns and
two sets of homilies for newly initiated Christians—On the Mysteries
and On the Sacraments. The second of these is perhaps a stenogra-
pher's version, taken down as it were in shorthand, of the sort of
text Ambrose produced in a more sophisticated edited form in On
the Mysteries. If it is authentic, the book includes the earliest known
version of the Roman canon (Eucharistic Prayer I in the present-day
or "Pauline" Roman Missal).

Ambrose's devotion to liturgical worship is evidenced in his
hymns and antiphons. A number of the fine prayers in the Ambrosian Missal are likely to be his, "especially those attached to the older
feasts".[41] On the other hand his connexion with "Ambrosian" chant
is less clear. Critics are divided as to whether its characteristics suggest
this kind of chant is especially primitive, or, to the contrary, notably developed. Yet both Augustine and Deacon Paulinus concur in
ascribing to Ambrose some sort of innovations in the matter of the
kind of chant used in church.[42] Finally, forty-two brief poems written to accompany a series of paintings of Old and New Testament
scenes on the walls of the Ambrosian Basilica (these were copied by
French pilgrims in the sixteenth century) are generally accepted as
his work, though the inscriptions like the frescoes themselves have
disappeared.[43] They prove that Ambrose was an iconophile. John of
Damascus would have been delighted.

Ambrose died on Holy Saturday, 397. He leaves history rec-
ommending to the clergy of Milan that an old priest, Simplicianus, should succeed him. Simplicianus would play an important
part in the conversion of Augustine, not least by recounting the
story of another conversion, that of the pagan philosopher Marius
Victorinus.

Ambrose was an original agent in Church life but not an original
mind. The historian Peter Brown draws an instructive contrast with,
precisely, Augustine.

---

[41] Paredi, Saint Ambrose, p. 344.

[42] Augustine, Confessions IX, 6, 7; Paulinus, Life of Ambrose 13.

[43] Paredi, Saint Ambrose, p. 345.

Ambrose, the fully educated bishop who read Greek, still belongs to the old world. He felt himself intimately bound to the vast prestige of the Christian scholarship of the Greek world, above all, to the great Origen of Alexandria. Augustine, the amateur, felt far more free to follow his own course: and paradoxically, in so doing, he came closer than did Ambrose to the spirit of the early Christian schools of Alexandria, and so, to a firm belief that a mind trained on philosophical methods could think creatively within the traditional orthodoxy of the Church.[44]

Nevertheless, it is Ambrose, not Augustine, who is the first of the Latin Doctors of the Church.

[44] Peter Brown, *Augustine of Hippo: A Biography* (London: Faber and Faber, 1967), p. 113.

12

Scholar and Monk: Saint Jerome

We know much more about Saint Jerome than might appear from the fact that the traditional date for his birth, 331, is contested and no one can be sure of his birthplace—which, however, must have been somewhere in the region where today Croatia, Slovenia, and Italy come together. Two towns figure in his early life: Aquileia, the predecessor of Venice as the great civil and ecclesiastical centre on the northern Adriatic, and Emona, the modern Ljubljana, now the Slovene capital. A plausible suggestion is that Jerome's family, who were wealthy enough to own land he later sold to support his Bethlehem monastery but from whom he was estranged by the choice of a monastic vocation, lived at some location that enjoyed reasonable access to those two cities.[1] Thanks to his copious letters and other texts that derive from the various controversies in which he was involved, lengthy periods of Jerome's life are extremely well documented. But there are also great gaps, especially for his early manhood.

The Early Years

Jerome was educated at Rome, along with his lifelong friend Bonosus, later to be a hermit on an island in the Adriatic. They were sent there so as to study under the grammarian Donatus, "the most celebrated schoolmaster of his time".[2] The topics studied were the correct use of language (Donatus' speciality) along with classical literature. Jerome would become the finest Latinist among the Fathers,

---

[1] J. N. D. Kelly, *Jerome: His Life, Writings, and Controversies* (London: Duckworth, 1975), p. 5.
[2] Ibid., p. 10.

competing with the best Roman prose writers of any period, and in the view of competent judges, occasionally excelling them. Later, classical literature would give him spiritual problems. As to a "knowledge of history, geography, general subjects, and indeed of moral behavior", this, in the words of the Oxford patrologist J. N. D. Kelly, "was not imparted directly, but was picked up incidentally, as the texts under examination [i.e., the classics of Roman literature] suggested topics to be developed".[3] Somewhere on the side he acquired a grasp of Roman law—perhaps a sign that his parents had wanted him to become a lawyer. Such initiation he had into philosophy for its own sake was probably delayed till he was living at Antioch, in the mid 370s, when he was well into middle age. In Rome he made good friends, including—fatefully for the future—Rufinus of Aquileia, and began to build up the well-stocked private library that accompanied him on his life's journey through Europe and the Near East.[4] He also lost his virginity, something that weighed on him in later life—especially if, as is possible, it followed his Baptism, which also took place in Rome, probably in the Lateran basilica.[5]

We next hear of Jerome in the autumn of 367, when he and Bonosus settled in Trier, presumably in the hope of advancing their careers since it was the residence of the emperors Valentinian I and his son Gratian. While at Trier he copied out for Rufinus (see *Letter 5*) two recent works by Hilary of Poitiers, sometimes called the "Athanasius of the West". Hilary's *On the Synods* was an analytic history of the Arian crisis: here Jerome's choice looks ahead to his own later role as a defender of orthodoxy. The other text he passed on, Hilary's *Tractate on the Psalms*, a commentary indebted to Origen, is a harbinger of Jerome's own transmission of Origen's exegetical work—until, that is, he turned against Origen and, in the course of so doing, against Rufinus as well. At Trier, perhaps under the influence of local monastics (whom we know from Augustine's *Confessions* to have lived nearby),[6] Jerome began to live the ascetic life, understood

---

[3] Ibid., pp. 12–13.

[4] On Jerome's library, see the remarkably full discussion in Meghan Hale Williams, *The Monk and the Book: Jerome and the Making of Christian Scholarship* (2006; repr., Chicago and London: University of Chicago Press, 2014), pp. 133–66.

[5] Jean Steinmann, *Saint Jerome* (London: Geoffrey Chapman, 1959), p. 19.

[6] Augustine, *Confessions* VIII, 6, 15.

as a life deliberately detached from worldly pursuits, and devoted instead to study and contemplation. Moving back to his home area, he found like-minded Christians at Aquileia and Emona: proto-monks or clerics living a common life, but also consecrated virgins. Soon, though, he had to move on again, owing to some trouble the nature of which is not recorded. In Kelly's words, "We may sus-pect ... that, not for the last time, his passionate temperament, his tactlessness, or his uncontrollable tongue, or some combination of these, had landed him in some major imprudence, some disastrous indiscretion."[7] *Letter* 11, written to the consecrated virgins, includes the words, "Human envy judges in one way, my dearest sisters, and Christ in quite another. The sentence of his court is not that of the tale-bearers' whispers."[8]

Jerome in the East

Jerome's aim was now to become a monk in the Holy Land, but his immediate goal on leaving Italy was Antioch whither he went in 374 via a leisurely journey, his library in tow, accompanied by a wealthy patron, Evagrius of Antioch, a former resident of Aquileia and the translator into Latin of Athanasius' *Life of Anthony*. (He should not be confused with Origen's radical disciple the monk-theologian Eva-grius of Pontus, though the two were contemporaries.) Kelly noted, "Even if he was driven out by the slanders which his friendship with the women had started, he ought, at the bottom of his heart, to have blessed this chance of fleeing to the East. It was there that his curiosity and his passion for asceticism and for travelling were alike drawing him. It was there that he was to discover his lifetime vocation."[9]

One aspect of this vocation was the acquisition of excellent Greek. Living for the first time in a Greek-speaking household, Jerome hugely improved his grasp of Greek, reading Aristotle's logical works and the *Isagoge* or introduction to philosophy of the Neoplatonist

[7] Kelly, *Jerome*, p. 34.

[8] Cited in Steinmann, *Saint Jerome*, p. 30. For the letters of Jerome as a source not only for his life but theology and exegesis, see Andrew Cain, *The Letters of Jerome: Asceticism, Biblical Exegesis, and the Construction of Christian Authority in Late Antiquity* (Oxford: Oxford Univer-sity Press, 2009).

[9] Steinmann, *Saint Jerome*, p. 31.

Porphyry (we have met both of these in connexion with John Damascene) and the commentaries on Aristotle's writings of Alexander of Aphrodisias—commentaries held in high esteem in later Greek and Arabic philosophy.

At the time Jerome arrived, the Church of Antioch was in internal schism and would remain so for some while. Leaving aside the imperially recognised Arian bishop (recognised, that is, by the Eastern emperor, Valens), the orthodox were divided into three camps. The first group, led from exile by Bishop Paulinus (not, of course, to be confused with the Milanese biographer of Saint Ambrose) and supported by Jerome's host Evagrius, were the "Old Nicenes". They held strictly to Athanasius' theology that in God there is a single *ousia* or hypostasis. Those two terms had been treated as synonymous in the original text of the Nicene Creed, though the 362 Council of Alexandria, approved by Athanasius, had said that not only the expression "one hypostasis" but also the expression "three hypostases" could have an orthodox sense.[10] The second group, the "Neo-Nicenes", were led by Bishop Meletius, also in exile. They accepted the theology of "one *ousia*, three hypostases" associated with the Cappadocian Fathers and notably Saint Basil. Basil's aim was to persuade the pope, Damasus, that this formula was indeed orthodox, and as a consequence to recognise Meletius as rightful Catholic bishop in Antioch. A third group, also with a bishop, Vitalis, were orthodox in Trinitarian doctrine but accepted the heretical opinion of Apollinarius of Laodicea, Vitalis' consecrator, that in the Word incarnate the divine mind of the Logos takes the place of what would otherwise have been the human mind of the man assumed. (This was the heresy which Gregory Nazianzen recognised to be a possible misreading of Athanasius.) In due course Jerome would have to take his own stand on all these issues.

Meanwhile Jerome was in a bad way, owing partly to poor health and partly to the unwanted return of sexual longings, but mainly, it may be conjectured, to recurrent doubt. Could he really bring himself to leave behind the sophisticated intellectual culture represented by Antioch and live forever after in the desert, in the company of mainly ill-educated speakers of Syriac? At Antioch, the "most populous and exciting city of the Near East", the "Christian style of life

---

[10] Henry Chadwick, *The Church in Ancient Society: From Galilee to Gregory the Great* (Oxford: Oxford University Press, 2001), pp. 416–19.

had an old-fashioned pagan zest to it."[11] It was now that he had the nightmare described in *Letter* 22, sometimes referred to as his "second conversion". He heard the divine Judge asking him whether he was a Christian, to which he replied, "Yes," only to hear in response the words, "You are lying. You are a disciple of Cicero, not of Christ; for your heart is where your treasure is."[12] For the next decade Jerome obeyed an oath he took then, never again to study the pagan classics. Later, he would adopt a more balanced view of the matter, and even in the decade of his abstinence from the classics, he could still be found alluding to them or echoing them. They were too firmly implanted in his mind to be wholly uprooted.[13] The dream steeled him to begin monastic life proper in austere conditions in a semi-desert area of northeast Syria. However, Evagrius brought him his post, his cave was roomy, he still had his library, and anchorites were available to copy out books he needed or at least wanted. According to *Letter* 17, he earned his keep by the labour of his hands, probably basket weaving, the economic baseline of monastic activity in the East. One should not be snide about Jerome's palatial cave. His letters from the desert describe real Gospel *metanoia*: a powerful experience of compunction and a sense of closeness to God and the angels. From his neighbours he picked up some Syriac. More importantly for the future, he resolved to learn Hebrew, no easy task. Kelly explains,

> He was grappling with a language completely different in structure from his own, without any grammar-books or traditions of grammatical or syntactical analysis to help him, and the Hebrew he was struggling with was written exclusively in consonants, without the points which were later invented to indicate the vowels. Yet, with his anonymous Jewish convert to start him off (there would be later successors), he was to acquire a mastery of the tongue far superior to that of any Christian writer before him (Origen not excluded) or for centuries after him.[14]

[11] G. W. Bowersock, *Julian the Apostate* (Cambridge, MA.: Harvard University Press, 1978), p. 94.

[12] Cited in Steinmann, *Saint Jerome*, p. 42.

[13] See Harald Hagendahl, *The Latin Fathers and the Classics: A Study of the Apologists, Jerome and Other Christian Writers* (Gothenburg: Göteborgs Universitets Aarsskrift, 1958).

[14] Kelly, *Jerome*, p. 50.

Jerome was now dragged into the Trinitarian dispute because the Meletians were pressurizing him to recognise "three hypostases" in God. Those who refused to do so, they said, must surely be Sabellians: those Christians who took Father, Son, and Spirit to be temporary modes of appearance of a primordially undifferentiated God. Jerome did not immediately see how a trio of hypostases, literally a trio of "subsistences", could actually be synonymous with the "three *personae*" in God, confessed by Latin Christians since the days of Tertullian. Conscious of his own Roman Baptism, he wrote in some concern to Pope Damasus, little thinking he would soon be Damasus' secretary and thus (to the minds of mediaeval Christians) a "cardinal" of the Roman Church.[15] Under pressure (it is proposed) from Meletian monks in the cave colony, Jerome returned to Antioch—and to another largely undocumented period in his life, between 376 (or 377) and 382, though it is known to have included his ordination as a priest by Paulinus, the "Old Nicene" bishop.[16]

As Jerome approached the age of fifty, he at last emerged as the author that would make him in time a Doctor of the Latin Church. He emerged first not as exegete, however, but as hagiographer and polemicist: hagiographer in *The Life of Paul the First Hermit*, a work notable for its appreciation of the beauty of nature, fascination with the marvellous, and the enthusiastic character of its piety (all continuing motifs in Jerome's later efforts at writing the lives of the saints);[17] polemical theologian in the *Altercation of a Luciferian with an Orthodox*, though no great dogmatic issue was at stake— Luciferians were not worshippers of Satan. Luciferians were simply Nicene Christians who insisted that bishops who had conformed to some version of Arianism or semi-Arianism could not, even if

[15] By the sixth century, "cardinalis" could be applied as an adjective to Roman presbyters, as in the correspondence of Gregory the Great; its extension to the (traditionally seven) Roman deacons and the bishops attached to the Lateran basilica came later; see Chadwick, *Church in Ancient Society*, p. 316.

[16] It was (probably) now that Jerome heard Apollinarius, and (again, probably) learned from his sane approach to Scripture, avoiding both a pedantic philology and the wilder flights of imaginative allegorism. Jerome's hermeneutics favoured allegorical explanation but only after the literal sense was established first.

[17] The life of Saint Paul shows Jerome still hankering for the pure eremitical monastic lifestyle, which he had really discovered he could not properly live; he would continue in this genre later, with lives of two monks in Syro-Palestine: Malchus and Hilarion.

they now accepted orthodoxy, continue in their sees. Though the treatise shows Jerome's reading of earlier Fathers (notably Tertullian, Cyprian, Hilary, and Athanasius), like most of the Latin Fathers (Augustine is the obvious exception) Jerome was no speculative thinker.

Meanwhile, the defeat of Valens by the Goths and his death in 378 at Adrianople (now Edirne in European Turkey) changed the political scene. Gratian, who, thanks to Ambrose, had become a pro-Nicene, made the fervently Nicene Theodosius his co-ruler in the East, the crucial step in ensuring that in the future the faith of Nicaea would be the faith of Christendom as a whole. In 381 Jerome hastened to Constantinople in time to hear Gregory Nazianzen deliver his *Five Theological Orations*, designed as these were to bring the Trinitarian crisis to an end by demonstrating the full divinity of the Son and the Spirit. It is presumed that Nazianzen, along with the other surviving Cappadocians Gregory of Nyssa and Nazianzen's cousin Amphilochius of Iconium (also present in Constantinople), alerted Jerome to the orthodoxy of the "one *ousia*, three hypostases" formula, as well as introducing him—directly, not just through Hilary—to the writings of Origen, of whom these Cappadocian bishops were, in matters exegetical, the disciples.

It was at Constantinople that Jerome began his massive work as a translator, starting with Eusebius' *Chronicle*—which is to be distinguished from the later and much fuller Eusebian *Church History*, the most important of our sources for the history of the Church before the first Council of Nicaea.[18] The *Chronicle* was meant to show the greater antiquity of biblical religion when compared with paganism. Jerome amplified the text where it dealt with Roman history and otherwise brought it up to date (which meant taking the story forward from 325 to 378, the date of the Battle of Adrianople). Much more important was his translation into Latin of the homilies of Origen. Beginning with homilies on Jeremiah, Ezekiel, and Isaiah, he would move on to Origen's sermons on the Song of Songs and

---

[18] Jerome left untranslated the work's first part, which goes by nations (with illustrative documentation), whereas its second part places the "ethnic" histories in synchronic parallel. The first (and presumably more important) part survives only in Armenian translation (with some gaps): Alden A. Mosshammer, *The Chronicle of Eusebius and Greek Chronographic Tradition* (Lewisburg, PA: Bucknell University Press, 1979).

Saint Luke's Gospel.[19] Origen is thought to have left 574 homilies at his death, only 21 of which have reached us in the original Greek, so students of Origen owe Jerome a lot, even if he touched up the texts stylistically, rendering many of them in the process, in Kelly's words, "more elegant and readable than the originals".[20] He also made his first foray into exegesis of his own—a study, both historical and figurative, of the call vision of the prophet Isaiah, making use of his newly acquired Hebrew but based on the Septuagint text. It was sent as a gift to Damasus, hence its misleading name, "*Letter* 18". In the words of the American Jerome scholar Meghan Hale Williams, "Whatever Jerome did and whomever he met at Constantinople, he made a fateful encounter there—with the literary legacy of Origen. It was under Origen's banner that he began, at Rome, to advance a new model for Christian scholarship as an ascetic practice, and to invoke the authority of the Hebrew text of Scripture."[21]

"Cardinal" Jerome

Jerome now had a new mission: to accompany Bishop Paulinus of Antioch to Rome as interpreter and adviser. Paulinus would go home but Jerome stayed, as he was found invaluable for his linguistic

---

[19] Kelly states, "Before many years there was to be a fierce explosion of anti-Origenism in which Jerome was to be deeply and passionately involved. At present, however, he was under the master's spell, fascinated by his prestigious scholarship and by the skill with which, by lavish use of allegorising and spiritualising methods of exegesis, he had seemingly cleared away many difficulties of the Bible and been able to read a Christian message out of the most anthropomorphic, legalistic, or even morally offensive passages of the Old Testament." Kelly, *Jerome*, p. 76.

[20] Ibid., p. 77.

[21] Hale Williams, *Monk and Book*, p. 29. Hale Williams points out that "unlike many of his Christian predecessors, Jerome devotes equal attention to the literal and allegorical senses of scripture. However, he associates them with separate exegetical traditions, whose status is markedly different.... The relation between the two primary senses of scripture was for Jerome a complex one. From one point of view, the spiritual sense was heavily privileged. Whereas the historical and literal meanings, associated with the Jews, had only a limited claim to truth, the allegorical or spiritual sense, associated with the Church, the true Israel, was the locus of salvation" (ibid., p. 115). And yet, "Not only did the historical sense precede allegorical interpretation; it also constrained it. Only when the literal meaning, literary context, and historical reference of a text had been clarified did it become available for higher exegesis." Ibid., p. 117.

knowledge, familiarity with the Christian East, and emerging literary skills. The pope used him as secretary, archivist, and resident specialist exegete, for it was now that Jerome began his huge project of replacing the existing Latin Bible, the *Vetus Latina*. He began with the four Gospels in a conservative revision made in the light of the Greek manuscripts he had to hand, which brought his version close to the fourth-century codices *Vaticanus* and *Sinaiticus*. The rest of the New Testament was, it seems, done by another hand or other hands.

Jerome also became the spiritual counselor of a number of Roman women of high rank and considerable wealth. He strongly urged them to some version of the ascetic life, whether by refusing to enter second marriages after the death of a spouse or by electing to remain virgins, and in each category, widow or virgin, living out an austere regime of prayer, fasting, and Scripture study—on which last topic he was uniquely well placed to assist. Soon, he was talked up as a possible successor to the pope who died in 384. But his relations with the women he directed were to be his undoing. Jerome aroused huge opposition among influential elites in Rome by his programme of encouraging these ladies, led by two widows, Paula and Marcella, to take up, in the incongruous setting of their grand houses, the lifestyle of the Fathers of the Egyptian Desert. (Among theological feminists, it has become customary to describe Paula as a "Desert Mother".) Jerome's letters of direction to Paula's youngest daughter, Eustochium, did not hesitate to castigate for their worldly lifestyle the Roman clergy and even the Roman ascetics. According to Bernard Green, "Jerome lambasted the Roman clergy with their stylist clothes and footwear, their jewellery and scents and coiffures, gossiping in the drawing rooms of rich women, dropping heavy hints about articles of furniture they would like to take home with them."[22] These letters were widely circulated (as no doubt he intended). He gave offence to a lot of people by his depreciation of the married life as a poor second best—but at least, he said, marriage "produces children who may embrace virginity", which he understood in exalted terms as consecration to the divine

---

[22] Bernard Green, *The Soteriology of Leo the Great* (Oxford: Oxford University Press, 2008), p. 10. Cf. Jerome, *Letter* 22.

Lover of the Song of Songs.[23] The possible contribution to the death of Paula's eldest daughter of the physical austerities he urged on her, together with his criticism of Roman ecclesiastics, meant that, once Damasus was dead, Jerome began to come unstuck. A pamphlet by the Roman layman Helvidius who claimed that after the birth of Jesus his mother led a normal married life, with intercourse and childbearing, elicited from Jerome the first of his really hard-hitting diatribes. Written in the spirit of such pagan satirists as Lucian, Horace, and Juvenal, he did not hesitate to include in his withering reply to Helvidius some unfavourable vignettes of particular persons—influential persons—who were still alive in Rome. There was probably justice in the attacks. As Henry Chadwick remarks laconically of Damasus' pontificate, "The maintaining of ethical probity in Roman society in this age was not easy."[24]

Jerome now returned to the Holy Land, taking with him Paula, Eustochium, and an entourage of pious women, but travelling by different routes so as to dispel gossip.

Jerome in the Holy Places

In Jerusalem Rufinus of Aquileia (Jerome's student friend) and Rufinus' Paula equivalent, the wealthy Roman matron Melania the Elder, had preceded Jerome's party. There Melania and Rufinus founded the first Latin monasteries: one for women, the other for men; these soon became renowned centres of learning and hospitality. Paula and Jerome did not wish to enter into competition with Melania and Rufinus. Instead, they created a similar system of dual monasteries, but at Bethlehem with the cost of building borne by Paula. It would be their home, and that of Eustochium, Paula's daughter, for the rest of their lives. Paula died in 404; Eustochium, in 419. Jerome, by far the oldest, was also the last to die, in 420, in (according to some calculations) his ninety-first year. The life lived in these houses was some version of the communitarian monasticism pioneered in Egypt by Saint Pachomius, a contemporary of

---

[23] Kelly, *Jerome*, p. 102.
[24] Chadwick, *Church in Ancient Society*, p. 317.

Saint Anthony in the Upper Nile Valley. Jerome would translate the Pachomian Rule, but not till 404 and for Latin-speaking monks in Egypt. These Latin monastics in the Holy Land would surely have much adapted the Pachomian model. Jerome's work now bore no relation to the agriculture and crafts of the Pachomian monastics, largely peasants as they were, in the Nile Valley.

In the first place, he was preaching. *Corpus Christianorum Series Latina* contains a hundred of his homilies preached in Bethlehem or Jerusalem, not included in Migne's *Patrologia Latina* since they were not believed to be his till the start of the twentieth century. He was also running a secondary school for boys where he lectured on Virgil and the Roman comic and lyrical poets—so much for the nightmare where a heavenly voice told him he was a Ciceronian not a Christian! He was running a hostel for visiting monks from all over the known world. And above all he was writing. He was finishing a translation of Didymus the Blind's *On the Holy Spirit* he had begun in Rome— fortunately enough, for the Greek original from the hand of Origen's greatest exegete-successor has not survived. He was translating Origen's homilies on Luke. He was writing commentaries, very Origenian in character, on Paul's letters to Galatians and Ephesians (as well as Philemon and Titus), where the first signs of disaffection with the more speculative side of Origen's mind begin to appear. He was also commenting, with plenty of help from Origen and the rabbis, on Old Testament books: Ecclesiastes and all the prophetic books, though the Jeremiah commentary remained unfinished at his death. He was producing an etymological dictionary of biblical proper names, a gazetteer of biblical place names, and a critical study of difficult sections of Genesis, again using rabbinic help. He was writing notes on the Psalms using a new Latin version based on reading the Greek in the light of the Hebrew. He was bringing out a corrected Latin version of various other books in the Septuagint's Greek text, notably Job, Proverbs, the Song of Songs, Ecclesiastes, and First and Second Chronicles, before taking the plunge and beginning a completely new text based exclusively on the Hebrew Bible.

When Augustine asked to see his revised Septuagintal books, Jerome said he had lost the manuscript; indeed, some of these corrected translations from Greek (Chronicles and the Solomonic books) have disappeared entirely. Augustine's request and Jerome's reply (in *Letter* 134) signal something very important: Jerome's beginning again from the

Hebrew did not go down well with contemporaries, whereas he himself was ever more convinced of its necessity. Kelly wrote:

> His intensive Biblical studies over the past decade had finally convinced him that, however revolutionary it might seem and whatever hostility it might provoke, the only ultimately satisfying Bible for Christians was one which reproduced the Hebrew original. In principle, of course, he was entirely right, even allowing for the fact (which he could not possibly know) that, being older, the Septuagint in many passages preserves a more ancient reading than the currently accepted Hebrew text (substantially the same as our "Massoretic" text). But he had an apologetic inducement which carried even more weight. It had become translucently clear, to himself and certain close friends, that their only hope of demolishing the arguments of Jewish critics was to take their stand on a text of the Old Testament which both parties were agreed was authentic.[25]

Rufinus and Augustine thoroughly disapproved, though the latter had to admit Jerome was right in regard to any hope of success in persuading Jews.[26] Part of the theological cost was the elimination of the additional books in the Alexandrian canon—what are often called the deuterocanonical books, sometimes omitted or printed as an appendix in Protestant Bibles. Their crime was, they did not exist in Hebrew. Jerome now saw them as second-rate texts. They might be used for edification but not to prove doctrine—though in practice he continued to cite them as though they were Scripture. Hale Williams remarks of Jerome's new Latin Old Testament that, despite the contemporary opposition, "over time ... its prestige rose, to the point that by the seventh century Jerome's version of the Hebrew Scriptures had largely overcome the Old Latin text used in the late

---

[25] Kelly, *Jerome*, pp. 159–60. But the debt to Judaism Jerome was happy to contract was not wholly textual as distinct from interpretative. Relying especially on his commentaries on Isaiah and Zechariah, Hale Williams suggests that "wherever Jerome invokes the *Hebraica veritas* in a context that does not limit the phrase to a narrowly textual meaning, we ought to consider the possibility that he was thinking not of the Hebrew text alone but of the entire arena of scriptural interpretation in which he believed the Jews to be specially expert" (Hale Williams, *Monk and Book*, p. 92). Compare her defence of Jerome's claims to have consulted Jewish teachers in ibid., pp. 121–32, relying on the English abstract of an unpublished 1997 dissertation by Hillel I. Newman at the Hebrew University of Jerusalem.

[26] Augustine, *The City of God* XVIII, 43.

antique church."[27] In the sixteenth century, the Council of Trent would recognise this displacement by calling the Hieronymian text the "Vulgate" or "Common Version".

Four Controversies

The last decades of Jerome's life were dominated by four controversies. The first, into which he was drawn by Roman correspondents, was with a Roman monk, Jovinian. Jovinian called into question the concept of a "more perfect life attainable by ascetic practices".[28] Baptismal regeneration was what counted, said Jovinian; there will be no differentiation of reward as between one Christian and another in the life to come. The scriptural account of the Last Assize (Last Judgment; see Rev 20:11–15) knows only the two most general categories: sheep and goats, which Jovinian understands as the baptised and the unbaptised—not, as Jerome maintained, those who have borne, respectively, good and bad fruit, a criterion open to multiple variations.[29] The treatise against Jovinian predicted that victory for his anti-ascetical and pro-egalitarian doctrines would lead to worldliness and immorality in Church and society.

The second controversy concerned Origen. Origen's contribution to the understanding of Scripture had been uniformly praised, not least by Jerome in his so-called pioneer patrology, *On Famous Men*. Origen's admirers largely ignored the more audacious if tentative suggestions about protology and eschatology found chiefly in the Alexandrian theologian's speculative essay *On First Principles*. Where necessary they quietly corrected Origen's excessively hierarchical ("Subordinationist") view of the relations of Father, Son, and Spirit. But Epiphanius of Salamis, a Palestinian monk now bishop in Cyprus, who had hosted Jerome and Paula on their journey to the East (his *Panarion*, so we saw, would be enormously useful to John Damascene), had decided Origen was the Church's heretic-in-chief,

---

[27] Hale Williams, *Monk and Book*, pp. 65–66.

[28] Kelly, *Jerome*, p. 181.

[29] Jerome, *Against Jovinian* 2, 22; see D. G. Hunter, *Marriage, Celibacy, and Heresy in Early Christianity: The Jovianist Controversy* (Oxford: Oxford University Press, 2007).

the true inspirer, in Epiphanius' opinion, of the dreaded Arius. Epiphanius sent a delegate to Jerusalem to invite the two Latin abbots, Rufinus and Jerome, to disclaim Origen's doctrines, before showing up in person later that year, 393. Rufinus demurred, confident not least of the sympathy of his own bishop, John I of Jerusalem, the successor of the better known Cyril of Jerusalem, author of the *Mystagogical Catecheses*, instructions for the newly baptised. Jerome, however, agreed—perhaps distinguishing in his own mind between Origen as exegete and Origen as doctrinal theologian. Jerome's *Letter* 61 set out the case that, yes, he had borrowed many things from Origen's exegesis but always guarding carefully against reproducing his doctrinal errors.

Meanwhile, Rufinus, resettled in Italy, embarked on an ambitious programme of Latin translations of the Greek Fathers—the Cappadocians, Evagrius of Pontus—and, fatefully, Origen; he preceded a translation of *On First Principles* by putting into Latin the first book of an *Apology for Origen* by Origen's pupil Pamphilus (co-authored with Eusebius of Caesarea), as well as writing a work of his own. Rufinus called the latter *The Falsification of Origen's Works*. Here he propounded the largely indefensible thesis that Origen's works had been interpolated by heretical hands. This conviction naturally influenced the way Rufinus set about translating *On First Principles*. So, for instance, when he came across passages that struck him as doctrinally odd, he replaced them with other relevant passages of a more conventional nature from elsewhere in Origen's writings. To Jerome's indignation, Rufinus quoted him (though without actually naming him) in the Preface to the first two books of *The Falsification of Origen's Works*. Jerome, Rufinus reported, had said Origen surpassed all other Christian writers. Origen was second only to the apostles as a teacher in the Church. But by now, Jerome was an official anti-Origenist. Rufinus, in effect, threw down the gauntlet, confronting Jerome with his own rapturous admiration for Origen in earlier life. Jerome at once set to work on a literal translation of *On First Principles* meant to show, indeed, to rub in, how matters really stood. In his *Against Rufinus* (a preemptive strike—reports reached Bethlehem that Rufinus was preparing a treatise against him), Jerome explained he had ever cited Origen only so as to warn Latin readers against his erroneous thinking. In his 401 *Apology against Jerome*, Rufinus pointed out that "if after acclaiming Origen for thirty years he now denounced him as a heretic, he was surely passing sentence on himself."[30]

The third controversy (after those with Jovinian, and about Origen) concerned the priest Vigilantius, who, writing from southwest Gaul, had attacked the veneration of the relics of the martyrs and other saints, as well as praying to them, lighting candles in their honour, and the practice of all-night vigils—and indeed the entire ascetical system of virginity, fasting, and monastic withdrawal from the world. In the last respect, it was another version of Jovinian's critique but now married to an attack on what would later be called popular Catholicism. In Kelly's words, "Had he been gifted with foresight, Jerome would have had the satisfaction of knowing that the practices and austere disciplines he was defending ... were to become the accepted norm of western Catholicism, and were to be officially justified by substantially the same apologetic as he was sketching out".[31]

The fourth and last controversy concerned Pelagius, who in the wake of the 410 attack on Rome by the Gothic leader Alaric had fled, accompanied by his highly combative disciple Caelestius, first to North Africa and then to the Holy Land. Like Jovinian, Pelagius stressed the nobility of the baptismal calling—but, unlike Jovinian, he was worried by the mediocrity of the Christian practice of so many of the baptised. In the words of Yves-Marie Duval, Pelagius was at one and the same time "the adversary and the successor of Jovinian".[32] He combated the Roman monk's denial of the salvational utility of asceticism, but he agreed with Jovinian that in principle, human persons, notably after Baptism, can avoid each and every sin. Pelagius' view of human nature was optimistic; his view of supernatural divine aid, minimalist.[33]

---

[30] Kelly, *Jerome*, p. 250. Moreover, since Jerome had published his literal *On First Principles*, Christians now had open access to everything that was worst in Origen. Naturally, this elicited from Jerome an *Apology against Rufinus* later that year. Too late, Augustine also wrote to them, imploring them to resume their friendship (this is Augustine's *Letter* 73). Meanwhile, Rufinus continued to publish many translations of Origen's homilies and commentaries, suggesting "how artificially the Origenistic issue had been blown up in the West". Ibid., pp. 256–57.

[31] Ibid., p. 290.

[32] Yves-Marie Duval, *L'affaire Jovinien: D'une crise de la société romaine à une crise de la pensée chrétienne à la fin du IVe et au début du Ve siècle* (Rome: Institutum Patristicum Augustinianum, 2003), p. 285.

[33] In Kelly's summary of his teaching, "[Pelagius] rejected as Manichaean, as well as stultifying to endeavour, the notion that human nature has been corrupted by original sin transmitted from Adam, and can raise itself only by God's help. Although a habit of sinning has set in,

In 410 Jerome's commentaries on the prophets had reached Ezekiel. He used the occasion of Ezekiel's prophetic call to comment on the synergy or cooperation between God and man. "When we bear fruit we are pruned by the Father so as to bear more fruit."[34] Jerome then broke off work to help refugees arriving in Palestine after the Goths' sack of Rome. In 411 Pelagius also reached Palestine, in his case from Africa. In Jerusalem Pelagius would find Bishop John receptive: Greek theology was keener on giving free will a high place in theological anthropology than was usually the case in the West. Jerome had no quarrel with free will, but he was clear that, to avoid evil and do good, human persons need the continuous help of God, as the Ezekiel commentary, when he resumed it, underlined. From 412 to 414, Jerome mounted an attack, seeing in Pelagius, as he thought, the posthumous spokesman of Rufinus, and, behind Rufinus, of Origen.[35] This was by no means entirely foolish: in his *Expositions* of the Pauline letters, Pelagius had indeed used Rufinus' abbreviated paraphrase of Origen's commentary on Saint Paul's Letter to the Romans. Jerome's *Letters* 130 and 133 are his first response to Pelagianism. In *Letter* 130 he explains that "where there is grace, this is not a reward for works done but the free gift of the Giver, so that the apostles' saying [Rom 9:16] is fulfilled, 'It depends not on man's will or exertion, but on God's mercy'. Certainly [Jerome went on] it belongs to us either to will or not to will. Nevertheless this liberty of ours is ours only by God's mercy."[36] In *Letter* 133 Jerome denies the claim that man can choose if he can live without sin—such a theory makes man like God, confutes the lives of the saints, and goes counter to such scriptural texts as Romans 3:23: "All have sinned and fall short of the glory of God."

---

a man is always free to shake it off, and by the exercise of his will to choose either right or wrong. Indeed, so far from there being any necessity of sinning, a man is in principle able to live without sin. Regarding sin as a voluntary act, he denied that new-born babies, who have no choice, can be guilty of it, yet he upheld the traditional practice of having them baptised. Assuredly men always need God's grace; but Pelagius defined grace, not as an inner power transforming them but as their original endowment with rational will, the divine forgiveness they obtain through baptism, and the illumination provided by the law of Moses and the teaching and example of Christ." Kelly, *Jerome*, p. 310. Kelly's summary is based on Robert F. Evans, *Pelagius: Inquiries and Reappraisals* (London: A. & C. Black, 1968).

[34] Jerome, *Commentary on Ezekiel* IV, 15, 8. Translation is the present author's.

[35] Giuseppe Caruso, O.S.A., *Ramusculus Origenis: L'eredità dell'antropologia origeniana nei pelagiani e in Girolamo* (Rome: Institutum Patristicum Augustinianum, 2012), pp. 531–58.

[36] Jerome, *Letter* 130, 12, cited in Kelly, *Jerome*, p. 313.

The implication that man needs no external supernatural aid makes nonsense of prayer, fasting, and continence.

Jerome's later *Dialogue against the Pelagians*, in its third book, shows how in the meantime Augustine had converted him to the strict doctrine of original sin. "That holy man and eloquent bishop Augustine not long ago wrote to Marcellinus ... two treatises on infant baptism in opposition to your heresy."[37] Adam's Fall is not "the precondition of mortality, it is a true fault passed down from progenitor to posterity."[38] Jerome was now marked down as a foe to the "enemies of grace". Hooligans, rumoured to be partisans of Pelagius, attacked the double monastery. Jerome and Eustochium, now abbess since her mother's death and taking her niece Paula the Younger with her, made their escape from the burning buildings. The news of the outrage was ill-received in the West. Jerome had the satisfaction of knowing that after this episode Pelagius was expelled from Jerusalem (and indeed from Palestine), though he complained that some of Pelagius' accomplices were still hanging around on the coast at Jaffa. By early 419, Jerome and Paula the Younger seem to have been back in a reconstructed monastery at Bethlehem. In *Letter* 154, the last we have from Jerome (it was discovered only in 1910), Jerome urges no leniency so far as Pelagians are concerned. With it, in J. N. D. Kelly's words, he "disappears from our view".[39] It might well have been the public exit he would have wanted. He is the second of the Latin Doctors, and the third and greatest of them, Augustine, would surely have sympathised with his last wishes—to give Pelagians no relief.

---

[37] Jerome, *Dialogue against the Pelagians* III, 19, trans. W. Fremantle, G. Lewis, and W. G. Martley, in *Nicene and Post-Nicene Fathers*, ed. Philip Schaff and Henry Wace, 2nd series, vol. 6 (Buffalo, NY: Christian Literature Publishing, 1893).

[38] Caruso, *Ramusculus Origenis*, p. 620.

[39] Kelly, *Jerome*, p. 331.

13

The Christian Plato: Saint Augustine of Hippo

With the possible exception of Cicero, more is known about Saint Augustine than about any other figure from Antiquity. We know far too much about him for that knowledge to be readily manageable. As with any life, however, it is always possible to state the broad outlines.

Early Life and Career

Augustine was born in 354 at Thagaste (now Souk Ahras) in the Roman province of Numidia, corresponding roughly to present-day northeast Algeria. He was the son of a small landowner, Patricius, a pagan, and his Christian wife, Monnica. Brought up to accompany his mother to church,[1] he received the rudiments of an education from a local elementary teacher (a "grammaticus") at Thagaste before moving on at the age of fifteen to secondary school at Madaura. Madaura was a Numidian town famous as the birthplace of the second-century writer Apuleius, who combined philosophy with novel writing. Perhaps (who knows?) hearing his name triggered Augustine's own ineradicable propensity to write books. Finally, for the equivalent of a university education, he transferred in 375 to Carthage, the city of Tertullian and Cyprian, capital of the neighbouring province of Africa Proconsularis. There, he trained as a rhetor, the principal way to enter public service at a senior level. Augustine developed a love of fine Latin style, which put him off the Scriptures as represented by the Old Latin Bible with its "humble vulgarity".[2]

---

[1] At one point, when seriously ill, Baptism might have been conferred but he recovered.

[2] Henry Chadwick, *Augustine of Hippo: A Life* (Oxford: Oxford University Press, 2009), p. 12.

Higher education was paid for by a patron who was a Manichee sympathiser—a friend to the dualist religion founded by a Persian would-be prophet, Mani. Born in 216, Mani held that the teachings of the Buddha, Zoroaster, and Jesus himself were incomplete. The completion was now at hand—in the revelations he himself had received and recorded in a number of writings, now extant only in fragments. Manichaeism possessed an elaborate cosmology, reminiscent of the Gnostics, and an equally elaborate governing hierarchy. The fullest set of Manichee writings are in Chinese, testifying that the "Religion of Light" spread quite as far eastward as it did westward. From Algeria to China, it was Christianity's main competitor until the rise of Islam.[3]

Augustine spent ten years as a Manichee "hearer", the equivalent of a layman in this syncretistic sect whose leaders were celibate monastics. In double-quick time, he landed posts, first as a private teacher of rhetoric at Carthage and Rome, where Manichees were influential, and then, in 384, with the additional support of the leader of the traditional pagan contingent among the Roman senatorial aristocracy, as public orator—that would be a State appointment—at Milan. Milan, as the life of Ambrose testifies, was one of the places to which the court of the Western Roman Empire periodically migrated.

Not all rhetors had more than a superficial acquaintance with the language of philosophy. Augustine was different. Owing to reading Cicero's now lost treatise *Hortensius*—a plea to its readers to make the pursuit of wisdom the chief purpose of their lives—Augustine was always a searcher, even though much of his philosophical culture may have reached him secondhand either through mediatorial figures (much of what he knew of Plato's thought came through Cicero and Cicero's contemporary Varro), or through anthologies of key passages. He became dissatisfied with Manichaeism, whose teachings struck him as in conflict with natural knowledge. For similar reasons he also lost confidence in astrology—it was at odds with the astronomical science of his day. His attraction to both the Manichees and the astrologers reflected a reluctance to believe the universe was ruled by chance.[4]

[3] S. N. C. Lieu, *Manichaeism in the Later Roman Empire and Medieval China: A Historical Survey* (Manchester: Manchester University Press, 1985).

[4] Serge Lancel, *Saint Augustine* (London: Student Christian Movement Press, 2002), p. 49.

Once freed from these dubious belief systems, he was tempted by the scepticism of the so-called New Academy whose principal tenet ran, It is probable that nothing is certain. This was not much of an improvement when considered as a basis for life. So Augustine was fortunate to discover the alternative, deeply religious, and, indeed, ascetic development of the Platonic tradition represented by the founder of Neoplatonism, the mighty Plotinus.

Yet he could not accept a religious philosophy that remained totally silent on the Christ of his childhood worship.[5] Paganism as such, remarked the ancient historian Peter Brown, "meant nothing to Augustine".[6] At Milan he heard the preaching of Ambrose. By his allegorical interpretations of Old Testament texts, Ambrose turned the Jewish Bible into a richly coded preparation for both Christ and evangelical morality. In effect, Ambrose cleared away objections to the Scriptures Augustine had learned from the Manichees. Moreover, Ambrose's preaching gave him for the first time the notion that—in his own words, in the early treatise *On the Happy Life*—the "idea of God rules out every corporeal consideration, as does likewise the idea of the nature of the soul since, of all beings, the soul comes closest to the being of God."[7] That amounted to metaphysical liberation from the constraints of philosophical materialism. Yet even more than this can plausibly be claimed for those sermons. Pope Benedict XVI goes so far as to say that it was from the preaching of Ambrose that Augustine "found the key to understanding the beauty and even the philosophical depth of the Old Testament and grasped the whole unity of the mystery of Christ in history as well as the synthesis between philosophy, rationality, and faith in the *Logos*, in Christ, the Eternal Word who was made flesh".[8]

The Ambrosian sermons Augustine heard at Easter 386 would have included a number of Plotinian themes: the sovereignty of the Good, the origin of evil, ascent to God, the heavenly fatherland, the liberation involved in bodily death, the perpetual life of the blessed. (These motifs will resound not only in such early writings as

[5] Augustine, *Confessions* III, 4; V, 25.

[6] Peter Brown, *Augustine of Hippo: A Biography* (London: Faber and Faber, 1967), p. 41.

[7] Augustine, *On the Happy Life* I, 4. Translation is the present author's.

[8] Pope Benedict XVI, *Church Fathers: From Clement of Rome to Augustine* (San Francisco: Ignatius Press, 2008), p. 171.

Against the Academics and the *Soliloquies*, but in the *Confessions* too.) They were Neoplatonic themes that assisted the intellectual appropriation of Christian revelation. The Milanese priest Simplicianus, who would succeed Ambrose as bishop, recounted to Augustine (we noted the episode in the chapter but last) the conversion of the Neo-Platonist philosopher Marius Victorinus, in which Simplicianus had played a part. Augustine found the story inspirational. A man who had defended Roman paganism with "thundering eloquence", now "blushed not to be the child of Your Christ, and an infant at Your fountain, submitting his neck to the yoke of humility, and subduing his forehead to the reproach of the Cross".[9]

Augustine had some personal experience of the call to the transcendent God in a characteristically Plotinian manner, via a profound journey inwards, into the depths of the soul. By reference to the Greek prepositions *en* (meaning "in") and *ek* (meaning "out), it might be termed a process of "enstasy" that issued in "ecstasy". It was a going into the self so as to go outwards towards God. In his *Confessions* he described it like this: "Warned [by these books] to return to myself, I entered my innermost being led by your guidance.... I entered, and saw with my soul's eye, feeble though it was, I saw above the eye of my soul, above my mind, the unchangeable light, not the ordinary light that all may see, nor a light of the same kind but stronger, as though that light would have a more dazzling brilliance, and by its power fill everything. No, it was not that but different, far different."[10] He had somehow heard in his heart a distant echo of the divine Word to Moses "I AM WHO I AM" (Ex 3:14)—which, for Augustine, means above all that God is eternal and unchangeable.[11] It gave him his distinctive "name" for God: *Idipsum* or "the One Who Is Himself".

We can hear the music of the *Enneads* and Exodus played contrapuntally when in the *Soliloquies* Augustine explains just how he

---

[9] Augustine, *Confessions* VIII, 3, trans. R. S. Pine-Coffin (London: Penguin, 1961); unless otherwise indicated, citations from the *Confessions* are from this translation. The episode figures importantly in the presentation of the "ecclesiastical form of faith" in Joseph Ratzinger, *Introduction to Christianity*, trans. J. R. Foster (London: Burns and Oates, 1969; San Francisco: Ignatius Press, 1990), pp. 63–64. Citations refer to the Ignatius Press edition.

[10] Augustine, *Confessions* VII, 16.

[11] Augustine, *Sermons*, 7, 7. There are nearly fifty places in his written corpus where Augustine discusses Exodus 3:13–15; see Emilie zum Brunn, *St. Augustine: Being and Nothingness* (New York: Paragon House, 1988), pp. 97–119.

had surmounted the scepticism of the New Academy. What provides certainty is the light of God, who is the invisible sun of the soul. "As in this visible [physical] sun we may observe three things: that he is, that he shines, that he illuminates: so in that God most far withdrawn whom you would fain apprehend, there are these three things: that He is, that He is apprehended, and that He makes other things to be apprehended."[12] As time went on, this metaphysically oriented Plotinian Christianity would be rendered ever more biblical in its content and manner. Yet it would never be left behind. Augustine's chief French-language biographer Serge Lancel commented: "Ideas of Plotinian origin which, swiftly modified by specifically Christian additions—the Prologue to the Gospel of Saint John, Saint Paul's Epistles, complemented by them and re-assimilated through them, would lastingly form the intellectual framework of the Augustinian doctrine of the universe, God and mankind."[13]

This was by no means an unconscious process. Augustine knowingly embraced the contribution of what he deemed true philosophy to the setting forth of divine revelation. In On Christian Teaching, he declared: "If those who are called philosophers, and especially the Platonists, are found to have said anything that is true and in harmony with our faith, we are not only not to shrink from it, but to claim it for our own use from those who have unlawful possession of it."[14] Augustine thus becomes an icon for the characteristically Catholic understanding of the way philosophy can be integrated with theology in the faith-reason relationship.[15] A Presbyterian student of Augustine's theology, Eugene TeSelle, took the point, stating, "Though they have come through different channels they emanate from the same source, the eternal Word; there is, so to speak, a pre-established harmony between them, and therefore it is no surprise that they assert the same things, using different words."[16]

---

[12] Augustine, Soliloquies I, 15, trans. C.C. Starbuck, in Nicene and Post-Nicene Fathers [NPNF], ed. Philip Schaff, 1st series, vol. 7 (Buffalo, NY: Christian Literature Publishing, 1888). Citations from the Soliloquies are from this translation.

[13] Lancel, Saint Augustine, p. 87.

[14] Augustine, On Christian Teaching II, 40, 60, trans. James Shaw, in NPNF, ed. Philip Schaff, 1st series, vol. 2 (Buffalo, NY: Christian Literature Publishing, 1887).

[15] Benedict XVI, Church Fathers, pp. 179–80.

[16] Eugene TeSelle, Augustine the Theologian (London: Burns and Oates, 1970), p. 73.

It was not, however, long before he saw the limits of Neopla-tonism in its services to Christianity. According to John M. Rist,

> Augustine soon noticed what he took to be arrogance (*superbia* = *tolma*) among the Neoplatonists themselves. Oddly enough, he thought, recognition of intelligibles (and correspondingly disvaluing sensibles) had provided no antidote to the very vice which Plotinus himself sometimes claimed to be the root of sinfulness in the soul.... The Platonists—in this like Docetists or Gnostics—were too proud to be able to recognize the inherent humility of the Incarnation; of itself, recognizing the intelligibles neither healed the philosophers nor substituted for Christ.[17]

For Augustine knew now that the eyes of his soul were in need of healing. In the *Soliloquies*, where he dialogues with Reason herself, he wrote: "Now I, Reason, am that in the mind which the act of looking is in the eyes. For to have eyes is not the same as to look; nor again is to look the same as to see. Therefore the soul has need of three things: to have eyes, such as it can use to good advantage, to look, and to see."[18] And Augustine proposed that faith, hope, and charity, respectively, meet just this trio of needs. Without those "theological" virtues "no mind is healed, so that it can see, that is, understand its God."[19] The quest is supremely worthwhile, for the vision of God is the "end [the goal] of [all] looking"; it is blessedness itself.[20]

In search of healing, Augustine's fervent wish was to approach Baptism and follow a specifically Christian form of the ascetic path towards wisdom. But delight in sexual relations, not least with his two successive concubines, stood in the way. Augustine's *Confessions* tells us how the issue was resolved. It was, in effect, a tale of two trees.[21] There had been a pear tree which as a child he robbed of its fruit for the sheer sake of the petty crime involved, just because it was forbidden—a parable of Adam's Fall. But now there was a second tree,

---

[17] John M. Rist, *Augustine: Ancient Thought Baptized* (Cambridge: Cambridge University Press, 1994), p. 104.

[18] *Soliloquies* I, 12.

[19] Ibid.

[20] Ibid., I, 13.

[21] This conceit comes from Lancel, *Saint Augustine*, p. 21, based on *Confessions* II, 4–10; VIII, 12.

a tree that was a parable of redemption. It was the fig tree under which he was sitting in his garden at Milan when he heard the voice of a child at play crying, "Take and read, take and read." He then picked up the Pauline epistles at the famous Romans text (13:14) about laying aside a sensual life and putting on instead the Lord Jesus Christ.[22] It was his so-called "moral" conversion. Now intent on continence, a prebaptismal retreat at an estate in the Lombard countryside—Cassiciacum, now Cassago di Brienza, just south of Como—saw him engaged in discussions with a small circle of friends and pupils, including his mother, on the themes of truth, happiness (or "blessedness", *beatitudo*), and the sovereign good, topics inspired at once by the *Enneads* and by the Psalter.[23]

Augustine was baptised in Milan at Easter 387. Once baptised and after writing two short treatises, *On the Immortality of the Soul* and the first draft of an *On Music*, he was to return to Africa; but the death of his mother and the political and military hazards of an insurgency (directed against the young emperor Valentinian II, who gave Ambrose such trouble) delayed him at Rome in what would prove a productive year for his literary output. While there, awaiting a declaration of the safety of the waters, he drafted the first of his anti-Manichee writings, a two-part work: *On the Morals of the Catholic Church* and *On the Morals of the Manichees*. Augustine was now clear that not only to see with the "eyes of the mind" but to "attain virtue", the soul "must follow as it would a guide something that transcends it; and that something is the selfsame cause of that good, in other words, God; and to reach God is to attain beatitude".[24] If *On the Morals of the Manichees* looks back, *On the Morals of the Catholic Church* looks ahead, starting a "process of building love—a Christianised Platonic love—into the classical structures of virtue".[25] Morals for Augustine are quintessentially theocentric since, while he redefines all forms of virtue as forms of love, he also holds that as a "result

---

[22] Augustine, *Confessions* VIII, 29.

[23] Augustine was tapping a rich vein; see, translated from the Swedish, Ragnar Holte, *Béatitude et sagesse: Saint Augustin et le problème de la fin de l'homme dans la philosophie ancienne* (Paris: Etudes augustiniennes, 1962).

[24] Lancel, *Saint Augustine*, p. 123, commenting on Augustine, *On the Morals of the Catholic Church* I, 9.

[25] Rist, *Augustine*, p. 161.

of their love of God ... men are able to react morally to whatever situation may arise in the course of their lives."[26] One of his claims in these works was that Catholic Christianity made a better setting for the ascetic life than did Manichaenism, a harbinger of his later plan for attaching monasteries to churches in North Africa.

From the same period, we have the curiously entitled *On the Quantity of the Soul*, where Augustine argues that the soul is not extended in space, so its "quantity" must be a question of power and capacity. We also have the first book of his treatise *On Free Will*, a topic where his intellectual legacy would eventually be mired in much misunderstanding.[27] As Henry Chadwick remarks in his posthumously published life of Augustine, "The religious and philosophical quests are fused together in his mind, and this will remain true to the end of his life."[28] It would also be true of a distinguished latter-day Augustinian, Joseph Ratzinger—far more true than what is claimed by those who regarded Ratzinger's theology (and pontificate) as marked by "Augustinian pessimism". Chadwick notes that, in ancient Christianity, Boethius sought to loosen a little that Augustinian synthesis of philosophy-with-theology. The same would be true, in the High Middle Ages, of Saint Thomas.

Monk, Priest, Bishop

Back in Africa—indeed, back at Thagaste—Augustine set up his own monastery for celibate laymen, *servi Dei*, "servants of God"—that is, professional ascetics or (a term I rather favour) "proto-monastics". The Thagaste monastery would be a fruitful seed-ground for his writing. Here he produced *On Genesis, against the Manichees*; many of the *On Diverse Questions* (a series of answers to enquirers); *On the Teacher*, where he substitutes for the Platonic doctrine of "anamnesis" (the soul remembering what it knew in a previous existence) a teaching about Christ the Logos of God as the inner pedagogue—what would later be called Augustine's "doctrine of illumination"; and *On*

---

[26] Ibid.

[27] John Rist, *Augustine Deformed: Love, Sin, and Freedom in the Western Moral Tradition* (Cambridge: Cambridge University Press, 2014).

[28] Chadwick, *Augustine of Hippo*, p. 31.

True Religion, written for his erstwhile Manichee patron, where he would use the language of deification otherwise associated with the Greek Fathers, especially (as we have seen) Cyril of Alexandria and the Cappadocians.[29]

Deification, for the early Augustine, is the height of the enjoyment of God (*fruitio Dei*) made possible by *otium*—literally "idleness" but metaphorically "contemplation", a thought which possibly echoes the second of the great Neoplatonist masters, Porphyry, the biographer of Plotinus. But as *On True Religion* makes clear, Christianity can fulfil Platonism only if the Word incarnate is acknowledged, the act of faith in Jesus Christ leading on from philosophy to salvation.[30] For the mature Augustine, deification will be, therefore, the result of the atoning activity of the God-man, who adopts the human beings he elects as his brethren, making them sons and daughters of God.[31] That is one aspect of Augustine's growing realisation in the lay monastery at Thagaste that what Christian revelation adds to the philosophers is, above all, knowledge of the "temporal dispensation" whereby, through God's freely enacted plan in history, mankind is brought to its intended goal.[32] The crucial importance of such "salvation history" was something that Irenaeus, say, would have taken for granted. But Irenaeus' way to Christ was not so complex as was Augustine's. Not that, since the time of his conversion, Augustine was unaware that "at least in the case of creation *ex nihilo* and of the Incarnation, the historical must become part of any account of 'reality', however 'Platonic' it might otherwise be."[33] But his grasp of saving history and its ultimate implications could be—and was— strengthened and improved.

In 391 Augustine moved with his fellow "servants of God" from Thagaste to Hippo (now Annaba, on the Algerian coast) in search of a better site for his monastery—little thinking it would lead to his being ordained a priest, very much against his wishes, by the elderly bishop who wanted Augustine to succeed him (an outcome verified

---

[29] See also *Letter* 10, of the same date, to his pagan friend Nebridius.

[30] Augustine, *On True Religion* 50.

[31] Gerald Bonner, "Augustine's Conception of Deification", *Journal of Theological Studies*, n.s., 37 (1986): 369–86.

[32] TeSelle, *Augustine the Theologian*, pp. 130–31.

[33] Rist, *Augustine*, p. 58.

four years later). The monk-priest at Hippo continued his literary struggle against the Manichees,[34] though the more urgent need was to oppose "Donatists": African Christians who might be described as "Catholic sectarians", if the phrase is not a contradiction in terms. This—to be considered shortly—was a problem bequeathed to him by the regional triumph of Cyprianic ecclesiology.

Augustine's self-education in theology (for this is what these writings represent) was still progressing. The keynote address he gave at the 393 Council of Hippo, now known as *On Faith and the Creed*, suggests he was not quite clear about the place of the Spirit in the immanent Trinity. "With respect to the Holy Spirit ... there has not been as yet, on the part of learned and distinguished investigators of the Scriptures, a discussion of the subject full enough or careful enough to make it possible for us to obtain an intelligent conception of what also constitutes His special individuality (*proprium*)."[35] He also needed to clarify his doctrine of creation vis-à-vis the Neoplatonists, a task he began in the unfinished *Literal Commentary on Genesis* of these few presbyteral years.[36] At the same time, he started to comment on the Psalter, which he had loved ever since his conversion. There his supreme theme was humility, whose primacy in the Christian life he underlined in the contemporaneous *On the Sermon of the Lord on the Mount*. The book would start a trend of giving the Beatitudes a high place in the moral theology of Latin Catholics, though not all would write as he did: "I understood that only One is truly perfect and that the words of the Sermon on the Mount are completely realized in only One—in Jesus Christ himself. The whole Church, instead—all of us, including the Apostles—must pray every

---

[34] Augustine, *On the Usefulness of Believing*; Augustine, *On the Two Souls*; Augustine, *Against Fortunatus*.

[35] Augustine, *On Faith and the Creed* 9, 19, trans. S.D.F. Salmond, in *NPNF*, ed. Philip Schaff, 1st series, vol. 3 (Buffalo, NY: Christian Literature Publishing, 1887). See my account of *On the Trinity* below, where the *proprium* of the Spirit is at last declared to be *Amor*, "love". "Whereas for Augustine the Spirit was always connected with 'ordering' ... the connection of order with love takes longer to develop." Rist, *Augustine*, p. 156n15.

[36] As Eugene TeSelle explains, he evolved "what one might call a two-stage understanding of creation as first the positing of 'matter' (corporeal and spiritual) and then the formation of this material substratum by the influence of the Word and its stabilization by the Spirit; there is, to use Augustine's own later terminology, first *existence*, the coming forth of matter as something other than God, and then *conversion*, ... matter's being changed for the better and becoming similar to God in some respect." TeSelle, *Augustine the Theologian*, p. 138.

day: 'Forgive us our sins as we forgive those who sin against us'."[37]
He began, too, expositions of the Pauline letters, above all, Romans
and Galatians, and finished his *On Free Will*, a work which later on
led to accusations he had once been a proto-Pelagian.[38] Continuing with the series of *Diverse Questions*, he had occasion to mention
for the first time the fateful words *peccatum originale*—which, Lancel
points out, may mean either "sin of origin" (an origin that brings the
human race some kind of penalty or punishment) or "original sin"
(implying the transmissibility of guilt). This second meaning became
the more distinctively Augustinian opinion, reflecting Augustine's
view that Adam was a kind of transindividual personage in whom
all human persons, present or future, lived a common life. Until the
moment of the Fall, Adam's soul was the common soul of the human
race. It was one way of understanding Paul's teaching on the two
Adams, each with its own solidarity because the common humanity in the old Adam would be reconstituted in the new unity of
the Body of Christ, who was himself the second—and permanently
redeeming—"transindividual" Person. The notion recurs in the early
twentieth-century Russian Orthodox theologian Sergei Bulgakov.

Writing as a newly made bishop, the 397 *On Christian Teaching*[39]
would be important for biblical hermeneutics. So much will become
plain in the later Latin Fathers, notably in the use made of it by
Gregory the Great and, after Gregory, by the English monk known
to history as the Venerable Bede. The Donatist theologian Tyconius
had already written a "rule-book" for interpreting the Bible, the *Book
of Rules*, and Augustine admired its approach to the interpretation of
biblical symbolism.[40] But Augustine thought that almost every area
of human knowledge could and should be drawn on to illuminate the
Scriptures—so much so that a single person would never be able to

---

[37] Augustine, *On the Sermon of the Lord on the Mount* I, 19, 1–3.

[38] Brown, *Augustine of Hippo*, pp. 148–49. For an elaborately argued case for the converted
Augustine's consistency on the topics of free will and divine aid, see TeSelle, *Augustine the
Theologian*, op. cit., pp. 156–65, a discussion continued on pp. 278–94. But TeSelle does not
find the same consistency on the matter of "election" (predestination). Ibid., pp. 177–82.

[39] *On Christian Teaching* was not finished till almost the end of his life when he added a
Book IV on homiletics (homilies, he wrote then, should instruct, please, and move).

[40] See Pamela Bright, *The Book of Rules of Tyconius: Its Purpose and Inner Logic* (Notre
Dame, IN: University of Notre Dame Press, 1988); Augustine makes much use of the work
in *On Christian Teaching* III, 30–37.

master the information required without some kind of set of handy aids, a prompt for the later invention of encyclopaedias.

At a more fundamental level, Augustine's *On Christian Teaching* works with two key distinctions: a distinction between reality and sign, and a further distinction between enjoying realities and using them. They were notions he found it possible to deploy across a wide range of theological areas. Reality and sign: that is a helpful combination for sacramental theology, where signs point to realities and sometimes embody them. Enjoying and using: that is a helpful combination for ethics, where other persons are to be enjoyed by us and never simply used as nonpersonal realities may be. "For Augustine the distinction merges into his view of the temporal as that which we must pass through to reach the things eternal. Everything short of the final goal in God becomes a subordinate object of our love, and in that sense is 'used' (by which Augustine does not mean 'exploited')."[41]

In this period when Augustine was at the height of his powers, he began to write the *Confessions*, which he would finish in 401. Bishop Paulinus of Nola, the wealthy layman-turned-ascetic, had asked for an account of his conversion.[42] This gave him an opportunity, not least, to reflect on the role in his life of the primacy of God's grace: a truth of which he had learned from the letters of Saint Paul. The *Confessions* were not simply an act of self-defence. In TeSelle's words, "The writing of the *Confessions* was probably occasioned by a combination of internal and external factors—his new renown as a bishop, inquiries about his earlier life, attacks on his integrity, his own reflections on classical culture, his new understanding of grace, all of them together requiring a massive re-examination and reinterpretation of his own life."[43] Augustine now wrote the last of his anti-Manichaean works.[44] But then the struggle with Donatism took over as priority number one.

---

[41] Chadwick, *Augustine of Hippo*, p. 61.

[42] "Augustine ... did not need to look far to find an audience for the *Confessions*. It had been created for him quite recently, by the amazing spread of asceticism in the Latin world" (Brown, *Augustine of Hippo*, pp. 159–60). For Paulinus, see D. E. Trout, *Paulinus of Nola: Life, Letters and Poems* (Berkeley, CA: University of California Press, 1999).

[43] TeSelle, *Augustine the Theologian*, p. 189.

[44] The chief among such writings are *Against Adimantus, Against Faustus, Against Secundinus*, and the *On the Nature of the Good*.

Donatism, Pelagianism

The heart of Donatism is the claim that the holiness of the Church cannot survive the perpetuation of the apostolic succession by bishops who have committed acts of apostasy—or at least betrayal (typically, the handing over of the Scriptures to pagan persecutors for them to destroy)—even if the bishops in question have subsequently repented and undergone reconciliation.[45] The Church's holiness, one of her essential marks, requires us to reject an apostolic succession carried on by such means. The Donatist claim ran as follows. During the Diocletianic persecution (in the opening years of the fourth century), the Catholic primate Caecilian had been consecrated by a *traditor*, a word which means at once a "hander-over" (of the Scriptures) and a "betrayer". The Donatus who gave Donatism its name was the successor of a bishop substituted at Carthage in 312 to take Caecilian's place. As Donatists saw matters, the "consecrating hands" of *traditores* "transmitted pollution, not Christ's apostolic pastoral commission", such that "all sacraments of this compromising church were rendered invalid."[46] All churches outside North Africa were apostate by association. Augustine sought public debates with Donatist leaders in continuing argument over both the history and the ecclesiology of the dispute.[47] Against the background of acts of violence committed by Donatist partisans, and concluding that persuasion had failed, he swung round to supporting the idea of an appeal to the imperial power. In 405, accordingly, the emperor Honorius promulgated a new law equating the Donatist schism with heresy on the grounds of its requirement of re-Baptism, a first step towards the elimination of the Donatist Church with State assistance.[48]

[45] The classic study in English is W. H. C. Frend, *The Donatist Church: A Movement of Protest in Roman North Africa* (Oxford: Clarendon Press, 1952); but its overall thesis—the religious dispute was the presenting issue only for deeper social and ethnic divisions—has been much criticized; see, for example, Brown, *Augustine of Hippo*, pp. 217, 227–28.

[46] Henry Chadwick, *The Church in Ancient Society: From Galilee to Gregory the Great* (Oxford: Oxford University Press, 2001), p. 382.

[47] Augustine's principal anti-Donatist works are *On Baptism against Petilianus*, *Against Crescentius*, and *On Baptism against the Donatists*.

[48] "Augustine's conversion to the use of coercion brought sharp criticism from some fellow Catholics. In later ages his arguments came to be disastrously exploited by inquisitors, ecclesiastical and secular, who neglected his crucial proviso that the form of correction must be seen to be a loving familial chastisement, a minimal force, absolutely excluding torture or death even for cases of violence." Chadwick, *Augustine of Hippo*, p. 113.

By that date, Augustine knew that Cyprian, the premier Doctor and martyr of the Church in Africa, had himself supported re-Baptism over against the teachings of the bishop of Rome. Cyprian was the spiritual giant of Christian Africa. Augustine could hardly write an "Against Cyprian".[49] Cyprian was "the glory of the African churches"[50]. He could stress that at least only Cyprian had not broken communion with his opponents, nor had he maintained, as the Donatists had come to do, that sinful ministers cannot baptise. In his writings on Donatism, Augustine stressed the geographical universality of the Church (she was hardly confined to a couple of provinces in North Africa), and how it was a "mixed body" made up of wheat and tares, left to grow together until the Final Judgment. On the one hand, he distinguished between the sacramental communion, *communio sacramentorum*, and on the other, the assembly or society of the saints, the *congregatio* or *societas sanctorum*. Tares could belong to the first in a way they could not to the second. It must be borne in mind that Augustine was not a modern ecumenist who takes for granted the fruitfulness of schismatic rites. He recognised the validity of the Donatist sacraments. But he allowed their rites no salvific value so long as participants remained outside the unity of the Church. After an imperially sponsored conference in Carthage in 411, the Donatist bishops were obliged either to accept communion with the Catholics or to surrender their sees and go into exile. Augustine did not object to these arrangements. But he did his best to smooth the passage of the less inflexible among the Donatist episcopate.[51]

Meanwhile a new crisis was upon him. The British monk Pelagius, a popular ascetic guide in Rome, had read Augustine's *Confessions* in 404 or 405.[52] He was scandalised by some words addressed by their author to God: "Give what you command and command what you will."[53] For Pelagius, grace was a gift of divine aid for the easier accomplishing of what we should be able to do anyway once our free

[49] In his *Reconsiderations*, indeed, Augustine describes the seven books of his *On Baptism, against the Donatists*, as an attempt to wrest the moral ownership of Cyprian's "letters and acts" from the Donatists, and restore them to the Catholics in Africa. *Reconsiderations* II, 18.

[50] Chadwick, *Augustine of Hippo*, p. 9.

[51] Augustine gave his own comments in the 412 *To the Donatists after the Conference*, and had a last word on the rupture in *Against Gaudentius* of 419 or 420.

[52] For an overview of Pelagius' life and doctrine, see Brinley Roderick Rees, *Pelagius: Life and Letters* (Woodbridge, UK: Boydell and Brewer, 1998).

[53] *Confessions* X, 29, 40. Translation is the present author's.

will commands us to act as we ought. His commentary on the Pauline epistles showed he knew Augustine's exposition of Saint Paul, and disagreed with it.

Modern writers are inclined to say that for Pelagius the root cause of Augustine's misconceptions was an underappreciation of Christian Baptism whereby we are born again.[54] And it is true that Augustine's experience of the faithful in the Church of North Africa made him sceptical about the likelihood of a total break with a sinful past.[55] Brown instances *Sermon* 131, where Augustine calls the convert not someone restored to perfect health but, as with the wounded man on the road to Jericho, someone saved from death by the "oil" of the baptismal anointing—that someone, he thought, is likely to spend the rest of his life convalescing in the "inn" of the Church.[56]

Augustine took Pelagianism to be not an exaltation of Baptism but a "hidden doctrine of self-redemption".[57] In 412 Augustine published his first anti-Pelagian text, *Merits and Remission*, in principle a response to a rather obscure Syrian monk, an erstwhile member of Jerome's community at Bethlehem who shared some of Pelagius' concerns. Rufinus the Syrian was alarmed at the "traducianist" notion that inherited sinfulness confers guilt such that unbaptised babies, dying in infancy, hereafter are destined for punishment—albeit of a mild variety. Little children, thought the Syrian Rufinus, have no need of absolution. The Baptism of infants brings divine adoption, not the forgiveness of sins.[58] (He had evidently not noticed the signs of infant egotism spotted by Augustine in the *Confessions*.) More important for the wider debate was Pelagius' radical disciple Caelestius, a legally trained Roman aristocrat and the first Pelagian spokesman to be

---

[54] Torgny Bohlin, *Die Theologie des Pelagius und ihre Genesis* (Uppsala: Uppsala Universitets Aarskrift, 1957), pp. 29–43. "The innocence that Pelagius was concerned to defend was not the innocence of babies: it was the *innocence of the post-conversion state*—of the adult who had 'turned away from his sins'. His criticism of the doctrine of original sin ... was determined by the fear that once a sin was regarded as 'natural' rather than 'voluntary', it would be allowed to survive the geological fault between a man's past and his present that Pelagius associated with conversion and with the rite of baptism." Peter Brown, "Pelagius and His Supporters: Aims and Environment", *Journal of Theological Studies*, n.s., 19 (1968): 105; internal citation from Augustine, *On the Deeds of Pelagius* VI, 16.

[55] Brown, "Pelagius", p. 107.

[56] Ibid., pp. 110–11.

[57] Hubertus B. Drobner, *The Fathers of the Church: A Comprehensive Introduction* (Peabody, MA: Hendrickson, 2007), p. 405.

[58] See Chadwick, *Church in Ancient Society*, pp. 449–50.

episcopally challenged. That same year, 412, Ambrose's future biographer, Paulinus of Milan, had accused Caelestius of erroneous teaching during a gathering of bishops in North Africa. *Inter alia*, Caelestius had said that nothing can be easier than to change our will by an act of will. With his customary psychological acumen (and a dash of irony), Augustine replied, "I could say with absolute truth and conviction [that men were not sinless] because they did not want to be sinless. But if you were to ask me why they did not want to be so, then we are getting out of our depth."[59] For Augustine, the freedom to will differently from how one has willed before "can only be the culmination of a process of healing" (cf. the situation of the man beaten up on the Jericho road).[60] Willing efficaciously to be sinless is not something that can be turned on or off like a tap. Even for unfallen Adam, so Augustine thinks, the will required divine assistance so as to persist in continued good actions. Augustine would eventually conclude that only the saints in glory who cannot sin—because they do not want to—enjoy the "to-be-longed-for necessity" that is perfect freedom, freedom perfectly attuned to the Good, to God.[61]

Though reactions to Pelagius (and even more to Caelestius) in Africa were clearly negative, sympathy for him further east showed the matter was by no means settled. A synod at Diospolis, presided over by the metropolitan of Palestine, exculpated Pelagius, though Augustine thought he "had been disingenuous, using ambivalent language".[62] A quartet of further works followed from Augustine's hand,[63] the last of which, *On the Grace of Christ and Original Sin*, was dispatched to the Pelagian leaders at the moment of Augustine's apparent triumph, for it coincided with their expulsion from Rome (by an imperial rescript issued at Ravenna, not by the pope who, however, found it difficult to object). Yet a legal—or even a canonical—penalty does not furnish a theological answer. Lancel is, therefore,

---

[59] Augustine, *Merits and Remission* II, 17, 26, quoted in Brown, *Augustine of Hippo*, p. 373.

[60] Ibid.

[61] Augustine, *The Incomplete Work against Julian* 5, 61.

[62] Chadwick, *Church in Ancient Society*, p. 453.

[63] In 412 Augustine wrote *On the Spirit and the Letter*, but the topic was really the relation of law and grace; it influenced the mediaeval hymnographer Adam of Saint Victor—but also, fatefully, Martin Luther. In 415 he followed this up by his *On Nature and Grace*—a reply to Pelagius' *On Nature*, which had just reached him. There followed in 416 *On the Deeds of Pelagius*, a response to the exoneration of Pelagius at the (Palestinian) Synod of Diospolis, and in 418 *On the Grace of Christ and Original Sin*.

correct to write: "For the bishop [i.e., Augustine], the most difficult part still remained—to define the conditions in which original
sin is transmitted and, always affirming the need for divine grace, to
safeguard what might remain of human freedom after accepting that
most serious of determinisms—the determinism of predestination.
He would be led to this—and his own approach to the frontiers of
heresy—by the repercussions of the controversy with Julian of Eclanum."[64] It was in the heat of that controversy that he allowed himself
to make a disastrous claim: we should speak, after the Fall, not of a
"free will" but of a "slave will".[65]

Julian of Eclanum (a town in Campania) was a young married
bishop, either living continently or as a widower. In the first place, he
took issue with what he considered Augustine's disparagement of the
conjugal life. This was not so much—as in the earlier debate between
Jovinian and Jerome—a matter of Augustine exalting the virginal state
(though he *did* exalt it). Julian's chief worry lay elsewhere. Augustine held the post-Fall exercise of procreative sexuality to be inevitably
compromised by the resistance of the bodily passions to reason. The
marriage act, when it issued in conceiving a baby, was the all-too-
appropriate means for the transmission of original sin.

This discussion, lacking in temperateness on both sides, soon became
one about the orthodoxy of Augustine's—and therefore the African
Church's—teaching on grace. At stake in Julian's mind was the justice
of God, but to Augustine's mind, God's justice was an attribute quite
as inscrutable as any other in the divine nature. There was also a further
concern: the sheer scope of the redemption (or lack of it). "Julian took
Augustine to imply that Adam's Fall had wider and more momentous
consequences than the redemptive work of Christ; [the Fall] involved
the entire race, whereas in Augustine's theology Christ died only
for the elect."[66] Julian and the other south Italian bishops who agreed
with him were soon removed from their sees by papal fiat, despite a
plea to the patriarch of Constantinople who happened to be Nestorius.
The Council of Ephesus, meeting in 431, confirmed their deposition.

Monks in Africa and Provence who read the exchange were deeply
worried by Augustine's insistence on the restricted number of the

[64] Lancel, *Saint Augustine*, p. 342.
[65] Augustine, *Against Julian* II, 8, 23.
[66] Chadwick, *Church in Ancient Society*, p. 467.

predestined and—in the inference they drew from this—the seeming uselessness, in the case of the nonelect, of salvifically oriented moral and ascetical effort. In an effort to convince them, in 426 he wrote, for the Africans, *On Grace and Free Will*, where he underlined the incapacity of will to contribute to salvation, and *On Rebuke and Grace*, which sought to answer the question, Then what is the point of rebuking faults? For the Gallic monasteries, he wrote in 427 *On the Predestination of the Saints* and *On the Gift of Perseverance*, where he called for extreme discretion in the way a doctrine of predestination is preached. Understandably, this counsel did not do very much to allay the monks' anxieties. Monastic theologians in southern Gaul—Vincent of Lérins, John Cassian, and Faustus of Riez—remained unconvinced.

These treatises for disquieted monastics remain today the most controversial of Augustine's writings. Especially contentious is Augustine's attempt to restrict the force of 1 Timothy 2:4, with its affirmation that God wills "all men to be saved". Augustine took that to mean *either* that God wills all kinds of individuals to be saved, *or* that God wills many to be saved. *Some* numerical restriction was probably inevitable by virtue of Cyprian's soteriological teaching received as it was throughout the African Church: without Baptism, infants are excluded from salvation. Indeed, it is hard to see what surrogate for saving faith might be available to a baby. The notion of the "limbo of the children" was later invoked in recognition of this crux for thought. A document circulated in the name of Pope Celestine defended Augustine's reputation, but declined to debate what it described as certain profound questions where censure would be inappropriate. One patristic scholar has called Augustine's denial that God willed all mankind's salvation a "teaching that could never be given official Roman endorsement".[67]

The compensating virtue of Augustine's last treatises remains their Christo-centricity:[68] the predestining, prevenient grace which

---

[67] Bernard Green, *The Soteriology of Leo the Great* (Oxford: Oxford University Press, 2008), p. 77.

[68] Among these treatises of the 420s, *On Grace and Free Will* and *On Rebuke and Grace* were written for monks in North Africa; *On the Predestination of the Saints* and *On the Gift of Perseverance* for monks in Gaul. His warning that his thesis should not be preached to ordinary people did not augur well for its future. "Thus, while successive popes maintained the condemnation of Pelagianism, they never accepted Augustine's later teaching on predestination." Green, *Soteriology of Leo the Great*, p. 78.

draws individuals from their sin is the same grace by which the "man assumed" in the womb of Mary was brought into unity with God the Word on their behalf.

Great Works

Meanwhile Augustine had been working furiously, amid the many distractions of a Late Antique bishop, on completing a number of his most substantial works. That meant his *Discourses on the Psalms* (begun as long ago as 392, finished in 420), *On the Trinity* (begun in 399, finished in 419), his second attempt at a *Literal Commentary on Genesis* (begun in 401, finished in 414), the *Tractates on John* (begun in 407, finished in 417), the *Tractates on the Letters of John* (also begun in 407, but finished in 416), and the second most celebrated of all his works—after the *Confessions*, that is—the *City of God* (begun in 413, finished in 426). In 419 or 420 Augustine wrote *On the Nature and Origin of the Soul*, a text which showed he still had not fully made up his mind about the soul's origin, declaring it more important to know how the soul might achieve its future salvation. The delays in bringing to a successful conclusion the works he had begun are readily understood. In John Rist's words,

> Much of his time was taken up by his liturgical and pastoral duties, his episcopal role and that which *de facto* followed from it as a magistrate, and by ecclesiastical politics. Completion of large books, such as *The Trinity* and *The City of God*, was constantly delayed, partly in the former case because of changes of plan and the difficulty of the subject-matter, but also to allow for time to satisfy pressing local concerns and the constant demands of correspondents.... As a result of all of this Augustine's life was hectic, as his writings bear witness.[69]

Among these works, *On the Trinity* and *The City of God* stand out as preeminent. The first was written quite simply to show that the Trinity was the one true God, as Augustine explained at its

---

[69] Rist, *Augustine*, p. 10. The role as judge was especially demanding: "Since the ruling of the apostle Paul that Christians should not sue each other in the lawcourts, bishops were expected to provide an arbitration service, which might be a delicate task." Chadwick, *Church in Ancient Society*, p. 147.

opening. Books I and II speak of the rule of faith—the interpretation of the Scriptures by their "Catholic expounders"—as it applies to the Church's Trinitarian monotheism,[70] with an accent on the unity, indivisibility, and equality of Father, Son, and Spirit in being and action.[71] He had long since left behind the rational Neoplatonic doctrine of a triad of emanation that he found in Plotinus' biographer Porphyry. It had delayed a proper linkage of Trinitarian theology to the revelation of God in salvation history. In these opening books, Augustine also suggests hermeneutical criteria for sorting out statements about Christ as "in the form of God" and "in the form of a servant", and, in cases where such statements are about him, "in the form of God", when they concern him as "from" God or simply as divine. Such disentanglement is a necessary preliminary to a coherent New Testament Trinitarianism.

Books II, III, and IV raise the question of how to distinguish Old Testament-type Trinitarian theophanies from New Testament Trinitarian missions. The theophanies are executed by angels,[72] and, if they manifest the Trinity, do so not in a "proper" fashion but only by signs.[73] The missions, by contrast, denote the Father actually sending the Son in the Incarnation and Atonement—and into human minds, to reveal him there by the truth of the Word—and, moreover, actually sending the Holy Spirit at Pentecost so as to make human persons, who exist in time, turn towards the eternal God.

Book V introduces the concept of "relation" as the key concept in understanding the Triune Persons. We do not speak of the Persons in any hypostatically distinctive way by "substantial" predication, since

[70] Augustine, *On the Trinity* I, 4, 7, trans. Arthur West Haddan, in *Nicene and Post-Nicene Fathers, First Series*, vol. 3, ed. Philip Schaff (Buffalo, NY: Christian Literature Publishing, 1887). Citations from *On the Trinity* are from this translation.

[71] "Augustine's basic frame of reference for understanding the Trinity is the appropriation of Nicaea", while "the most fundamental conception an articulation in 'Nicene' Trinitarian theology of the 380s of the unity among the Three is the understanding that *any action of any member of the Trinity is an action of the three inseparably*." Michel René Barnes, "Rereading Augustine's Theology of the Trinity", in *The Trinity*, ed. Stephen Davis, Daniel Kendall, S.J., and Gerald O'Collins, S.J. (Oxford: Oxford University Press, 1999), pp. 154, 156. Italics in original.

[72] Apart from the numerous references to "the angel of the Lord" in connexion with such Old Testament theophanies as the Burning Bush, the giving of the Law on Mt. Sinai is considered to be angelically mediated in Galatians 3:19, Acts 7:53, and Hebrews 2:2.

[73] Augustine, *On the Trinity* II, 17, 32.

everything that is true of their substance, the single divine nature, is true of them precisely without distinction. Nor do we ever speak of them by "accidental" predication, since in the divine there is no possibility of mutations or alterations. It remains for us to speak of them "relationally"—they personalize the same divine nature by the way they relate to each other.[74] Father and Son are related to each other as Begetter and Begotten; they are related to the Spirit as the Giver to the Gift, the gift (that is) of "a certain unutterable communion" between Son and Father.[75]

Books VI and VII are governed by a continuing anxiety about Arianism, perhaps reflecting Augustine's first encounters with actual Arians—refugees from the Gothic invasion of Italy, or, as Henry Chadwick thinks, Gothic soldiers sent to fight their co-religionists the Vandals, who were threatening Africa from their strongholds in Spain.[76] These books emphasise once again the equality of the Triune Persons—one way of expressing the consubstantiality thesis of the First Council of Nicaea[77]—while also seeking to establish the "special attributes of each of the persons",[78] as reflected in their distinctive roles in creation and salvation. There, "wisdom" is especially appropriate for the Son or Word, "love" (touched on, however, only briefly at this point) for the Holy Spirit.

Books VIII to XIV show Augustine trying to describe the Trinity in a different way—still employing faith and, he urges, charity, but working now by means of analogies, which are drawn either (and more shortly) from a triadic analysis of what love is, or (at much greater length) from human powers more generally. When knowing and loving by faith and charity the Trinity, Augustine concludes that the mind itself does indeed image that Trinity—but only in the Age to Come, when the knowing and loving in question come to bear not on the "temporal dispensation" of salvation, the work of Christ

[74] Not at first acquainted with the Cappadocian theology that gave Christian Trinitarianism its classic expression in the East, Augustine appears to have been led to this concept by his discovery of Gregory Nazianzen's *Orations*, which Rufinus (Jerome's friend-turned-foe) had recently translated. See Irénée Chevalier, *Saint Augustin et la pensée grecque: Les relations trinitaires* (Fribourg: Collectanea Friburgensia, 1940).

[75] Augustine, *On the Trinity* V, 11, 12.

[76] Chadwick, *Augustine of Hippo*, p. 119.

[77] Basil Studer, "Augustin et la foi de Nicée", *Recherches augustiniennes* 19 (1984): 133–54.

[78] Augustine, *On the Trinity* VI, 10, 11.

and the Spirit in time, but on its intended outcome in the life of eternity. This by definition is unavailable to us now.

Book XV recapitulates what has gone before and includes a fuller—and historically highly influential—discussion of the place of the Holy Spirit within the eternal Trinity. The Spirit's place—his hypostatic particularity—is to be *Amor*, the love breathed forth as the communion of love of Father and Son. Hinted at earlier in the work, this is now incorporated into a wider plea. Our best similitude for the processions from the Father of the Son and Spirit is a mind expressing the whole of itself in a word, and breaking forth in the love which that same act of expression provokes. In *On Faith and the Creed*, Augustine has his answer to the dubium he recorded while still a priest. It will provide the framework for the "Augustinian-Thomistic" account of the Holy Trinity to this day.

The City of God, Augustine's meditation on history and eschatology where two cities—one of God, the other of earth; one of charity, the other of self-love—are intertwined till the End, was prompted by the fall of Rome to Alaric's Gothic army in 410, an event that sent shockwaves around the Roman world even though the principal capital of that world was now Constantinople.[79] In Books I to IV, Augustine defends Christianity against the claim that it bore responsibility for this débâcle. Book I reflects on the fact that, though a city fell, both pagans and Christians were safe in its churches. For Books II, III, and IV, the fall of Rome is not the result of banning pagan sacrifices; rather, Rome was grievously damaged already by its worship of false gods. Book V contrasts God with fate or destiny—and lauds the emperor Theodosius the Great, who replaced pagan worship with Christian cultus in both East and West. Books VI to X constitute a refutation of both polytheism and whatever is erroneous from a Christian standpoint in the Platonic tradition.[80] The opening ten books, accordingly, furnish Augustine's mature view of the limits of pagan wisdom and virtue—and access to salvation.[81] Books XI to

---

[79] See Gerard O'Daly, *Augustine's "City of God": A Reader's Guide* (Oxford: Oxford University Press, 1999).

[80] In the *City of God*, "The solutions of the new Christian literature must always 'stand out the more clearly' by always being imposed upon an elaborately constructed background of pagan answers to the same question." Brown, *Augustine of Hippo*, p. 306.

[81] John Marenbon, *Pagans and Philosophers: The Problem of Paganism from Augustine to Leibniz* (London and Princeton, NJ: Princeton University Press, 2015), pp. 23–41.

XIV describe the origin of the two cities, Books XV to XVIII their development, and Books XIX to XXIX their goals or ends. The remaining nineteen books constitute a reconstruction of the soteriology of Scripture, read in a way that is at once protological, historical, and eschatological.

The City of God has been described as "a book about being otherworldly in the world".[82] It is a simplification of Augustine's thesis to suppose that he identified the city of God with the Church, for the city's membership does not fully coincide with membership of the visible Church. Some who are in the Church do not belong to the city of God, and there may be others who belong to the city of God yet do not belong to the Church.[83] In any case, the "dividing-line between the two 'cities' is invisible, because it involves each man's capacity to love what he loves".[84] Nor did Augustine identify the earthly city with the now officially Christian Roman State. That State is not per se contrary to the city of God, but no State could ever be its even partial embodiment since States for Augustine take their rise from Adam's Fall (though at one point he muses on what might be the possibilities of a *christianum imperium* if a believing emperor legislated with consummate wisdom for the regeneration of society[85]). But Augustine does not offer, as his mediaeval and modern disciples did, a worked-out theory of the "spiritual earthly city", *civitas terrena spiritualis*, a Christian State perfectly aligned with the divine city.[86] Indeed, his "view of the nature of moral evil entails that it is impossible to construct an institutional utopia in this life".[87]

Augustine's picture of history in its relation to the End can be described, with Lancel, as looking at a painted triptych—a painting with three panels. On the left, there is all previous historical time which Augustine sought to lay out with the sources at his disposal. On the right, there is all future time, a period indefinitely but not infinitely long. At the centre, there is the brief but crucial timespan from Incarnation to Passion and Resurrection, "a few short years in that immense expanse of time but which gave the whole its entire

[82] Brown, *Augustine of Hippo*, p. 324.
[83] Lancel, *Saint Augustine*, p. 403.
[84] Brown, *Augustine of Hippo*, pp. 322–23.
[85] Augustine, *The City of God* II, 17, 18.
[86] Cf. Lancel, *Saint Augustine*, p. 405.
[87] Rist, *Augustine*, p. 48.

meaning, of being the history of salvation".[88] In this account, so Chadwick observes, Augustine "seeks to offer a conscious alternative to Platonism, which can find little significance in the space-time process, and to discern a grand parabola of divine providence in human history."[89]

In 426 or 427 Augustine penned his *Retractationes* or *Reconsiderations*, a unique book for the ancient world, and one that involved the now septuagenarian bishop reading the many tens of thousands of his own words. There was not much time left. In 429 the Vandals crossed the straits of Gibraltar. On August 28, 430, when the bishop died, they were at the gates. Though the province fell to Vandal rule, the siege of Hippo had not been carried through. So Augustine's collection of books—the books he had written and, evidently, from the evidence of the *Reconsiderations*, had conserved—survived and was transferred, by what means is unknown, to the apostolic library (the library of the popes) at Rome. By its mediation, Augustine became the principal Christian teacher of the West.

---

[88] Lancel, *Saint Augustine*, p. 408. Lancel mentions as a plausible alternative reading to his own the German Benedictine Basil Studer's thesis that the climax of the book comes at the end of Book X (X, 32, 3)—Augustine's proclamation of the Christian religion as the universal way of salvation. The rest of the work simply confirms the proclamation's truth. See Basil Studer, "Zum Aufbau von Augustins *De civitate Dei*", in *Collectanea Augustiniana: Mélanges Tarcisius J. van Bavel*, II, ed. B. Bruning, M. Lamberigts, and J. van Houtem (Leuven: Petters, 1990), pp. 937–51. That would have the advantage of explaining the decisive turn by which Book X is the last on paganism and Book XI the first to introduce the dialectic of the two cities.

[89] Chadwick, *Augustine of Hippo*, p. 136.

14

Preacher of the Mysteries: Saint Leo

Saint Leo was born some time towards the end of the fourth century, of Tuscan parents.[1] He became a deacon in the Church of Rome, where he soon acquired great influence, always exercised in favour of orthodoxy. Thus, he kept the pope of the day, Celestine I, well informed about Nestorianism; in 430, by which time he was arch-deacon of Rome, he encouraged the monastic theologian John Cassian to write his treatise *On the Incarnation of the Lord* (*De incarnatione Domini*) against Nestorius.[2] Leo made sure that Celestine's successor, Sixtus III, held fast to the essentials of an Augustinian theology of grace. So Sixtus refused to rehabilitate Augustine's root-and-branch opponent on that topic, Julian of Eclanum. Leo was also well regarded by the imperial court, which entrusted him with a diplomatic mission in Gaul. In fact he was there when he was elected pope in the late summer of 440.

He would prove an especially "Petrine" bishop of Rome. Leo held that the transmission to the Roman bishop, in a unique mode of the authority of Saint Peter, made the existing pope the "primate of all bishops" as Peter was chief of the apostles. This conviction coloured all his activity. It received liturgical expression in his annual homilies

[1] For Leo's life, see J. N. D. Kelly, "St. Leo I", in *The Oxford Dictionary of Popes* (Oxford: Oxford University Press, 1986), pp. 43–45.

[2] Cassian's treatise linked Nestorianism to Pelagianism, a conceptual affinity noted by Bishop Charles Gore in his 1883 essay "Our Lord's Human Example". According to Lionel Wickham, "The Nestorian Christ is the fitting Saviour of the Pelagian man" (Lionel Wickham, "Pelagianism in the East", in *The Making of Orthodoxy: Essays in Honour of Henry Chadwick*, ed. Rowan Williams [Cambridge: Cambridge University Press, 1989], p. 210). See Donald Fairbairn, *Grace and Christology in the Early Church* (Oxford: Oxford University Press, 2003), which explores the contrasts between, on the one hand, the Antiochene school (Theodore of Mopsuestia and Nestorius), and, on the other, Cyril of Alexandria and Cassian.

on the anniversary of his enthronement. It would not have gone down so well with Cyprian in his later period.

Leo's liturgical preaching was outstanding not only for its doctrinal coherence but also for its strong sense of the presence of the mysteries of Christ's life, Death, and Resurrection by way, specifically, of their liturgical commemoration. In a number of the preambles to his sermons, he describes the mysteries of the life of Christ—his Nativity or Epiphany, or his Death and Resurrection—as taking place *hodie*, "today".[3] In this way, he proved an inspiration for the early twentieth-century Benedictine reviver of a high doctrine of the Liturgy, Dom Odo Casel, the founder of the school of thought called *Mysterientheologie*, "the theology of the mysteries".[4]

Casel's fellow Benedictine, Dom Bernard Green, a monk of Ampleforth, describes the sermons like this: "These sermons offered more than pastoral encouragement. They were major theological statements intended for a sophisticated audience who were following the whole cycle.... The liturgical year was still only newly developing but he proved its first systematic commentator."[5] Leo presented the cycle of feasts and other celebrations, a cycle that renews the mysteries of the life of Christ as so many opportunities to "see Christ both as the mystery that transforms life (*sacramentum*) and the pattern that shapes behavior (*exemplum*) while at the same time it opens the heart in love".[6] And "he taught [Christians] they were saved by participating in the liturgical cycle of the Church and by taking home into daily life the patterns of behavior that Christ in the liturgy demanded of them."[7]

Leo was a vigorous pope, maintaining a strong line against not only Pelagians but also the Manichees, who had made something of a comeback in the Rome of his time. He sought to impose a uniform ecclesiastical discipline in Italy. In Spain, he urged the bishops, who

---

[3] M.B. de Soos, *Le mystère liturgique d'après saint Léon le Grand* (1958; repr., Münster: Aschendorff, 1972).

[4] For a brief overview, see Aidan Nichols, O.P., "Odo Casel Revisited", *Antiphon: A Journal for Liturgical Renewal* 3, no. 1 (1998): 12–20.

[5] Bernard Green, *The Soteriology of Leo the Great* (Oxford: Oxford University Press, 2008), pp. 1, 7.

[6] Ibid., p. 59.

[7] Ibid., p. 61.

lived under an Arian Visigothic government,[8] to do whatever they could to oppose "Priscillianism"—named for Priscillian of Avila, a bishop who headed an ascetic movement accused of incorporating elements of Gnosticism or Manichaenism.[9] With regard to North Africa, Leo made himself available for settling disputes in the Church in Africa, which, as the career of Cyprian shows, had her own robust tradition of autonomy exercised by regional councils. And in Gaul, he took steps to prevent the see of Arles[10] from acquiring quasi-patriarchal status, presumably because that would have interposed another sort of impediment to papal influence—though there was also the question of the due rights of metropolitans.[11] In eastern Illyria,[12] Leo sought to strengthen the authority of the Roman patriarchate, though requiring his vicar, who was based in Thessalonica, to respect the rights of local metropolitans.[13]

Leo's chief claim to fame in later history is his issuing of the Tome of Leo—otherwise, *Letter 28*—to Flavian of Constantinople. The Tome played a major, some would say a decisive, role in the Christological dispute of the mid-fifth century.[14] The Tome was spurned by the 449 Council of Ephesus, which condemned Flavian, a supporter of the settlement that had followed the 431 Council of the same name, and acclaimed Eutyches, a Constantinopolitan archimandrite who had proposed a radical version of Monophysitism incompatible with that settlement. After the union, Eutyches opined, the humanity of Jesus was no longer "consubstantial" with that of his mother, and therefore

---

[8] Visigoths were barbarians who had settled in the western portions of the Roman Empire.

[9] Henry Chadwick, *Priscillian of Avila: The Occult and the Charismatic in the Early Church* (Oxford: Clarendon Press, 1976).

[10] Arles (Latin, *Arelate*) was a major centre in the Christianization of the country.

[11] The Greek-born Zosimus, who became pope in 417, had accorded a suprametropolitical status to Arles: its "becoming the seat of the Gallic prefecture made the bishop aspire to greater authority" (Henry Chadwick, *The Church in Ancient Society: From Galilee to Gregory the Great* [Oxford: Oxford University Press, 2001], p. 454). But the purpose might have been to create a "papal vicariate" there. Ibid., p. 510.

[12] The southeast of the Balkans, an area that in terms of civil governance had been transferred to the Eastern Roman Empire.

[13] For Leo's church-political activity, see Trevor G. Jalland, *The Life and Times of Leo the Great* (London: Society for the Promotion for Christian Knowledge, 1941).

[14] "Decisive" was the adjective chosen by Jaroslav Pelikan in *The Christian Tradition*, vol. 1, *The Emergence of the Catholic Tradition* (Chicago and London: University of Chicago Press, 1971), p. 264.

not with ours either.[15] At this synod, later acclaimed by Monophysites as the Fourth Ecumenical Council or "Ephesus II", Dioscorus of Alexandria, Cyril's successor, refused to allow Leo's Tome to be read since its teaching was so manifestly compatible with the objectionable 433 Formulary of Reunion, whereby Cyril had made modest concessions to Antiochene thinking. In the mêlée that ensued, only one of the three Roman delegates is known to have escaped, making his way overland on foot to a neighbouring port. He was more fortunate than Flavian, who died of his ill-treatment. Dioscorus, believing himself to be cut off from communion with Leo, embarked on the extraordinary act for an Alexandrian patriarch of excommunicating the Roman pope. Leo in turn declared the Ephesian synod an "assembly of robbers" (*latrocinium*) and appealed to the emperor Theodosius II for vindication. Regrettably, Theodosius had already enacted the depositions of Antiochene bishops called for by Dioscorus and his episcopal supporters, ordering the burning of the writings of the last great Antiochene theologian-exegete, Theodoret of Cyr. The following year, 450, the emperor succumbed to a riding accident, but the brother-in-law, Marcian, who succeeded him, repealed the relevant decrees and made the necessary organisational arrangements—this time neither at Ephesus nor Nicaea but in sight of his own imperial residence, across the water.

The replacement Council met in the Church of Saint Euphemia at Chalcedon in 451. By its celebrated Christological Definition, it promulgated the doctrine of the single Person but two natures of the Saviour in terms that were in general keeping, if not always exact verbal alignment, with Leo's Tome.[16] Leo was, however, displeased by the canon of the Council of Chalcedon, which accorded Constantinople a comparable status to Rome on the ground that both were the *imperial* cities. He delayed his formal acceptance of the Council for two years and even then refused to admit the lawfulness of

---

[15] "Eutyches proposed a version of the Alexandrian Christology which effectively denied the reality of Christ's humanity after the union, and accordingly undermined the 'theology of the Emmanuel' just as surely as did the *homo assumptus* christology of Nestorius and his supporters." J. Mark Armitage, *Leo the Great's Theology of Redemption* (Strathfield, New South Wales: St. Paul's Publications, 2005), p. 5.

[16] For a splendid account of the Definition, see Chadwick, *Church in Ancient Society*, pp. 578–82.

the canon in question. The Orthodox archbishop of Constantinople still has the title "bishop of New Rome"—arguably the basis of his claim to be an "ecumenical" patriarch, a patriarch with an actually or potentially universal role.

Had Leo gone in person to the *latrocinium*, the extreme Cyrilline party would have found him a tough nut to crack. His personal courage was shown in his dealings with barbarians. In 452 he journeyed to the north Italian city of Mantua so as to confront Attila the Hun, whom he dissuaded from invading central and southern Italy. Hunnic movements in a westwards direction sparked a chain reaction, forcing other tribal groups to cross the imperial frontiers in search of comparative safety—as well as pickings. Leo would be less successful three years later with one of their leaders, the Vandal Gaiseric, when he met him outside the walls of Rome. But though he could not prevent the seizure and looting of the city, he gained guarantees that there would be neither arson nor the killing of citizens.

Leo I died in 461. For some generations, the syllabus for the baccalaureate degree in theology at the (traditionally Anglican) University of Oxford has closed the timespan of its patristics course by reference to that date, in this way giving silent yet eloquent tribute to Leo's importance for the universal Church.

A Kerygmatic Theology

Leo did not write formal theology. He was essentially a preacher who got across his message via both homilies and letters. The letters would have been finished off in the papal chancery where a notable contemporary theologian, Prosper of Aquitaine, served as chief secretary— rather in the way Jerome had assisted Pope Damasus.[17] That has led to a question about how much of their content is Leo, how much Prosper.[18] But Leo is not likely to have bowed to secretarial management, since he had his own, exceptionally well-focussed view of

[17] N. W. James, "Leo the Great and Prosper of Aquitaine: A Fifth Century Pope and His Adviser", *Journal of Theological Studies*, n.s., 44 (1993): 554–84.

[18] A highly sceptical view of Prosper's role is found in Green, *Soteriology of Leo the Great*, pp. 193–201.

what Christian preaching entails. As the Australian patrologist Mark Armitage explains, "So far as Leo is concerned ..., the task of the preacher is to proclaim the *mysterium* or *sacramentum* of the incarnation, passion, and exaltation of Jesus Christ [i.e, the way those events are the expression in time and space of the acts of the eternal Son of God], and to encourage the imitation of his *exemplum* [i.e., the example the God-man gave us precisely in his humanity]."[19]

Armitage goes on to say that "this proclamation, this 'kerygma', in turn demands a christology which, in order to account for the twin categories of *sacramentum* and *exemplum*, is constructed around the principle of the double consubstantiality."[20] By "the double consubstantiality", Armitage means the twofold consubstantiality of one who is both *consubstantialis Patri*, consubstantial with the Father, and *consubstantialis matri*, consubstantial with his mother and thus with all mankind.

Leonine Christology

The formula *consubstantialis Patri, consubstantialis matri* has been drawn from Leo's writings. (An excellent example is to be found in Leo's *Letter* 31, read in the Office of Readings of the Roman Missal for December 17.[21]) It functions, however, not as a frequently occurring tag (in point of fact its appearance is rather rare) but as what has been called the "matrix concept" that lies behind a variety of formulations Leo uses so as to speak of the dual character of the Word incarnate in his twofold substance, twofold nature, twofold form, or twofold status—all common Leonine expressions.[22] The theology of the two natures suits Leo's stylistic "predilection for antitheses and rhythmic parallelism", but more importantly, like Irenaeus and Athanasius he

---

[19] Armitage, *Theology of Redemption*, p. 18.

[20] Ibid., pp. 18–19. The couplet *sacramentum/exemplum* appears to go back to Augustine. Commenting on the soteriology of Book IV of Augustine's *De Trinitate*, Eugene TeSelle explains: "Christ's death and resurrection is both a *sacramentum* of the current death and reneal of the inner man and an *exemplum* of the future death and resurrection of the outer man." Eugene TeSelle, *Augustine the Theologian* (London: Burns and Oates, 1970), p. 176.

[21] Saint Leo's letter can be found at http://www.liturgies.net/Liturgies/Catholic/loh/advent/december17or.htm.

[22] TeSelle, *Augustine the Theologian*, p. 9.

sees the foundation of the work of redemption in "the *being* of Christ, not merely in his *acts*".[23]

Leo's Christology, it is suggested, is neither Alexandrian nor Antiochene (the two principal Christologies on offer at Chalcedon) so much as it is distinctively Latin, having in the above-mentioned approach a family resemblance to the Christology of Tertullian, the first theological writer of the Latin Church.[24] In his sermons and letters (which often share passages by recycling), Leo applies this principle of double consubstantiality in conjunction with two other controlling convictions in his thought.

The first of these is the *communicatio idiomatum*, whereby what is predicated of one substance can be ascribed to the other owing to the single subject who personalizes both. This, we can suppose, is what redeemed Leo's emphasis on the dual consubstantiality in the eyes of strict Cyrillians. Cyrillians, like their master Cyril of Alexandria, were very keen on the single subjectivity of the incarnate Word. We have encountered the "exchange of properties" before, in connexion with, precisely, Cyril's thought.

The second major auxiliary idea is not so much a positive principle (like the *communicatio idiomatum*) as it is a negative one. It is the principled avoidance of both Nestorianism and Eutychianism (radical Monophysitism) since each of these heretical views makes it impossible for Christ to be *Emmanuel*, "God with us". Nestorianism does that because there is no single subject of the natures. Eutychianism does that because after the union the humanity assumed effectively ceases to exist. That reflects a specifically fifth-century problematic, the problematic of Chalcedon itself—but the general principle that the human form or substance of Christ mediates his divine form or substance (Christ is the Mediator between God and man) might well be said to be entirely typical of Augustine, another Latin-speaking North African in the tradition of Tertullian.[25] So we can see why Leo's Christology has been called typically Latin: it is Tertullianic (if with—presumably serendipitous—Cyrilline overtones), and it is

---

[23] Alois Grillmeier, S.J., *Christ in Christian Tradition*, vol. 1, *From the Apostolic Age to Chalcedon, 451*, 2nd ed., trans. John Bowden (Mowbrays: London and Oxford, 1975), p. 531.

[24] Basil Studer, *Trinity and Incarnation: The Faith of the Early Church* (Edinburgh: T&T Clark, 1993), pp. 199–210.

[25] Armitage, *Theology of Redemption*, p. 10.

Augustinian.[26] The foundational Christological statement was that Christ is one single Person, *Persona*, in each of his states or natures, *status* or *natura*, as Tertullian had claimed in his polemic *Against Praxeas*, and Augustine had echoed in his letter to the proconsul of Africa, Volusianus, who was deciding whether or not to become a Christian.[27] "The Mediator appeared," Augustine explained, "joining both natures in the unity of the person."[28]

The Tome of Leo was not without its critics. Leo's statement there that "each form does what is proper to it in communion with the other" seemed to some to overstress the independence of the two natures and thus undermine the unity of a Christ who (if Leo were correct) acted sometimes as God, sometimes as a human being. This was the reason for the hesitation of Cyrillian-minded bishops at Chalcedon who, to the embarrassment of the Roman representatives, spent five days minutely comparing the Tome with Cyril's writings so as to check the consonance between them. This was not surprising: for Leo, Cyril was above all the Cyril who two years after Ephesus had made a compact with Syrian bishops of the Antiochene school in the Formulary of Reunion; Leo read the more rigorously Cyrilline texts, like the *Twelve Anathematisms*, in the light of that formulation.[29] In the words of an Orthodox patrologist, "The common European interpretation of the Acts of Chalcedon as the triumphant vindication of Leo's theology is historically misplaced."[30] For John McGuckin, detailed scrutiny of the Chalcedonian decree shows how in various respects the decree was as much a corrective to Leo's Tome as it was a substantiation of it. In the Definition as eventually promulgated, "Leo's attribution of separate actions to natures had been decidedly dropped, and his terms only inserted as one key sentence in a sea of Cyrilline citations" (the sentence in question is the one that reads "the property of each nature being preserved and concurring in one *prosôpon*

---

[26] Bernard Green states, "Leo was to become Augustine's most significant but also most discriminating disciple." Green, *Soteriology of Leo the Great*, p. 22.

[27] Tertullian, *Against Praxeas* 27; Augustine, *Letter* 137. See Hubertus Drobner, *Person-Exegese und Christologie bei Augustinus: Zur Herkunft der Formel "Una Persona"* (Leiden: Brill, 1986).

[28] Augustine, *Letter* 137, 9.

[29] Green, *Soteriology of Leo the Great*, p. 52.

[30] John McGuckin, *Saint Cyril of Alexandria and the Christological Controversy* (Crestwood, NY: Saint Vladimir's Seminary Press, 2004), p. 236.

[person]").[31] The same modern commentator would acknowledge, however, that "the *intent* of Leo was to teach substantially the same doctrine as Cyril, that is of the single subjectivity of the Word presiding over his incarnate condition, perhaps with a more stressed sense of the distinction of natures, which in common Latin parlance had no other meaning attached to the word than 'natural properties'."[32]

And indeed, Leo had made a strong statement of the unity, *unitas*, of the divine and human natures, in a sentence in *Letter* 28 that immediately precedes the already cited affirmation about how "each form does what is proper to it in communion with the other." "There is," Leo had written, "no falsehood in the unity since the lowliness of the manhood and the altitude of Deity find their meeting-place there." Furthermore, he expected the reference to that "communion", *communio*, of Christ's divine and human operations to be taken with full seriousness. In Armitage's words, "Each form, *forma*, may accomplish what is proper to it ... but it does not do so in independence of the other, but in *communio*, with the result that what emerges is not so much two distinct sets of activity as a single set of activity viewed under two *proprietates*, 'properties'—for which the best translation might in this context be 'aspects', properties or aspects corresponding with the two facets of the double consubstantiality."[33]

Accordingly, on this view of the Tome, Leo did not mean to say Christ sometimes acted as God and sometimes as man, a claim which would disable us from using the positive principle of the *communicatio idiomatum*. Rather, in each mystery of Christ's life, Death, and exaltation, we can discern in some aspect or aspects the divine form, while in another aspect or aspects we see the human form.

Each mystery, then, can be viewed from two perspectives. In each Christological mystery, there is a manifestation both of divine glory and of human humiliation, or even—in Leo's favoured term—*contumelia*, "degradation". In a comparison used by Leo: in each mystery there can be perceived both the emperor and the slave of the emperor's enemy—the enemy who is the Devil, the oppressor of men. Coming to amicable terms with the Antiochenes after the Council of Ephesus,

[31] Ibid., p. 238.
[32] Ibid., p. 234. Italics added.
[33] Armitage, *Theology of Redemption*, p. 86.

Cyril had already admitted that "the different attributes [glorious, humble] could be referred to the two conditions [form of God, form of a slave], if it were agreed that there was only one subject of reference in Christ."[34] Leo sounded remarkably Cyrilline when in the Tome he declared, immediately after the controversial "each form does what is proper to it" passage, "We must say this again and again: one and the same is truly Son of God and truly son of man."

For Bernard Green, Leo's assertion of the proper activity of each form is nonetheless surprising. In his preaching, while recognising the distinction between the natures of Christ, Leo had aimed to "coordinate their contribution to salvation".[35] It might have been expected that this short passage from the Tome, which Green does not hesitate to call a "blunder", would dismay orthodox readers in the Greek East.[36] Some translators sought to "save" Leo by taking the subject of the verb "does" (agit) to be "Christ", not the disparate "forms", and taking the noun "form" (forma) to be not a Latin nominative (and thus the subject of the verb) but a Latin ablative (and thus a term for Christ's mode of action).[37] Possibly Leo thought it would suffice, in the anti-Nestorian sections of the Tome, to assert the full divinity of Christ—not realising that Nestorius' real error lay in ascribing to the Saviour a double prosôpon, the duality of "two Sons", to which his own language of two forms, understood as subjects of activity, could provide an opening. If so, he soon corrected himself in his post-Chalcedon letter to the monks of Palestine (Letter 124, dated 453) where the acts of the God-man are "distinguished not by way of contrasting the natures but rather by affirming their complementarity".[38]

A Narrative Theologian

Leo did not write biblical commentaries. Nor, to judge from the extant sermons, did he preach on the Old Testament as such—a

---

[34] McGuckin, Christological Controversy, p. 193. In this respect, Cyril's later formulations anticipate the Tome of Leo, but also, perhaps, surpass it in clarity, if it is true that the thinking behind Leo's letter "largely reproduced Augustine's less focussed christology". Ibid.

[35] Green, Soteriology of Leo the Great, p. 218.

[36] Ibid., p. 221.

[37] George L. Prestige, "The Greek Translation of the Tome of St. Leo", Journal of Theological Studies 31 (1930): 183–84.

[38] Green, Soteriology of Leo the Great, p. 242.

huge contrast with Ambrose, who died more or less when Leo was born. Leo's Christological speculation derives from the celebration of the Liturgy and from concern with the mission of the Church, not from biblical exegesis. Nevertheless, in Mark Armitage's view, Leo can appropriately be called a "narrative theologian" (a term borrowed from later twentieth-century theology, both Protestant and Catholic[39]) in the same sense in which such very different figures as Irenaeus and Cyril of Alexandria can be called such. How can they be called such? They can be called "narrative theologians" insofar as these Fathers sought to identify and explore the central story line—the "narrative"—of Scripture as it runs from creation to apocalypse. There are two reasons for extending this description to Leo's case.

To begin with, Leo stands within "a Latin tradition which stretches from Hilary through Ambrose, Jerome, and Augustine and on to Bede and the authors of the middle ages according to which (1) everything in the Old Testament represents a prefiguration of Christ, and (2) the Christ therein prefigured is Christ the body (that is, the church) as well as Christ the head."[40] That idea was classically expressed by the gifted Donatist theologian Tyconius, who (as we have seen) influenced Augustine, but it was a generally pervasive one in patristic thinking.

There is a further reason for calling Leo a "narrative theologian" that turns on a more distinctively Augustinian and post-Augustinian motif. To cite Armitage again,

Western writers from Augustine onwards operate within a salvation-historical framework according to which history is divided into the periods *ante legem* [before the (Mosaic) Law], *sub lege* [under the (Mosaic) Law], and *post legem* [after the (Mosaic) Law] ...—the last of which [the epoch after the Law] is in practice divided into the periods before and after the conversion of Constantine and the assumption by the empire of her providential role in God's plan for the redemption of the world.[41]

---

[39] Early examples of each are George W. Stroup, *The Promise of Narrative Theology: Recovering the Gospel in the Church* (Louisville, KY: John Knox Press, 1981); Terrence W. Tilley, *Story Theology* (Collegeville, MN: Liturgical Press, 1985). For a critique, see Francesca Aran Murphy, *God Is Not a Story: Realism Revisited* (Oxford: Oxford University Press, 2007).

[40] Armitage, *Theology of Redemption*, p. 19.

[41] Ibid.

That means, then, that when Leo recounts the Christological mysteries on the feasts that commemorate them, he is aware not only of
how they fulfil the Old Testament narratives that prefigure them.
He is also conscious of how they initiate developments that charac-
terise the mission of the Church, the mission that flows from those
founding Christological events, reaching out to Leo's own time. In
Armitage's words, "Leo's entire prophecy/fulfillment approach to
soteriology is informed by the fact that he sees the work of Christ in
terms not simply of a typological fulfillment but also of an effective
universalisation—a making available and knowable to all—of the
redemption recounted in the Old Testament",[42] hence the great
importance he gives to the Epiphany, the visit of the magi, in his
sermon cycle, and his refusal to disassociate the Nativity from the
Epiphany. The magi are the first witnesses to "universalisation", to
the universal significance of the Incarnation.

A Theology of Redemption

Leo has a very rich doctrine of how that universalisation works out in
practice—how, in other words, redemption happens for Jack and Jill
in the Gentile world. He has his own special idiom for realised redemption, turning on the notions of *novus ordo*, *nova nativitas*, and *nova origo*:
"new order", "new birth", "new origin".[43] The blessing of the Gentile nations comes about through their incorporation into the "new
order" and "new birth" that results from Jesus' own "new origin" in
the assumption of humanity by God the Word. That incorporation is
safeguarded by the mysteries of his life and Death, and it leads to the
deliverance of pagan peoples from diabolic captivity.[44]

So Jesus ushers in a new age "firstly, by instituting a new kind of
pure, incorrupt humanity [though the entry of the Word into Mary's
womb]; secondly, by preserving that new humanity in the face of
temptations and attacks—that is, in the face of the temptations and
attacks hurled at him by the devil throughout his life and in particular

[42] Ibid., p. 54.
[43] See especially Leo, *Sermon* 22.
[44] Armitage, *Theology of Redemption*, p. 68.

in his passion; and thirdly, by handing on to believers this new, demon-conquering humanity when they imitate his new nativity in the font of baptism."[45] This divine-human innovation, as we might call it, fulfils all the essential Old Testament promises. Thus, there is a new creation, as promised in the Hebrew Bible. The Gentiles enter the true Israel, as promised in the Hebrew Bible. Israel is restored from exile in the sense of liberated from demonic captivity, as promised in the Hebrew Bible. Taken together, these blessings can be said to add up to nothing less than the "re-origination" of the human race.[46]

This reoriginated humanity must pass through its own equivalent of the Saviour's Paschal Mystery—a process which will require our participation in that same mystery. We are to be strengthened by testing, through sharing in the mystery of Christ's Cross. Here Leo stresses especially the overcoming in union with Christ of our fear of suffering and death.[47] Renovated humanity is then to be raised up, exalted. This will come about through a sharing in the post-Crucifixion mysteries, the mysteries of Christ's Resurrection and Ascension.[48]

One particular episode which, in the life of Christ, ushers in the mysteries of both the Death and the exaltation is especially important for Leo. This is the mystery of the Transfiguration of Christ, which for Leo underlines the interconnexion of these Sorrowful and Glorious Mysteries: the Passion, the supreme expression of the humiliation of the Word-made-flesh, and the Resurrection, his entry into reacquired glory.[49] In this very Latin patristic pope, we glimpse a fascination with the Thabor event that we might associate more readily with the Christian East, where the Transfiguration is a mystery around which theological meditation ever circles, from

---

[45] Ibid.

[46] Ibid., p. 71.

[47] Leo, *Sermons* 54, 59, 67. "Christ, inasmuch as he is *consubstantialis nobis*, embraces the *infirmitas* of fear and suffering in order that, living in solidarity with him, we might be empowered to overcome it." Armitage, *Theology of Redemption*, p. 96.

[48] "Because the flesh of Christ has been glorified, our own flesh, which, concorporated with him, is now *connaturalis* and *consubstantialis* with his, is, by way of a certain solidarity, as good as glorified ..., inasmuch as, if we continue to imitate Christ by *conversatio sancta* and *doctrina divina*, we (the body) shall inevitably participate in the glorification of the flesh which he (the head, to whom we are inseparably and organically united), even now experiences." Armitage, *Theology of Redemption*, p. 122.

[49] See the analysis of *Sermon* 51 in ibid., pp. 97–102.

Maximus Confessor in the seventh century to the Russian Diaspora writer Vladimir Lossky in the twentieth.

Leo's teaching on the reorigination of humanity in Christ has significant implications for the Christological disputes of the fifth century. If Jesus had no connexion with the old creation, as Eutychianism implied, he could not embody a transition to the new creation. If, as Nestorianism implied, he was essentially confined by the limits of the old creation, then he would have no power to bring in the new. This connexion between a proper understanding of the mysteries and a correct solution to the problems of metaphysical Christology is emblematic of Leo's entire theology. For Leo, the overall structure of salvation history rules out-of-court the defective Christologies both of Eutyches and of Nestorius. Leo presents Christ as the fulfillment of the divine promise to Abraham that in his— Abraham's—seed all the nations of the earth shall be blessed. If Jesus were not human as Abraham is human (as Eutyches contends), then this promise has not yet had its fulfillment. Likewise, if in this seed of Abraham the presence of the Son of God is not personally invested (as Nestorius would say), then the divine power to confer universal blessing has not yet been exercised. In Armitage's words (and it is his well-argued case I am following),

> If, embracing [what Leo calls in *Sermon 26*, on the Nativity] the *ratiocinatio humana* [the human, all too human, reasoning] of Eutyches and Nestorius, we fail to acknowledge that Christ is *consubstantialis Patri, consubstantialis matri* [consubstantial with the Father, consubstantial with his mother], we shall completely undermine the proposition that in Jesus God has fulfilled his promises to Abraham. In the process, we *de facto* separate ourselves from the justifying faith of Abraham—the faith that God will fulfil his covenant promises.[50]

What is said here of the Incarnation can also be said of the Atonement, the Paschal Mystery, where Leo presents Christ as both *Hostia*, the "victim", and *Veritas redemptionis*, the "truth of redemption", terms which indicate the two forms of the Word incarnate, who is, respectively, human, in the form of a servant (the *Hostia*), and divine, in the

[50] Ibid., pp. 27–28.

form of God (the *Veritas redemptionis*). As *Hostia*, he is "consubstantial" with the Old Testament types which he fulfils and transforms. As *Veritas redemptionis*, he is "consubstantial" with the God who acts in and through him to bring the narrative of salvation history from old dispensation to new dispensation, from worship in types and shadows to worship in the Spirit.[51] Christ is both the human "victim", in continuity with the Old Testament types, the cultic sacrifices, and the figures associated with them, such as Abel, Melchizedek, Isaac, Moses, Aaron, Elijah, David, and he is also the divine "truth of the redemption" empowered to make that crucial transition from Old Testament worship to worship in spirit and truth. Eutyches cannot do justice to this continuity of Jesus Christ with the saints of the Old Testament. "Leo may (unfairly) accuse Eutyches of denying the reality of Christ's human flesh, but his more penetrating insight is that Eutyches denies the reality of Christ's historical status."[52] By contrast, Nestorius cannot do justice to the way Jesus Christ transcends those saints. "The Christ of Nestorius stands in continuity and solidarity with the saints of the Old Testament, but, because he does not truly share the *natura, forma, substantia*, or *status* of his Father, he is effectively trapped within the succession of the Old Testament saints, and cannot add the *veritas redemptionis* which consists in *ipsa misericordia, ipsa veritas*, and *ipsa vita*",[53] very mercy, very truth, very life.

In their differing—indeed, opposing—ways, these Christologies deny the fundamental proclamation of the Church that Christ fulfils the Law and the Prophets, and, in so doing, they destroy the coherence of the salvation-historical narrative.[54] "Leo's theology of promise and fulfillment demands that Christ should be truly human in order that he can stand in continuity with the Old Testament saints, but, because the revelatory and redemptive function which he exercises is God's, he needs to be *consubstantialis Patri* also. In the teacher of *salutaris doctrina* [saving doctrine] we need to discern the form of God as well as the form of humanity."[55]

---

[51] Ibid., p. 52. Armitage admits, however, that Leo does not employ the vocabulary of consubstantiality in this context.

[52] Ibid., p. 64.

[53] Ibid.

[54] Ibid., p. 57.

[55] Ibid., p. 62.

And once again, Leo's soteriological thinking leaps ahead to the consequences for the calling of the nations through the mission of the Church. In *Sermon 68*, he finds it highly significant that after the Crucifixion, "a Roman soldier shows himself readier than the priests of Israel to recognise the Son of God. Just as the incarnation is followed immediately by adoration of the magi, so also the crucifixion is followed by the confession of the (presumably Gentile) soldier. In either case [Christmas, Good Friday] a *sacramentum* of redemption is acknowledged by a representative of the nations."[56] Indeed, in *Sermon 59*, also on the Crucifixion, Leo declares that in the Cross, the altar of the Jewish Temple, *ara templi*, has given way to the altar of the entire world, *ara mundi*. In Leo's words, "For you drew all things unto yourself, Lord, and when you had stretched out your hands all the day long to an unbelieving people that gainsaid you, the whole world at last was brought to confess your majesty."[57]

Leo on the Christian Life

Leo's account of the Christian life starts as is only to be expected, with holy Baptism. For Leo, as *Sermon 24* shows, the baptismal font is comparable to the Blessed Virgin Mary's womb. The Holy Spirit fills Mary so that the divine Son can take from her a pure example of our humanity in a "new order" and "new birth". The same Holy Spirit fills the baptismal font so that the believer can derive from it a share in the same new order and birth. Here the font "becomes a kind of sacrament of Mary's womb; in each case a material and earthly substance is rendered pure and heavenly by the operation of the Spirit, and in each case a new humanity reconstituted in the image, likeness, and form of God rises out of it."[58]

Perseverance in living out the new birth is not of course to be taken for granted. "Christ's saving work delivers us from the necessity of servitude to Satan, but we are still free to enslave ourselves to

---

[56] Ibid., p. 58.

[57] Leo, *Sermon 59*, 7, trans. Charles Lett Feltoe, in *Nicene and Post-Nicene Fathers*, ed. Philip Schaff and Henry Wace, 2nd series, vol. 12 (Buffalo, NY: Christian Literature Publishing, 1895).

[58] Armitage, *Theology of Redemption*, p. 73.

sin to a lesser or greater degree, and, in particular, those who are not
baptised have yet to appropriate for themselves the benefits of the
complex of incarnation, passion, and resurrection."[59] Leo thought
it more important to teach the universality of God's saving outreach
than to worry, with the later Augustine, about the de facto limitations of its extent. In the words of Bernard Green, "While Leo was
unambiguous in asserting the universality of the divine salvific will,
he did not feel it necessary to speculate further why that universal will
should not be universally efficacious."[60]

For Leo, the baptised Christian experiences a yearly climax to his
life in Christ in the seasons of Lent and Eastertide, when the catechumens are preparing for initiation. Leo had confidence in the efficacy
of the liturgically reactivated saving events.[61] He presents Lent as "a
microcosm of the Christian life in which the nations enter into the
nova creatura [the new creation] and the devil seeks to drag them back
into *vetustas* [the former life of the 'old man']."[62] The power of the
Cross is made efficaciously present in the Paschal celebration such
that at Easter the *sacramentum* of Christ's deliverance of humanity is
also made effectively present. Thus, "the devotions of Lent coupled
with the saving mysteries of Passiontide and Easter represent a time
in which, with the nations flocking to the baptismal font, even this
residual [Satanic] power is fatally eroded."[63]

Yet the Church at all times needs to combat Satanic assault by the
living out of the Beatitudes, to which Leo devotes one of his most
celebrated sermons, *Sermon 95*. He underlines the crucial importance
for Christian living of the Beatitudes just as Augustine had done before
him in his treatise *On the Lord's Sermon on the Mount*. This is also the
place to find Leo's mystical theology, which emphasises *pax*, "peace"—
understood as peace proceeding *from* the love of God and consisting
in perfect concord with God's will. The Beatitude that reads, "Blessed
are the peacemakers, for they shall be called sons of God" (Mt 5:9),
represents for Leo the topmost rung of the ladder of mystical ascent.

---

[59] Ibid., p. 80.

[60] Green, *Soteriology of Leo the Great*, p. 81.

[61] For a modern attempt to imitate his approach, see Aidan Nichols, O.P., *Deep Mysteries: God, Christ and Ourselves* (Lanham, MD: Lexington Books, 2019).

[62] Armitage, *Theology of Redemption*, p. 81.

[63] Ibid., p. 80.

This should not be disassociated, however, from Leo's more mundane teaching on prayer, fasting, and almsgiving, which in effect constitute his ascetical theology, as described in *Sermon* 12, a homily for the December fast in the year 450.[64] The connexion between the two is that the latter, the evangelical practices, are signs of living in the world of the new creation whose expected outcome is mystical peace in God.

---

[64] Thirty-four of his extant ninety-six sermons are concerned with fasting. Green, *Soteriology of Leo the Great*, p. 86.

15

Biblical Moralist: Saint Gregory the Great

Saint Gregory was born about 540 into a family of wealthy Roman noblemen who had already produced two popes, Felix III, in the late fifth century, and Agapetus I, who had died only a couple of years before Gregory was born.[1] Gregory's family was intensely devoted to the Church: his parents, Gordian and Sylvia, were venerated as saints; his sisters were consecrated virgins living, albeit within the family home, a life of prayer and self-denial. Their brother was trained in rhetoric and (most likely) law, and in 572 he became prefect of Rome, a position once of huge influence but subsequently, with the decline of the role of the imperial Senate, not quite so significant. In 574 he abandoned public life to become a monk, converting into a monastery the family mansion on the Caelian Hill. His community appears to have used an eclectic mix of monastic rules, one of them being that of Saint Benedict, for whom Gregory personally conceived a great admiration, as appears from his popular work *The Dialogues* where, however, Benedict had to share the honours with other recent saintly figures in the Italian countryside.

By Gregory's own admission, these monastic beginnings were the happiest period of his life, but they were brought to a sudden end by his ordination as a deacon in 578 and subsequent dispatch to Constantinople. There he served as papal representative both to the emperor from whom he sought political and military help against Germanic intruders in central Italy, and also to the patriarch with whom he clashed over the theology of the Resurrection (Gregory wanted a more robust statement of the corporeality of the risen body). It is assumed—rather than demonstrated by documents—that

---

[1] For the life of Saint Gregory and its context, see R. A. Markus, *Gregory the Great and His World* (Cambridge: Cambridge University Press, 1997).

his mandate will have extended to discussion of the regional schism caused by the posthumous condemnation at Justinian's 553 Council of Constantinople (the Fifth Ecumenical Council) of either the persons or the writings of three Antiochene theologians: Theodore of Mopsuestia, Theodoret, and a Syrian bishop who had accused Saint Cyril of Apollinarianism, Ibas of Edessa. In North Africa and northern Italy, there were those who saw this action as a threat to the Chalcedonian settlement. The support of the Antiochenes had been crucial in getting the Tome of Leo accepted. In reality the decree was aimed at softening Monophysite resistance to Chalcedon, not at ditching the Council altogether. But two great sees, Milan and Aquileia, broke off communion with both Constantinople and Rome. The momentous character of that action is plain to historians who recall how Saint John Chrysostom, on his exile from Constantinople, had written letters of complaint to the greatest bishoprics in the West—to Rome, yes, but also to Milan and Aquileia.[2] Gregory's own "line" on the "Three Chapters" dispute was that the condemnation of the Antiochene divines could not be taken seriously as a rejection of Chalcedon if the latter's authority were simultaneously reaffirmed. His own Christology was close to the "Neo-Chalcedonianism" favoured by Justinian. The Saviour was both "of" two natures and also "in" them.[3]

Though neither aspect of his mission could be called a marked success and he was still in deacon's Orders, Gregory was elected pope in 590. It cannot have harmed him that he had made important friends in Constantinople, both ecclesiastical and civil, and kept up correspondence with them on return to Rome.[4] His early letters as pope bewail his now permanent removal from monastic *otium*, from "sacred idleness"—that is, the contemplative life. One of the first letters in the Gregorian letter collection, written to the emperor Maurice's sister, Theoctista, is typical. "Under the colours of episcopacy, I have been brought back to the world, in which I am subject to as many worldly responsibilities as I remember myself to have had in my life as a layman. For I have lost the high joys of my peace, tumbling

[2] John Chrystostom, *Letter* 155.

[3] Henry Chadwick, *The Church in Ancient Society: From Galilee to Gregory the Great* (Oxford: Oxford University Press, 2001), p. 668.

[4] Listed in Markus, *Gregory the Great*, pp. 11–12.

down inwardly, though I seem to have ascended outwardly. That is why I grieve to have been thrust so far from my Creator's face. Every day I strive to be outside the world and outside the flesh."[5] But Gregory would go on to prove himself one of the most vigorous popes of the patristic era, and a highly influential figure for its medi-aeval successor-epoch, not least in matters of spiritual theology and attitudes to pastoral care.

Gregory's sense of the burdens of his new office is partly to be explained by the contemporary breakdown of civil governance not just at Rome but through much of Italy. Gothic and imperial armies fought indecisively for decades in a plague-ravaged countryside before a new threat arose from across the Alps in the shape of the Lombards. Gregory organised food supplies and the marshalling of troops, safeguarding Rome from sack by the Lombard king Agilulf by promising an annual tribute. His policies were simple: the pursuit of peace and the conversion of the Lombards to Catholic Christianity. Further afield, in the Germanic kingdoms in Gaul and Spain, he worked through metropolitans with a view to regularising the election of bishops and the maintenance of clerical celibacy or at least continence. In Africa Gregory sought to defuse what he took to be a revival of Donatism. In the East, he maintained the position of the Roman see as a court of appeal from Oriental bishops, and opposed the adoption of the style "ecumenical patriarch" by Constantinople. Though he rejected the description of his office as that of a "universal pope [i.e., father]", which, he said, would contravene the episcopal ordering of local churches (where each bishop is a "father-in-God"),[6] it should not be thought he was a minimiser of papal claims. While conceding that Antioch and Alexandria were associated with Rome

[5] Gregory the Great, *Letters* I, 5, cited in *The Thought of Gregory the Great*, by G. R. Evans (1986; repr., Cambridge: Cambridge University Press, 1988), p. 123. At the opening of the *Dialogues*, Gregory makes a pertinent and psychologically insightful comment on "how the mind works": "First we lose a prized possession but remain aware of the loss; then as we go along even the remembrance of it fades, and so at the end we are unable any longer to recall what was once actually in our possession. That is why, as I have said, when we sail too far from shore, we can no longer see the peaceful harbour we have left." St. Gregory the Great, *Dialogues*, trans. Odo John Zimmermann, O.S.B. (New York: Fathers of the Church, 1959), p. 4.

[6] Pope Gregory VII would have no such doubts in his 1075 *Dictatus papae*, one of whose propositions ran, "That only the Roman pope is universal."

as Petrine sees, he reserved the title *sedes apostolica* for Rome alone. It was the head of the churches, being governed by the vicar of Peter, prince of the apostles.[7] At Rome itself, he sought to improve liturgical worship, perhaps founding a chant school to this end: at any rate, the belief he had done so helps to explain the appearance of the term "Gregorian chant". As at Canterbury, on the mission to the Anglo-Saxons, which gave him enduringly high repute in England,[8] he promoted monks to positions of influence wherever that was possible, following a wider trend of two centuries' growth in the Church in the Mediterranean world.[9]

Gregory's literary production was dominated by exegesis. The earliest work, the *Moralia in Job* (or, in English, "Moral Commentary on the Book of Job"),[10] began life in Constantinople as talks to members of his monastery whom he had brought with him as his entourage. As pope he wrote a set of short homilies on the Gospels, some more extended homilies on the Book of Ezekiel (preached during the Lombard siege), and an "Exposition" of the Song of Songs, most of which is lost, as well as a commentary on one of the historical books of the Old Testament, First Samuel (in the Vulgate, that is called the "First Book of the Kings"), extant now only as reworked by a twelfth-century monk, Peter of Cava. We no longer have his commentaries on the Heptateuch, the prophetic books, and the Book of Proverbs. Doubtless, their tenor was much the same as the exegetical writings that survive. Gregory's approach to Scripture was allegorical in the spirit of Ambrose and therefore of Origen. The *Moralia in Job*, a sprawling composition, was ransacked in later generations for its teachings on the moral life and asceticism, the ideas behind it coming mainly from Augustine.[11] Gregory's *Liber Regulae Pastoralis* (*The Book of the Pastoral Rule*, or *The Rule for Pastors*), dating from the early years

---

[7] Gregory the Great, *Letters* II, 39.

[8] The early life of Gregory was written by a monk of Whitby in Yorkshire. Bertram Colgrave, ed., *The Earliest Life of Gregory the Great, by an Anonymous Monk of Whitby* (Cambridge: Cambridge University Press, 1985).

[9] Andrea Sterk, *Renouncing the World yet Leading the Church: The Monk-Bishop in Late Antiquity* (Cambridge, MA: Harvard University Press, 2004).

[10] Robert Louis Wilken, "Interpreting Job Allegorically: The *Moralia* of Gregory the Great", *Pro Ecclesia* 10, no. 2 (2001): 213–26.

[11] Not surprising if "in all essentials it was Augustine's conceptual structures that shaped the world of his imagination." Markus, *Gregory the Great*, p. 40.

of his pontificate, was rapidly translated into Greek and later into Anglo-Saxon and became in J.N.D. Kelly's words the "textbook of the mediaeval episcopate".[12] A total of over 850 letters survive, though some of these may have been the work of papal clerks and simply signed off by the pope. A good number concern landed properties outside Italy donated or bequeathed to the Roman Church as a source of income.[13] The notion of the apostolic see as an investment corporation opened the way, alas, to the financial scandals that dogged the mediaeval and later modern papacy.

Action and Contemplation

The *Book of the Pastoral Rule* (*Liber Regulae Pastoralis*, sometimes known as *On Pastoral Care*) announces as its main theme the difficulty of combining the active and contemplative lives. This had become a concern for Christian ministers, above all for bishops, almost as soon as the trend to have monk-bishops set in. Both Augustine (writing on Martha and Mary) and John Cassian (not actually a bishop but pondering in his *Conferences* the spiritual life of the many monks who were becoming bishops) gave thought to how contemplation could be pursued in the midst of the multiple demands of ministerial existence—especially in a time of widespread societal breakdown.

For Gregory the Great, it was a major preoccupation. As the Anglo-Hungarian patrologist Robert Markus points out, there are several "mini-treatises" along these lines in the *Moralia in Job*.[14] It was possible, so Gregory discovered, to think of the divergent tendencies of action and contemplation not as pulling the person apart—though he often experienced it personally in that manner—but as, in different ways, assisting each other to the benefit of both. In the *Homilies on Ezekiel*, he wrote, "We must note that just as the right order of the life is to tend from the active to the contemplative, so [nonetheless] the soul often reverts profitably from the contemplative to the active, so that the contemplative life having kindled the mind, the active life might

---

[12] J.N.D. Kelly, "St. Gregory I", in *The Oxford Dictionary of the Popes* (Oxford: Oxford University Press, 1986), p. 67.

[13] Chadwick, *Church in Ancient Society*, pp. 661–62.

[14] Markus, *Gregory the Great*, p. 20.

be the more perfectly led. For the active life should convey us to the contemplative, but sometimes the contemplative life should send us back to the active life from what the mind turned in on itself beheld."[15] A bishop's preaching activity was an obvious example. Not just a fruit of contemplation, it could also be a means of return to contemplation. In preaching, a minister can refind himself Mariologically. He can become the "mother" of the Lord, as he brings forth Jesus in others.[16]

There was also a Christological argument pertinent to this both/ and, rather than either/or, of action and contemplation. Gregory employed it in his *Pastoral Rule*. The acceptance of the difficult burden of contemplation and action together was one of the messages of the life of the Saviour himself. As Gregory asked rhetorically in the *Pastoral Rule*, "With what disposition of mind does one who might be conspicuous in profiting his neighbours prefer his own privacy to the advantage of others, when the Only-begotten Son of the supreme Father Himself came forth from the bosom of the Father into the midst of us all that He might profit many?"[17]

The question of how monks and bishops should live raises the wider issue of ecclesiology at large. Gregory's ecclesiology worked with a threefold ordering: firstly, *rectores*, literally "rulers", his most common name for bishops, though he also spoke of them as *praedicatores*, "preachers", and *doctors*, "teachers" or "doctors"; secondly, *continentes*, namely, monastics; and thirdly, *conjugati*, the married laity. The *Pastoral Rule* focusses on the *rector* (i.e., the bishop): "what sort of man he should be, what sort of a life he should lead, how he should deal with his subjects".[18] Tutored by his earlier reflections in the

---

[15] Gregory the Great, *Homilies on Ezekiel* II, 2, 11, cited in R. A. Markus, *Gregory the Great*, pp. 24–25.

[16] In a remarkably gender–fluid sermon on the Gospels, commenting on the words of Jesus about his disciples, "Here are my mother and my brethren" (Mt 12:49), Gregory remarks: "We should know that a person who is Christ's brother and sister through his belief becomes his mother by preaching. He brings forth, as it were, the Lord Jesus, whom he introduces into the heart of the person listening; he becomes his mother, if through his words the love of the Lord is produced in his neighbour's heart." Gregory the Great, *Homilies on the Gospels* 3, 2 (this homily is placed first in the sequence given in Jean-Paul Migne's *Patrologia Latina*).

[17] Gregory the Great, *Pastoral Rule* I, 5, trans. James Barmby, in *Nicene and Post-Nicene Fathers*, ed. Philip Schaff and Henry Wace, 2nd series, vol. 12 (Buffalo, NY: Christian Literature Publishing, 1895).

[18] Markus, *Gregory the Great*, p. 29.

Moralia in Job, much of this boiled down for Gregory to a matter of speaking: How should a bishop speak, when, what, to whom, and how much? He stressed the need for careful adaptation to audience. In the words of the *Moralia*, "Any teacher must touch the hearts of his audience with the same doctrine, but not in the same expressions if he is to build all into a single virtue of charity."[19] He adopted a doublet already found in Augustine: the bishop's aim must be *prodesse* not *praeesse*, to "be of use", not to "be in charge".[20]

The emphasis on speech meant that Gregory often interpreted ruling as teaching. The ultimate aim of Christian teaching is to feed contemplation, chiefly through the exposition of the Scriptures, which can bridge the gap between the three main orders in the Church (rectors, monasticism, the married laity) by encouraging that contemplative ardour which is or should be the common spiritual ideal of all these parties. In Markus' words, "Gregory's image of the Church is that of a vast community of contemplation, its members ranked according to the level they are able to attain."[21]

Keeping close to Gregory's own idiom, the historian of mediaeval Christian thought Gillian Evans sums up in the following words Gregory's account of the aims of a preacher in the *Moralia in Job*:

> The primary task of the preacher or *rector* is not only to preach but to do so to such effect that his people are righteous; in this lies the true glory of a priest. A vast progeny of faithful souls is produced by the fertility of holy preaching. It is as though the Church, the Bride of the Word of God, were filled with the Holy Spirit and became "with young" by preaching; as though she suffered the pains of childbirth in exhorting her children; and brought them forth at last by converting their hearts.[22]

The conversion Gregory had in mind is not simply moral conversion, conversion to ethical righteousness, though it includes that. It is also an anagogical process, helping the hearers to make progress

---

[19] Ibid., p. 30.
[20] Ibid., pp. 43–44.
[21] Ibid., p. 33.
[22] Evans, *Thought of Gregory the Great*, p. 82, echoing *Moral Commentary on Job* XI, 14, 22; VI, 36, 55; XIX, 12, 19.

in the contemplation that anticipates homecoming in the Kingdom of Christ and his Father. In the *Homilies on Ezekiel*, Gregory speaks of the *cantum bonae praedicationis*, the "song of good preaching", as not only delighting the Lord for whom the Church longs but enabling the Bridegroom's friends to "hear the word of life so that they may come to live in their heavenly home".[23] Preaching is about helping people to want heaven and to get there.

The Interpretation of Scripture

The bottom line of preaching for Gregory is always Scripture. Gregory's approach to the Bible was clearly akin to that of Augustine, from whom he drew so much, if without Augustine's nuance and delicacy. His view of what the Greek Fathers would have termed the "outer wisdom" of secular learning was largely identical with Augustine's. Secular learning is useful when it helps sacred learning. Around the time of Gregory's birth, the monastic founder Cassiodorus had created in Italy a study-centre where the two (sacred and secular) were quite deliberately held together. In the *Moralia in Job*, justifying the semi-mythological names given to star constellations in chapter 9 of the Book of Job (astronomers still use them today), Gregory affirms that if the biblical authors could use names given to creatures by worldly sages (i.e., by knowledgeable pagans), then "there is no reason why 'spiritual men' should not make use of the words of the carnal in order to further spiritual understanding."[24] And what was at stake here was indeed primarily for Gregory biblical understanding. Interest in secular disciplines is justified to the degree that it promotes understanding of Scripture. Here Gregory could look to Augustine's *On Christian Teaching*, notably Book II of the same, which had also inspired Cassiodorus' approach in his *Institutes of Divine and Human Learning*.

Immersion in Gregory's writing has left on many readers—at any rate when contrasted with Augustine's corpus—the impression of a

---

[23] Evans, *Thought of Gregory the Great*, p. 84, with an internal citation of *Homilies on Ezekiel* II, 2, 4.

[24] Markus, *Gregory the Great*, p. 38.

narrowing in metaphysical range.[25] Robert Markus has an explanation for this. In a world where learned paganism had virtually disappeared (the relapse of peasants into traditional forms of magic was a
different matter), and unbelievers (except in the form of barbarian
soldiery) were more or less unknown, the principal preoccupation of
a "rector", who was also a preacher and teacher, was with the failure of moral practice among a nominally Christian mass population.
Consequently, as with the commentary on Job, Gregory's exegetical
interests were predominantly focussed on Scripture's "moral"—what
the Greeks called its "tropological"—sense: the meanings the Bible
carries that are relevant to ethical manners of life, to the modes (*tropoi*) of moral behavior. In Markus' words, "How to be a Christian,
how to live the fullest Christian life: this was Gregory's central preoccupation in all his preaching; and this was the question into which
the anxieties of his age had shaped themselves. Naturally, it helped to
give his exegesis a predominantly moral direction."[26]

For Gregory the Bible is light and food for the soul, but the way
exegesis draws on these illuminating and nourishing resources is
by encouraging renewal of life—which means ongoing conversion by
repentance, self-denial, and the attitude and practice of charity. That,
however, is not in a moralistic—a restrictedly moral—sense because
these dispositions are meant to open up the soul, like a flower under
the sun's rays, to a life of contemplating God. In his *Homilies on Ezekiel*, Gregory declares, "The words of God grow with the reader,"
divina eloquia cum legente crescent: words approvingly quoted by the
1992 *Catechism of the Catholic Church* in its account of the life of faith.[27]
In proportion to the reader's own faith and love (as brought to bear
on the text), the Scriptures can themselves deepen faith and love.
Dom Jean Leclercq, in a classic study of monastic theology, will call

[25] "Gregory is a theologian without deep intellectual anxieties. His own active struggle was
with the difficulty of maintaining a balance between the demands of this world and his long-
ing for the next, and he wrote accordingly on the spiritual life, and on pastoral care. Augustine
woke in the night sometimes because an unsolved philosophical or theological problem was
worrying him [cf. *On Order* I, 3, 6–7]. Gregory took the solutions arrived at by those before
him largely for granted. Chalcedon seemed to him a resting-place for the old debates on
points of doctrine. This calm and assurance gave Gregory's theology a maturity and settled air
which is new in the Latin West." Evans, *Thought of Gregory the Great*, p. 55.

[26] Markus, *Gregory the Great and His World*, p. 41.

[27] *Catechism of the Catholic Church*, no. 94.

Gregory the Great "the doctor of desire".[28] In Gregory's own expla-nation, "Unless the readers' minds extend to the heights, the divine words lie low, as it were, uncomprehended.... It often happens that a scriptural text is felt to be heavenly, if one is kindled by the grace of contemplation to rise to heavenly things. And then we recognize the wonderful and ineffable power of the sacred text, when the reader's mind is permeated with heavenly love.... For according to the direc-tion the reader's spirit takes, so the sacred text rises with him."[29]

The Word sought in daily *lectio*, with faith, obedience, and humil-ity, as the reader, helped by the Holy Spirit, feeds on the text in the house of the Church, ever growing in the desire for God and thus detachment from a sinful world: Gregory's spiritual approach to Scripture had enormous influence on biblical commentators in the West throughout the mediaeval period.[30]

One respect in which Gregory differs from Augustine (and where his influence was less benign) is in his more broad-brush (some would say cavalier) attitude to the biblical text's literal sense. For Augustine in *On Christian Teaching*, a true interpretation of Scripture is always in conformity with charity, with the love of God and neighbour. But Augustine did not draw the conclusion that *any* interpretation that fosters charity is in and of itself a right reading of the text. One might be approaching the desired goal of Scripture but doing so by a wrong route so far as some particular text was concerned.[31] Gregory was not too bothered about this.[32] That might be owing to his exalted doc-trine of charity. The root of the virtues has its soil in participation in a sacred order that spans all realities: "Through love, one participates in God and in the corporate body of Christ, creating a harmony and concord throughout the cosmos, the Church, and society, and in the Christian himself."[33]

[28] Jean Leclercq, O.S.B., *The Love of Learning and the Desire for God: A Study of Monastic Culture*, trans. Catharine Misrahi (New York: Fordham University Press, 1961), pp. 33–43.

[29] Gregory, *Homilies on Ezekiel* I, 7, 8–9, cited in Evans, *Thought of Gregory the Great*, p. XX.

[30] See René Wasselynck, "L'influence de l'exégèse de saint Gregore le Grand sur les com-mentaries bibliques médiévaux (VIIème–XIIème siècle)", *Recherches de théologie ancienne et médiévale* 32 (1965): 157–205.

[31] Augustine, *On Christian Teaching* II, 6.

[32] Paul Meyvaert, "Gregory the Great and the Theme of Authority", in *Benedict, Gregory, Bede and Others* (London: Variorum Reprints, 1977), pp. 3–12.

[33] Carole Straw, *Gregory the Great: Perfection in Imperfection* (Berkeley, CA: University of California Press, 1988), p. 92.

A Doctor of the Mysteries

Gregory's concern with the organisation of the Christian community and the interpretation of the Bible makes him a characteristic representative of the Latin patristic tradition. That tradition commonly strikes modern students as both less cosmological and less mystagogical than its Greek counterpart. Its practical, exegetical bent may not be at variance with the speculative and mystical emphases of the Greek Fathers. But it is, it would seem, at best complementary to those emphases, certainly not a mirror of them. That is not entirely fair. I have just mentioned Gregory's surprisingly "transcendentalist" notion of charity, which outruns not only ethics but even the account found in the Thomist school for which charity is supraethical in that it is a "theological"—God-attaining—virtue. But there is more. In an overall study of Gregory's writing, Carole Straw places immediately after her introduction a chapter entitled "Microcosm and Mediator"—the very title chosen by Lars Thunberg for his evocation of the world view of Saint Maximus. Surely no one could dispute the absorbing interest of the Confessor in cosmology and mystagogy.[34] Straw is claiming for Gregory, *avant la lettre*, a Maximian affinity. This most Roman of popes appears to have suffered from too ready an identification of the Latin tradition with exhortation and pragmatics.

Justifying her choice of title, Straw writes with reference to the *Moral Commentary on Job*, "As the whole universe consists of visible and invisible things, in creating man God 'gathered together another world in miniature', making him an admixture of flesh and soul, dust and spirit. Like the rest of the universe, he shares invisible causation, the spirit. And like most of creation, he shares visible effect, the body."[35] So much might be a commonplace of ancient Stoicism, were Gregory not to explain, later in this treatise, how "where we have fallen, there we lie that we may rise again.... If we have fallen from the invisible because of the visible, it is fitting that we strive to rise again through the visible to the invisible."[36] As Straw explains, drawing this time on the *Dialogues*,

---

[34] See Chapter 7 above.

[35] Straw, *Gregory the Great*, p. 39, with reference to the *Moral Commentary on Job* VI6, 15, 18.

[36] *Gregory the Great, Moral Commentary on Job* XXVI, 12, 18, in Straw, *Gregory the Great*, p. 29.

In Gregory's sacramental vision, carnal signs mediate between this world and the next. Carnal means attain spiritual ends, and the things of this world are often vehicles of spiritual experience. The soul can be bruised through the body: ascetic practices and the suffering of external adversities can help chasten and improve the soul. Though they be dusted with the sin of the world, ordinary human activities can become sacrifices offered to God, linking man with the world beyond, just as the daily sacrifice of the Mass mediates between worlds, and the sacrifice of Christ mediates continually with God.[37]

Though, truth to tell, Gregory cannot compete with Maximus as a speculative thinker, the phrase "mediator between God and men" (I Tim 2:5), occurring as it does over fifty times in Gregory's biblical commentaries, denotes, as it would for Maximus, a "midpoint gathering and reconciling every contrariety".[38] In both theologians, opposites are turned into remedies.

Being mortal and unrighteous, we were at a great distance from the Righteous and Immortal One. But the Mediator of God and Man appeared between us, the mortal and unrighteous and the Immortal and Righteous One, sharing mortality with men, and righteousness with God. Since through our depths we were so far away from the heights, he joined in himself the lowliness and highness together, and this became for us a way of return, for he joined our depths with his heights.[39]

This objective work of the Redeemer—the greater mysteries—must be appropriated subjectively. This happens above all through the lesser mysteries of the sacraments, in particular the Mass—the "sacrament of the Lord's Passion", as Gregory calls it,[40] where the Christian "meets Christ's sacrifice in ordinary life"[41] and is called upon to take up his own cross, in both passivities and activities, in sufferings and in active works.

---

[37] Straw, *Gregory the Great*, pp. 47–48.

[38] Ibid., p. 151.

[39] Gregory the Great, *Moral Commentary on Job* XXII, 17, 42, in Straw, *Gregory the Great*, p. 151.

[40] Gregory the Great, *Moral Commentary on Job* XIII, 23, 26. Translated passage is the present author's.

[41] Straw, *Gregory the Great*, p. 159.

The Mission to the English

Indeed, Gregory's best-known practical initiative—the sending of the monk Augustine to Canterbury—must itself be framed in the context of a Doctor of the greater mysteries of the world's salvation. The mission to the English Gregory launched in 597 was motivated in part by his belief that, on the eschatological timeline, time was growing short. His realistic picture of the state of that part of the earth's surface best known to him—central Italy, with its intractable problems (political, economic, medical)—made Pope Gregory I the most apocalyptically minded senior Churchman since the end of the apostolic age. His predictions for an imminent end of the world were of course not verified. But from them issued the urgency with which he sponsored this mission to England—to what for a Mediterranean Christian could only seem the very edge of planet earth: *ultima thule*. "What counted for him more than anything was the entire arc of salvation history, which continues to unfold in the obscure meanderings of time. In this perspective, it is significant that he inserted the news of the conversion of the Angles in the middle of his *Book of Morals*, a commentary on Job: to his eyes, the event constituted a furthering of the Kingdom of God which the Scripture treats."[42]

More significant in the long term than Gregory's revival of eschatology was the breakthrough in missionary thinking it entailed. So far, the Latin Church had understood its missionary remit as confined to the inhabitants of the Roman Empire. After the start of the Anglo-Saxon mission, it would understand its mission to be universal.

Historians stress, however, that Gregory did not envisage a new civil configuration for the Roman patriarchate, not only because the theological clock was moving towards apocalypse but also because he was and remained a loyal subject of the East Roman emperor at Constantinople. The kings and other leaders of the Germanic kingdoms founded in the wake of the contraction and eventually collapse of the Western Roman Empire he conceived as on the same level as high civil servants in the Byzantine Empire. He addressed them as "sons" and "daughters". The Byzantine emperors, by contrast, he addressed

[42] Pope Benedict XVI, *Church Fathers and Teachers: From Saint Leo the Great to Peter Lombard* (San Francisco: Ignatius Press, 2010), p. 46.

as "lords". In Markus' words, "Gregory's perspective on the Germanic nations [such as the Anglo-Saxons] was not very different from the official image held in Byzantine government circles."[43]

But, like the Byzantines (who conceived the other Christian States over whom they had no control whatsoever as parts of their "commonwealth"), he knew that theory was one thing, realities on the ground another. He was not really initiating a mission to a totally un-Christianised land. There were many survivors of the Romano-British Church, especially in Wales; there was the Irish or "Scotic" mission originating from Iona and affecting northern England; and there were Frankish clergy and laity at the Kentish court itself. Nor did the fact that the mission Gregory sent came directly from the pope mean it would succeed, headed though it was by a monk from his own monastery, Augustine—soon to be called "of Canterbury". Yet succeed it did, and the success exceeded Gregory's highest expectations.

Within five years, Augustine's party sent back representatives to Rome to procure Church plate, vestments, ornaments, relics, and books, with a report that sufficed to elicit from Gregory metropolitical rank for Augustine and the creation of a dozen suffragan sees. What he was not informed of was the strength of pagan sentiment in London, the planned base for what became instead the *Canterbury* province of the Latin Church. Nor did his informants properly understand the attitude of the British clergy they would encounter. The latter had come out of a form of Church life far more markedly monastic and charismatic than administratively episcopal and territorial. One way to put this would be to say: Cyprian's ecclesiology meant nothing to them.

Gregory's remaining gift was to pass on to Augustine and his colleagues the lesson of humility he himself had learned as monk, bishop, and exegete. "You should remember, dearest brother, amidst the outward things you do through the Lord's power, always to subject your inner self to the most meticulous judgment, and be aware of what you yourself are and how great is the grace shown to the people for whose conversion you have been granted the gift even of working miracles."[44] (Unfortunately, Augustine forgot this lesson

---

[43] Markus, *Gregory the Great*, p. 164.
[44] Gregory the Great, *Letters* XI, 36, cited in ibid., p. 181.

on a crucial occasion, the meeting with the British bishops, when he failed to rise from his seat as they entered.[45])

Gregory's initiative in the Anglo-Saxon mission was remembered in Continental Europe even when, aside from his writings, little else about him was recalled at Rome. In the words of one historian of the papacy in patristic times, "His neglect in Rome can be attributed almost certainly to his elevation of the monks as a rival centre of power to the clerical establishment. By the mid-seventh century the [secular] clergy had won the battle, and the eclipse of the monastic power bid obscured with it the celebrity of its instigator."[46] The nascent English Church, on the other hand, continued to return his concern with gratitude, granting him the title of their "apostle". In the words of J. M. Wallace-Hadrill, "The English felt drawn to Rome; that much is clear; but they reserved their love for the Pope who first helped them. It was Gregory the heir of Saint Peter, not of Rome impersonally, that the English liked first to think."[47] That claim makes a not unsuitable transition to the last figure to be discussed in this book, the Venerable Bede.

[45] Bede, *Ecclesiastical History of the English People* II, 2.

[46] Jeffrey Richards, *Consul of God: The Life and Times of Gregory the Great* (London: Routledge and Kegan Paul, 1980), pp. 260–61.

[47] J. M. Wallace-Hadrill, "Rome and the Early English Church: Some Questions of Transmission", *Settimane di Studio del Centro italiano di studi sull'Alto Medio Evo* 7 (1960): 1.

16

The English Contribution:
Saint Bede the Venerable

Saint Bede was born in 672 or 673 in what is now "Tyne and Wear", a region made up of adjacent parts of the historic counties of Northumberland and Durham. As a boy, he was given by his family as an oblate to one (or perhaps both) of the twinned monasteries of Saint Peter at Wearmouth (now called Monkwearmouth) and Saint Paul at Jarrow. Lying some seven miles apart, these monasteries, which followed a composite rule (possibly oral rather than written), had been founded by a Northumbrian nobleman, Benedict (or Benet) Biscop in 674 and 681, respectively.[1] During Bede's early life as a monk, they had a shared abbot, Coelfrith, who evidently recognised Bede's linguistic and intellectual gifts and ensured they had full scope. Bede expressed what he owed to these men in his *Lives of the Abbots of Wearmouth and Jarrow*, the main source for our knowledge of them.

Benet Biscop and Coelfrith made great strides in building up library resources for their monasteries, crossing to the European mainland so as to collect patristic texts. The texts were copies of the Bible—both part-texts and at least one "pandect", or entire Bible—brought from the scriptorium of Cassiodorus' monastery in southern Italy, as well as some texts by classical authors,[2] though these—apart from

[1] "Pre-Viking England lacked any normative monastic rule.... Some founders, most famously the great Northumbrian nobleman-abbots Wilfird and Benedict Biscop, constructed rules based heavily on St. Benedict's, but they did so by choice rather than obligation, and in an eclectic spirit." John Blair, *The Church in Anglo-Saxon Society* (Oxford: Oxford University Press, 2005), p. 80. See the full account in Henry Mayr-Harting, *The Coming of Christianity to Anglo-Saxon England*, 3rd ed. (Philadelphia: Pennsylvania State University Press, 1991), pp. 148–219.

[2] The classic attempt to establish the library's contents is M. L. W. Laistner, "The Library of the Venerable Bede", in *Bede: His Life, Times, and Writings: Essays in Commemoration of the Twelfth Centenary of His Death*, ed. A. H. Thompson (Oxford: Clarendon Press, 1935), pp. 237–66.

the Roman grammarians—were largely avoided by Bede in his own writing. The major exception there is Virgil, the chief stylistic influence on Bede's Latin poetry.

While we have the name of one of his teachers, Trumbehrt, a monk in the tradition of Saint Chad and thus of the Irish tradition of Saint Aidan,[3] Bede is usually regarded as largely self-taught. He implies as much in his *Letter to Bishop Egbert* (of York) on Church reform, written shortly before his death in 735.[4] Self-education, if that is the right phrase, included acquiring enough Greek to use a bilingual (Latin/Greek) copy of the Acts of the Apostles for his commentary on that biblical book (in two editions, the second making more use of the Greek to correct the first). He was assisted by the prodigious memory that enabled him to cross-reference Scripture with ease and locate relevant passages from, especially, Jerome, Augustine, Gregory, Ambrose, and the rather disorganised Spanish polymath Isidore of Seville.[5]

The mention of Trumbehrt discourages us from seeing Bede as a product of the "Roman", over against the "Celtic", Church. As the historian of Anglo-Saxon England John Blair insists, "England in the seventh and eighth centuries was influenced by Ireland on the one hand, Italy and Gaul on the other, but to think of these as two self-contained and contrasting 'packages' is unrealistic and unhelpful."[6] The prominence of the 664 Synod of Whitby, when Romans and Columbans (or Wilfridians and Ionans) quarreled about the dating of Easter, has given rise to misunderstanding. "There was no evident

---

[3] The library of Wearmouth-Jarrow may have possessed Hiberno-Latin texts in exegesis, cosmology, and computistics. Clare Stancliffe, "British and Irish Contexts" in *The Cambridge Companion to Bede*, ed. Scott DiGregorio (Cambridge: Cambridge University Press, 2010), pp. 69–83, especially pp. 81–82. Ancient Irish monasteries were, among other things, "educational centres where there were learned men who could explain the movements of the stars, the workings of the universe, the course, reason, and nature of human history, the purpose and ends of men." D. L. T. Bethell, "The Originality of the Early Irish Church", *Journal of the Royal Society of Antiquaries of Ireland* 3 (1981): 46, cited in Blair, *Church in Anglo-Saxon Society*, p. 77.

[4] Bede, *Letter to Bishop Egbert* 6.

[5] "Rather than the precious gift of synthesis, it would seem that he possessed the gift of *collation*, that is, of collecting, which he expressed in an extraordinary personal erudition, although it was not always ordered as might have been desired." Pope Benedict XVI, *Church Fathers and Teachers: From Saint Leo the Great to Peter Lombard* (San Francisco: Ignatius Press, 2010), p. 58.

[6] Blair, *Church in Anglo-Saxon Society*, p. 5.

barrier between British and Irish Christians, or the English converts of either, until the Easter controversy drove a wedge between them in the 660s, and marginalized both the British and the Irish non-conformists."[7]

Bede's entire life was spent as a monastic teacher, cantor, scribe, and author of not only biblical commentaries and books of homilies but also grammatical and topographical aids and a book on plainsong modes. He produced studies of chronology (texts on calendrical computation and two attempts at a world chronicle), cosmology, Church history, and hagiography (including an entire martyrology, which serves as the remote basis for the Roman Martyrology used today). He was an accomplished versifier, composing hymns in various metres as well as a book of poetic epigrams, no longer extant. The five-line vernacular poem known as "Bede's Death Song" may exemplify not his memory but his creativity. Bede was an avid searcher after historical documentation and well-informed oral report, sufficiently so for his *Ecclesiastical History of the English People* to be regarded by modern historians as largely credible and reliable even by their own exacting standards. Criticism is directed chiefly to his omissions—which may at times be indicators of bias and not simply the result of lack of information.[8] On a severe view of the latter, "Bede was merely the culmination of a project to construct a new English Christian identity, founded on Gregorian Rome, which encouraged a British cultural amnesia and cold-shouldered any help—if in fact there was any—on offer from the learned and well-organized Churches of western Britain."[9] As Margaret Deanesly pointed out, "The customs of the Welsh had been those of Gaul, Italy and the western church when Patrick and Illtud and Petroc and David converted the heathen and taught their fathers the due practices of the Christian life, long ago."[10]

[7] Ibid., p. 29.

[8] Nicholas Brooks, "From British to English Christianity: Deconstructing Bede's Interpretation of the Conversion", in *Conversion and Colonization in Anglo-Saxon England*, ed. Nicholas Howe and Catherine Katkov (Tempe, AZ: Arizona Center for Medieval and Renaissance Studies), pp. 1–30; more widely, see Nicholas John Higham, *(Re-)Reading Bede: The "Historia Ecclesiastica" in Context* (London: Routledge, 2006).

[9] Blair, *Church in Anglo-Saxon Society*, p. 33.

[10] Margaret Deanesly, *The Pre-Conquest Church in England* (London: Adam and Charles Black, 1963), p. 57.

In his later writings especially, and these include the *Ecclesiastical History*, Bede can also be presented as a reformer, aiming at the purification and renewal of society and Church. The conversion of England became as much a preoccupation as the living out of his monastic vocation through Liturgy, study, and teaching. In the words of the eminent American Bede scholar George Hardin Brown, "Although Bede's writings as a monk were directed to the spiritual life of the individual soul, in later life both his historical and exegetical writings emphasise the great need for societal and ecclesiastical reform. He was deeply committed to the salvific power of Christianity and was actively engaged in the apostolate for the salvation of his people. He used his authoritative writings, as the previous Fathers of the Church did, as instruments of reform."[11] To this accolade, however, a warning is appended. "He entertained no roseate expectations. He saw all mankind as being called from the exile of a lapsed world to the perfect world found only in God."[12] In that perspective, it is pertinent to note that a touching account of his death survives, the *Letter of Cuthbert to Cuthwin*. It is read on Bede's feast day, May 25, in the present Roman Liturgy of the Hours.

Bede would probably have been surprised to be included, albeit as a tailpiece, in a presentation of the Latin Fathers, since he frequently described himself, in his own writing, as "following in the footsteps of the Fathers", and he can therefore, if one wishes, be regarded as "between two worlds".[13] He was the first to formulate the quartet of four preeminent Latin Fathers—Ambrose, Jerome, Augustine, Gregory—choosing the number four so as to mirror the four evangelists in the New Testament canon. He could criticize as well as serve his patristic sources, as in his commentary on Habakkuk, where his predecessor as exegete was none other than Saint Jerome. That has led one modern student of Bede's Old Testament interpretation to remark, "The tag 'following in the footsteps of the Fathers' heralds not a programme of slavish imitation, but reflects instead Bede's

---

[11] George Hardin Brown, *A Companion to Bede* (Woodbridge, UK; Rochester, NY: Boydell Press, 2009), p. 16. For a discussion of what that "reform" would have consisted in, see Blair, *Church in Anglo-Saxon Society*, pp. 101–17.

[12] Brown, *Companion to Bede*, p. 16.

[13] Benedicta Ward, "Bede the Theologian", in *The Medieval Theologians: An Introduction to Theology in the Medieval Period*, ed. G. R. Evans (Malden, MA: Blackwell, 2001), pp. 57–64.

attempt to join the tradition of the Fathers by writing alongside them as a collaborator and partner—that is, as one of their own."[14]

The mediaeval Latin authors and their early modern successors certainly treated Bede as one of the Fathers. If asked why, they would no doubt have associated this status with, above all, the proven fruitfulness of his exegetical production. He was the single most common source of the patristic comments on the biblical text in that standard mediaeval (twelfth-century) compilation the *Ordinary Gloss*.[15] His homilies were the single biggest element in the ninth-century homiliary of Paul the Deacon, which, by incorporation into both the monastic and the Roman Liturgy of the Hours, "became the standard collection of readings for the night office" in the Western Church.[16] In the sixteenth century, Saint Robert Bellarmine drew a comparison between two contemporaries, Bede and John Damascene, each spreading light by their wisdom, Bede on the West, Damascene on the East, and Bellarmine was quoted accordingly in the 1899 rescript of Pope Leo XIII declaring Bede a Doctor of the Church. The same comparison has been made in our own day by the Orthodox patrologist Andrew Louth in the closing pages of his study of John of Damascus.[17]

Bede's extremely varied literary work lends itself to subdivision into at least three main categories: Bede as teacher, Bede as exegete, Bede as historian. In the context of patristic theology, the category "Bede as exegete" will be central. "Bede as teacher" will mean Bede as concerned to build up an educational culture able to assist people to understand the Scriptures. "Bede as historian" will mean Bede as writing a theologically informed history that can be seen as the continuation, in its own time and place, of the account of the "wonderful deeds of God" recorded in the salvation history that Scripture records. By implication, the Bible is in view throughout.

[14] Scott DiGregorio, "Bede and the Old Testament", in *Cambridge Companion to Bede*, p. 132.

[15] E. Ann Matter, "The Church Fathers and the *Glossa Ordinaria*", in *The Reception of the Church Fathers in the West: From the Carolingians to the Maurists*, ed. Irena Dorota Backus (Leiden: Brill 1997), pp. 83–111. On the *Ordinary Gloss* more widely, see Lesley Smith, *The Glossa Ordinaria: The Making of a Medieval Bible Commentary* (Leiden: Brill, 2009).

[16] Lawrence T. Martin, "Bede and Preaching", in DiGregorio, *Cambridge Companion to Bede*, p. 163.

[17] Andrew Louth, *St. John Damascene: Tradition and Originality in Byzantine Theology* (Oxford: Oxford University Press, 2002), pp. 283–88.

Bede as Teacher

The distinguished mediaevalist Benedicta Ward, nun of the Convent of the Incarnation at Fairacres, Oxford, in her comprehensive study of Saint Bede, divides the chapter on "Bede the Teacher" into three main sections: "learning to read and write", "learning about numbers", and "learning about the world".[18] These topics name the principal skills Bede deemed necessary for building up an educational culture capable of coming to terms with Sacred Scripture—though one might also add, under this heading "Bede as teacher", a reference to his gazetteers. (*On the Holy Places* was a concise summary of the book of the same name by Adamnan of Iona; its companion was a geographical dictionary Bede produced as an aid to following Saint Luke's narrative in the Acts of the Apostles.[19]) Addressing grammar, computing and chronology, cosmology and topography, "Bede's educational manuals were designed to provide basic instruction for reading, interpreting and expounding Scripture and history."[20]

Benedicta Ward's phrase "learning to read and write" covers three works. Bede's *On Orthography* is an alphabetical collection of entries on the meaning and proper use of Latin words, especially those that might trip up a beginner. It is better thought of as a reference work than as a manual for novices. By contrast, *On the Art of Metre* is definitely for beginners—the exposition moves from the letters of the alphabet, and their division into vowels and consonants, through syllables and the idea of metrical "feet" to metre itself. This was all with a view to teaching a pupil who had got the rudiments of Latin grammar from his earlier studies (else he would not be using the book) how he might "recognize and read correctly the verse forms found in hymns, metrical saints' lives, epigrams, the liturgical chants, as well as in classical Latin poetry".[21]

Then there is *On Figures of Speech and Tropes*, which introduces the student to figures of speech found in Scripture—a topic that

---

[18] Benedicta Ward, S.L.G., *The Venerable Bede* (1990; repr., London: Geoffrey Chapman, 1998), pp. 20–35.

[19] A more ambitious biblical gazetteer based on place names in Jerome and the Jewish historian Josephus is now thought not to be Bede's. Brown, *Companion to Bede*, p. 71.

[20] Ward, *Venerable Bede*, p. 21.

[21] Ibid., p. 22.

could be classified under rhetoric rather than grammar, but gram-marians often took it for their own (it could obviously be seen as belonging to the study of language). Bede was wary of encouraging monks to explore the Roman rhetorical tradition, which, by teach-ing strategies of persuasion, was, in his opinion, far too susceptible to heretical—or even diabolical—misuse. When discussing allegory, Bede adds an important section on typology in the Christological and ecclesiological sense of that word, the application of texts by the transfer of sense to Christ and the Church. He was himself highly experienced in the practice of such application, as is shown by, for example, his commentary on the Song of Songs, which, by influence direct or indirect, is entirely in the manner of Origen of Alexandria. In *On Figures of Speech and Tropes* Bede attempts, in George Hardin Brown's words, "a general theory of symbol applied to Christian salvific history",[22] and one inspired by the discussion of the relation between signs and things (realities) in Augustine's *On Christian Teaching*.

Through Augustine, Bede came across the "Book of Rules" of the maverick Donatist theologian Tyconius, whom, despite his ecclesi-ology, Augustine so admired. The English monk applied its seven ways of interpreting the symbolism of prophecy to the elaborate imagery of the Johannine Apocalypse—Bede's commentary on that book appears to have been his earliest entry into the field of Scripture scholarship.[23] Bede accepted the common patristic hermeneutic of a quartet of modes of biblical interpretation—literal, typical, tropo-logical or moral, and anagogical—for whose authority he refers his readers to Gregory the Great's *Moral Commentary on Job*.

Next we come to what Sister Benedicta calls "learning about numbers". Bede wanted his monastic pupils to know how to situate themselves in time, time secular and time sacred. This included some very basic notions: finger-counting, learning the numerical value of the letters of the Roman and Greek alphabets, becoming acquainted with traditional modes of measuring time or dating events, Greek, Roman and (for the start of the year and the names of the months) English, or Germanic. His chronological works also include the

---

[22] Ibid., p. 25.
[23] Ibid., p. 69.

largest possible temporal perspective—the six ages of world history, a notion he took from Augustine and Isidore but recalculated by a method of his own. That the world had six ages on its temporal trajectory reflected the six phases or "days" of its creation according to the Book of Genesis, and the conventional six stages in the life of an individual from babyhood to senility: appropriately enough since, as Bede explained in the second and longer of his works on chronology, man is a microcosm of the world and thus of the ages of the world. Bede had made his own calculations about the length of these six historical ages. He described the seventh age as running parallel with the six ages in what we might term "eschatological time": it is the unfinished time of all the just who have ever lived from Abel to the Final Judgment. The eighth age would conclude, then, both the sixth and the seventh ages—both historical time and its accompanying eschatological parallel—being as it is the extended point where parallel lines of duration at last converge: the "age of eternal joy and eternal woe after the end of this world".[24]

The study of time could also include very specific issues, and above all, how to reckon correctly the date of Easter—a matter so potentially church-dividing between the Irish and Roman missions in England. It was indeed a convoluted question that entailed interrelating the Jewish lunar calendar with the Roman solar calendar, and thus calculating in advance the lunar and solar cycles, all in relation to the vernal equinox and the timing of the Jewish celebration of Passover. Benedicta Ward provides an extremely lucid account of this complex subject,[25] which for participants in the debate was strangely crucial since, to their minds, "here was the point where time crossed with eternity and all the symbolism of heaven and earth had to be focused to bring this into view."[26]

Finally, numbers were important to Bede in the context of symbolic interpretation of Scripture. Wherever the occurrence of a number could conceivably be made to "illuminate doctrine" or "clarify conduct", he would invoke it,[27] and if the upshot strikes moderns as

[24] Ibid., p. 31.
[25] Ibid., pp. 27–31.
[26] Ibid., p. 28.
[27] Ibid., p. 31.

impossibly fantastic, for contemporaries it savored of the harmony and concord of an overarching divine plan linking creation and salvation.

Learning something of the created world was also basic. Bede's contribution was modest in content if ambitious in title: *On the Nature of Things*. Drawing on writings from the Isidorian corpus both genuine and pseudonymous, and Pliny the Elder's *Natural History*, Bede offered his students a compact introduction to cosmology, writing as he did of the earth, stars, planets, atmosphere, the seas, the nature of seismic and volcanic activity, and the main geographical regions of the globe.

Bede as Exegete

As already mentioned, Bede's biblical commentaries have been highly regarded in the tradition. This was not only because, writing on some biblical books—notably Genesis and the Gospel according to Saint Luke—he assembled, albeit with contributions of his own, the comments of the earlier Latin Fathers, and this was highly convenient. It was also because he chose to write about some texts where the Latin Church had little if anything else to go on. His commentaries on Ezra and Nehemiah come into this latter category and so do, more surprisingly, his commentaries on the Catholic epistles, always excepting Augustine's *Tractates on the Letters of St. John*, which he knew and exploited.[28]

For understandable reasons, Bede's exegesis of the New Testament concentrates more on the literal sense concerning as it does the fulfillment of Old Testament prophecy, while his interpretation of the Old Testament is predominantly allegorical. That is not just because the Old Testament is, for Christians, the "Book of Foreshadowings". As Benedicta Ward points out, the historical narratives of the Hebrew Bible, with their focus on kings and war, were only too likely to confirm the prejudices of the Anglo-Saxon ruling class, prejudices that Bede's spiritual heroes, like the missionary bishop Aidan and his ascetic successor Cuthbert, sought to dislodge in favour of other priorities such as loving God and one's neighbour. "Admiration for warlike kings protected by God [was] a concept which tied in far too

---

[28] Brown, *Companion to Bede*, p. 34.

well with their unregenerate selves."[29] It was certainly an achievement to have created out of First Samuel, for instance, a "complete book of instruction in doctrine and conduct for contemporary Christians".[30] One could say of Bede what Peter Brown said of Augustine: for him, "the Bible was literally the 'word' of God. It was regarded as a single communication, a single message in an intricate code, and not as an exceedingly heterogenous collection of separate books."[31] But even then Bede recognised the importance of the literal sense not only in addressing the historical dimension, but also, more widely, in the necessary task of adjudication between different translations, which for him meant chiefly the Old Latin and the Vulgate Bibles with their backgrounds in, respectively, the Septuagint and the Hebrew text.

One noteworthy feature of his Old Testament exegesis is his interest in architecture: he has a free-standing study of the Desert tabernacle and another of the Jerusalem Temple, while his commentary on Ezra and Nehemiah naturally considers the second, post-exilic Temple, the problems of whose building exercised the author of those books. These and other sacred structures certainly gave him an opportunity for flights of imaginative allegorizing, legitimized by New Testament language about Christ as the New Temple and the Church community as the House of God built of living stones. In an Introduction to *On the Temple*, the Anglo-Saxon scholar Jennifer O'Reilly commented,

> The mental tour of the great building [Solomon's Temple] opens vistas on the historical journey of the chosen people journeying to the Promised Land, on the continuing journey of the new people of God towards the heavenly Jerusalem, a journey accomplished by the individual believer at death but continuing for the Church as a whole until the end of time. The work describes how the Church on earth can be built up spiritually to become more like that heavenly dwelling. It ends where it begins with the longing for the heavenly mansions but with the reader's understanding of that image extraordinarily enriched.[32]

[29] Ward, *Venerable Bede*, p. 55.

[30] Ibid., p. 68.

[31] Peter Brown, *Augustine of Hippo: A Biography* (London: Faber and Faber, 1967), p. 252.

[32] Jennifer O'Reilly, Introduction to Bede, *On the Temple* (Liverpool: Liverpool University Press, 1995), p. xxxii.

Bede's interest in constructed spaces may also reflect his appreciation of the church buildings in which he celebrated the monastic Liturgy and whose iconography he lovingly recalls.[33] It has been pointed
out that "the images adorning Biscop's churches ... served as visual
summaries of Scripture and of the relationship between the Old and
New Testaments, illustrated by means of didactic typology—devices
also employed by Bede in his writings."[34] One is reminded of the
set of poems Ambrose wrote to a series of paintings of matched Old
and New Testament scenes on the walls of the Milanese basilica that
would bear his name.

Bede as Historian

In the sense that he sought to find the most reliable sources available
for reconstruction of the past, Bede's approach to history writing
was at once critical and yet theological. He would not have appreciated the force of the word "yet" in my phrase "and yet theological".
Between the two qualities—researched and theological—there was to
his mind no incongruity. That is Benedicta Ward's inference from
the way Bede entitles his narrative of the Church in England a "Historia ecclesiastica". Theology is applied to a common account, historia,
rendering it in the process ecclesiastica. Through a "presentation of
what was generally agreed about past events", Bede's text "reveals
the pattern of redemption, the work of God in this world and in the
next".[35] In the Preface to the Ecclesiastical History of the English People,
Bede tells his readers he means to seek out the vera lex historiae, "the
true law of history"; but, for Ward, what this means is "a careful
record of popular report", which, to be fully useful for the edification of contemporary Anglo-Saxon people, must then be interpreted
"according to known truth revealed in Christ".[36]

Her phrase "popular report" is perhaps a little cavalier, even when
qualified by the words "careful record". Also in the Preface to the

---

[33] Bede, History of the Abbots of Wearmouth and Jarrow 6 and 9.

[34] Michelle P. Brown, "Bede's Life in Context", in DiGregorio, Cambridge Companion to
Bede, p. 19.

[35] Ward, Venerable Bede, p. 112.

[36] Ibid., p. 113.

Ecclesiastical History, Bede lists his authorities; where contemporary Northumbria is concerned, he appeals, in the manner of modern "oral historians", to witnesses with firsthand experience, while in the corresponding Preface to his prose *Life of Cuthbert*, he describes how he not only questioned such witnesses but submitted his account for checking and cross-checking to select individuals among his oral sources.[37]

But, to be sure, Bede "consistently reworked such accounts in order to present their inner truth in accordance with the insights of theology",[38] a "re-working" hardly unexpected in early Christian historiography—Bede would have noted it in Eusebius' *Ecclesiastical History*, translated into Latin by Rufinus, and the *Histories against the Pagans* of Orosius, which offered Augustine a specifically evangelical "take" on Roman decline in the *City of God*.

Of that "re-working", Ward goes so far as to say that, since "Bede's History is essentially concerned with the aspect of life in Anglo-Saxon England which related to the conversion of a people to Christianity", it has "more in common with the biblical commentaries than with the chronicles".[39] True, the *Ecclesiastical History of the English People*, like Bede's chronicles, is structured in terms of the six ages of the world, or the six ages of man; but that is because there is, in Bede's mind, a parallelism between, on the one hand, the creation of a new people of God on the British island of which England formed the larger part and, on the other hand, the creation of the original people of God of the Old and New Covenants.

If we may trust Benedicta Ward's judgment, Bede saw himself as writing in the "sixth age" not simply in terms of world history, or Church history in general, but in terms of the ecclesiastical history of the English people in particular. On her reading, Book I concerns the infancy of Christianity among the Anglo-Saxons. Book II deals with its childhood: recording the growth of the Church in England and the passing of the first generation of new Christians. Book III describes its fertile youth, when it began to propagate, notably in the new life of the Church of Northumbria, Bede's own native kingdom.

[37] C. J. Godfrey, *The Church in Anglo-Saxon England* (Cambridge: Cambridge University Press, 1962), pp. 210–12.

[38] Ward, *Venerable Bede*, p. 114.

[39] Ibid., p. 131.

Book IV evokes the mature age of the Church under its "princes", Archbishop Theodore and his assistant Abbot Hadrian, who held synods to lay down doctrine and discipline and through the school of Canterbury made possible a flowering of learning. Book V, with its coda in the closing letter to Egbert of York, conveys a contrasting sense that decline has already set in—hence the urgency of Bede's closing appeal to Egbert to sponsor a programme of monastic, clerical, and societal reform before it is too late.

By way of counterpoint, "each of the five books of the *Ecclesiastical History* is filled with the vision of those saints already at rest in the seventh age, though still available to toilers in the sixth. Bede's account of the English is therefore a world history in miniature, in which they take their place among the people of God awaiting 'the eighth age of the blessed Resurrection in which they shall reign forever with the Lord'."[40]

For his part, George Hardin Brown confesses that "such a religious historicity is strange to the reader today": Bede's historical outlook is "at once achronological (typical, symbolic, allegorical, timeless) and temporal (*continuous*, distinct, unique)".[41] And yet, the *Ecclesiastical History* is not just Bede's last work. It is the culmination of all his efforts in a variety of genres. Now that Bede's wider corpus is better known, it is unfashionable to call the "History of the English Church and People" his supreme achievement. But it can still be regarded as the cumulative climax of all he had done before.

> His many years as a teacher and writer of postclassical Latin, coupled with his impressive natural endowments, enabled him to write a well-structured, long and coherent treatise. His many years as an exegete honed his interpretative skills; the commentaries in the Gospels and Acts had especially practiced his talents for narrative, artistic selectivity, and the reconciliation of real and seeming contradictions. His work as a computist developed his special abilities for chronology, for fixing and relating events, and for understanding temporal sequence and relationships. His works of biography and hagiography had trained him to incorporate detail and sign into the larger fabric, to utilize reports, data, popular accounts, and miracle stories for studied

---

[40] Ibid., p. 115.
[41] Brown, *Companion to Bede*, p. 113.

effect. His expertise in poetry as well as rhetorical prose allowed him to use both forms effectively within the text, and his editorial expertise allowed him to edit and use letters and quotations effectively.[42]

In short, "all his training as grammarian exegete, literary artist, and chronologer" came together,[43] to produce this *gesta Dei per Anglos*, this account of the "deeds of God through the English".

Not inappropriately, then, Bede will be the only Englishman to appear in the *Paradiso* cantos of Dante's *Divine Comedy*, that deathless portrayal of the ultimate intended outcome (hell can hardly be called *intended*) of the entire saving history of God with men.[44]

---

[42] Ibid., p. 96.
[43] Ibid.
[44] Dante, *Paradiso* X, 130.

CONCLUSION

With the lives and teaching of the Fathers, the way is thrown open for the flowering of Christendom in Latin and Byzantine Christianity alike. This does not mean, though, that the Fathers, having served their purpose, are left behind—like a ladder which, useful for scaling a wall, can subsequently be abandoned. The Fathers retain their unique place in theological history. They are the accredited receivers of the biblical revelation, for no revelation is truly transmitted until it is received.[1] Joseph Cardinal Ratzinger (now Pope Emeritus Benedict XVI) stated, "The life-sustaining power of the scriptural word is interpreted and applied in the faith that the Fathers and the great councils have learned from that word. The one who holds to this has found what gives secure ground in times of change."[2]

In these words, Pope Benedict XVI is reminding his hearers that, in St. Peter's Basilica, the empty throne of the apostle, suspended by the architect above the high altar, is carried by four representatives of the patristic Church, two from the East and two from the West. Certainly, the Eastern Orthodox, for their part, will not recognise the understanding of the Scriptures taught at Rome unless they hear therein the voices of the holy Fathers. "The witness of the Fathers belongs, integrally and intrinsically, to the very structure of the Orthodox faith. The Church is equally committed to the *kerygma* of the apostles and to the *dogmata* of the Fathers. Both belong together inseparably. The Church is indeed 'Apostolic'. But the Church is also 'Patristic'. And only by being 'Patristic' is the Church continuously 'Apostolic'."[3]

---

[1] Joseph Cardinal Ratzinger, "[The] Importance of the Fathers for the Structure of Faith", in *Principles of Catholic Theology: Building Stones for a Fundamental Theology*, trans. Sr. Mary Frances McCarthy, S.N.D. (San Francisco: Ignatius Press, 1987), pp. 133–52.

[2] Joseph Cardinal Ratzinger, " 'Primacy in Love': The Chair Altar of St. Peter's in Rome", in *Images of Hope: Meditations on Major Feasts*, trans. John Rock and Graham Harrison (San Francisco: Ignatius Press, 2006), p. 34.

[3] Georges Florovsky, "The Ethos of the Orthodox Church", in *The Patristic Witness of Georges Florovsky: Essential Theological Writings*, ed. Brandon Gallagher and Paul Ladouceur (London: T&T Clark, 2019), p. 293.

Moreover, in the claim which my Preface staked out, the Fathers can also be, as they were for their contemporaries, singing-masters of the soul. "Truly, these are the 'Fathers' of the Church since from them, through the Gospel, she received life. Equally they are her builders ... on the one foundation laid by the apostles, namely: Christ."[4]

---

[4] Pope Saint John Paul II, apostolic letter *Patres Ecclesiae* (January 2, 1980), I. Translation is the present author's.

SELECTED BIBLIOGRAPHY AND FURTHER READINGS

A. General Works in English

Benedict XVI, Pope. *Church Fathers: From Clement of Rome to Augustine*. San Francisco: Ignatius Press, 2008.

———. *Church Fathers and Teachers: From Saint Leo the Great to Peter Lombard*. San Francisco: Ignatius Press, 2010.

Chadwick, Henry. *The Church in Ancient Society: From Galilee to Gregory the Great*. Oxford: Oxford University Press, 2001.

Davis, L.D., S.J. *The First Seven Ecumenical Councils (325–787): Their History and Theology*. Collegeville, MN: Liturgical Press, 1990.

Drobner, Hubertus B. *The Fathers of the Church: A Comprehensive Introduction*. Peabody, MA: Hendrickson, 2007.

Evans, G.R., ed. *The First Christian Theologians: An Introduction to Theology in the Early Church*. Oxford: Blackwell, 2004.

Ferguson, Everett, ed. *Encyclopaedia of Early Christianity*. New York: Garland, 1997.

———. *Personalities of the Early Church*. London: Routledge, 1993.

Margerie, Bertrand de, S.J. *An Introduction to the History of Exegesis*. Vol. 1, *The Greek Fathers*; Vol. 2, *The Latin Fathers*; Vol. 3, *Saint Augustine*. Translated by Leonard Maluf and Pierre de Fontnouvelle. Petersham, MA: St. Bede's Publications, 1991–1994.

Quasten, Johannes. *Patrology*. Vol. 1, *The Beginnings of Patristic Literature*; Vol. 2, *The Ante-Nicene Literature after Irenaeus*; Vol. 3, *The Golden Age of Greek Patristic Literature*; Vol. 4, *The Eastern Fathers from the Council of Chalcedon*. Utrecht: Spectrum Publishers, 1950. Repr., Allen, TX: Christian Classics, 1999.

Ramsey, Boniface. *Beginning to Read the Fathers*. 2nd ed. Mahwah, NJ: Paulist, 2012.

Wilken, Robert L. *The Spirit of Early Christian Thought*. London and New Haven, CT: Yale University Press, 2003.

Young, Francis, Lewis Ayres, and Andrew Louth, eds. *Cambridge History of Early Christian Literature*. Cambridge: Cambridge University Press, 2004.

B. Particular Bibliographies: Primary Sources in Translation

Saint Irenaeus

Irenaeus. *Against Heresies*. Translated by Alexander Roberts and William Rambaut. In *Ante-Nicene Fathers*, edited by Alexander Roberts, James Donaldson, and A. Cleveland Coxe, vol. 1. Buffalo, NY: Christian Literature Publishing, 1885. Available on the New Advent website.

———. *Proof of the Apostolic Preaching*. Translated by Joseph P. Smith, S.J. Ancient Christian Writers. New York: Newman Press, 1952.

Extracts

Grant, Robert M. *Irenaeus of Lyons*. London: Routledge, 1997.

Origen

Origen. *Commentary on the Epistle to the Romans*. Translated by Thomas P. Scheck. 2 vols. Washington, DC: Catholic University of America Press, 2001–2002.

———. *Commentary on the Gospel of John*. Translated and edited by Allan Menzies. In *Ante-Nicene Fathers*, vol. 9. Buffalo, NY: Christian Literature Publishing, 1896. Available on the New Advent website.

———. *Commentary on the Gospel of John*. Translated by Ronald F. Heine. 2 vols. Washington, DC: Catholic University of America Press, 1989–1993.

———. *Commentary on the Gospel of Matthew*. Translated by John Patrick. In *Ante-Nicene Fathers*, edited by Allan Menzies, vol. 9. Buffalo, NY: Christian Literature Publishing, 1896. Available on the New Advent website.

———. *Contra Celsum*. Translated by Frederick Crombie. In *Ante-Nicene Fathers*, edited by Alexander Roberts, James Donaldson, and A. Cleveland Coxe, vol. 4. Buffalo, NY: Christian Literature Publishing, 1896. Available on the New Advent website.

———. *Contra Celsum*. Translated by Henry Chadwick. 1953. Reprint, Cambridge: Cambridge University Press, 1980.

———. *Exegetical Works on Ezekiel*. Translated by Mischa Hooker. Edited by Roger Pearse. Ipswich: Chieftain Publishing, 2014.

———. *Exhortation to Martyrdom; On Prayer; On First Principles IV; Prologue to the Commentary on the Song of Songs; Homily XXVII on Numbers*. Translated by Rowan Greer. London: Society for Promoting Christian Knowledge, 1979.

———. *Homilies on Genesis and Exodus*. Translated by Ronald F. Heine. Washington, DC: Catholic University of America Press, 1982.

————. *Homilies on Joshua.* Translated by Barbara J. Bruce. Washington, DC: Catholic University of America Press, 2002.

————. *Homilies on Judges.* Translated by Elizabeth Ann Dively Lauro. Washington, DC: Catholic University of America Press, 2009.

————. *Homilies on Leviticus.* Translated by Gary Barkley. Washington, DC: Catholic University of America Press, 1990.

————. *Homilies on Luke.* Translated by Joseph Lienhard. Washington, DC: Catholic University of America Press, 1996.

————. *Homilies on Numbers.* Translated by Thomas P. Scheck. Downers Grove, IL: Intervarsity Press Academic, 2009.

————. *On First Principles.* Translated by Frederick Crombie. In *Ante-Nicene Fathers,* edited by Alexander Roberts, James Donaldson, and A. Cleveland Coxe, vol. 4. Buffalo, NY: Christian Literature Publishing, 1885. Available on the New Advent website.

————. *On First Principles.* Translated by G. W. Butterworth. London: Society for Promoting Christian Knowledge, 1936. Reprint, Gloucester, MA: Peter Smith Publishing, 1973.

Von Balthasar, Hans Urs, ed. *Origen: Spirit and Fire; A Thematic Anthology of His Writings.* Translated by Robert J. Daly, S.J. Washington, DC: Catholic University of America Press, 1984.

Extracts

Trigg, Joseph W. *Origen.* London: Routledge, 1998.

Saint Athanasius

Athanasius. *Against the Heathen.* Translated by Archibald Robertson. In *Nicene and Post-Nicene Fathers,* edited by Philip Schaff and Henry Wace, 2nd series, vol. 4. Buffalo, NY: Christian Literature Publishing, 1892. Available on the New Advent website.

————. *Contra gentes and de Incarnatione.* Translated by Robert W. Thomson. Oxford: Clarendon Press, 1971.

————. *Festal Letters.* Translated by Archibald Robertson and R. Payne-Smith. In *Nicene and Post-Nicene Fathers,* edited by Philip Schaff and Henry Wace, 2nd series, vol. 4. Buffalo, NY: Christian Literature Publishing, 1892. Available on the New Advent website.

————. *The History of the Arians.* Translated by M. Atkinson. In *Nicene and Post-Nicene Fathers,* edited by Philip Schaff and Henry Wace, 2nd series, vol. 4. Buffalo, NY: Christian Literature Publishing, 1892. Available on the New Advent website.

————. *The Letters of Saint Athanasius concerning the Holy Spirit.* Translated by C. R. B. Shapland. New York: Philosophical Library, 1951. Available on archive.org.

————. *The Life of Antony and the Letter to Marcellinus.* Translated by Robert C. Gregg. New York: Paulist, 1980.

————. *Life of St. Antony.* Translated by H. Ellershaw. In *Nicene and Post-Nicene Fathers*, edited by Philip Schaff and Henry Wace, 2nd series, vol. 4. Buffalo, NY: Christian Literature Publishing, 1892. Available on the New Advent website.

————. *On the Decrees.* Translated by John Henry Newman. In *Nicene and Post-Nicene Fathers*, edited by Philip Schaff and Henry Wace, 2nd series, vol. 4. Buffalo, NY: Christian Literature Publishing, 1892. Available on the New Advent website.

————. *On the Incarnation of the Word.* Translated by Archibald Robertson. In *Nicene and Post-Nicene Fathers*, edited by Philip Schaff and Henry Wace, 2nd series, vol. 4. Buffalo, NY: Christian Literature Publishing, 1892. Available on the New Advent website.

————. *On the Synods.* Translated by John Henry Newman and Archibald Robertson. In *Nicene and Post-Nicene Fathers*, edited by Philip Schaff and Henry Wace, 2nd series, vol. 4. Buffalo, NY: Christian Literature Publishing, 1892. Available on the New Advent website.

————. *Orations against the Arians.* Translated by John Henry Newman and Archibald Robertson. In *Nicene and Post-Nicene Fathers*, edited by Philip Schaff and Henry Wace, 2nd series, vol. 4. Buffalo, NY: Christian Literature Publishing, 1892. Available on the New Advent website.

Extracts

Anatolios, Khaled. *Athanasius.* London: Routledge, 2004.

The Cappadocians

Saint Basil

Basil. *Address to Young Men on Greek Literature.* Translated by F. M. Padelford. New York: American Book, 1901.

————. *The Ascetic Works of Saint Basil.* Translated by W. K. Lowther Clarke. London: Society for Promoting Christian Knowledge; New York: Macmillan, 1925.

————. *Letters.* Translated by Blomfield Jackson. In *Nicene and Post-Nicene Fathers*, edited by Philip Schaff and Henry Wace, 2nd series, vol. 8. Buffalo, NY: Christian Literature Publishing, 1895. Available on the New Advent website.

————. *On the Hexameron*. Translated by Blomfield Jackson. In *Nicene and Post-Nicene Fathers*, edited by Philip Schaff and Henry Wace, 2nd series, vol. 8. Buffalo, NY: Christian Literature Publishing, 1895. Available on the New Advent website.

————. *On the Holy Spirit*. Translated by Blomfield Jackson. In *Nicene and Post-Nicene Fathers*, edited by Philip Schaff and Henry Wace, 2nd series, vol. 8. Buffalo, NY: Christian Literature Publishing, 1895. Available on the New Advent website.

————. *The Rule of St. Basil in Latin and English: A Revised Critical Edition*. Translated by Anna M. Silvas. Collegeville, MN: Liturgical Press, 2013.

Extracts

Hildebrand, Stephen M. *Basil of Caesarea*. London: Routledge, 2018. Originally published: Grand Rapids, MI: Baker Academic, 2014.

Saint Gregory Nazianzen

Gregory Nazianzen. *Letters*. Translated by Charles Gordon Browne and James Edward Swallow. In *Nicene and Post-Nicene Fathers*, edited by Philip Schaff and Henry Wace, 2nd series, vol. 7. Buffalo, NY: Christian Literature Publishing, 1894. Available on the New Advent website.

————. *On God and Man: The Theological Poetry of Gregory Nazianzen*. Translated by Peter Gilbert. Crestwood, NY: Saint Vladimir's Seminary Press, 2001.

————. *Orations*. Translated by Charles Gordon Browne and James Edward Swallow. In *Nicene and Post-Nicene Fathers*, edited by Philip Schaff and Henry Wace, 2nd series, vol. 7. Buffalo, NY: Christian Literature Publishing, 1894. Available on the New Advent website.

Norris, F. W., ed. *Faith Gives Fulness to Reasoning: The Five Theological Orations of St. Gregory Nazianzen*. Translated by Lionel Wickham and Frederick Williams. Leiden: Brill, 1990.

Extracts

Daley, Brian E. *Gregory of Nazianzus*. London: Routledge, 1996.

Saint Gregory of Nyssa

Gregory of Nyssa. *Against Eunomius*. Translated by W. Moore, H. A. Wilson, and H. C. Ogle. In *Nicene and Post-Nicene Fathers*, edited by Philip Schaff and Henry Wace, 2nd series, vol. 5. Buffalo, NY: Christian Literature Publishing, 1893. Available on the New Advent website.

————. *Ascetical Works*. Translated by Virginia Woods Callahan. Washington, DC: Catholic University of America Press, 1967.

————. *Commentary on the Song of Songs*. Translated by Casimir McCambley. Brookline, MA: Hellenic College Press, 1987.

————. *The Great Catechism*. Translated by William Moore and Henry Austin Wilson. In *Nicene and Post-Nicene Fathers*, edited by Philip Schaff and Henry Wace, 2nd series, vol. 5. Buffalo, NY: Christian Literature Publishing, 1893. Available on the New Advent website.

————. *Homilies on Ecclesiastes: An English Version with Supporting Studies*. Translated by Stuart G. Hall. Berlin: de Gruyter, 1993.

————. *The Letters*. Translated by Anna M. Silvas. Boston, MA: Brill, 2006.

————. *The Life of Moses*. Translated by A.J. Malherbe and Everett Ferguson. New York: Paulist, 1979.

————. *The Lord's Prayer and the Beatitudes*. Translated by Hilda C. Graef. New York: Newman Press, 1954.

————. *On Faith*. Translated by H.A. Wilson. In *Nicene and Post-Nicene Fathers*, edited by Philip Schaff and Henry Wace, 2nd series, vol. 5. Buffalo, NY: Christian Literature Publishing, 1893. Available on the New Advent website.

————. *On the Holy Spirit, against Macedonius*. Translated by William Moore and Henry Austin Wilson. In *Nicene and Post-Nicene Fathers*, edited by Philip Schaff and Henry Wace, 2nd series, vol. 5. Buffalo, NY: Christian Literature Publishing, 1893. Available on the New Advent website.

————. *On Not Three Gods*. Translated by H.A. Wilson. In *Nicene and Post-Nicene Fathers*, edited by Philip Schaff and Henry Wace, 2nd series, vol. 5. Buffalo, NY: Christian Literature Publishing, 1893. Available on the New Advent website.

————. *On the Soul and the Resurrection*. Translated by William Moore and Henry Austin Wilson. In *Nicene and Post-Nicene Fathers*, edited by Philip Schaff and Henry Wace, 2nd series, vol. 5. Buffalo, NY: Christian Literature Publishing, 1893. Available on the New Advent website.

————. *On Virginity*. Translated by William Moore and Henry Austin Wilson. In *Nicene and Post-Nicene Fathers*, edited by Philip Schaff and Henry Wace, 2nd series, vol. 5. Buffalo, NY: Christian Literature Publishing, 1893. Available on the New Advent website.

————. *The Soul and Resurrection*. Translated by Catherine Roth. Crestwood, NY: St. Vladimir's Seminary Press, 1993.

Extracts

Meredith, Anthony. *Gregory of Nyssa*. London: Routledge, 1999.

Saint Cyril of Alexandria

Cyril of Alexandria. *Against the Blasphemies of Nestorius.* Translated by Edward Bouverie Pusey. Oxford: Parker; London: Rivingtons, 1881. Available online at Roger Pearse's website of additional texts by early Church Fathers at https://www.tertullian.org/fathers/.

———. *Against Those Who Are Unwilling to Confess That the Holy Virgin Is Theotokos.* Translated by George Dragas. Rollinsford, NH: Orthodox Research Institute, 2004.

———. *Commentary on the Gospel of John.* Translated by David Maxwell. 2 vols. Downers Grove, IL: InterVarsity Press Academic, 2013–2015.

———. *Commentary on the Gospel of Luke.* Translated by Robert Payne Smith. Oxford: Oxford University Press, 1859.

———. *Commentary on Isaiah.* Translated by Robert C. Hill. Brookline, MA: Holy Cross Press, 2008.

———. *Commentary on the Twelve Prophets.* Translated by Robert C. Hill. 3 vols. Washington, DC: Catholic University of America Press, 2007–2012.

———. *Festal Letters 1–12.* Translated by P. R. Amidon. Washington, DC: Catholic University of America Press, 2009.

———. *Glaphyra on the Pentateuch.* Translated by Nicholas P. Lunn. 2 vols. Washington, DC: Catholic University of America Press, 2018–2019.

———. *Letters 1–110.* Translated by John I. McEnerney. Washington, DC: Catholic University of America Press, 1987.

———. *On the Unity of Christ.* Translated by J. A. McGuckin. Crestwood, NY: St. Vladimir's Seminary Press, 1995.

———. *Scholia on the Incarnation of the Only Begotten.* Translated by Edward Bouverie Pusey. Oxford: Parker; London: Rivingtons, 1881. Available online at Roger Pearse's website of additional texts by early Church Fathers at https://www.tertullian.org/fathers/.

———. *That Christ Is One.* Translated by Edward Bouverie Pusey. Oxford: Parker; London: Rivingtons, 1881. Available online at Roger Pearse's website of additional texts by early Church Fathers at https://www .tertullian.org/fathers/.

Extracts

Russell, Norman. *Cyril of Alexandria.* London: Routledge, 2000.

Denys

Parker, John. *The Works of Dionysius the Areopagite.* 2 vols. London and Oxford: James Parker, 1897–1899. Available online at Roger Pearse's

website of additional texts by Early Church Fathers at https://www
.tertullian.org/fathers/.

Pseudo-Dionysius. *The Complete Works*. Translated by Colm Luibheid.
Mahwah, NJ: Paulist, 1987.

Saint Maximus

Allen, Pauline, and Bronwen Neil, eds. and trans. *Maximus the Confessor and
His Companions: Documents from Exile*. Oxford: Oxford University Press,
2002.

Maximus the Confessor. *The Ascetic Life and the Four Centuries on Charity*.
Translated by Polycarp Sherwood, O.S.B. Westminster, MD: Newman
Press, 1957.

——. *The Disputation with Pyrrhus of Our Father among the Saints Maximus
the Confessor*. Translated by Joseph P. Farrell. South Canaan, PA: St. Tikhon's Monastery Press, 1990.

——. *On the Cosmic Mystery of Jesus Christ: Selected Writings from St. Maximus the Confessor*. Translated by Paul M. Blowers and Robert Louis
Wilken. Yonkers, NY: Saint Vladimir's Seminary Press, 2003.

——. *On Difficulties in the Church Fathers: The Ambigua*. Translated by Nicholas Constas. 2 vols. Cambridge, MA: Harvard University Press, 2014.

——. *On Difficulties in Sacred Scripture*. Translated by Nicholas Constas.
Washington, DC: Catholic University of America Press, 2018.

——. *Selected Writings*. Translated by George C. Berthold. London: Society for Promoting Christian Knowledge, 1985.

Extracts

Louth, Andrew. *Maximus the Confessor*. London and New York: Routledge,
1996.

Saint John Damascene

John Damascene. *Exposition of the Orthodox Faith*. Translated by E. W. Watson and L. Pullan. In *Nicene and Post-Nicene Fathers*, edited by Philip
Schaff and Henry Wace, 2nd series, vol. 9. Buffalo, NY: Christian Literature Publishing, 1899. Available on the New Advent website.

——. *Three Treatises on the Divine Images*. Translated by Andrew Louth.
Crestwood, NY: St. Vladimir's Seminary Press, 2013.

——. *Writings*. Translated by Frederic H. Chase. Washington, DC:
Catholic University of America Press, 1958.

Tertullian

Tertullian. *Against Hermogenes*. Translated by Peter Holmes. In *Ante-Nicene Christian Library*, vol. 15. Edinburgh: T&T Clark, 1870.

————. *Against Marcion*. Translated by Peter Holmes. In *Ante-Nicene Christian Library*, vol. 7. Edinburgh: T&T Clark, 1868.

————. *Against Praxeas*. Translated by Peter Holmes. In *Ante-Nicene Christian Library*, vol. 15. Edinburgh: T&T Clark, 1870.

————. *An Answer to the Jews*. Translated by S. Thelwall. In *Ante-Nicene Christian Library*, vol. 18. Edinburgh: T&T Clark, 1870.

————. *The Apology*. Translated by S. Thelwall. In *Ante-Nicene Christian Library*, vol. 11. Edinburgh: T&T Clark, 1869.

————. *On the Flesh of Christ*. Translated by Peter Holmes. In *Ante-Nicene Christian Library*, vol. 15. Edinburgh: T&T Clark, 1870.

————. *On the Prescription of Heretics*. Translated by Peter Holmes. In *Ante-Nicene Christian Library*, vol. 15. Edinburgh: T&T Clark, 1870.

————. *On the Resurrection of Christ*. Translated by Peter Holmes. In *Ante-Nicene Christian Library*, vol. 15. Edinburgh: T&T Clark, 1870.

————. *The Testimony of the Soul*. Translated by S. Thelwall. In *Ante-Nicene Christian Library*, vol. 11. Edinburgh: T&T Clark, 1869.

The above texts, and other minor treatises, were republished as *Ante-Nicene Fathers*, vol. 3, edited by Alexander Roberts, James Donaldson, and A. Cleveland Coxe. Buffalo, NY: Christian Literature Publishing, 1885. Available on the New Advent website. See also the Tertullian Project website with details of post-Victorian English translations of texts.

Extracts

Dunn, Geoffrey D. *Tertullian*. London: Routledge, 2004.

Saint Cyprian

Cyprian. *The Lapsed* and *The Unity of the Catholic Church*. Translated by Maurice Bévénot, S.J. Washington, DC: Catholic University of America Press, 1957.

————. *Letters*. Translated by Robert Ernest Wallis. In *Ante-Nicene Fathers*, edited by Alexander Roberts, James Donaldson, and A. Cleveland Coxe, vol. 5. Buffalo, NY: Christian Literature Publishing, 1886. Available on the New Advent website.

————. *Selected Letters*. Translated by Allen Brent. Crestwood, NY: St. Vladimir's Seminary Press, 2007.

————. *Treatises.* Translated by Robert Ernest Wallis. In *Ante-Nicene Fathers*, edited by Alexander Roberts, James Donaldson, and A. Cleveland Coxe, vol. 5. Buffalo, NY: Christian Literature Publishing, 1886. Available on the New Advent website.

Saint Ambrose

Ambrose. *Commentary of St. Ambrose on the Gospel according to St. Luke.* Translated by Íde M. Ní Riain. Dublin: Halcyon, 2001.
————. *Exposition of the Christian Faith.* Translated by H. de Romestin, E. de Romestin, and H. T. F. Duckworth. In *Nicene and Post-Nicene Fathers*, edited by Philip Schaff and Henry Wace, 2nd series, vol. 10. Buffalo, NY: Christian Literature Publishing, 1896. Available on the New Advent website.
————. *On the Holy Spirit.* Translated by H. de Romestin, E. de Romestin, and H. T. F. Duckworth. In *Nicene and Post-Nicene Fathers*, edited by Philip Schaff and Henry Wace, 2nd series, vol. 10. Buffalo, NY: Christian Literature Publishing, 1896. Available on the New Advent website.
————. *On the Mysteries.* Translated by H. de Romestin, E. de Romestin, and H. T. F. Duckworth. In *Nicene and Post-Nicene Fathers*, edited by Philip Schaff and Henry Wace, 2nd series, vol. 10. Buffalo, NY: Christian Literature Publishing, 1896. Available on the New Advent website.
————. *On Virgins.* Translated by H. de Romestin, E. de Romestin, and H. T. F. Duckworth. In *Nicene and Post-Nicene Fathers*, edited by Philip Schaff and Henry Wace, 2nd series, vol. 10. Buffalo, NY: Christian Literature Publishing, 1896. Available on the New Advent website.
————. *Seven Exegetical Works.* Translated by Michael P. McHugh. Washington, DC: Catholic University of America Press, 1972.
————. *Theological and Dogmatic Works.* Translated by Roy J. Deferrari. Washington, DC: Catholic University of America Press, 1963.

Extracts

Ramsey, Boniface. *Ambrose.* London: Routledge, 1997.

Saint Jerome

Jerome. *Against Jovinian.* Translated by W. H. Fremantle, G. Lewis, and W. G. Martley. In *Nicene and Post-Nicene Fathers*, edited by Philip Schaff and Henry Wace, 2nd series, vol. 6. Buffalo, NY: Christian Literature Publishing, 1893. Available on the New Advent website.
————. *Against the Pelagians.* Translated by W. H. Fremantle, G. Lewis, and W. G. Martley. In *Nicene and Post-Nicene Fathers*, edited by Philip Schaff

and Henry Wace, 2nd series, vol. 6. Buffalo, NY: Christian Literature Publishing, 1893. Available on the New Advent website.

———. *Against Vigilantius*. Translated by W. H. Fremantle, G. Lewis, and W. G. Martley. In *Nicene and Post-Nicene Fathers*, edited by Philip Schaff and Henry Wace, 2nd series, vol. 6. Buffalo, NY: Christian Literature Publishing, 1893. Available on the New Advent website.

———. *Apologia for Myself against the Books of Rufinus*. Translated by W. H. Fremantle. In *Nicene and Post-Nicene Fathers*, edited by Philip Schaff and Henry Wace, 2nd series, vol. 3. Buffalo, NY: Christian Literature Publishing, 1892. Available on the New Advent website.

———. *Commentary on Daniel*. Translated by Gleason L. Archer Jr. Grand Rapids, MI: Baker Book House, 1958.

———. *Commentary on Ezekiel*. Translated by Thomas P. Scheck. Mahwah, NJ: Paulist, 2017.

———. *Commentary on Isaiah*. Translated by Thomas P. Scheck. Mahwah, NJ: Paulist, 2015.

———. *Commentary on Matthew*. Translated by D. H. Williams. Washington, DC: Catholic University of America Press, 2008.

———. *The Dialogue against the Luciferians*. Translated by W. H. Fremantle, G. Lewis, and W. G. Martley. In *Nicene and Post-Nicene Fathers*, edited by Philip Schaff and Henry Wace, 2nd series, vol. 6. Buffalo, NY: Christian Literature Publishing, 1893. Available on the New Advent website.

———. *Letters*. Translated by W. H. Fremantle, G. Lewis, and W. G. Martley. In *Nicene and Post-Nicene Fathers*, edited by Philip Schaff and Henry Wace, 2nd series, vol. 6. Buffalo, NY: Christian Literature Publishing, 1893. Available on the New Advent website.

———. *Prefaces* [to the biblical books Jerome retranslated]. Translated by W. H. Fremantle, G. Lewis, and W. G. Martley. In *Nicene and Post-Nicene Fathers*, edited by Philip Schaff and Henry Wace, 2nd series, vol. 6. Buffalo, NY: Christian Literature Publishing, 1893. Available on the New Advent website.

Extracts

Rebenich, Stefan. *Jerome*. London: Routledge, 2002.

Saint Augustine

Texts by various translators and editors in the following:

Nicene and Post-Nicene Fathers, 1st series, vols. 1–8. Buffalo, NY: Christian Literature Publishing Company, 1887–1888. Available on the New Advent website.

The Works of Saint Augustine: A Translation for the Twenty-First Century. New York: New City Press, 1990–.

Saint Leo

Leo. *Letters*. Translated by Charles Lett Feltoe. In *Nicene and Post-Nicene Fathers*, edited by Philip Schaff and Henry Wace, 2nd series, vol. 12. Buffalo, NY: Christian Literature Publishing, 1895. Available on the New Advent website.

———. *Sermons*. Translated by Charles Lett Feltoe. In *Nicene and Post-Nicene Fathers*, edited by Philip Schaff and Henry Wace, 2nd series, vol. 12. Buffalo, NY: Christian Literature Publishing, 1895. Available on the New Advent website.

———. *Sermons*. Translated by Jane Patricia Freeland, C.S.B.J., and Agnes Josephine Conway, S.S.J. Washington, DC: Catholic University of America Press, 1996.

Extracts

Neil, Bronwen. *Leo the Great*. London: Routledge, 2009.

Saint Gregory the Great

Gregory the Great. *The Book of Pastoral Rule*. Translated by George E. Demacopoulos. Crestwood, NY: Saint Vladimir's Seminary Press, 2007.

———. *The Dialogues*. Translated by Odo John Zimmermann. Washington, DC: Catholic University of America Press, 2002.

———. *Forty Gospel Homilies*. Translated by Dom David Hurst. Kalamazoo, MI: Cistercian Publications, 1990.

———. *Homilies on the Book of the Prophet Ezekiel*. Translated by Theodosia Gray. Center for Traditionalist Orthodox Studies: Etna, CA, 1990.

———. *Letters*. Translated by John R. C. Martin. 3 vols. Toronto: Pontifical Institute of Mediaeval Studies, 2004.

———. *Moral Reflections on the Book of Job*. Translated by Brian Kerns, O.C.S.O. 5 vols. Collegeville, MN: Liturgical Press, 2014–2019.

———. *On the Song of Songs*. Translated by Mark DelCogliano. Collegeville, MN: Liturgical Press, 2012.

———. *The Pastoral Rule*. Translated by James Barmby. In *Nicene and Post-Nicene Fathers*, edited by Philip Schaff and Henry Wace, 2nd series, vol. 12. Buffalo, NY: Christian Literature Publishing, 1895. Available on the New Advent website.

————. *Register of Letters*. Translated by James Barmby. In *Nicene and Post-Nicene Fathers*, edited by Philip Schaff and Henry Wace, 2nd series, vols. 12–13. Buffalo, NY: Christian Literature Publishing, 1895. Available on the New Advent website.

Extracts

Moorhead, John. *Gregory the Great*. London: Routledge, 2005.

Saint Bede the Venerable

Bede the Venerable. *On the Song of Songs and Selected Writings*. Translated by A. G. Holder. New York: Paulist, 2011.
————. *The Reckoning of Time*. Translated by Faith Wallis. Liverpool: Liverpool University Press, 2004.
————. *On the Temple*. Translated by Sean Connolly. Liverpool: Liverpool University Press, 1995.
McClure, Judith, and Roger Collins, eds. *The Ecclesiastical History of the English People*. Translated by Bertram Colgrave. Oxford: Oxford University Press, 1994.

C. Particular Bibliographies: Secondary Sources

Saint Irenaeus

Minns, Denis, O.P. *Irenaeus*. London: Geoffrey Chapman, 1994.
Osborn, Eric. *Irenaeus of Lyons*. Cambridge: Cambridge University Press, 2001.
Parvis, Sara, and Paul Foster, eds. *Irenaeus: Life, Scripture, Legacy*. Minneapolis, MN: Fortress, 2012.
Payton, James R., Jr. *Irenaeus on the Christian Faith: A Condensation of "Against Heresies"*. Cambridge: James Clarke, 2012.

Origen

Clark, Elizabeth A. *The Origenist Controversy: The Cultural Construction of an Early Christian Debate*. Princeton, NJ: Princeton University Press, 1992.
Crouzel, Henri. *Origen: The Life and Thought of the First Great Theologian*. Edinburgh: T&T Clark, 1989.
De Lubac, Henri. *History and Spirit: The Understanding of Scripture according to Origen*. Translated by Anne Englund Nash. Greek and Latin Translation

by Juvenal Merriell of the Oratory. San Francisco: Ignatius Press, 2007. Original French title published in 1950 by Éditions Montaigne, Paris.

Heine, Ronald. *Origen: Scholarship in the Service of the Church.* Oxford: Oxford University Press, 2010.

Trigg, Joseph W. *Origen: The Bible and Philosophy in the Third Century Church.* Routledge: Abingdon, 1998.

Saint Athanasius

Anatolios, Khaled. *Athanasius: The Coherence of His Thought.* London: Routledge, 1998.

Brakke, David. *Athanasius and the Politics of Asceticism.* Oxford: Clarendon Press, 1995.

Cross, F. L. *The Study of St. Athanasius.* Oxford: Clarendon Press, 1945.

Gwynn, David M. *Athanasius of Alexandria: Bishop, Theologian, Ascetic, Father.* Oxford: Oxford University Press, 2012.

Pettersen, Alvyn. *Athanasius.* London: Geoffrey Chapman, 1995.

Weinandy, Thomas G. *Athanasius: A Theological Introduction.* Farnham: Ashgate, 2007.

The Cappadocians

General

Barrois, George A. *The Fathers Speak.* Crestwood, NY: Saint Vladimir's Seminary Press, 1980.

Dumitraşcu, Nicu, ed. *The Ecumenical Legacy of the Cappadocians.* Basingstoke: Palgrave Macmillan, 2015.

Gregg, R. C. *Consolation Philosophy: Greek and Christian Paideia in Basil and the Two Gregories.* Cambridge, MA: Philadelphia Patristic Foundation, 1975.

Meredith, Anthony. *The Cappadocians.* London: Geoffrey Chapman, 1995.

Saint Basil

Fedwick, Paul Jonathan, ed. *Basil of Caesarea: Christian, Humanist, Ascetic.* Toronto: Pontifical Institute of Mediaeval Studies, 1981.

Hildebrand, Stephen M. *Basil of Caesarea.* Grand Rapids, MI: Baker Academic, 2014.

———. *The Trinitarian Theology of Basil of Caesarea.* Washington, DC: Catholic University of America Press, 1997.

Rousseau, Philip. *Basil of Caesarea.* Berkeley, CA: University of California Press, 1994.

Silvas, Anna M. *The Asketikon of St. Basil the Great*. Oxford: Oxford University Press, 2005.

Saint Gregory Nazianzen

Beeley, Christopher A. *Gregory of Nazianzus on the Trinity and the Knowledge of God: In Your Light We Shall See Light*. Oxford: Oxford University Press, 2008.

McGuckin, John Anthony. *Saint Gregory of Nazianzus: An Intellectual Biography*. Crestwood, NY: Saint Vladimir's Seminary Press, 2001.

Ruether, Rosemary Radford. *Gregory of Nazianzus: Rhetor and Philosopher*. Oxford: Oxford University Press, 1969.

Saint Gregory of Nyssa

Coakley, Sarah, ed. *Re-thinking Gregory of Nyssa*. Oxford: Blackwell, 2003.

Laird, Martin. *Gregory of Nyssa and the Grasp of Faith: Union, Knowledge, and Divine Presence*. Oxford: Oxford University Press, 2004.

Ludlow, Morwenna. *Gregory of Nyssa. Ancient and (Post)Modern*. Oxford: Oxford University Press, 2007.

Maspero, Giulio, and Lucas Francisco Mateo-Seco, eds. *The Brill Dictionary of Gregory of Nyssa*. Leiden: Brill, 2010.

Saint Cyril of Alexandria

McGuckin, John Anthony. *St. Cyril of Alexandria and the Christological Controversy*. Crestwood, NY: St. Vladimir's Seminary Press, 2004.

Weinandy, Thomas G., O.F.M. Cap., and Daniel A. Keating, eds. *The Theology of St. Cyril of Alexandria: A Critical Appreciation*. London and New York: T&T Clark, 2003.

Wessel, Susan. *Cyril of Alexandria and the Nestorian Controversy: The Making of a Saint and Heretic*. Oxford: Clarendon Press, 2004.

Denys

Coakley, Sarah, and Charles M. Stang. *Re-thinking Dionysius the Areopagite*. Oxford: Wiley, Blackwell, 2009.

Golitzin, Alexander. *Et introibo ad altare Dei: The Mystagogy of Dionysius Areopagita, with Special Reference to Its Predecessors in the Eastern Christian Tradition*. Thessalonica: Patriarchikon Idruma Paterikôn Meletôn, 1994.

Louth, Andrew. *Denys the Areopagite*. London: Geoffrey Chapman, 1989. Repr., London: Continuum, 2001.

Riordan, William. *Divine Light: The Theology of Denys the Areopagite*. San Francisco: Ignatius Press, 2008.

Rorem, Paul. *Pseudo-Dionysius: A Commentary on the Texts and an Introduction to Their Influence*. New York: Oxford University Press, 1993.

Saint Maximus

Allen, Pauline, and Bronwen Neil, eds. *The Oxford Handbook of Maximus the Confessor*. Oxford: Oxford University Press, 2015.

Blowers, Paul M. *Maximus the Confessor: Jesus Christ and the Transfiguration of the World*. Oxford: Oxford University Press, 2016.

Nichols, Aidan. O.P. *Byzantine Gospel: Maximus the Confessor in Modern Scholarship*. Edinburgh: T&T Clark, 1993.

Saint John Damascene

Janosik, Daniel J. *John of Damascus: First Apologist to the Muslims*. Eugene, OR: Pickwick, 2016.

Louth, Andrew. *St. John Damascene: Tradition and Originality in Byzantine Theology*. Oxford: Oxford University Press, 2002.

Sahas, Daniel J., ed. *John of Damascus on Islam: The Heresy of the "Ishmaelites"*. Leiden: Brill, 1972.

Schadler, Peter. *John of Damascus and Islam: Christian Heresiology and the Intellectual Background to Earliest Christian-Muslim Relations*. Leiden: Brill, 2017.

Tertullian

Daly, C.B. *Tertullian the Puritan and His Influence: An Essay in Historical Theology*. Dublin: Four Courts, 1993.

Osborn, Eric. *Tertullian: First Theologian of the West*. Cambridge: Cambridge University Press, 1997.

Rankin, David. *Tertullian and the Church*. Cambridge: Cambridge University Press, 1995.

Saint Cyprian

Benson, Edward White. *Cyprian: His Life, His Times, His Work*. London: Macmillan, 1897.

Brent, Allen. *Cyprian and Roman Carthage*. Cambridge: Cambridge University Press, 2010.

Burns, J. Patout. *Cyprian the Bishop*. London: Routledge, 2002.

Fahey, M.A. *Cyprian and the Bible: A Study in Third Century Exegesis*. Tübingen: Mohr Siebeck, 1971.

Sage, Michael M. *Cyprian*. Philadelphia: Philadelphia Patristic Foundation, 1975.

Saint Ambrose

McLynn, Neil B. *Ambrose of Milan: Church and Court in a Christian Capital.* Berkeley, CA: University of California Press, 1999.

Moorhead, John. *Ambrose: Church and Society in the Late Roman World.* London: Longman, 1999.

Paredi, Angelo. *Saint Ambrose: His Life and Times.* Notre Dame, IN: University of Notre Dame Press, 1964.

Saint Jerome

Cain, Andrew, and Josef Lössl. *Jerome of Stridon: His Life, Writings and Legacy.* London and New York: Routledge, 2009.

Kelly, J. N. D. *Saint Jerome: His Life, Writings, and Controversies.* London: Duckworth, 1975.

Williams, Megan Hale. *The Monk and the Book: Jerome and the Making of Christian Scholarship.* 2006. Reprint, Chicago and London: University of Chicago Press, 2006.

Saint Augustine

Bonner, Gerald. *St. Augustine of Hippo: Life and Controversies.* 3rd ed. Norwich: Canterbury Press, 2002.

Brown, Peter. *Augustine of Hippo: A Biography.* 2nd ed. London: Faber, 2000.

Chadwick, Henry. *Augustine of Hippo: A Life.* Oxford: Oxford University Press, 2009.

Lancel, Serge. *Saint Augustine.* London: Student Christian Movement Press, 2002.

O'Daly, Gerard. *Augustine's "City of God": A Reader's Guide.* Oxford: Oxford University Press, 1999.

Rist, John M. *Augustine: Ancient Thought Baptized.* Cambridge: Cambridge University Press, 1994.

Scott, T. K. *Augustine: His Thought in Context.* New York: Paulist, 1995.

Teselle, E. *Augustine the Theologian.* London: Burns and Oates, 1970.

Van der Meer, Frederick. *Augustine the Bishop: The Life and Work of a Father of the Church.* London: Sheed & Ward, 1961.

Saint Leo

Armitage, J. Mark. *Leo the Great's Theology of Redemption.* Strathfield, New South Wales: St. Paul's Publications, 2005.

Green, Bernard. *The Soteriology of Leo the Great*. Oxford: Oxford University Press, 2008.

Jalland, Trevor. *The Life and Times of St. Leo the Great*. London: Society for Promoting Christian Knowledge, 1941.

Saint Gregory the Great

Caradini, John, ed. *Gregory the Great: A Symposium*. Notre Dame, IN: Notre Dame University Press, 1995.

Demacopoulos, George E. *Gregory the Great: Ascetic, Pastor, and First Man of Rome*. Notre Dame, IN: Notre Dame University Press, 2015.

Evans, G. R. *The Thought of Gregory the Great*. Cambridge: Cambridge University Press, 1986.

Markus, R. A. *Gregory the Great and His World*. Cambridge: Cambridge University Press, 1997.

Neil, Bronwen, and Matthew Dal Sarto, ed. *A Companion to Gregory the Great*. Leiden and Boston, MA: Brill, 2013.

Richards, Jeffrey. *Consul of God: The Life and Times of Gregory the Great*. London: Routledge and Kegan Paul, 1980.

Straw, Carole. *Gregory the Great: Perfection in Imperfection*. Berkeley, CA: University of California Press, 1988.

Saint Bede the Venerable

Blair, Peter Hunter. *The World of Bede*. London: Martin Secker and Warburg, 1970; Cambridge: Cambridge University Press, 1990.

Brown, George Hardin. *A Companion to Bede*. Woodbridge, UK; Rochester, NY: Boydell Press, 2009.

DeGregorio, Scott, ed. *The Cambridge Companion to Bede*. Cambridge: Cambridge University Press, 2011.

Ward, Benedicta. *The Venerable Bede*. 2nd ed. London: Geoffrey Chapman, 1998.

NAME INDEX

Aaron (biblical character), 283
Abel (biblical character), 223, 283, 309
Abraham (biblical character), 30, 45, 107, 121, 282
Adam (biblical character), 28, 30, 32–33, 50, 67, 125–26, 154, 170, 178, 185n15, 242n33, 244, 250, 255, 260–61, 267
Adamnan of Iona, 307
Adam of Saint Victor, 260n63
Agapetus I (pope), 287
Agilulf, 289
Aidan, Saint, 303, 310
Alaric, 242, 266
Albert, Saint, 142
Alexander of Alexandria, 59, 89
Alexander of Aphrodisias, 231
Alexander of Thessalonica, 59
Alexander the Great, 35
Ambrose of Milan, Saint, 112, 212–27, 231, 234, 246–48, 251, 279, 290, 303, 305, 312
Ambrosius, 212
Amphilochius of Iconium, 234
Anatolios, Khaled, 61–62, 63–64
Andrei Rublev, Saint, 121
Anthony of Egypt, Saint, 79, 221, 238
Antonianus (bishop), 206
Antoninus Pius (emperor), 14
Apuleius, 245
Apollinarius of Laodicea, 103, 231, 233n16
Arcadius, 220
Aristotle, 167, 186, 230, 231
Arius, 52, 58–59, 69, 74, 74n57, 122, 214, 241

Armitage, Mark, 274, 277, 279–80, 281n48, 282, 283n51
Athanasius, Saint, 58–79. 89, 103, 170, 193, 126n56
  Christ and redemption, 274–75
  on Christ's nature, 118
  History of the Arians, 213–14
  on Holy Spirit, 94, 100, 101
  on hypostasis, 92, 122, 123, 231
  influence of, 155, 177, 222, 234
  Life of Anthony, 221, 230
  Logos and unity, 205
  Trinity and hypostasis, 91
  Trinity and interpenetration, 174
Attila the Hun, 273
Augustine of Hippo, Saint, 185, 193, 234, 238, 245–68, 268, 291, 300, 303, 305, 309
  City of God, 42, 313
  Confessions, 219, 222, 224, 229
  contrasted with Ambrose, 226–27
  Donatist Crisis, 211
  fluency in Greek, 212
  on God as *corpus*, 193
  on infant baptism, 244
  influence of, 279
  influence on Bede, 308
  interpretation of Scripture, 294–95
  on Isaiah, 112
  and Jerome, 238, 239
  on letters of Saint John, 310
  mission to Canterbury, 299–301
  prodesse contrasted with *praeesse*, 293
  on salvation, 285
  on Scripture interpretation, 296, 311
  theosis, 103, 106
  on Trinity, 93, 94, 110, 120